# NORMATIVE ETHICS

## Dimensions of Philosophy Series
### Norman Daniels and Keith Lehrer, Editors

*Normative Ethics*, Shelly Kagan

*Introduction to Marx and Engels: A Critical Reconstruction,*
Second Edition, Richard Schmitt

*Political Philosophy*, Jean Hampton

*Philosophy of Mind*, Jaegwon Kim

*Philosophy of Social Science*, Second Edition,
Alexander Rosenberg

*Philosophy of Education*, Nel Noddings

*Philosophy of Biology*, Elliott Sober

*Metaphysics*, Peter van Inwagen

*Philosophy of Physics*, Lawrence Sklar

*Theory of Knowledge*, Keith Lehrer

*Philosophy of Law: An Introduction to Jurisprudence,*
Revised Edition, Jeffrie G. Murphy and Jules L. Coleman

FORTHCOMING

*Philosophical Ethics*, Stephen L. Darwall

# NORMATIVE ETHICS

Shelly Kagan

YALE UNIVERSITY

 WestviewPress

*A Division of HarperCollinsPublishers*

*Dimensions of Philosophy Series*

Copyright © 1998 by Westview Press, A Division of HarperCollins Publishers, Inc.

Published in 1998 in the United States of America by Westview Press, 5500 Central Avenue, Boulder, Colorado 80301–2877, and in the United Kingdom by Westview Press, 12 Hid's Copse Road, Cumnor Hill, Oxford OX2 9JJ

Library of Congress Cataloging-in-Publication Data
Kagan, Shelly.
  Normative ethics / Shelly Kagan.
    p.   cm. — (Dimensions of philosophy series)
  Includes bibliographical references and index.
  ISBN 0-8133-0845-3. — ISBN 0-8133-0846-1 (pbk.)
  1. Ethics.   I. Title.   II. Series.
BJ1012.K244   1998
170'.44—dc21                                                                      97-30631
                                                                                         CIP

The paper used in this publication meets the requirements of the American National Standard for Permanence of Paper for Printed Library Materials Z39.48–1984.

10   9   8   7   6   5   4   3   2   1

*For Elana, Rebecca, and Ari*

# CONTENTS

# Acknowledgments

My views on moral philosophy have been constantly and profoundly influenced by the conversations I have had and the books and articles I have read. But it is far too late in the day, I fear, to try to identify most of the specific points of influence. I know that I have shamelessly appropriated insights and arguments whenever they have seemed plausible to me—making them my own—and now I am no longer able to give detailed credit for most of these ideas. But credit and gratitude are most certainly due, to all those who have taught me: my colleagues, my students, and my teachers.

Special thanks should go to Gina Novick. It was Gina who first persuaded me to write this book. And then—years later—she read it in manuscript and showed me how to make it better.

*Shelly Kagan*

# 1

# PRELIMINARIES

## 1.1 What Normative Ethics Is

How should one live? There are few questions, I think, that are as gripping and as inescapable as this one. Unlike many of the other classical questions of philosophy, this question—the central question of moral philosophy—seems pressing and important. It matters what answers we come up with, for it matters what I do with my life. What I make of myself, how I live, what I do, what kind of person I become—these things are of vital concern to each of us, even if few of us normally reflect on them in a systematic or critical fashion.

Moral philosophy attempts to answer the question of how one should live. Because of the staggering difficulty and significance of the question, any attempt to provide an answer can seem arrogant, pretentious, or embarrassing. Who could be so foolish, so naive, or so dogmatic, as to think that they had themselves (finally!) arrived at the truth about how to live? Indeed, many of us have learned to pretend—or have even fooled ourselves into thinking that we believe—that there are no correct answers here, that ethics is all simply a matter of opinion.

And yet, on reflection, most of us do in fact think that there are right and wrong answers in ethics. Here is a simple example: it would be immoral to set a child on fire for the mere pleasure of watching him burn. Is there anyone who seriously doubts the truth of this claim?

Perhaps there is. (Human history has produced more than its share of demented or wicked individuals.) If so, such a person need read no further in this book. But for the rest of us—for those who think that there are indeed certain moral claims that are correct and others that are wrong—the question is not whether there are right answers in moral philosophy but only to what extent we can arrive at them. How far can we go toward systematizing our answers and defending them? To what extent do our moral views need to be revised? Can our moral theories be generalized and extended so as to provide answers where we do not already possess confident opinions?

Now in broad terms there are two possible ways to go about answering questions like these (or perhaps there are two possible ways to understand the questions). On the one hand, you might try to discuss in abstract terms the very possibility of systematization in ethics, the nature of moral justification, the various possible grounds for revising ethical claims, and so on. On the other hand, you might try to do the actual work of systematizing, revising, and extending our moral views. That is, rather than concentrating on "second-order" questions concerning the nature and possibility of a moral theory, you might instead concentrate on the "ground-level" project of presenting and defending a moral view. In this book, we will be concerned with moral theories of this second, substantive sort.

This same point can be made with the help of some contemporary jargon. Moral philosophy as a whole can be usefully divided into three basic areas: metaethics, normative ethics, and applied ethics. *Normative ethics*— the topic of this book—involves substantive proposals concerning how to act, how to live, or what kind of person to be. In particular, it attempts to state and defend the most basic principles governing these matters. Consider, for example, our earlier judgment that it would be immoral to set a child on fire for the pleasure of watching him burn. Presumably the immorality of such an act can be explained in terms of something more basic or fundamental—perhaps a moral prohibition against causing horrible pain to the innocent. And perhaps that prohibition could itself be explained in terms of something even more general, such as a right not to be harmed. The point right now is not to decide whether or not these particular suggestions are correct, but only to illustrate one way in which we can move toward more and more fundamental moral claims.

Is there, then, a single ultimate moral principle from which all other moral principles can be derived? The debate over whether there is, and if so, what it might be, is the concern of normative ethics. And even if there is no one single fundamental moral principle, we can still try to arrive at a complete *list* of the basic moral principles—or, at the very least, a list of some of the most important ones. Normative ethics, then, is concerned with stating and defending the most basic moral principles. (But this talk about "principles" should not be taken too literally. I don't mean to be assuming without discussion that the most basic moral claims are best described in terms of rules. It might be that we need to talk instead—or in addition—about the most basic rights, duties, virtues, or what have you.)

Since the most basic moral principles will probably be stated in rather general terms, it will not always be apparent what to do in particular situations or in morally complex cases. This will be especially true if there are several fundamental principles, since conceivably these might conflict (or appear to conflict) in some particular case. It may be a difficult matter to decide how such a conflict is to be resolved or how a fundamental principle is to be applied in some controversial area. Accordingly, the attempt to apply the general principles of normative ethics to particular difficult or complex cases is itself an important part of moral philosophy. It is called *applied ethics*, and doing it well can be a quite challenging and subtle undertaking. Not surprisingly, the moral judgments offered for particularly difficult cases remain controversial. There are on-going philosophical debates, for example, over issues like the morality of capital punishment, abortion, and affirmative action. Indeed, in some cases entire specialized subfields have developed, devoted to problems in medical ethics, business ethics, and so on. I think in fact that the entire field of political philosophy can legitimately be viewed in this way, as one (vitally important) branch of applied ethics—one devoted to problems about the justification of the state, the use of power, and the merits of alternative forms of government.

Think for a moment about what it would mean to have a theory concerning, say, the morality of abortion. Among other things, such a theory would presumably indicate the circumstances (if any) in which abortion would be morally justified, and the circumstances (if any) in which it would be morally unjustified. That is to say, the theory would itself have a certain degree of generality, covering more than one specific type of case. Although a theory of abortion would be less general and less fundamental than the *most* basic principles of morality, a theory of abortion would still be *more* fundamental and more general than any particular judgment that might be derived from it concerning whether a particular mother in her particular circumstances would be justified in having an abortion.

What this means is that the distinction between normative ethics and applied ethics does not rest upon any kind of sharp line. Really what we have is something like a continuum: moral claims differ in their degree of generality; they can be ranked as more or less basic. Since most moral claims will lie somewhere in the vast middle of this continuum, it will be somewhat arbitrary or a matter of convenience whether we classify them as belonging to normative ethics or to applied ethics. In the light of this, some moral philosophers don't draw any distinction between normative ethics and applied ethics at all. They just talk about there being various theories in normative ethics—and they note that some of these theories are more general, and others are less so, some more basic, and others more derivative.

I have no real disagreement with those who prefer to talk this way. My purpose in introducing the notion of applied ethics was simply to bring out this point that substantive moral claims can themselves be more or less fundamental. The theories to be discussed in this book lie pretty firmly on the "more fundamental" side of the continuum. We will not be discussing topics like capital punishment, or euthanasia (mercy killing), or affirmative action, that lie much further down the "applied" side of the continuum. This is an important part of what I mean when I say that the topic of this book is normative ethics.

The other main area of moral philosophy is *metaethics*. Metaethics is concerned with answering second-order questions of the sort I indicated earlier. Consider, for example, the claim that killing is always wrong. So long as it is normative ethics that we are doing, what we are concerned with is the substantive question of whether this claim is correct: is killing always wrong, or must an exception be made for self-defense (or war, or capital punishment)? And who, exactly, is it wrong to kill? Humans, animals, plants? Similarly, we want to know whether the wrongness of killing is fundamental and ultimate—or can it be derived from some even more basic moral principle? These, as I say, are typical questions that can be raised about the claim from the standpoint of normative ethics.

But there are other questions—very different types of questions—that can be raised about this claim as well. For example, when someone claims that killing is always wrong, what exactly does the word "wrong" mean? Can we give an adequate definition of moral terms like "right," "wrong," "good," and "bad"? Similarly, the claim that killing is always wrong seems to be ascribing a property to acts of killing. (Compare the claim that "killing is always difficult," which ascribes to acts of killing the property of being difficult.) But what kind of property is "wrongness"? It doesn't seem to be a property of the sort that the five senses or the sciences can tell us about. But, then, is it a natural property or an empirical property at all? And if not, what other kind of property could it be? Furthermore, how can we know whether killing actually has this strange property? Indeed, how can we know anything about ethics at all? Are there really objective, moral facts, waiting to be known? If so, what kinds of facts are moral facts? How do they differ from ordinary, empirical facts? How do such moral facts fit into a world of scientific facts? And if there aren't really any moral facts, then just what is going on when someone makes a moral claim like the claim that killing is always wrong?

Obviously enough, questions of this sort are quite different from the substantive moral questions raised by normative ethics. Providing answers to these questions would not directly involve taking a position on the substantive *content* of morality—that is, which acts are required, which forbidden, what kinds of people are good, what kinds of people are bad, and so on. Rather, answering these questions would require taking a stand with regard to the *nature* of morality. What is the function of moral discourse? What is the place of values in the world of persons and things? What is the *point* of morality? These second-order questions are the concern of metaethics.

Unlike the distinction between normative ethics and applied ethics—where almost everyone agrees that there is no sharp line—many moral philosophers have thought that there is indeed a sharp logical distinction to be drawn between normative ethics and metaethics. Not only that, it has seemed to many as though whatever particular positions you happen to take in one of these areas (say, metaethics) this will still leave you completely free with regard to the positions you can take in the other area (that is, normative ethics). For example, it seems as though two people could agree completely concerning the nature of morality, the existence of moral truths, and so on, while still disagreeing with each other as to whether or not killing is always wrong. And similarly, two people might agree that killing is indeed always wrong, while holding radically different views concerning the nature of morality, the possibility of moral knowledge, and so forth. Accordingly, some philosophers have held that when doing either metaethics or normative ethics (including applied ethics) one can completely disregard the other area. (Indeed, having drawn a very sharp line between metaethics and normative ethics, some of these philosophers argued that the sole concern of moral philosophers qua philosophers should be with metaethics. Normative ethics was to be left to sermons and editorials; philosophers—it was claimed—could make no distinctive contributions to it.)

I think, however, that metaethics and normative ethics do not actually have anything like this kind of independence from one another. Here is an easy example. When doing normative ethics we try to defend and justify substantive moral claims. But to do this, obviously enough, we have to have views about what it is you need to do to provide a moral claim with a good defense. That is, in doing normative ethics we will be presupposing some kind of account—either a developed one or at least a working understanding of one—of justification in ethics. But the topic of justification in ethics is itself one that actually belongs to metaethics. In short, doing normative ethics requires having views about metaethical issues. What's more, depending on the details of your views about what counts as a good justification in ethics, it may well turn out that some substantive normative claims are easier to defend than others. So normative ethics and metaethics may not actually be independent of one another after all.

Of course, even if it is granted that in this and other ways your views in metaethics can have an influence on your views in normative ethics, it might still be true that there is indeed a sharp line to be drawn between these two areas of moral philosophy. After all, metaethics is concerned with the second-order questions about the nature and point of morality, while normative ethics is concerned with ground-level questions about how one ought to live. And it certainly seems as though there is a sharp distinction between these two different kinds of questions.

In fact, however, I believe that here too (as with the distinction between normative ethics and applied ethics) we are actually faced with a continuum rather than a sharp line. For as we go deeper in our attempt to articulate the fundamental moral principles, relatively specific first-order claims about the content of morality give way gradually to more general overall characterizations of morality's content; and as these in turn become more general still, we find ourselves making what increasingly come to seem like second-order claims about the very nature of morality. This is especially so when we attempt to provide a basis or foundation for the substantive moral claims of normative ethics. Such foundational theories will inevitably grow out of and appeal to larger metaethical conceptions of morality's purpose and point. That is, in the course of defending a given theory about the foundations of normative ethics, when we try to explain why it is that the various features of that theory should seem attractive and plausible, inevitably the claims we make will themselves simply be metaethical claims about the nature of morality. At a deep enough level, normative ethics does not merely draw upon metaethics—it simply becomes metaethics. (This point will, I hope, become clearer in the second half of the book, when we actually begin considering rival theories about the foundations of normative ethics.)

So there is a continuum here too. As soon as you begin to try to defend a normative claim *within* morality, you are inevitably making a "meta" claim *about* morality. Thus, the shift from a perspective that is purely first-order to a perspective that is at least partially second-order has begun. Theories may differ in the degree to which this second-order perspective dominates, but for the most part it is only a matter of degree.

Nonetheless, the fact remains that the focus of a discussion in moral philosophy will be quite different if one concentrates on abstract second-order questions about the nature of morality, rather than on the ground-level project of stating in general terms the content of morality and providing a basis for it. In this book, as I have said, the focus will be on attempts to state and defend substantive moral claims. This is the other important part of what I meant in saying that the topic of this book is normative ethics.

Let me hasten to add that in saying that this book will be about normative ethics and not applied ethics or metaethics, I certainly do not mean to be suggesting that these other areas of moral philosophy are not important. They are indeed important; and they are difficult as well. And, of course, as I have just been arguing, there aren't actually any sharp lines separating normative ethics from these other areas. But for all that, it seems possible and worthwhile to focus on normative ethics—and that is my intent.

Actually, however, the focus will be somewhat more narrow than that. I have suggested that the central question of moral philosophy as a whole, and of normative ethics in particular, is how one should live. I take this question to be sufficiently general that it is an open matter what an adequate answer would concentrate on. Plausibly enough, one might think that an adequate answer would primarily be concerned with issues about what one should do and how one should act. But one might hold that an adequate answer would concentrate instead on describing what kind of person one should be, rather than what one should do. And there are other possibilities as well. Ideally, no doubt, we would consider all the most important theories for each type of approach—making no assumption at the outset about which aspect is most central in answering how to live.

Of course, it is also plausible to think that a complete normative theory will have something to say about each of these aspects—that is, about what to do, what kind of person to be, and so on. Yet even if this is right, it might be that in picking one of these aspects to concentrate upon, we run the risk of failing to present some of these theories in the strongest possible light. This is, however, a risk I am going to take. I am going to organize our examination of the rival theories of normative ethics by focusing on the question of how one should act. Which acts are morally better or worse than others? Which acts are morally permissible, which ones morally required, and which ones morally forbidden—and what makes them so? Our central concern in this book will be examining rival theories on this score. Other aspects will come into view now and again, but they will not be center stage. (I should note that this focus is quite typical for contemporary normative ethics, although not universal.)

Focusing on the moral status of acts in this way also means that certain topics in normative ethics will receive little or no discussion, and what discussion there is will be disjointed and scattered in different locations. For example, I will have nothing at all to say about the topic of free will, and precious little to say about a number of closely connected topics, such as the nature of moral agency, and moral responsibility, as well as questions of punishment, praise, and blame. Similarly I will have very little to say about the nature of our moral obligations to animals, although this topic too deserves careful consideration.

I note all of this not so much by way of making an apology, but rather as a warning. This book is not intended to be an exhaustive encyclopedia of all the topics of normative ethics—not even all the most interesting ones. It is meant only to be an introduction to some of the most important theories and topics. And this last qualification—that the book is only an introduction—is meant quite seriously as well. There is much more that can be said about every single topic that I will be discussing. My goal is not at all to provide a full and complete examination of the various theories and arguments that we will be considering. Rather, I simply want to give a sense of what some of the main issues in normative ethics are. This involves pointing out what is attractive and what is problematic about the various views to be discussed. But I never take myself to be offering definitive arguments for or against a given view. There is always more that needs to be said than what I will attempt to say here.

## 1.2   What Normative Ethics Is Not

The rival normative theories we will be considering are theories about how people ought to act, morally speaking. This point is worth emphasizing:

they are theories about how people *ought* to act. This means, among other things, that they are not claims about how people *do* act. After all, we all know that people at least sometimes fail to do what they are morally required to do. Perhaps this happens only rarely; perhaps it happens far more frequently than we normally think. Regardless, it is important to be clear about this distinction between what ought to be and what is: a claim about how people ought to act should not be mistaken for a description of how people actually do act. And this means that you cannot disprove a given claim about how people should act merely by pointing out that they do not actually act that way: perhaps they should, but simply fail to do what they are morally required to do. This is not to say that descriptions of how people actually act are irrelevant to ethics. All *sorts* of empirical claims may be relevant to defending ethical claims. But it is still important not to confuse the two kinds of claims.

It is also important not to confuse the substantive moral claims of normative ethics with mere descriptions of the moral beliefs or ethical codes of some group or society. It is one thing to tell us how a given society *thinks* people should act. It is quite another thing to tell us whether this is indeed the way that people really, genuinely *should* act. If what you are looking for is a description of the moral code of some society or culture—that is, if what you want is a careful description of what some group of people thinks or has thought we should do—then you can and must turn to the writings of sociology, or anthropology, or history. But if what you want to know is the correct (or true, or most valid, or best) set of moral beliefs—that is, if what you want is a careful account of what people really should do—then this cannot be settled by an appeal to the social sciences. You must turn instead to normative ethics. For it is normative ethics that attempts to state and *defend* the substantive moral claims. And defending a moral claim— showing that it really does tell us the truth about how people ought to act—is something quite different from merely reporting what this or that group has thought about the matter.

I am certainly not suggesting that no group or society has ever managed to arrive at correct moral views. Doubtless most groups are right about at least some things morally, and perhaps there is some group (or individual) that is right about everything morally (though I must say, I doubt it). But the mere fact that a given group makes some moral claim does not—just by that very fact alone—prove that the moral claim is correct. Indeed, this is true for all subjects, and not just ethics: the mere fact that somebody says something doesn't prove that what they say is so. So if our concern is to find out what people really ought to do, then we must start *evaluating* the various rival theories of normative ethics, considering the evidence and arguments that can be offered for or against them. Ultimately, that is, what we need to assess are the *reasons* that can be offered for accepting or rejecting a given moral claim.

Of course, the study of the moral beliefs of different cultures can be helpful in a number of ways. It can open our eyes to the fact that different groups have disagreed about moral questions—even on some of the matters that seem most self-evident to us. If nothing else, this may deepen our desire to discover to what extent our own moral views can be defended. And it may leave us more open to the possibility of deciding that it is actually some of our own moral views that are mistaken and in need of revision. Furthermore, the study of the moral beliefs of other groups can help us discover arguments for or against some position—arguments that we might otherwise have overlooked but that are worthy of careful consideration. And, of course, the study of the moral beliefs of other groups can be interesting in its own right.

All these same things are true with regard to studying the theories of the great moral philosophers, living and dead. Learning about these philosophers can be fascinating in its own right and can drive home to us the realization that the problems of normative ethics, and of moral philosophy in general, are deep and difficult, and even thoughtful and brilliant people can disagree about the answers. And—not surprisingly—studying the writings of moral philosophers is one of the best ways to discover rival moral theories, as well as some of the most interesting and compelling arguments for and against these theories. (Although here, too, it should go without saying, describing what a given philosopher believes about morality is quite another matter from deciding what morality actually requires.)

Nonetheless, in this book, no attempt at all will be made to describe the views of any particular philosopher or those of different societies. We will be going directly to the rival theories of normative ethics themselves—the rival claims about how people should act and the arguments for and against these claims.

So the substantive moral claims of normative ethics should not be confused with descriptive claims about what people actually do, or about what various groups (or individuals) think people should do. But there is something else normative ethics should not be confused with: the law. Determining what people morally should do is not the same thing as determining what the *law* says they should do. For the law may permit some particular act, even though that act is immoral; and the law may forbid an act, even though that act is morally permissible, or even morally required.

Here, too, easy examples can bring out the point. In the American South, before the Civil War, slavery was legal. But despite the fact that slavery was legally permitted, we would certainly want to insist that slavery was *morally* forbidden: it was *immoral* to treat enslaved people as they were treated—indeed, it was morally reprehensible—and the truth of this claim is not altered by the fact that such treatment was permitted by the law. Similarly, to take a more contemporary example, opponents of abortion think that abortion is typically (or perhaps even always) morally forbidden—despite the fact that current law generally permits it. And if the law ever changes, so as to prohibit most (or all) abortions, there will doubtless be many other people who nonetheless will think that abortions are still typically (or perhaps even always) morally permissible—despite the fact that the law forbids it. In short, what the law says is one thing; and what morality says may well be another.

Once again, this is obviously not to say that the law is typically immoral, simply that morality and the law should not be confused. Nor does it deny the possibility that if the law requires or forbids some act this may sometimes be relevant to whether or not the act is in fact morally required or forbidden. Some think there is a moral duty to obey the law; others think that the fact that something is required by the law provides at least *some* support for thinking that morally one ought to do it. Whether any such theses about the law and morality are true is itself a question to be debated within normative ethics (or perhaps applied ethics). But none of this alters the point that the temptation to confuse morality and the law should be resisted. (The temptation is sometimes made more inviting by a tendency to speak of "the moral law"; but the moral law should not be confused with the kind of law passed by governments.)

So claims about what people should do from the moral point of view should not be mistaken with claims about what people should do from the legal point of view. Nor, of course, should they be confused with claims about what people should do from the aesthetic point of view, or the economic point of view, or the patriotic point of view, and so on. Any of these specialized standpoints may yield claims about how people "ought" to act, and at least in some cases they may well be relevant to determining how people really should act from the moral point of view. But it is the moral point of view itself that is our concern in normative ethics, and none of these other standpoints should be mistaken for it.

There remains one other point of view whose relationship to morality deserves special mention: rationality. We certainly often talk about what it would be rational for people to do—whether a given act is rationally required, or whether it would be irrational (rationally forbidden) to perform some act, and so on. Can this point of view, too, like the others, differ from the moral point of view? Could it ever be rational to act immorally? Could it ever be irrational to perform an act that is morally required? Or do rationality and morality necessarily coincide?

This is perhaps the deepest and most difficult question in all of moral philosophy. But answering it requires, among other things, an adequate account of rationality—and this is itself an obscure and contested topic in philosophy. So I propose, for the most part, to simply put this question aside. Our concern will be to articulate the demands of the moral point of view, and to see to what extent rival claims within normative ethics can be defended. We will be asking only how people ought to act, morally speaking; we will not here pursue the crucially important—but nonetheless distinct—question of the degree to which rationality endorses the demands of morality.

Restricting our project in this way does not, however, undermine its significance. Most of us take ourselves to be quite prepared to act as we morally should, if only we can determine just what it is that morality asks of us. At the very least, we feel inclined to give considerable weight to moral considerations. But most of us experience confusion and uncertainty, at least upon occasion, concerning what morality really demands. It would be no small accomplishment to arrive at an adequate understanding of which acts are morally permitted, which forbidden, and which required. The various rival theories concerning these matters constitute the field of normative ethics—and it is this which shall be our concern in this book.

## 1.3  Defending Normative Theories

There is more than one theory about how we should act. (This is so even when we restrict our attention to theories of normative ethics—theories about how we should act from the standpoint of morality.) What's more, these different theories are genuine *rivals;* they are not merely alternative ways of saying the very same thing. They disagree—not always, to be sure, but sometimes—about precisely which acts are morally permitted, required, or forbidden. Since they disagree, they cannot all be right: we must choose between them. But what is to guide our choice? On what grounds are we to accept or reject a normative theory? How can a moral claim be defended?

As we have already noted, this general topic belongs to metaethics, not normative ethics. But as we also pointed out, it is very difficult to see how you could even get started on normative ethics without at least a rough and ready view concerning the nature of justification in ethics. Given the scope of this book, to say a lot would be to say too much, but it does seem necessary to say at least something.

Consider how different defending an ethical theory will have to be from defending a scientific one. In choosing between scientific theories, we can appeal to empirical evidence. We can do experiments, testing predictions against observation. But none of this seems available in ethics. Imagine trying to do an experiment to test some fundamental moral claim, for example, that killing is wrong. Suppose I grab someone off the street, stab him in the chest, and watch him die. What am I looking for? What kind of observation will support (or undermine) the claim that killing is wrong? (Would it help if I gathered other observers as well?) Experiments and empirical evidence just don't seem to be of any real help in proving things in ethics.

Now in fact this conclusion isn't quite right. If I want to prove that your giving your grandmother something to drink was an immoral act, it may well be relevant to show that you gave her cyanide-laced tea, which in turn caused her death; and proving these things is indeed a matter of empirical evidence. So we certainly shouldn't say that empirical evidence is never relevant to ethics. Indeed, it may be relevant a great deal of the time. After all, consider how a prohibition against giving someone cyanide is to be defended: it can be derived from our more familiar moral principles—but only when we add the empirical observation that cyanide causes death. Perhaps, then, in a similar fashion, but more generally, many of the less fundamental moral principles can themselves be derived from even more basic moral principles—but again, only when the latter are combined with appropriate empirical claims about the world. If this is so, then empirical claims can play a significant role in justifying moral principles.

Whether this is really so or not, and to what extent, is something concerning which different normative theories will disagree (as we shall see). But almost everyone agrees that this empirical approach to defending moral principles cannot extend to all of ethics. Sooner or later we seem to come to moral principles that are not themselves based on or (even partly) derived from empirical claims. So how are these "purely ethical" principles to be defended?

Some people conclude that if ethics cannot be based on empirical evidence all the way down, the ultimate moral principles must be matters of mere opinion, or personal taste. But this conclusion is too hasty as well. After all, there are other areas of inquiry besides ethics where defending a claim is not ultimately a matter of empirical evidence and experiments. Consider mathematics or logic: defending the Pythagorean theorem, for example, is hardly a matter of drawing triangles and then measuring the sides to see if they add up properly. Yet no one is tempted to say that mathematics is all a matter of personal opinion or tastes.

I certainly do not mean to suggest that arguments in ethics look very much like arguments in mathematics. (The nature of the similarities and differences is too complex to explore here.) The point is just that there are ways to defend a claim other than an appeal to empirical evidence. One can still *argue* for or against a conclusion, and the various arguments can be more or less compelling, to varying degrees. So when someone offers a moral principle, we can still ask what *reasons* there are to accept it; and we can also consider what reasons there may be to reject it instead. Then we can go on to the delicate task of determining which side, on balance, has the stronger case to be made for it, which side seems the most plausible in the light of all the relevant arguments.

All this is well and good, but just what do arguments in ethics look like? (That is, what do they look like in cases other than those where one principle is straightforwardly derived from another one that is more basic?) What sorts of reasons can we offer in defense of—or against—a theory in normative ethics?

One thing we can do is to point out the extent to which a given theory fits—or fails to fit—our various moral intuitions. In particular, we often have strong, immediate reactions to the description of real or imaginary examples. Even a schematic example, with only a few details filled in, can often be enough to evoke a sharp intuitive judgment that an act of the kind described would be morally forbidden (or required, or optional). I made use of this common phenomenon at the start of the chapter, when I put forward the claim that it would be immoral to set a child on fire for the pleasure of watching the child burn. As soon as we think about the possibility of someone doing this, we have the compelling intuition that such an act would be morally forbidden. Such moral intuitions about hypothetical cases are difficult to disregard. If some proposed moral theory gives what intuitively strike us as the wrong answers about such hypothetical cases, then we are inclined to take this as a significant (or perhaps even decisive) argument against that theory. We expect an adequate moral theory to provide a good fit for our moral intuitions; so showing that a theory generates and supports the intuitively correct answers can be an important aspect of defending it.

Of course, finding a theory that fits well with our intuitions is often a difficult matter, particularly when it is the most basic principles of morality that we are after and that we are trying to put together into a complete theory. For the more general the theory, the more cases it will cover. And this raises the very real possibility that no theory will provide a perfect fit for all of our intuitions. In some cases, of course, this isn't especially troubling. On reflection, most of us are inclined to dismiss at least some of our intuitions as resulting from prejudice, bias, or failure to think clearly. And sometimes our intuitions are weak, uncertain, or wavering; obviously, our commitment to accommodating such intuitions isn't very strong. But even when it comes to stable and considered judgments about specific cases, we may not be able to find a theory that can accommodate all of our intuitions. In order to find a theory that provides the best fit with our considered intuitions as a whole, we may have to accept a theory that nonetheless clashes with some particular intuitions.

All of this makes the task of determining how well a given theory fits our intuitions much less straightforward. There will often be the potential for a good deal of debate over the relative importance of the various intuitive and counterintuitive implications of the given theory. Showing that a proposed normative theory fits our considered intuitions rather well overall can therefore be a demanding and significant aspect of defending it.

Just how important this aspect is will depend, of course, on how much confidence we have in the intuitions. But moral philosophers differ considerably as to how much weight considered intuitions about specific cases should be given. Some philosophers take the extreme position that certain intuitions should be treated as *givens*—no theory that fails to accommodate them can possibly be acceptable. Other philosophers take the equally extreme position that such intuitions should be given no weight whatsoever—

the mere fact that a theory has counterintuitive implications is no argument against it at all. Most philosophers take a position somewhere between these two extremes: the extent to which a theory coheres with our intuitions about cases is one relevant consideration in evaluating that theory; but it may not be a decisive one.

Yet what else can there be besides the appeal to intuitions about cases? In fact, rather a great deal. A moral principle may strike us as intuitively plausible in its own right—above and beyond its implications for specific cases. Or it may be derivable from a more general theory that itself strikes us as attractive and plausible. So, in addition to intuitions about cases, we also have to consider intuitions about principles and theories. If we're lucky, these intuitions about principles will be in harmony with our intuitions about cases; but if we are unlucky, there may be some tension here as well—and then we will have to ask just which theory is it that provides the best overall fit with our intuitions, taking both sorts of intuitions into account.

But there is more than this that needs to be considered as well. For it is always worth asking whether a given theory has a plausible *rationale*. If a theory prohibits a certain kind of act, what exactly is it about acts of that sort that makes it appropriate to prohibit them? If a theory holds that a particular factor has relevance in a certain range of cases, what exactly is it about that factor that explains why it is relevant at all—and what explains why it is only relevant in the specified range of cases and not more generally? If a theory holds that morality has such and such a feature, can we explain why morality should have a feature like that? Does it make *sense*?

Imagine a slaveholder who feels, intuitively, that it is permissible to treat blacks in ways that it would never be permissible to treat whites. Such a person may well be able to find principles that fit his intuitions about cases; presumably these will be principles that discriminate between people on the basis of skin color. Now what should we say about this case? Obviously, it is not that there is no difference between black and white—differences in skin color are perfectly real differences. But what we still want to know—and what the slaveholder should still ask himself—is why this difference should *make* a difference. What could possibly explain why skin color should have any moral relevance at all? Pressed to offer a plausible explanation for his racist principle, the slaveholder may come to see that none can be offered, and that the principle cannot be defended after all. (When pressed, he might admit that differences in skin color are not themselves of any direct moral relevance; but he might insist nonetheless that differences in race are highly correlated with extreme differences in intelligence and in character—that blacks are, for example, stupid and lazy. Conceivably, there might be a plausible explanation of why these further features should matter morally. But now the slaveholder's position can be defeated by showing that his principle rests on empirical assumptions that are simply false.)

Someone who thought that intuitive fit was all that mattered in defending a moral principle might point out that the slaveholder's racist principle never matched *our* intuitions, and so the example may not show anything more than that you shouldn't consider a principle to be adequately defended until it matches your own intuitions. But I think that the example does show more than this. We were imagining that the racist principle did fit the slaveholder's intuitions about cases, and yet it seems to me that he himself should be able to see that the principle has not been adequately justified if he cannot provide it with a plausible rationale. Similarly, even if we *shared* the slaveholder's racist intuitions, it would not be appropriate to consider the intuitive fit an adequate defense of the principle, given that there is no plausible explanation of why skin color should make a difference morally. Thus, providing a normative theory with a plausible rationale is itself an important aspect of defending it.

Of course, there will be room for considerable disagreement over what constitutes a plausible explanation for a moral principle or theory. Whether a proposed explanation strikes us as plausible or implausible will depend on our overall conception of the nature of morality. Ultimately (as I noted in 1.1), we will have to evaluate possible explanations in the light of our metaethical account of morality's purpose and point. But none of this undermines the basic point that an important component of evaluating a normative theory is seeing whether it can be provided with a plausible rationale; it only repeats the earlier observation that sooner or later normative ethics turns into metaethics.

A friend of intuitions might still insist that even here all we are doing is bringing in still more intuitions to be accommodated as best we can. If so, I do not think that any serious disagreement still remains between us. For once "intuitions" is being used this broadly, it is just another word for opinions, judgments, and beliefs. The position we have arrived at is this: in defending a moral theory, we must see how well that theory fits in with a wide variety of judgments that we are inclined to make about many different matters. We have opinions about cases, about principles, about the nature of morality, about what counts as an adequate explanation, and more. Some of these opinions are fairly specific, others are more general; some are arrived at rather "intuitively" and spontaneously, others only after considerable reflection; some are extremely difficult to give up, others are more easily abandoned. We try to find the moral theory that provides the best overall fit with this eclectic set of beliefs. But if—as seems overwhelmingly likely—no theory can actually accommodate all of the relevant initial beliefs, we revise the set: we alter our beliefs, and reevaluate our theories, until we arrive as best we can at a theory that seems on balance to be more plausible than any of its rivals. Ultimately, then, defending a normative theory is a matter of arguing that it provides the best overall fit with our various considered judgments.

If something like this picture is correct, then defending (or attacking) a normative theory will virtually never be an open and shut matter. Almost any normative theory is likely to have its counterintuitive aspects, and people can sincerely disagree as to which theory is, on balance, the most attractive. That is why there are few or no "knockdown" arguments in ethics (or anywhere, for that matter). All you can do is point out the attractive features of your own favored theory, explain why you are prepared to live with its various unattractive features, and try to show that the alternatives are even worse.

What this means is that you will not be able to persuade everyone of the truth of your position. So be it: you cannot persuade everyone. But that does not relieve you of the obligation to try to defend your moral views, and to revise them if you cannot. For each of us must decide how to live; and given the importance of that decision, it behooves us to examine whether our own moral views can indeed be defended.

Of course, the process of justification that I have been describing is a complex and open-ended one. Few people will have the time (or the inclination) to go very far by way of examining alternative theories and assessing the relative weights of their various attractive and unattractive features. In any event, it should certainly be emphasized that even the arguments and discussions that follow in this book are sketchy and incomplete. Indeed, since overlooked but significant features of old theories might always be brought to our attention, and new theories might always be put forward, the process of evaluation and justification can perhaps never be completely finished. It must always be tentative.

Nonetheless, however tentative our conclusions, it should be noted that in principle the process of justifying your moral views could take you rather far from where you started—this, despite the fact that "all" you are doing is trying to find a theory that fits your various "intuitions." For it is always a possibility that getting to a theory that provides the best fit overall may involve rejecting a large number of intuitions with which you began. Although it need not be the case, it certainly *could* be the case that experience and reflection will lead you to a moral theory rather unlike the one that you initially found plausible.

It may be best to conclude this section by admitting that not everyone would accept the account I have just been giving of what it is to defend an ethical theory. The topic of justification in ethics is a controversial one, and the approach I have been suggesting is by no means universally accepted. Now in point of fact, I think that in practice everyone does accept an approach pretty much like this—whether or not they realize it. But the fact remains that many do not realize it, and would reject my account. Still, to enter into this debate more carefully would be to write a book on metaethics or on justification in general, not normative ethics. So perhaps the matter is best left here. (Since I believe that the same basic approach to justification is also used in other areas of philosophy—and indeed in all inquiry whatsoever!—a full defense of my view would certainly require a very different sort of book.)

## 1.4   Factors and Foundations

Whether a given action is required, permitted, or forbidden is typically a function of several different morally relevant factors. Much of the work of normative ethics is a matter of articulating these various *normative factors,* and discovering how they interact so as to determine the moral status of an act.

An example should help to make this idea of a normative factor clearer. Suppose that someone is drowning in the lake, and the only way she can be saved is if I row out to her in a boat and pull her in. Should I do it? Presumably, the fact that my act would have a good result—it would save a life!—is one morally relevant factor in determining the rightness or wrongness of the act. In particular, if the act is permitted—or perhaps even morally required—this is in large part due to the very fact that my act would help bring about this good result, and there is no other way to achieve it. The goodness or badness of results is thus a morally relevant normative factor— a factor that can help determine the moral status of an act.

It certainly doesn't seem to be the only such factor. Suppose that the only boat at hand is not mine, but rather belongs to someone else. If I am to rescue the drowning woman, I must steal it (even though I plan to return it later). Here we have a second relevant normative factor: the fact that performing the act requires violating the property rights of the boat's owner. Whether I should still take the boat out or not depends on which of these two factors is more important, morally speaking. If, as I suppose, I should still take the boat, this is because saving a life outweighs property rights (at least in this case). And if anyone takes the opposite position, and believes that morally I shouldn't take the boat, this is presumably because they think that property rights here outweigh the chance to save a life. Whatever your answer, it seems plausible to think that there are now two normative factors that are at work in this case, and the moral status of the act depends on which factor outweighs the other.

There are other factors that might come into play as well. If the woman drowning is my wife, it might well be thought that I have a special obligation to try to rescue her—an obligation stronger than my general obligation to try to save the lives of strangers—and this will then provide a third factor that contributes to determining what it is that I should do. On the other hand, if I myself run a serious risk of drowning in the course of a rescue attempt (even though what's most likely is that we will both make it safely back to the shore), this may well provide a fourth relevant factor: perhaps, because of the potential risk to me, undertaking a rescue remains optional, rather than being morally required.

Obviously, this list of potentially relevant normative factors is far from complete. The four we have mentioned—the chance to save lives, violation of property rights, special obligations to one's wife, potential cost to the individual agent—are only offered as examples. But even this limited sample should be sufficient to help fix the basic idea of a morally relevant factor; and the example of the drowning woman (in its different versions) nicely illustrates the way in which the various relevant normative factors together determine the moral status of a given act.

Now some of the phrases that I have just been using are somewhat ambiguous. If I say of a given factor, for example, that it can "help determine the moral status of an act," then what I am saying can potentially be understood in two different ways: I might be making a claim about how we can *figure out* what the moral status of a given act is. Or I might be making a claim about what *makes* the given act have the particular moral status that it does. So let me state explicitly that when I use phrases like this, it is the latter (metaphysical, or ontological) claim that I have in mind, rather than the former (epistemological) one. That is, as we try to produce an adequate theory of the normative factors, what we are after is an account of what it is that actually makes it be the case that different acts have the status that they do. In the original version of the example of the drowning woman, if rowing out is indeed morally required, then it is the very fact that there is a life that can thus be saved that explains why this is so. It is not merely that thinking about the fact that a life can be saved is a pretty useful thing to do when trying to decide whether rowing out is really required or not. No, the fact that a life can be saved is what *makes* it be the case that the act in question is required. The same thing is true for other, and more complex, cases. If several different normative factors come into play—as in the final version of the example of the drowning woman—then it is the interaction of these very factors that grounds the ultimate moral status of the act; it is the relevant normative factors themselves that together make it be the case that the act has the particular overall moral status that it does.

However, I do not mean by any of this to deny the fact that knowledge of the normative factors can be an invaluable guide in trying to figure out what it is that we should do. After all, if the normative factors are what make it be the case that any given act has the particular moral status that it does, then someone with an adequate understanding of the normative factors and how they interact would be in a good position to decide just what the moral status of a given act really comes to (assuming, of course, that this person also knew all the relevant details about the particular act in question). Nor do I take this to be merely a hypothetical, ideal possibility— one available in principle, but never actually put into practice. For I take it that often enough people do in fact try to figure out how they should act by trying to identify the various normative factors that are relevant in the given case. Similarly, when we think about various examples—whether real or imaginary—we often assess the moral status of the relevant act by identifying the relevant factors and thinking about how these factors would interact. In short, since the factors determine (metaphysically speaking) the moral status of the act, thinking about the factors can help us determine (epistemologically speaking) the status of the act as well.

Of course, I would not want to overstate the role that thinking about the normative factors has or should have in our moral decision making. Often enough, no doubt, one simply inspects the situation—and acts. Little or no moral reflection may take place; involved appeals to moral theory may be inappropriate or impossible. Sometimes one simply has to make a judgment and act on it. In fact, this may be the most common case. As long as we are talking about individuals with a proper moral education and a good character, this may well be enough. (And if we are *not* talking about people with a good moral character, then throwing in a heavy dollop of moral theory is hardly likely to improve their choices!)

Despite this point, however, there still seems to me an important place in moral deliberation for an adequate theory of the normative factors. For we do in fact often appeal to the presence or absence of various factors in deciding how we should act. This is especially so in complex or controversial cases, where our spontaneous judgments and intuitions may leave us uncertain and confused—or in sharp disagreement with the opinions of others. One way we often try to make progress in such cases is by systematically considering the various factors that are at play. (It is with just such difficult cases that applied ethics is especially concerned, and so arguments in this area typically take the form of a careful investigation of the normative factors that are at work in the given case.) Obviously enough, to the extent that we do find ourselves making use of a theory of normative factors, it is important that that theory be a correct one.

But whatever practical implications a theory of the normative factors may have for guiding our moral deliberations, there still remains the intrinsic theoretical interest we have in possessing an adequate account. To the extent that we find ourselves intrigued by the question of how we should act, we will want to know not only what the correct answer is, in any given case, but why it is the correct answer. It is just this knowledge that an adequate theory of the normative factors would provide. To sum up: insofar as normative ethics is concerned with describing the fundamental principles that determine how we should act, much of what we need is to be found in a theory of the normative factors.

A good deal of what we want to accomplish in normative ethics, then, involves arriving at an adequate account of the factors. Unfortunately, having argued this, I must now confess that it would be far beyond the scope of this book to try to offer anything like a complete account. At best, I can only hope to provide a reasonable description of at least some of the most important normative factors. This will be our concern in Part

One. As we will see, however, providing even this much is not at all a trivial task.

First of all, a large number of purported factors have been proposed at one time or another, and people disagree as to which of these really count—that is, which of them genuinely belong on an accurate list of the potentially relevant normative factors. Second, even when there is some agreement that a particular factor belongs on the list, it is often a difficult and controversial matter to try to specify the precise content and contours of that factor. For example, suppose that we tentatively agree that one morally relevant factor is whether or not a given act will help bring about good results; we will still need to spell out exactly what it is that makes one outcome better or worse than another, and this topic is itself both complex and controversial. Finally, there remains the task of articulating how the various factors interact. When more than one factor comes into play, how do the different factors combine so as to determine the ultimate (overall) moral status of the act? And when different factors conflict, which ones outweigh the others? (The answer presumably doesn't have to be the same in every case: it may depend on the details.) The fact is, the discussion of even one normative factor can quickly become astonishingly complex. So our own discussion of the various normative factors will often do little more than scratch the surface. I hope to say enough, however, to give a sense of what I take to be the most difficult and interesting questions surrounding each of the basic types of factor.

Although a major component of normative ethics is concerned with describing the normative factors—what they are and how they interact—this does not at all exhaust the field. For we want to know not only which factors genuinely have moral relevance—but what it is that makes these the relevant factors in the first place. It is important to be clear about the nature of this new question. I am not here asking what makes a given factor relevant in some particular case: obviously, this is a matter of the details of the specific case. Rather, I am asking what is it that explains why a given factor ever makes a difference to the moral status of any act at all. To put the point another way, only certain of the many factors that have been discussed at one time or another have any genuine moral relevance. Even if we are confident what the relevant factors are, we still need to know what *explains* their relevance. Just what is it that explains why the genuinely relevant normative factors have the relevance that they do? What is the basis of their moral significance?

To answer this question is to offer a theory about the *foundations* of normative ethics. It is to offer an account of what grounds the normative factors. Obviously, it would be helpful at this point if I could now go on to quickly mention some familiar examples of foundational theories—to fix the idea and to make the contrast with normative factors intuitively clearer. Unfortunately, the most important foundational views are less familiar than the normative factors themselves, and they are sufficiently complex that I cannot easily offer examples here. So for the time being, we will have to make do with the mere *idea* of a foundational theory—a theory that attempts to explain the basis of the truly relevant normative factors. Not surprisingly, there are rival theories in this area as well, and they will be our concern in Part Two.

What may be somewhat surprising, however, is the extent to which these two areas of normative ethics—factors and foundations—can be discussed independently of one another. That is, it seems as though much of the discussion of the normative factors can take place without relying on any particular view about the foundations (a belief that is reflected in the structure of this book: the detailed examination of the normative factors takes place in Part One, while the various foundational theories are not even introduced until Part Two). Similarly, although perhaps to a lesser extent, foundational theories can be evaluated without relying on any particular view about the normative factors. So even though eventually we want to connect our views about the normative factors with our views about the foundations, it seems as though we can make at least some headway with each of these independently of the other. This is, at any rate, the practice in a good deal of contemporary moral philosophy: investigation at the level of the normative factors is typically done without making explicit theoretical commitments at the foundational level; and rival foundational theories are often assessed independently of their implications for the factoral level.

On the other hand, I certainly do not mean to be suggesting that investigations concerning either one of these levels (factoral or foundational) can or should be brought to a conclusion without any regard at all for our views about the other level. For our views about factors and foundations must cohere, and there is no particular reason to think that any given foundational theory will be compatible with any given theory about the factors. Foundational theories are not neutral with regard to what emerges at the factoral level; on the contrary, it seems quite likely that, once sufficiently specified, any particular foundational theory will support rather specific conclusions concerning the normative factors. To put the same point the other way around, any given account of the normative factors will be compatible with only some but not all theories concerning the foundations. At the very least, therefore, we must make sure that our views concerning the two levels can be coherently combined. But beyond this, we can also use our theories about a given level to help us refine or revise our views about the other level.

Ideally, after all, appeal to the correct foundational theory would help resolve any unsettled disputes we might have about the normative factors. It would enable us to see just which factors genuinely have direct moral significance, and it would answer questions about the precise nature of these factors, their relative weights, and how they interact. Indeed, since it is the correct foundational theory—whatever that turns out to be—that provides the basis for and explains the various normative factors, it should not surprise us if these various disputes about the normative factors could not be completely resolved in the absence of an adequate foundational theory.

Similarly, one significant consideration in guiding our choice between rival foundational theories will be the extent to which a given theory generates and supports our favored account of the normative factors. Although foundational theories can be assessed "in their own right" in terms of the relative plausibility of the various rationales with which they can be provided, it is certainly the case that many people will want to reject any foundational theory that fails to generate what they take to be a plausible account at the factoral level. And for any given basic approach to the foundations, we can revise and fine-tune the details of the theory with an eye to their implications at the factoral level. In principle, then, appeal to the correct account of the normative factors—and the need to find a foundational theory that will support that account—can help resolve unsettled disputes about the nature of the foundations.

Sooner or later, therefore, we will want to bring our views about the factors and our views about the foundations into contact with each other. But that does not mean that we have to develop our views about both levels simultaneously. As I have already suggested, to a surprising extent the two areas can be investigated independently of one another. (Perhaps this should not surprise us after all, since theorizing about the normative factors typically draws rather heavily upon intuitions about cases, while theorizing about the foundations draws more heavily upon metaethical intuitions about the nature of morality.) Ultimately, a complete theory of normative ethics will need to have a plausible account of both the factors and the foundations, and how the two are combined. But we can begin our investigation by focusing initially on the factors alone. Investigation of the foundations can follow later.

# Part One

# FACTORS

# 2

# THE GOOD

## 2.1  Promoting the Good

In this first half of the book, we are going to examine various factors that might be thought to possess moral relevance at the normative level. But the list of potential "candidate" factors is virtually unlimited; how should we decide which ones to discuss? My suggestion is quite simple. Most of us (the readers of this book, at any rate) share a common moral outlook which we might call *commonsense morality*. People may differ about the details, but at least the broad features are familiar and widely accepted. Even those people who reject commonsense morality—whether in whole or in part—are typically quite familiar with it (it may influence their moral intuitions, for example, even if these are intuitions that, on reflection, they are prepared to disavow). I implicitly appealed to commonsense morality in the example of the drowning woman (in 1.4), when I was trying to give intuitively plausible examples of morally relevant factors. I was counting on your acceptance of commonsense morality—or, at least, your familiarity with it. Since commonsense morality recognizes and endorses the four factors that I mentioned, I assumed that you would either accept these factors yourself or else recognize them as factors that many other people regard as relevant.

This feature seems to me to be a desirable one when selecting factors for more extended examination as well: since we will obviously have to limit our discussion, it makes sense to select factors that we will all recognize as being widely accepted. So I propose to let the common moral outlook continue to be our guide, at least so far as setting the agenda goes: the factors that we will discuss in Part One will be those that are recognized by commonsense morality. Note that we can do this without necessarily *endorsing* the views of commonsense morality. We are only letting commonsense morality set the agenda for discussion; we are not assuming that all of the factors it recognizes are of genuine moral relevance.

It is somewhat arbitrary where we begin, but for reasons that will emerge as we go along, I think the best factor to consider first is this: the goodness of outcomes. This is a factor that I think virtually everyone recognizes as morally relevant. It may not be the *only* factor that is important for determining the moral status of an act, but it is certainly at least *one* relevant factor. If an act will have bad results, that is a reason not to perform it; if, on the other hand, it will have good results, then that is a reason *to* perform it.

Sometimes, of course, no matter what we do, the outcome will be bad. Then all we can do is make the best of a bad situation. But this is still a matter of the goodness of outcomes. All other things being equal, we should pick the act where the outcome will be the least bad overall, for that will be the act with the *best* outcome (of those available to us). Similarly, and more happily, sometimes we have to choose between two acts *both* of which will have good outcomes. In such cases, all other things being equal, we should pick the act with the *better* of the two outcomes.

This talk of "all other things being equal" is just another way of recognizing that goodness of outcomes may not be the only morally relevant factor that comes into play in any given case. Even if a particular act would lead to better results overall than any other act available to the agent, perhaps there could still be *other* factors that oppose performing the given act, so that, on balance, the act is morally forbidden. If so, then in cases where this happens other things are *not* equal—and so "all things considered" the morally best act may not be the act with the best *results*. We won't start asking until the next chapter when, if ever, the goodness of outcomes can be "outweighed" in this fashion. But the point to be emphasized, once more, is this: even if goodness of outcomes is not the only factor, it is certainly at least *one* morally relevant factor. So, all other things being equal, we should pick the act with the best results. We should pick the act that best promotes the good.

It is important to understand that in saying that the moral status of an act is determined (at least in part) by its results, this is meant to include *all* of its results. It is not only the immediate, or short term, results that matter: long term results, side effects, indirect consequences—all these matter as well, and they count just as much as short term or immediate consequences. If, for example, I must choose between an act with a small immediate positive effect—but no other later effects—and an alternative act that will have no immediate effect, but will eventually produce a lot of good, it is the second act I should perform. Similarly, if an act will have both good results and bad results, then these must *all* be taken into account. The question is: how good or bad will the results be overall, on balance, taking into account all of the results; and how does this compare to the overall results of the other acts available to the agent?

Now it was probably obvious all along that talk of "good outcomes" or "good results" was meant to include all of the results and all of the consequences. But for all that, it must be noted that these terms are indeed being used here in a somewhat nonstandard fashion. For normally when we talk of the "results" or "outcomes" or "consequences" of an act, we mean to be restricting our attention to those events taking place *after* the act that are *caused* by the act. It is only if the act literally produces some later event that we call that event one of the act's results or consequences. For example, if the later event would have happened anyway, we don't normally consider it part of the consequences of the act. But for our purposes in normative ethics, we need to give these terms a "wider," more inclusive sense than is normal. In thinking about the goodness of outcomes, what matters is not the goodness of what I literally produce myself, but rather the goodness of everything that ultimately happens, the goodness of the "upshot."

An example should make this clear. Suppose five people are in danger of losing their lives, but if I try to rescue any of them at all, I will only be able to save one of them. Luckily, however, there is someone else willing to perform the rescue—and she will indeed be able to save all five, provided that I don't get in the way. (If I am in the way, she won't be able to save any.) Now what should I do? If I sit back and let the other person perform the rescue, I don't actually produce any good at all myself, whereas if I do try to perform the rescue, my act would at least produce the good outcome of one life saved. So should we say that I ought to try to perform the rescue, since this is the act that will have better results, in the normal narrow sense of that term?

But this is clearly the wrong answer. Even though I will save one, the other four will die. Yet were I only to sit back and allow the woman to rescue all five, then no one would die at all! This second outcome is obviously the better one from the moral point of view, even though in terms of the narrow consequences of my act this may not be the best choice. What this shows, of course, is that in thinking about goodness of outcomes as a morally relevant factor, our real concern should be with the overall upshot—how good or bad things will be if I act in one way rather than another—rather than with what I myself produce. Accordingly, when we talk of the results, consequences, or outcome of an act, let us understand these terms in a wide sense, a sense that encompasses everything that happens, the entire upshot. (The example also shows, incidentally, that sometimes the act with the best results will be the "act" of doing nothing at all.)

So when we look at the results of an act we want to look at everything that happens. This stretches the normal notion of "results" somewhat, but seems to be necessary to get at the morally relevant concept. But we may need to stretch the notion of "results" in a second way as well: in principle we may need to look not only at what *will* happen (if the act is performed) but also at what *is* happening (when the act is performed). In some cases this may be a fairly obvious point. For example, a given act may itself be quite difficult to perform. In deciding whether that act has good results overall, we will surely want to include, say, the physical pain the agent suffers *while* performing the act, and not only the good and bad results that may come after the act is completed.

Other examples will be more controversial, and will depend on the specific theories (yet to come) concerning exactly what features make an outcome good. On at least some views, however, the occurrence of an act of a given type may in itself be a good or bad thing that can happen; if so, then in assessing the goodness of outcomes we will want to include the agent's act itself as a potentially significant part of the "outcome" of the act.

Even if we stretch the term this far, it may seem obvious, at any rate, that there can be no need to take into account—as part of the act's "outcome"—what happens *before* the agent acts. After all, no act can alter the past, and so whatever good or bad events occurred in the past will be the same no matter what the agent does now; so the past cannot be relevant in determining whether one act has a better outcome than another. In fact, however, this too will depend on the details of one's theory of the good. On some views it will matter whether the past and the future "fit" together in certain ways (for example, we might think the outcome is better if certain people who have done evil in the past are punished in the future). On views like this, we might say that what matters is how well the course of world history goes. The upshot of some act might be that history as a whole goes less well, even though we wouldn't see this if we looked merely at what happens during or after the act. I think we should leave room for the possibility of such views, and so we will have to stretch the notions of "outcome," "results," and "consequences" so that they include absolutely everything that happens if an act is performed—past, present, and future.

This is certainly not to say that absolutely everything that happens *does* affect the goodness of the outcome. (Obviously, much, or most, of what happens is neither good nor bad in itself.) We still need an account of exactly which features go into making one outcome better than another. And this will, in fact, be our major concern in this chapter. But one final preliminary point still needs to be clarified. When we say that one morally relevant factor in determining the moral status of an act is whether that act will promote the good, we do not mean to be taking into account every kind of moral goodness that an act might produce. Our concern, rather, is only with *intrinsic* goodness.

Many things with moral value possess only *instrumental* value. They are valuable only insofar as they can contribute to producing other goods (or eliminating various bads). Thus, for example, medicine, air conditioners, automobiles, and money all possess instrumental value; they are useful means for acquiring or producing other goods (or eliminating bads): among other things, they can be used to produce various pleasures and to eliminate or avoid various pains. For most of us, these things are valuable *only* because of this instrumental value. On reflection we would agree that we do not really value these things for their own sake, or in themselves. They are merely instrumental goods, not intrinsic goods. In contrast, most of us value pleasure for its own sake; we think of it as something good in itself—not merely as a means to getting something else (though it may be that as well). Similarly, we think of pain as something bad in itself, something to be avoided not merely because of what else it might produce, but for its own sake. That is to say, we take pleasure to be intrinsically good, and pain to be intrinsically bad.

In determining the moral status of an act, it is only the intrinsic value of the results that matters. It would seem foolish, for example, to prefer one of two outcomes that were similar in terms of all the intrinsic goodness that they contained, simply because the first contained a far larger amount of instrumental good. After all, instrumental goods matter only because they can produce intrinsic goods. Ultimately, then, all that really matters are the intrinsic goods (and the intrinsic evils). So insofar as an act's moral status depends on the goodness of its outcome, what it depends on is the intrinsic goodness of the outcome.

This is not to deny that for many practical purposes it is handy to evaluate outcomes in terms of the instrumental goods they may contain. I might, for example, reasonably choose between two acts on the basis of which will produce more money for me—knowing all the while that money is of merely instrumental value. But in such cases I also know and expect that the extra money can eventually be put to work to produce some extra good that I value for its own sake. That is, I reasonably take the short term difference in instrumental goods as evidence of a long term difference in intrinsic goods. Ultimately, however, what really justifies my choice is this long term difference in intrinsic goodness.

Of course, all of this still leaves us with the difficult task of deciding exactly what is of intrinsic value (or intrinsic disvalue). What makes one outcome intrinsically better than another? This is the question we will be exploring in the rest of this chapter.

## 2.2  Well-Being

In principle, the intrinsic goodness of an outcome might depend on several different types of factors. That is, just as the moral status of an act might depend on the interplay of several different morally relevant factors—one of which is the goodness of the act's outcome—the goodness of the outcome may itself depend on the interplay of several different subfactors. (And the subfactors may themselves depend on several further factors—the "subsubfactors." Since such talk can quickly get clumsy, typically I will simply call them all "factors," whatever their level. It is, at any rate, largely a matter of convenience and custom whether we view the "subfactors" as forming a genuinely unified single "factor" at the next higher level—or instead view talk of the "factor" as merely being shorthand for referring to the group of subfactors.)

As we shall see, it is controversial exactly what factors go into making one outcome better than another. But once more there is a point on which virtually everyone agrees: one such factor is how well off people are. That is, all other things being equal, one outcome is better than another if people are better off in that outcome. And, all other things being equal, if people are less well off, if their lives are going less well, then the outcome is worse.

As before, talk of "other things being equal" is to remind us that this may not be the *only* factor that matters; but it is, at least, *one* of the factors that matters. The higher the level of well-being, all other things being equal, the better the outcome.

But what, exactly, is well-being? What is it for someone's life to go better or worse? What does someone's being better or worse off consist in?

It is important to understand what we are *not* asking in raising these questions. We are not asking what sorts of things may have a causal impact on well-being. Obviously enough, almost anything at all might, in the right circumstances, affect someone's level of well-being. And certain things will have an effect in almost all circumstances: money, a job, and opportunities, for example, will almost always raise your level of well-being; and poverty, disease, and enemies will almost always lower your well-being. But these things are only a means to raising or lowering your level of well-being. They have instrumental value (or disvalue) because of the impact they can have on how well off you are. But they are not themselves what well-being (or ill-being) *consists* in. What we want to know, then, is what is it that *constitutes* being well off? (Not: what are the *means* to being well off?) We want to know: what are the "components" of well-being?

One important and popular answer is this: well-being consists in the presence of pleasure and the absence of pain. The more pleasure and the less pain that a life contains, the better the life. Increase the amount of pleasure that a person experiences (or decrease the amount of pain), and you make that person better off; increase the pain (or decrease the pleasure), and you make her worse off.

Now in point of fact, pretty much everyone believes at least this much: the presence of pleasure and the absence of pain is at least one component of well-being. (It is quite hard to deny this. The value of pleasure and the disvalue of pain seem virtually self-evident to anyone experiencing them.) But the particular view I have in mind makes a bolder claim; it holds that well-being consists *solely* in the presence of pleasure and the absence of pain. Pleasure and pain are the *only* elements that directly constitute how well off a person is.

We can put this same point another way. If we ask ourselves what are the intrinsic goods by virtue of which a life worth living *is* a life worth living, the answer—according to this view—is pleasure, and only pleasure. Similarly, the only intrinsic evil by virtue of which a life is less worth living is pain. This view—that well-being consists solely in the presence of pleasure and the absence of pain—might be called *welfare hedonism.*

Actually, there are at least four different hedonistic views that need to be distinguished. *Psychological hedonism* is the claim that—as a matter of empirical, psychological fact—everyone's ultimate goal is to pursue their own pleasure and minimize their own pain. *Ethical hedonism* is the claim that—as a matter of normative ethics—what everyone *should* do morally is to try to maximize pleasure and minimize pain. From a logical standpoint, at least, since these two views make no claims about what has or lacks intrinsic value, they need to be distinguished from *value hedonism,* which is the claim that pleasure is the only intrinsic good and pain the only intrinsic evil. But even this last view needs to be distinguished from welfare hedonism, which limits itself to the somewhat more modest claim that *well-being* consists solely in the presence of pleasure and the absence of pain. (After all, one might accept welfare hedonism and yet still believe that there are other intrinsic goods that have nothing to do with well-being.)

Some people are attracted to all four hedonistic claims. But it is only welfare hedonism with which we are concerned here, since it is only welfare hedonism that purports to be and limits itself to being a theory about the nature of well-being. So, for our purposes, we can put these other versions of hedonism aside and use the term "hedonism" to refer to welfare hedonism.

Of course, the fact of the matter is that life is not one unending run of intense pleasure, unblemished by any pain, and so the hedonist needs to tell us how to rank lives that are mixtures of various sorts of pleasures and pains. However, the basic idea here is fairly simple and obvious: add up the pleasures and subtract the pains. The greater the "sum" (that is, the higher the net balance of pleasure minus pain), the better the life. But since not all pleasures are equally good, and not all pains are equally bad, the view needs to be made somewhat more complicated. Still, a solution is not beyond our reach. Intuitively, it seems, the longer a pleasure lasts, the better; and the more intense the pleasure is, the better as well. So by multiplying intensity times duration, we can calculate the quantity of pleasure a given pleasant experience contains. Similarly, we can calculate the quantity of pain by multiplying the intensity of the pain times the duration of the pain. By adding up the total quantity of pleasure and then subtracting from this the total quantity of pain, we arrive at a measure of how good a life someone has had as a whole—their overall level of well-being. (Different calculations, but along similar lines, will allow us to make judgments about how well off a person is at a time, or during a certain period, or how much a person's level of well-being would vary under different outcomes.)

Advocates of such *quantitative hedonism* need not believe that we can actually make the relevant calculations, at least not with very much precision. But they can still claim that the basic ideas expressed here capture real and important insights into the nature of well-being: well-being is simply a matter of pleasure and pain; and the value or disvalue of pleasures and pains is simply a matter of their intensity and duration.

One important implication of quantitative hedonism is that quantity for quantity, all pleasures are equally valuable. Of course, people will differ from one another with regard to what sorts of things *give* them pleasure: you may derive great pleasure from listening to opera, while I find the experience painful; I may enjoy bird-watching, while you find it boring. From a practical standpoint, therefore, it will clearly be important to get our facts straight about what exactly gives pleasure to whom. But so long as we are indeed talking about equal quantities of pleasure, it doesn't matter where the pleasure comes from. Similarly, some things (such as great art) may be rich and fruitful sources of large quantities of intense and abiding pleasure, while other things (such as watching television) are at best sources of minimal, mild, and fleeting pleasure. So from a practical standpoint it may well be rational to invest more energy in contemplating art than in watching television. But so long as we are talking about equal quantities of pleasure, it doesn't matter where the pleasure comes from: a unit of art-based pleasure is of no greater value than a unit of television-based pleasure.

This, at any rate, is the view of quantitative hedonism. But it is at just this point that some think quantitative hedonism goes astray. Many find it very hard to believe that one kind of pleasure is no more valuable than another (unit for unit). After all, if *quantity* of pleasure is all that matters, this seems to lead to some pretty bizarre conclusions. Consider the life of a contented pig, wallowing in the mud: it might be filled with pleasure, a far greater quantity of pleasure than can be found in the life of a person. Yet who would want to trade places with the pig? Who thinks that the pig has a better life?

Pressed to defend our preference for a human life over a porcine existence, a natural suggestion is this: pigs might have a greater quantity of pleasure, but humans can have pleasures of a much more valuable *kind*. Unlike pigs, humans can experience love, friendship, and art; they can have the pleasures of discovery, creativity, and understanding. We seem drawn to the thought that such "spiritual" or "mental" pleasures are simply of a higher quality than the mere "physical" or "bodily" pleasures that are all that are available to the pig—and that these "higher" pleasures are of greater intrinsic value than the "lower" pleasures. If this is right, then when judging the level of well-being of some individual (whether human or non-human) we must take into account not only quantity but also *quality*. (Perhaps a new formula could achieve this by multiplying intensity times duration times a "quality rating"—but we need not pursue this question. We can also put aside, for the sake of simplicity, the question of whether quality can also affect the value of *pains,* as well as pleasures.)

Such *qualitative hedonism* will be resisted by advocates of quantitative hedonism, who may claim that the appeal of qualitative hedonism is based on a simple mistake. As we have already observed, and as the quantitative hedonists themselves would stress, the sources of the so-called higher pleasures typically lead to far greater *quantities* of pleasure than do the sources of the so-called lower pleasures. So from a practical point of view, it typically makes sense to prefer the experiences of the higher pleasures—for these experiences will simply contain more pleasure! But this doesn't show that a given quantity of higher pleasure is any more valuable than the *same* quantity of lower pleasure. In and of itself, quality just doesn't make a difference to the intrinsic value of (a unit of) pleasure.

In reply, the qualitative hedonists will simply deny that they are making any such mistake. Admittedly, sources of higher pleasures typically yield far greater quantities of pleasure than do sources of lower pleasures; but even when we take this into account—even when we focus on similar quantities of pleasure—we still find ourselves attracted to the thought that a given quantity of higher pleasure is more valuable than the same quantity of lower pleasure.

Like many of the other controversies in normative ethics that will be discussed in this book, I will not try to settle here which side is correct or which side has the stronger argument. For reasons discussed earlier (in 1.3) it should not surprise us if intelligent and thoughtful individuals can sincerely disagree as to which view seems most plausible when all the arguments are taken into account. (It is also worth bearing in mind that here—as elsewhere—further arguments might be offered on either side.) Consequently, all one can do—on this question, as on the others that will follow—is to weigh the various arguments of each side and to decide for oneself.

Of course, even if we agree with the qualitative hedonist, that higher pleasures are more valuable than lower pleasures, we are still in need of some test to tell which of two pleasures is the more valuable (that is, higher in quality). The most plausible suggestion that has been made is this: ask the experts. That is, ask those who have experience with both sorts of pleasures. If those who have experience with both pleasure X and pleasure Y prefer to have X rather than Y (given a choice between equal quantities of either), then we can reasonably conclude that X is the more valuable pleasure.

It must be admitted that applying this test is not without its difficulties. As often as not, it may be impossible to find someone who genuinely has first-hand experience with both kinds of pleasures. How many lovers of opera really know what it is like to be totally absorbed watching game shows on television? And what human being has had the experience of being a pig wallowing in the mud? Still, the qualitative hedonist can admit these practical difficulties while insisting that the basic idea behind the test is correct: pleasures can differ as to their quality; and these differences in quality would be reflected in the preferences of those who had experienced them.

A remaining worry is this. Is qualitative hedonism genuinely a form of *hedonism?* The welfare hedonist claims that pleasure (and the absence of pain) is all that matters intrinsically for well-being. If one holds that quantity of pleasure is not all that matters, but that quality matters too, has one abandoned the commitment to hedonism? People's intuitions on this question seem to differ, although it is not clear what turns on the answer other than the label. Even if the so-called qualitative hedonist is not genuinely a hedonist, the position she holds might still be the truth.

However, pushed this far, we might want to go farther. If the value of our various experiences can vary—depending on what *kind* of pleasures they are—perhaps other experiences may have value, too, even though they are not pleasures at all! Perhaps certain experiences have a high quality and contribute to our well-being, even though it would be stretching things to say they are pleasant. At the very least, it might be grossly misleading to focus on whatever pleasure they contain, as this might be quite irrelevant to their value.

Perhaps, then, the position we should actually accept is this: all that intrinsically matters for determining one's level of well-being are the various experiences one has—one's mental states. Some mental states are more valuable than others, and pleasure is presumably one such kind of valuable experience (or one aspect of an experience that may make it valuable). But it is not the only kind of valuable experience (or the only aspect of an experience that can give it value). In short, perhaps we should simply accept a *mental state* theory of well-being.

Strictly speaking, of course, hedonism is a version of a mental state theory (or perhaps: it is a family of mental state theories). It agrees that your mental states are what determine your level of well-being, and it holds a particular view as to which mental states have value (namely, the pleasant ones). But we are now considering the possibility of theories that move beyond hedonism in allowing other kinds of experiences to have value as well. Of course, any fully specified mental state theory would need to tell us exactly what kinds of experiences have what kind of value. And it should be noted that, other than hedonism, there have been relatively few attempts to do this. But even if one is uncertain as to exactly which kinds of experiences contribute to well-being, and by how much, one might be quite convinced as to the fundamental truth of mental statism: your mental states are the only things that directly determine your level of well-being.

Many people find the idea of mental statism quite compelling. It lies behind the common saying that "What you don't know can't hurt you." What else *could* constitute well-being other than having the right mental states? Yet mental state theories seem to leave something important out, for there are cases in which all mental state theories lead to answers that are difficult to accept.

Imagine a man who dies contented, thinking he has achieved everything he wanted in life: his wife and family love him, he is a respected member of the community, and he has founded a successful business. Or so he thinks.

In reality, however, he has been completely deceived: his wife cheated on him, his daughter and son were only nice to him so that they would be able to borrow the car, the other members of the community only pretended to respect him for the sake of the charitable contributions he sometimes made, and his business partner has been embezzling funds from the company, which will soon go bankrupt.

In thinking about this man's life, it is difficult to believe that it is all a life could be, that this life has gone about as well as a life could go. Yet this seems to be the very conclusion mental state theories must reach! For from the "inside"—looking only at the man's experiences—everything was perfect. We can imagine that the man's mental states were *exactly* the same as the ones he would have had if he had actually been loved and respected. So if mental states are all that matter, then—since this man got the mental states right—there is nothing missing from this man's life at all. It is a picture of a life that has gone well. But this seems quite an unacceptable thing to say about this life; it is surely not the kind of life we would want for ourselves. So mental state theories must be wrong.

A defender of the mental state approach might insist that the businessman's life must have gone well, since he was happy. But those who think something important was missing from this man's life need not be impressed by this answer. Some will deny that the man was genuinely happy: he *thought* he was, but in reality, he was not; perhaps the example shows that there is more to happiness than having the right sorts of mental states. Others will agree that the businessman was indeed happy; but they will argue that this only shows that there is more to well-being than happiness, since something is certainly less than ideal about the deceived man's life. In short, whatever we feel about the correct account of happiness, the example still seems to show that mental state theories are wrong: having the best kind of mental states is just not enough.

To be fair, some mental state theorists may not think that our deceived businessman had the very best kinds of experiences—perhaps it would be better to have experiences of adventure or discovery. But it seems we could compose a comparable story whichever mental states are best. Indeed, if we want, we can imagine an "experience machine" that electronically stimulates your brain, giving you whatever experiences you think most valuable. The effect is so perfect that it will feel ("from the inside") *exactly* as though you were climbing mountains, composing symphonies, or what have you. In reality, you are simply floating in a tank in the scientist's lab—but once you are hooked up, all memory of this will disappear, and you will have exactly the mental states endorsed by your favorite mental state theory.

Would you want to spend your life hooked up to an experience machine? If not, then it seems that mental state theories must be wrong—all of them. For life on the experience machine gets the mental states exactly right; so if something is missing from a life on the experience machine—if it is not the best kind of life imaginable—then there must be more to well-being than having the right kind of experiences.

But what is missing? A natural response to these examples—the deceived businessman, the experience machine—is that these people don't really have what they *want*. They *think* they do, but they don't. The businessman wanted to be loved and respected. He thought he was—from the inside it *seemed* that he was, he had the same mental states as someone who was— but still he wasn't *really* loved and respected, even though that was what he *wanted*. Similarly, the person on the experience machine may, say, have the very same mental states as someone who is climbing a mountain, and climbing a mountain may be what he most wants to do. But since he obviously is not really climbing any mountains, he doesn't truly have what he wants—to climb mountains! In short, what is missing from all of these examples is that the person's preferences are not actually satisfied; things are not in fact the way they want them to be.

The point could be put this way: what we want out of life is to have what we *want* out of life, and what we want is almost always far more than merely having certain kinds of experiences. For example, if you want to be a great and famous novelist, then your desire is only satisfied if you have in fact written a great novel, and your work is well-known by others. Merely having the experiences is not enough to actually satisfy the desire. (It should be noted that "satisfy" is being used here in a somewhat technical sense: a desire is satisfied, in this sense, if and only if the very thing that is desired actually occurs. This concept should not be confused with the *feeling* of satisfaction that often accompanies our believing that our desires have been met.)

These thoughts suggest a desire-based or a *preference* theory of well-being. According to the preference theory, well-being consists in having one's preferences satisfied. To the extent that your preferences or desires are satisfied, you are better off; to the extent that your preferences or desires are not satisfied, you are less well off. (Of course not all of your preferences are equally important to you, so we would probably want to make the view more complicated, holding that the stronger the desire, the greater the contribution to well-being made by the satisfaction of that desire. But we won't pursue these details here.)

Not surprisingly, mental state theorists will argue that the attractiveness of the preference theory is based on a confusion. Unlike our make-believe examples, they will note, in real life there is actually only one way to achieve the very same mental states one would have if the corresponding "external" states of affairs really existed—and that is to actually bring about the external states of affairs. For example, the only way to have the very same experiences as someone climbing a mountain is to actually climb a mountain. So from a practical standpoint, we are justified in simply aiming at the *external* states, knowing that, if we can achieve these, the mental states will follow. Thus, aiming at the external states has instrumental value; it is the best means to the mental states. But this should not mislead us into thinking that the external states have *intrinsic* value, making a direct contribution to well-being; only the mental states themselves do that.

Preference theorists, however, may not be impressed by this argument. They will, of course, admit that in real life a given set of experiences and the corresponding external states of affairs go pretty much hand in hand—we don't get the one without the other. But this doesn't show that it is the former and not the latter that matters. We may have to think about various kinds of make-believe examples to find cases where we would have the mental states without the corresponding external reality; but when we do think about such cases, we see quite clearly that what we value is *more* than merely having the right mental states. Our preferences concern external reality, too, and not only experiences. Of course, it is certainly true that *one* of the things we all have preferences about is having the right mental states. (I want to experience pleasures and not pain; I want to have the experiences of loving and being loved; I want to experience the accomplishment of my various goals; and so on.) So a preference theory will certainly recognize that my mental states are one of the things that help determine my level of well-being. But mental state theories go wrong in claiming that mental states are the only thing that directly determine my level of well-being. My other preferences matter too; and they must be satisfied as well if I am to be completely well off.

Once more, I won't try to settle this dispute. But I do want to consider two other possible objections to the preference theory. Both try to show that the theory yields unacceptable results. The first objection notes that, according to the preference theory, I am made better off by the satisfaction of my various desires, regardless of the subject matter of the given desire. Suppose, then, that I am a fan of large prime numbers, and so I hope and desire that the total number of atoms in the universe is a prime. Imagine, furthermore, that the total number of atoms is, in point of fact, prime. Since this desire is satisfied, the preference theory must say that I am better off for it, that my life is the better for it. (I don't *know* that my desire is satisfied, of course. But as already noted, the question of whether a desire is satisfied should not be confused with the question of whether one realizes it and consequently has a feeling of satisfaction.)

But this is absurd! The number of atoms in the universe has nothing at all to do with the quality of my life. It makes no difference at all to my level of well-being. (Were the number really even, this would not leave me *worse* off!) So the preference theory must be false.

One possible explanation of what has gone wrong is this. My preferences can range over anything at all—including things that have nothing to do with me or my life. But the brute satisfaction of *these* preferences cannot plausibly be claimed to make me better off; so an *unrestricted* preference theory is unacceptable. The only plausible approach will be in terms of a *restricted* preference theory: we will have to find the particular subset of my desires that concern my life, and claim that it is only the satisfaction of *those* desires that constitutes my well-being.

(The mental state theorist, of course, will insist that this misdiagnoses the problem. The real source of the absurdity is in thinking that the mere satisfaction of a desire—any desire—can, in and of itself, make me better off, even if I never know about it, and so even if it never has any effect on my mental states. But the preference theorist may reply that she has already admitted that one of the things we care about are our mental states, in particular knowing that our desires have been satisfied. So the preference theorist can acknowledge that if one of my desires is satisfied without my knowing about it, I am still not as well off as I might have been—since my desire to *know* about it is not satisfied.)

The second objection to the preference theory—even in its restricted form—is this. Many of my desires, including desires about my life, are based on misinformation, sloppy thinking, inexperience, prejudice, bias, and various other kinds of error or irrationality. I might want something, for example, because I am misinformed as to its nature, and I falsely believe I will enjoy having it. It seems implausible to claim that giving me what I want in a case like this makes me better off. (Well, strictly speaking, knowing that I had gotten my way might give me some mild feeling of satisfaction, and this would presumably make me slightly better off; but what seems implausible is the claim that satisfying this mistaken desire leaves me better off in and of itself.) Yet I do in fact have such mistaken (or crazy, or irrational) desires among my desires, and so the preference theory apparently has to say that satisfying these desires does indeed improve my level of well-being.

To avoid this result, we need to distinguish between *actual* preference theories and *ideal* preference theories. As the name suggests, actual preference theories claim that well-being is a matter of the satisfaction of your actual desires—the desires you do in fact have, whatever their basis. As we have just seen, this has the counterintuitive implication that satisfying even your irrational or misinformed desires leaves you better off. In contrast, ideal preference theories claim that well-being is a matter of the satisfaction of your "ideal" desires—that is, the desires you *would* have if you were fully informed, thinking clearly, free from prejudice and bias, and so on. Since you would not have misinformed, crazy, or irrational desires under such ideal conditions, they are not among your ideal desires; so, on this view, satisfaction of such desires does not contribute to your well-being. It seems, then, that preference theorists who want to avoid the second objection should embrace an *ideal* preference theory. (Of course, assuming that they want to avoid the first objection as well, they will actually need to embrace a *restricted* ideal preference theory.)

But once we have made the move to an ideal preference theory, we may want to move even further. After all, what exactly is it that explains why it is only ideal desires whose satisfaction will contribute to well-being? Why does having what we want leave us better off in those cases—but only in those cases—where the desires in question are ideal desires? We cannot say: having what we want makes us better off by virtue of the very fact that these are the things we want. For this view actually supports the *actual* preference theory, rather than the ideal preference theory. (The things we want include everything that we *do* want—not just those things we would want if informed; and some of the things we *would* want if we had ideal preferences we do not in fact already want.)

A tempting thought is this. Having the things we would want—if only we were fully informed, rational, free from bias, and so forth—is valuable, because these are the things that are truly worth having! That is, if we were fully informed, and so on, we would be in an ideal position to *recognize* which things have value and which things do not. And then our preferences would follow accordingly: we would prefer to have what has more value over what has less.

But this means that the appeal to preferences is not doing any actual work in explaining the source of the value. It is not that the various goods that we would want were we ideally informed are valuable because we would desire them; rather, we would want these goods because we would be able to *see* that they are indeed valuable, *independently* of our wanting them.

Thus we are led to *objective* theories of well-being, theories that hold that being well off is a matter of having certain goods in one's life, goods that are simply worth having, objectively speaking. Similarly, there may be certain objective bads or evils, the having of which simply leaves one worse off. Possession of the relevant goods and the absence of the relevant evils is what constitutes well-being. And the goods and evils themselves have intrinsic value or disvalue independently of our desires (actual or ideal); indeed, they have the particular value they have regardless of whether anyone is in a position to realize this.

Of course, any fully specified objective theory will need to provide us with a list of the various objective goods and evils that together determine one's level of well-being. Different objective theories will provide different lists. Indeed, it is possible to view hedonism as a kind of objective theory—one with a very short list! (Pleasure is the only objective good; pain the only objective evil.) But most objective theories will go beyond hedonism in offering longer lists—lists that include other mental states, and indeed include various external states of affairs as well (that is, they will include more than mental states alone). Typical goods on such lists might include accomplishment, creativity, health, knowledge, friendship, freedom, fame, and respect.

The preference theorist will hasten to point out that goods like these are typically desired by us (and certainly would be desired under ideal conditions), so the preference theory too can recognize the contribution these things make to well-being. And the hedonist will hasten to point out that goods like these are typically of crucial instrumental value in achieving the most pleasant mental states, so hedonism too will recognize the contribution these things make to well-being. The objective theorist, however, thinks that both these approaches miss the mark: the hedonist goes wrong in failing to recognize that these goods have intrinsic value, and not merely instrumental value; the preference theorist goes wrong in failing to see that the intrinsic value these goods possess is had objectively—it is not based on or somehow derived from the fact that we do or would desire them.

Yet if desire is not the basis of the value of these goods, what is? And what is it, if anything, that unifies the various items on the list? Why do these things, and only these things, have objective value? Not surprisingly, answers to these questions are difficult to come by, and different objective theorists offer different answers. Many proposals take the form of *perfectionism:* the objective goods are those that are elements in an ideal or perfect human life, one which fully realizes the distinctive and essential characteristics of human nature. Of course, even within a broadly perfectionist approach there is room for considerable disagreement, both with regard to what constitutes human nature and—accordingly—what goods are elements in the perfect human life.

But however we settle these questions, a difficulty remains. As we have seen, the objective theorist holds that possession of the objective goods makes one better off—regardless of whether or not one realizes this. This seems to have the implication that your life could be made better off by the possession of some "good" even though you yourself dislike it and would greatly prefer to be without it: since the good possesses objective value, your own opinion on the subject is quite irrelevant. Your life could be going well even though you are unhappy with almost all its central features! Thus, like the other theories of well-being, the objective theory too seems to lead to unacceptable results.

Some objective theorists may be willing to live with this implication of their theory. Others, however, may try to resist it, by claiming that although the value of the objective goods is not *based* on one's preferences or pleasure, nonetheless it is true for each objective good that if one possessed it, one would be glad to have it. But it is hard to see what could guarantee the truth of this fortunate convergence of objective value and desire or enjoyment. Indeed, critics of objective theories may well think that there simply *is* no way to guarantee this result: if we want convergence of goodness and desire or enjoyment, then we must build desire or enjoyment right into the definition of goodness. That is to say, we must appeal to either hedonism or a preference theory.

This then brings us full circle. Each theory of well-being has its attractive features, but none is without its drawbacks. Although there is considerable agreement that well-being is a central factor in determining the goodness of an outcome, there is nothing approaching agreement as to what exactly well-being consists in. As always, this does not mean that no single view is correct; it does, however, mean that each of us will have to decide for himself or herself which view is the most plausible one on balance—once all of the arguments of each side have been considered.

It is worth noting, finally, that despite this philosophical disagreement as to the precise theoretical basis of well-being, there is in fact a considerable consensus concerning most real-life cases. Advocates of the various theories may differ as to whether various goods are merely instrumental to well-being or are instead directly constitutive of well-being. But when considering realistic cases, we find that most plausible views are in a fair amount of agreement as to who is well off and who is not. So from a practical standpoint, at least, our inability to resolve the theoretical dispute may not be debilitating.

## 2.3   The Total View

Let's suppose that you've come away from the previous section with an adequate theory of well-being. It will be a theory of *individual* well-being, that is, a theory that tells us what it is for a given individual to be better or worse off. Such a theory is obviously useful for us, given our belief that well-being is at least one factor that determines the overall goodness of outcomes. But we can't use it as it stands, till we decide what to do about the fact that there is more than one person in the world. (There are, of course, millions and billions of people in the world; but the logical problem arises as soon as there are two!) For each person—let us suppose—we can form a judgment concerning how well off that person is and how that person's level of well-being would vary under different outcomes. But what do we do with all of this information? Whose well-being are we to take into account, in deciding which outcome is better?

One possible view is this: each one of us should take into account only his or her own level of well-being. If this view is correct, then when I say that a given outcome is better, what I should mean is that it is better in terms of my own well-being. And when you say that a given outcome is better, what you should mean is that it is better in terms of *your* well-being.

This view doesn't deny that one person's well-being can be affected in various ways by the level of well-being of another. Nor need it deny that the outcome that is best for one person might well be best for many others as well. It is just that when any given person evaluates an outcome in terms of well-being, all that *counts*—directly, in and of itself—is that particular person's level of well-being. Someone's saying that the outcome is good is just a way of saying that it is good *for them*.

A different possible view holds that each one of us should take into account *everyone's* level of well-being. When I say that a given outcome is better, then, I mean that it is better counting everyone—not just me. And when you say that a given outcome is better, you mean the same thing: better, counting everyone.

Of course, this second view would be very similar to the first, if each of us counted everyone, but only for a very small amount, while counting ourselves for a great deal. So let's add, straight off, that according to this second view each of us should not only count everyone but should count everyone *equally*.

Now we agreed at the start of this chapter that one factor that determines the moral status of an act is the goodness of the outcome of that act. And we also agreed that well-being is at least one subfactor that helps determine the goodness of an outcome. But now we see that we have to decide how this factor—goodness of outcome—is to be understood: is the morally relevant factor only how good the outcome is *for me,* or is the morally relevant factor how good the outcome is *overall,* taking *everyone's* well-being into account?

So long as we clearly bear in mind that what we are asking is what matters from the *moral* point of view, I think that most of us will agree that everyone's well-being needs to be taken into account. If an act will benefit me, this is certainly a good result; but if it will benefit others as well, this is an even better result, morally speaking. Indeed, an act might have good results, from the moral point of view, even if there is no benefit in it for me at all. I pretty much took all this for granted previously: for example, in discussing the case of the drowning woman (in 1.4), I assumed we would all agree that saving the woman's life was a good result. And I assumed I could say this even without knowing whether my own level of well-being would somehow be improved by my act as well. So when we are considering goodness of outcomes as a factor that can help determine the moral status of an act, everyone's well-being counts.

(What could tempt us to think otherwise? Well, we might get the question of what counts, morally speaking, confused with the question of what counts from the *rational* point of view—or we might think the two must coincide (see 1.2). And then we might also hold the view that the only thing that I can count from the rational point of view is my own well-being. But if you do indeed accept this last claim about rationality—and I for one see no reason to believe it—then it seems much more plausible to *deny* that the rational point of view and the moral point of view must coincide. For it is extremely implausible to suggest that *morally* speaking, no one counts but myself.)

In talking about goodness of outcomes as a morally relevant factor, then, we are not just talking about goodness from a "personal" point of view or a "subjective" point of view—what's good for some particular individual. We are, rather, talking about goodness from what is sometimes called an "objective" point of view, an "impartial" point of view, or an "impersonal" point of view. (None of these labels is perfect, and the last is particularly unfortunate: talk of what is good from the "impersonal" point of view might suggest that we are considering a standpoint that has nothing to do with persons! Better labels might be that of the "transpersonal" or "omnipersonal" point of view. But use of "impersonal" in this context is pretty well established.)

Suppose we agree then that goodness of outcomes is a matter of the overall objective good, the goodness of the results taking everyone's well-being into account. This immediately raises a new problem, given that what is good for one person may not be good for another.

Imagine a very simple case. Suppose I must choose between producing outcome A and outcome B, and my choice will only affect two people. If I pick A, Anatole will be better off than if I pick B; but if I pick B, Belinda will be better off than if I pick A. So outcome A is better for Anatole, and B is better for Belinda. But which outcome is better taking *both* of these people into account? (Strictly, we should have asked: which outcome is better taking *everyone* into account? But since no one else is affected, these seem to come to the same thing in this case.)

Obviously, what would be best of all would be an outcome in which both Anatole *and* Belinda are benefited. Unfortunately, however, this is impossible, and only *one* person can be benefited. But who should it be? Is the outcome better if Belinda is benefited, or is it better if Anatole is benefited?

A natural proposal is this: it depends on who will benefit *more*. For example, if Anatole will be much better off in A than in B, while Belinda would only be slightly better off in B than in A, then A is the better outcome overall: admittedly, Belinda is the "loser" in A, but she does not lose very much; while if we picked B, then *Anatole* would be the loser, and would lose much more (that is much more than what Belinda loses in having A rather than B).

Now consider a slightly more complicated case. Suppose that Beatrice will be affected by the choice too. Like Belinda, Beatrice is better off in B than in A. Finally, suppose that although it is still true that Anatole stands to benefit more than does either Belinda or Beatrice individually, this isn't true by very much. When we tell the story this way, the natural suggestion seems to be that *B* is the better outcome. Admittedly, the benefit to Belinda isn't as big as the benefit to Anatole would have been, and the benefit to Beatrice isn't as big as the benefit to Anatole would have been; but when you consider the benefits to both Belinda *and* Beatrice, this just seems to outweigh the "loss" to Anatole. Intuitively, that is, the individual benefits to Belinda and to Beatrice add up to a greater "total" benefit than we would get by benefiting Anatole by himself.

Generalizing, then, we might say that one outcome is better than another—at least so far as well-being is concerned—if the total benefit of having that outcome rather than the other is greater. But if we do state the point this way, we have to be careful not to lose sight of the basic, underlying idea that how good an outcome is depends on *everyone's* level of well-being in that outcome. That is, it's not just a matter of those who happen to get an extra *benefit* from that outcome.

Not surprisingly, we can often make comparisons between outcomes more easily if we put everyone else aside and focus only on those whose level of well-being varies from one outcome to the next; indeed, as we have just seen, we can often make the comparisons more easily still if we focus only on the *differences* in the levels of well-being (that is, the extra benefits). But for all that, the underlying idea really seems to be this: how good an outcome is depends on the *total* amount of well-being in that outcome. Ultimately, that is, the goodness of an outcome is not just a matter of the extra *boosts* to well-being that an outcome happens to contain (compared to the others); it is really a matter of *all* the well-being that it contains. All other things being equal, then, the greater the total amount of well-being, the better the outcome. Call this the *total* view.

It is important to avoid a common misunderstanding about this view. It does not say that goodness of an outcome is a matter of *how many* people are better off in that outcome; it is not a matter of "majority rules." Often, of course, the outcome with the greatest total amount of well-being will indeed be the outcome that benefits the greatest number of people. This is true, for example, in the case of Anatole, Belinda, and Beatrice. But it is also possible to have cases where this is not true. Suppose that Belinda and Beatrice would actually only be very slightly better off in B than in A, while Anatole will be *much* better off in A than in B. In this case, we can imagine, the total benefit to Belinda and Beatrice of having B rather than A is still less than the benefit to Anatole of having A rather than B; that is, even though only one person would benefit from A, while two would benefit from B, it is A that has a greater total amount of well-being. According to the total view, then, this is the better outcome.

It should be noted that all this talk about comparing who gets benefited more presupposes that it makes sense to talk about how *much* someone benefits, and whether this is more or less than someone else. Similarly, talk of adding up the total amount of well-being in a given outcome presupposes that it makes sense to talk about *measuring* a person's level of well-being—giving it a number that we can meaningfully compare to someone else's number—and then adding these numbers up. That is, this entire approach presupposes that it makes sense to talk about *interpersonal comparisons of well-being*. (Since another term for "well-being" is "utility," these are also often called "interpersonal comparisons of *utility*.") Yet it is often thought that there is something deeply problematic about such comparisons. It is sometimes suggested that such comparisons are simply meaningless, or perhaps meaningful but in principle impossible to make. Other times it is suggested that although in theory it may be possible to make the comparisons, in actual practice they cannot be made, or cannot be made with any kind of precision.

There are obviously a number of different objections being raised here (although they are often run together), and we do not have the space to try to answer them adequately. One point that does seem worth making, however, is that in evaluating the plausibility of a given objection we do well to keep in mind the details of our particular theory of well-being. (I see no reason to assume that interpersonal comparisons of well-being will be equally problematic regardless of what theory of well-being we hold.) For example, suppose we are hedonists. Then to claim that interpersonal comparisons are simply meaningless is equivalent to saying things like this: it makes no sense to say that one person is in more pain than another. This seems quite implausible. On the other hand, it does seem plausible to suggest that we often cannot compare the intensity of two people's pains with any great precision.

Perhaps this last point should be conceded more generally. In real life we are often unable to make anything more than rough and imprecise comparisons. But we certainly do seem to be able to do at least that much in many cases. And often our judgments, although rough, are sufficient to enable us to say that one outcome is better than another. So I am inclined to think that any general skepticism about the possibility of making interpersonal comparisons of well-being is probably misguided. On the other hand, it must be admitted that in most cases the assignment of precise numbers will probably be beyond us.

Of course, even if for all practical purposes precise numbers are not available to us, there still may be a fact of the matter as to exactly how much better off one person is than another. (In practice, all sorts of measurements may elude us, even though there is still a fact of the matter as to precisely what some quantity comes to.) Alternatively, it may be that the fact of the matter is that, even in principle, interpersonal comparisons of well-being can only be rough and imprecise. Even if this is so, however, the total view may still be correct: perhaps the total amount of well-being contained in an outcome can only be specified roughly and imprecisely; but for all that, it might still be true that when one outcome does contain a greater total amount of well-being than another, it is the better outcome.

In what follows, I will occasionally assign numbers when comparing levels of well-being. This will help to make the examples clear, but nothing should turn on the precise numbers used, nor on the numbers being precise. Consequently, even those who think that interpersonal comparisons of well-being cannot be precise—not even in principle—need not reject, for that reason alone, the arguments to come. (However, those who dismiss the possibility of interpersonal comparisons altogether will definitely need to reject a certain amount of what follows.)

Difficulties of measurement aside, there are two other issues concerning the total view that should be mentioned, even if only briefly. (They are too complex to pursue in any detail here.) The first is this. According to the total view, the greater the total amount of well-being, the better the outcome (all other things being equal). But there are two ways that we can increase the total: (1) we can make the people who actually exist better off; or (2) we can increase the *number* of people who exist, adding extra happy people. Now virtually everyone agrees that the first method does indeed make the outcome better: if you have a group of people, then the better off they are, the better the outcome. But it is far less clear whether the *second* method of increasing the total actually makes for a better outcome. Does the mere fact that an outcome contains *extra* happy people make the outcome better, in and of itself? Suppose the first outcome contains one billion people, all at a high level of well-being, while the second outcome contains one billion and *one* people, all at that same high level. The "original" people are no better off in the second outcome—does the mere addition of the *extra* person make the outcome better?

Many people comfortably answer yes. Such people can continue to accept the total view, since this is the answer it supports. Others, however, are inclined to think that the mere addition of extra happy people does not make an outcome better. Accordingly, such people must reject the total view, and find an alternative account of the contribution that well-being makes to the goodness of an outcome.

One common proposal is the *average view*—which holds that the greater the *average* level of well-being in an outcome, the better. (To get the average, take the total amount of well-being, and divide by the number of people in the outcome.) Now in those cases where the number of people is the same in both outcomes, the average view will still agree with the answers given by the total view. But in cases where one outcome has more people than another, the two views may differ. Since adding the extra happy people may increase the total without increasing the average, the total view will have to say the second outcome is better, while the average view can deny this. To return to our example, adding the one extra person to the original billion people will increase the total amount of well-being, but it does nothing to increase the average level of well-being. So the average view can hold that the second outcome is no better than the first.

There are, however, various problems with the average view. First of all, if the extra happy person is at a *higher* level of well-being than the original people, then the addition of the extra person may actually *increase* the average. So the average view will have to hold that the outcome with this extra, above-average person is better. And while some may find this intuitively acceptable—certainly friends of the *total* view will find this congenial—others may feel that the average view here fails to capture the original intuition that the mere addition of *extra* people cannot make for a better outcome. Furthermore, if the extra person is *below* average—even if only by a very small amount—then the second outcome will have a *lower* average, and so the average view will have to hold that it makes things *worse* to have this extra person. But many will find it hard to believe that the mere addition of an extra happy person can make an outcome worse. (It may not make things better; but that is a far cry from saying it makes things worse.)

Thus those who are dissatisfied with the total view in its application to "different number cases" may find the average view unacceptable as well. In point of fact, finding an acceptable principle to govern different number cases may turn out to be a surprisingly difficult undertaking. In what follows, however, I will—if only for the sake of simplicity—assume the truth of the *total* view. Luckily, this choice should affect little of the ensuing discussion.

The final question about the total view concerns the well-being of *animals* (or, more precisely, nonhuman animals). When comparing the goodness of outcomes, does the well-being of animals count too?

Most people will readily agree that animals count too. If one can eliminate, say, the pain and suffering of a dog or even a bird, this makes the outcome better. But do animals count as *much* as people? If a cat's well-being is increased by a certain amount, does this make the same contribution to the goodness of the outcome as would a comparable increase in the well-being of a *person*?

Many think not. They hold that although animals count, they count for less than people. The well-being of animals matters, but it gets less *weight* than does human well-being. Such a view could get quite complex, assigning different weights to different *kinds* of animals: for example, perhaps highly intelligent animals like apes and dolphins count for a great deal; dogs and cats somewhat less; birds and fish even less; and insects not at all. Clearly, adopting a position of this sort would require a certain amount of revision in the total view (which, as it stands, treats all increases in well-being equally).

It seems possible, however, that our inclination to count the well-being of animals for less than that of humans is instead simply a matter of prejudice and confusion. Of course, in many cases the welfare of an animal might not be affected as much as the welfare of a human would be: slapping a cow, for example, might not cause as much pain as would slapping a human child. But if we are genuinely comparing the same *amount* of pain, it is hard to see why the pain of a cow should count for less than the pain of a human: after all, the cow is, by hypothesis, in just as much pain. Perhaps, then, unit for unit, the well-being of animals should count just as much as the well-being of people. And if this is the position we take, we can continue to accept the (unrevised) total view. (Holding this view, it should be noted, is fully compatible with claiming that some of the most valuable components of well-being—those elements that make the greatest contribution to individual well-being—may not be available to animals. For example, animals cannot enjoy poetry. Once again, however, this does not give us any reason to count animals less when we are talking about *comparable* elements of well-being.)

The moral status of animals is a difficult and controversial topic. What's more, it is obviously of considerable practical significance. But we will not consider it further here. Indeed, except for one or two brief remarks, the special moral issues that arise for animals will not be considered again. I want to emphasize, however, that this omission is a response to the complexity of the topic, not a claim about its unimportance.

## 2.4 Equality

Is the total amount of well-being the only factor that affects the goodness of an outcome? Many people think not. For if the total is all that matters, then it doesn't matter how the well-being is *distributed*. So long as the total amount of well-being is the same, it doesn't matter who receives how much.

Suppose we have two possible outcomes—each with ten people, and each with a total of 1,000 units of well-being. (Units of well-being are sometimes called "utiles"; hedonists often favor the term "hedons.") In the first outcome, each of the ten people has 100 units. In contrast, in the second outcome, nine of the people have only 50 units each, while the tenth person has all of the remaining 550 units!

As far as the total view is concerned, these two outcomes are equally good—since the total amount of well-being is the same in both. Yet almost everyone is drawn (at least initially) to the thought that the first outcome is far better than the second. For in the first outcome the well-being is distributed *equally;* everyone is at the same level of well-being. But in the second outcome, there is a huge difference between the level of the one well off individual and everyone else. And this inequality seems to make the second outcome worse.

Cases like this seem to support the conclusion that the total amount of well-being is not all that matters intrinsically in determining the goodness of an outcome. Distribution of the well-being matters too, and in particular, equality matters.

Now this conclusion is not necessarily inconsistent with the total view. One could understand the total view as merely holding that the total amount of well-being is *one* factor that can contribute to the goodness of an outcome, so that—all other things being equal—the greater the total, the better the outcome. One could believe this and yet still hold that the total amount of well-being is not the *only* factor that matters intrinsically: equality (or, more generally, distribution) matters too.

Obviously, however, the view that equality matters *is* opposed to any view that says that *all* that matters is well-being. Let us call a view of this bolder type—one that claims that well-being is *all* that matters—*welfarism*. And let us call the view that says that equality matters too, *egalitarianism*. What most of us believe, then, is that welfarism is mistaken: distribution matters too, and in particular, equality matters. We are not welfarists, but egalitarians.

(A word about this terminology might be in order. I have defined the welfarist as holding the "extreme" or "pure" view that welfare is the *only* factor that matters, whereas—in contrast—I have defined the egalitarian as merely holding the "moderate" view that equality is *one* of the factors that matters. The reason for the nonsymmetrical treatment of these terms is that virtually everyone accepts at least "moderate" welfarism, and virtually no one accepts "pure" egalitarianism; so the interesting question concerns the choice between pure welfarism and moderate egalitarianism. For simplicity, therefore, I'm using the unadorned, unqualified labels "welfarism" and "egalitarianism" to refer to the two positions at the heart of the controversy.)

It might be thought that the welfarist is inconsistent in not admitting that equality of distribution is one factor that helps to determine the goodness of outcomes. After all, when explaining and defending the total view we observed that from the moral standpoint it seems that everyone counts equally. (That's why we have to add together the total of *everyone's* well-being, counting everyone equally.) It seems, then, that the total view recognizes, and indeed presupposes, the importance of equality. So how can it be denied now?

There are, however, two importantly different notions of equality at issue, and an advocate of the total view can consistently endorse the importance of one while rejecting the other. The total view holds that people are equal in this sense: in and of itself, each unit of well-being makes an equal contribution to the overall goodness of an outcome, regardless of *whose* well-being it is. (The welfare of blacks counts as much as the welfare of whites, an increase in the well-being of a woman counts as much as a comparable increase in the well-being of a man, my welfare counts neither more nor less than yours, and so on.) But accepting this does not entail that it matters in and of itself whether everyone is at an equal level of well-being. The equal *importance* of well-being simply does not entail the importance of equal *levels* of well-being.

Thus it is not true that the welfarist is somehow being inconsistent in not recognizing the intrinsic value of equal distribution. Welfarism can consistently embrace one claim about equality (people matter equally) without embracing the other claim (equal distribution matters).

By the same token, however, this also means that the welfarist cannot attempt to dismiss egalitarianism on the grounds that welfarism has *already* taken the significance of equality into account. For the egalitarian can correctly observe that it is only one kind of equality that matters for welfarism, whereas the egalitarian thinks that *both* kinds of equality are important.

So the question remains: does equality of distribution matter? Is equality—that is, equality in the distribution of well-being—one of the factors that determines the goodness of an outcome? (For simplicity, we can now revert to the practice of letting "equality" be shorthand for "equality of distribution," since that will be our focus for the rest of this section.)

As we have seen, most people do find themselves intuitively drawn to the thought that equality does matter. But the welfarist argues that belief in egalitarianism is due to a natural mistake. To understand it, the first thing to bear in mind is that in real life we cannot directly distribute well-being itself; all that we can do is to distribute resources—the *means* to well-being—hoping thereby to produce well-being indirectly. The second thing to note is that so far as the distribution of *resources* is concerned, equality does indeed matter, as a way of maximizing the total amount of well-being produced; that is, it matters *instrumentally*. From a practical standpoint, then, it will often make sense to aim at equal distribution. This tempts us (says the welfarist) into thinking that equal distribution matters in and of itself—and so equal distribution of well-being must matter as well. But the egalitarian is wrong to ascribe intrinsic value to the equal distribution of well-being. First of all, it is only equality of resources that matters—not equality of well-being. Secondly, equality matters at best only instrumentally; it has no intrinsic value.

The welfarist's argument is a difficult one, so let's consider it at greater length. The heart of the argument turns on the observation that equality often has *instrumental* value; more precisely, equality often has instrumental value when we are concerned with the distribution of *resources*. This is because most resources, for example money, display "diminishing marginal utility": the more money you have, the smaller the increase to your well-being that will be produced by an extra dollar. This means that we can typically produce the greatest total amount of well-being by distributing resources equally.

Suppose, for example, that we have two people—a man and a woman—and a million dollars to be distributed between them. One possible distribution would be to give the woman the entire million dollars, leaving the man with nothing. Here, presumably, the woman will be at a high level of well-being, while the man will be at a low level. Alternatively, we could give the man one thousand dollars, leaving the woman the million less the thousand. When compared to the first outcome, the level of well-being of the poor man will increase dramatically; in contrast, the wealthy woman's level of well-being will go down only slightly. (When you are poor, an extra thousand dollars produces a lot of well-being; when you are wealthy, it may barely matter.) So the *total* amount of well-being produced by the money will be greater in the second scenario. And if we took another thousand dollars and "shifted" it as well, we would have an even *greater* total amount of well-being. (Perhaps the poor man would not gain quite as much extra well-being this time as from the first thousand, but it would still be much greater than what the wealthy woman would lose.) All other things being equal, then, we would keep getting a greater and greater total "bang for our bucks" the closer we came to having the money distributed equally. We could expect to produce the greatest total amount of well-being in the scenario in which the man and the woman each have half the money. That is to say, equal distribution of money may be instrumentally valuable as a way of achieving the greatest total amount of well-being.

This may not be true in every single case, but it seems true often enough: equal distribution of resources helps to achieve the highest possible total amount of well-being. Reasonably enough, then (the welfarist continues), we find ourselves drawn to the thought that equality matters. But it is a mistake—albeit a natural one—to take this to mean that there is any *intrinsic* value in the equal distribution of *well-being*.

In this light, consider once again the example from the start of this section: in the first outcome, ten people have 100 units of well-being each; in the second, one person has 550 units, while the other nine have only 50 units each. In thinking about this case, it is natural to bring to bear our intuitions from real-life cases of distribution—treating the example as though it concerned the distribution of, say, units of money. Then the first outcome would indeed be better, since the total amount of well-being would be higher. But if we keep in mind that what the example actually involves is the distribution of well-being, and not the distribution of resources, we will see that these initial intuitions are misleading: by hypothesis the total amount of well-being is the *same* in both outcomes; there is, therefore, no reason to prefer the first outcome, no reason to prefer the outcome where well-being is distributed equally. Or so argues the welfarist.

But not everyone will be convinced by this argument. No doubt many will indeed find that when they reexamine their convictions, keeping in mind the potential confusions just noted by the welfarist, the commitment to egalitarianism has disappeared. But others may find that even when all of the welfarist's points are kept firmly in mind, they are still drawn to the thought that one outcome can be better than another by virtue of the fact that it contains a more equal distribution of well-being. They will insist that it is the welfarist who is mistaken in claiming that, so long as the total amount of well-being is the same, it is a matter of indifference from the moral point of view whether one person has a higher level of well-being than another. In short, they may remain convinced that equality matters—not only instrumentally, but intrinsically.

Of course, any committed egalitarian will need to say just *how much* equality matters. In our original example, both outcomes have the same total amount of well-being; they are "tied" from the perspective of the total view, and the egalitarian makes the (relatively modest) claim that the fact that one outcome has more equality than the other helps to break the tie. But sometimes an outcome with greater equality will have a *smaller* total amount of well-being. What should we say then? Is the importance of equality limited to breaking ties? Or can an increase in equality be valuable enough to outweigh a possible loss in terms of the total amount of well-being—so that on balance an outcome with greater equality but a smaller total will sometimes be better than an outcome with a greater total but less equality?

Most egalitarians would be prepared to say that in at least some cases a loss in total well-being can be outweighed by a gain in equality. (For example, an outcome where nine people have 50 units of well-being and one person has 600 may still be worse overall, because of the inequality, than an outcome where all ten people have 100 units of well-being—despite the fact that the first outcome has a slightly higher total.) On the other hand, few egalitarians would be prepared to say that no matter how small the gain in equality, and no matter how large the loss in terms of total well-being, the outcome with greater equality is always better overall. (For example, suppose the choice is between an outcome with one person at 550 and nine at 50, and an outcome where everyone is at 10 units of well-being. Despite the greater equality, many would think the second outcome is worse overall.)

So egalitarians need to offer some principle governing *trade-offs* between equality and total well-being. They need to produce a trade-off schedule, indicating what kinds of gains in equality will outweigh what kinds of losses in well-being. To make things even more complicated, since one outcome may have less inequality than another, even though it does not have perfect equality, the egalitarian also needs to offer a method of measuring degrees or *amounts* of inequality.

Most egalitarians have not gone very far toward providing these things. They content themselves with intuitive judgments involving a few simple cases, and they do not try to articulate and defend precise methods of measuring inequality, or principled methods of adjudicating trade-offs. Ultimately, however, the egalitarian will have to provide (and defend) these more detailed principles as well.

There are several other aspects of the egalitarian position that stand in need of further specification as well. For example, does it matter whether there is inequality at any given *moment,* or is the relevant issue rather one of whether different people's *lives* are equally good? Similarly, does equality between different generations—living at different times in history—matter, or does inequality matter only among individuals living at the same time? And does equality matter only among members of an interacting community, or is it an issue even when comparing groups that have never had any contact with each other?

Different answers to these questions will produce a variety of different egalitarian positions. A fully specified egalitarian view will need to take a stand on these, and other, issues. Unfortunately, we cannot pursue them further here. But although would-be egalitarians clearly have their work cut out for them, none of this shows that the various detailed egalitarian principles cannot be adequately articulated and defended.

There is, however, one further problem that deserves our attention. Frequently, when pressed to defend the importance of equality, egalitarians fo-

cus on the plight of the worse off—that is, those who have less under un-
equal distributions. Equal distribution is seen as attractive since it improves
the lot of those who would otherwise be worse off. But in point of fact,
equality is not always better for the worse off. Sometimes it does not improve their position at all; other times it actually makes it even worse. After
all, one way to eliminate the inequality between the haves and the have
nots is simply to lower the level of the haves down to the level of the have
nots, leaving the have nots where they are. If equality matters in and of itself, then we must say that this is an improvement. Many, however, will
find this quite implausible.

Now it is difficult to be confident about our intuitions here, since in cases
of this sort the gain in equality comes at the cost of a loss in total well-being.
Perhaps, then, the loss in total well-being outweighs the gain in equality, so
that on balance the egalitarian outcome is worse; this would still be compatible with thinking that equality is *one* of the things that matters.

Accordingly, it may be difficult to be decide whether one believes that (1)
in cases of this sort, equality is simply of no value whatsoever, or (2) equality does indeed have value in and of itself—but in such cases this value is
outweighed. On reflection, however, some may find that they are not egalitarians after all. The egalitarian is committed to saying that *whenever* there
is an increase in equality, there is at least one *aspect* with regard to which
the outcome is better (even if it is, on balance, outweighed); and many will
find this implausible. They will suggest that our concern should not be with
equality per se, but rather with the plight of the worse off. Typically, no
doubt, an increase in equality helps those at the bottom; but when it does
not, it is of no value at all.

Perhaps, then, to the extent that distribution matters, this factor should
be captured in terms of a principle that gives greater weight to improving
the well-being of those who are worse off: the *lower* the level of someone's
well-being (in absolute terms), the *greater* the extent to which increasing
their well-being by a certain amount improves the goodness of an outcome.
Comparably sized increases in well-being for those at a higher absolute
level will simply have less weight, so will result in a smaller increase in the
outcome's goodness.

Advocates of such a principle of *weighted beneficence* will still need to tell
us *how much* more important it is to help the worse off. An extreme position would hold that *any* increase in the level of the very worst off individuals—no matter how small—outweighs any loss to the better off individuals—no matter how large (provided, of course, that the "better off" are not
thereby brought below the original level of the worst off). This extreme position is sometimes called *maximin* (since it holds that the best outcome is
the one with the highest minimum level, that is, the one that maximizes the
level of the worst off). However, many who are sympathetic to weighted
beneficence do not want to give this kind of absolute ("lexical") priority to

helping the very worst off. They prefer more moderate versions—with finite rather than infinite weightings—so that if the gain to the worse off is small enough it can be outweighed by a *sufficiently* large gain for the better off.

Here is one final complication. Weighted beneficence makes the individualistic, noncomparative judgment that how much an increase in well-being matters depends on one's level of well-being. Egalitarianism makes the relational, comparative judgment that it matters whether one's level of well-being is higher or lower than another's. Conceivably, however, *both* judgments are true. This means that in principle it should be possible to accept both egalitarianism and weighted beneficence. Instead of pursuing these and other complications any further, however, let's ask whether there are any additional factors that may affect the goodness of an outcome.

## 2.5  Culpability, Fairness, and Desert

Imagine that there has been an explosion. Two people have received similar injuries and need our help. Unfortunately, we cannot help both of them: we must choose whether to aid Boris, or Glinda. Which outcome would be better?

Let us assume that the same size loss in overall well-being will befall whoever we leave unaided (and no one else will be affected); so the total amount of well-being is the same in both outcomes. And let us also assume that Glinda and Boris start out at the same level of well-being; so considerations of equality (or of weighted beneficence) do not distinguish between the two outcomes either. We might conclude, then, that the outcome in which we aid Glinda is neither better nor worse than the outcome in which we aid Boris.

Suppose, however, that the explosion is Boris's fault. Unlike Glinda, who is totally free from blame and not at all responsible for the explosion, Boris is partially responsible for what happened: perhaps he was careless in mixing certain chemicals, or he negligently forgot to throw the safety switch. Then we might want to say that it is not a matter of moral indifference whether it is Glinda or Boris that is aided. Since we cannot help both, it is more important to aid innocent Glinda than culpable Boris: the outcome in which it is Boris that is helped is *worse* than the outcome in which it is Glinda that is helped. It is less *fair*. This suggests that *fairness* is a further factor that can itself contribute to the goodness of an outcome.

Now in point of fact, the notion of fairness is somewhat amorphous and seems to pick out different features in different contexts. Often, indeed, to say of something that it is unfair is to say nothing more than that it is illegitimate or unjustified. But the common strand in many attributions of unfairness is this: an outcome (or process) is unfair if the treatment received by the various individuals concerned fails to reflect the presence or absence of morally relevant differences between them.

In the case of Glinda and Boris, the morally relevant difference has to do with the fact that Glinda is blameless and not at all responsible for the explosion, while Boris is at least partly at fault. This difference in *culpability* or *responsibility* seems to make it appropriate that if only one of the two can be aided, it should be Glinda. Indeed, we might want to go even further. Even if Boris's injuries are somewhat more severe than Glinda's, so that a greater total amount of well-being would be produced by helping Boris, it might still be better to aid Glinda, in light of Boris's greater culpability.

One way to capture a view like this would be to discount the importance of well-being, given culpability. Glinda is totally nonculpable, and so the potential loss to her well-being is given its full weight. Boris, in contrast, is somewhat culpable, and so although his potential loss in well-being is fully as large as Glinda's, it is discounted, and thus counts for less. That is, given the *culpability discount rate,* the contribution that Boris's well-being makes to the goodness of the outcome is less than that made by Glinda's well-being. That is why the outcome in which Glinda is helped is the better outcome.

We could make the position more subtle still by having a larger and larger discount rate, the greater one's degree of culpability. If Boris was only slightly at fault, the discount rate will be small (and so a unit of his well-being would count almost as much as a unit of Glinda's). On the other hand, if Boris was quite reckless in his disregard of the dangers, the discount rate would be large (and so a unit of his well-being would not count nearly as much as one of Glinda's).

A view like this will of course be rejected by a welfarist, since it assigns *intrinsic* significance to matters of culpability. The welfarist will argue instead that culpability is at best of *instrumental* importance: from a practical standpoint, if we give lower priority to helping the culpable, this will provide an incentive to all to take greater care; and so, in the long run, this will increase the total amount of well-being. But this doesn't show that *in and of itself* the well-being of the culpable matters less.

Of course, if you are convinced of the intrinsic significance of culpability, then you will think that it is actually the welfarist who is mistaken. But there is still an important point of agreement between the welfarist and such an advocate of the culpability discount rate: both sides agree that in and of themselves, increases in well-being are always of positive intrinsic value; even if the well-being of the culpable counts for less, it is still a good thing. (Admittedly, if the discount rate can go all the way to 100 percent, so that a person's well-being can be *completely* discounted, then even this point of agreement can disappear; but even here, increasing well-being will never be a *bad* thing.)

However, because of this very point of agreement, some may think that a culpability discount rate doesn't yet go far enough. The effect of the discount rate is to make it less important that someone's level of well-being be improved. But it is still better, all other things being equal, if well-being is increased—even the well-being of the culpable: an increase in well-being is always of positive intrinsic value (or, at least, never a bad thing). *Retributivists,* however, hold that some people *deserve* to suffer. If one is sufficiently evil and morally blameworthy, then it may in fact be a good thing if one undergoes a *loss* of well-being. When it comes to morally evil people, an increase in well-being is of no positive intrinsic value at all; it is, instead, an intrinsically *bad* thing: increasing the well-being of evil individuals *decreases* the overall goodness of an outcome.

Consider Boris and Glinda once again: suppose that Boris deliberately caused the explosion, hoping to harm Glinda, but accidentally got caught in the blast himself as well. And imagine that we can in fact help *both* of them. Should we? So long as all we believe in is a culpability discount rate, we must say that the outcome will be better if we help Boris as well. (Or, at least—if the discount is here 100 percent—helping Boris will not make the outcome worse.) But the retributivist may insist that helping Boris does indeed make the outcome *worse* than it would be were we to help Glinda alone. Here, it is a *bad* thing for Boris's well-being to be increased. In short, it is only reasonably decent and moral individuals who deserve to be well off; if Boris is bad enough, then it would be better were he to suffer.

Once more the welfarist will claim that this assigns intrinsic value where there is only instrumental value. (If we punish evildoers this will have a deterrent effect on those who might otherwise do evil; so in the long run this will increase the total amount of well-being.) And this time, the welfarist may be joined by those who believe only in the more modest culpability discount rate. But the retributivist will insist that it is a deep and significant mistake to assume that well-being is always of value. In and of itself, well-being is neither good nor bad: it is only deserved well-being that is intrinsically good; undeserved well-being is intrinsically bad.

If the retributivist view is correct, then the total view is mistaken as well—insofar as this view is understood to embody the claim that the contribution that well-being makes to the goodness of an outcome is simply a matter of the total amount of well-being. We will need, instead, a revised understanding of the total view: what matters (other things being equal) is the total amount of *deserved* well-being.

For similar reasons, if retributivism is correct, then the egalitarian may need to revise her view as well. After all, is inequality genuinely a bad thing, if the reason that the worse off are worse off is because they *deserve* to be?

It is, of course, open to the egalitarian to claim that even *deserved* inequality has intrinsic negative value (although perhaps considerations of desert outweigh considerations of equality, so that *on balance* deserved inequality is a good thing). But most egalitarians, I imagine, will not find this the most plausible view. They will want to claim, instead, that inequality is a bad thing precisely when it is *undeserved*; that is to say, it is only when individuals are equally deserving that equality has intrinsic value. (It was easy to overlook this point during the initial discussion of inequality, since it was natural to assume that all of the people in the examples were equally deserving.)

One way to understand the disagreement between the retributivist and the advocate of the more modest discount rate is to see them as differing over what exactly one *deserves*, given culpability. The retributivist claims that when one is sufficiently culpable, one deserves to suffer. This is a noncomparative, nonrelational judgment: regardless of how well others are doing, it is a good thing if the sufficiently guilty undergo a loss of well-being. In contrast, the advocate of the culpability discount rate makes a comparative or relational judgment: given that not everyone can be helped, the guilty deserve to do less well than the innocent. But he rejects the noncomparative judgment that it is intrinsically better if the guilty suffer: if the culpable can be aided without thereby lowering the level of others, then this would be a good thing; there is no value in the guilty suffering unnecessarily.

Whichever view of desert one adopts, a more precise specification of the *grounds* for making desert claims will still need to be provided. For example, should the retributivist hold that evil intentions are sufficient for someone to deserve punishment, or must the person first have actually performed an immoral act? Similarly, is culpability genuinely necessary before the discount rate sets in, or is it sufficient if you are partly *responsible* for something bad happening? (You might be responsible for causing an unforeseeable accident, even though not blameworthy.) An adequate account would need to provide plausible answers to questions like these.

So far, we have considered only one general category of desert claims. These are cases involving what might be called *moral desert*—that is, cases where (roughly speaking) someone deserves something because of the moral or immoral nature or impact of his acts (or perhaps his intentions). But questions of desert can arise in many other areas as well—areas that don't particularly involve moral concerns. For example, you can deserve to win a prize, or a contest, by virtue of your greater skill or superior performance; you can deserve to make a discovery, by virtue of your perseverance and insight; you can deserve to lose your money, by virtue of your carelessness or gullibility; and on and on. As even these few examples make clear, *what* it is that you deserve can vary tremendously, as can the grounds *by virtue of which* you deserve it: it may be a matter of talent, character, deeds, effort, or accomplishments (or the lack of any of these things).

As noted, many of these desert claims arise in situations that are not, in themselves, moral contexts; and the various features of the individual by virtue of which the desert claims are made may not possess in themselves any particular moral relevance. But for all that, one might want to claim that desert can affect the goodness of outcomes in these cases as well. That is, one might want to offer the *general desert thesis* that an outcome is better, all other things being equal, if people in it have the things they deserve.

Of course, this general thesis may strike many as implausible. Some kinds of desert may simply have no impact on the goodness or badness of an outcome. (You may "deserve to lose your money" to the con artist; but do we really think it better if you do?) But this still leaves open the possibility that some categories of desert *do* indeed affect the value of an outcome. As we have already seen, many find it plausible to think that moral desert has this kind of significance. Perhaps, then, other types of desert can be identified as having this kind of significance as well.

What, then, is the connection between culpability, desert, and fairness? It is basically a matter of broader and broader categories. Many people are inclined to believe that moral desert can affect the goodness of an outcome. Culpability is a *particular* feature that can help determine moral desert, but there may be others as well (such as nonculpable responsibility for something bad). Furthermore, beyond such cases of "negative" moral desert, some features may mark an individual as being unusually morally *meritorious*—and so deserving of a *greater* level of well-being than the average. Similarly, there may be other *kinds* of desert—that is, types of desert other than moral desert—that can affect the goodness of an outcome.

Now when people do not have what they deserve to have, it is often appropriate to call the outcome *unfair:* in such outcomes the distribution of goods and evils among individuals may not properly reflect the presence or absence of morally relevant differences between them. Thus it seems perfectly appropriate to say, as well, that fairness is itself a factor that can affect the goodness of outcomes.

But fairness is, in turn, a broader category than desert. And so, in some cases, issues about fairness can arise that do not involve, or may even militate against, considerations of desert. For example, people may be *entitled* to things that they do not particularly deserve. (If you win the race, you are entitled to the prize—even if you didn't deserve to win. If your parents write you out of the will, you are not entitled to their money—even if you deserve it more than your sister, who will inherit everything.) Now if someone is entitled to something, it may be unfair if they are deprived of it—regardless of whether they deserved to have it in the first place. And so some may want to hold that, other things being equal, an outcome is better if people have the things they are entitled to. This, then, would be a case of fairness affecting the goodness of an outcome, but on grounds other than desert. And there may well be others as well.

These are all still cases where talk of what is fair or unfair points to distributive factors that affect the goodness of outcomes. But there are still other cases where the factors being pointed to are not most naturally understood in this way at all (see, for example, the discussion of the principle of fair play, in 4.3). Accordingly, given the wide variety of concerns that might be intended when a charge of unfairness is raised, it is always best to press the person making the charge to specify more precisely what kind of factor he has in mind. Only then are you in a position to see whether this is indeed a factor that has genuine moral significance and, if it is, whether that factor has been inappropriately disregarded in the case at hand.

## 2.6  Consequentialism

What factors help to determine the goodness of an outcome? So far we have considered individual well-being, and distributive concerns such as equality, fairness, and desert. Of course, as we have seen, not everyone will agree that all of the members of this list have intrinsic moral significance. (The welfarist, for example, rejects all but the first.) But we might also wonder whether there are any significant omissions: should further factors be added to the list? From a logical point of view, of course, virtually anything could be said to have intrinsic value. One could hold that, other things being equal, one outcome is better than another if it contains more tin foil, or fewer hub caps. These particular views are obviously implausible; but that doesn't show that we have already canvassed all the most serious proposals.

As far as commonsense morality is concerned, the factors that we have examined are, I believe, the most important determinants of the intrinsic goodness of an outcome. But a more controversial suggestion may merit brief mention as well: some have held that certain goods, such as knowledge or beauty, have a value that goes beyond their contribution to well-being. The existence of beauty, for example, may have a value in and of itself—independently of whatever contribution to well-being it may happen to make. Indeed, some have gone so far as to hold that the existence of a naturally beautiful world would be a good thing—even if there were no sentient creatures to appreciate it. (Of course, unlike beauty, there couldn't be any *knowledge* without the existence of sentient creatures; but for all that, the intrinsic value of knowledge might not be exhausted by the contribution it makes to individual well-being.) Similarly, and even more radically, it might be suggested that the existence of well-functioning ecosystems has intrinsic value, or the maintenance of endangered species—above and beyond the contribution these things make to individual well-being.

If any claims of this sort are true, then the goodness of an outcome can also be affected by what we might call *impersonal* values ("impersonal" since these values are not ultimately a matter of individual well-being or its distribution). Such a possibility should not be dismissed out of hand. But most people are inclined to deny the existence of such values, or to deny that these can represent genuinely *moral* values—precisely because of their impersonal nature—and so I will not consider them further.

Imagine, then, that we have arrived at an adequate account of the various factors that can help determine the goodness of an outcome. Let's call this a *theory of the good*. (Sometimes such an account is called a *value the-*

*ory;* but since one might intend any number of things by the term "value," it is perhaps slightly less ambiguous to talk about a theory of *the good.*)

Of course, it goes without saying that to actually achieve anything like an adequate theory of the good would require a far more detailed investigation than what we have undertaken. But suppose we had such an account. We would then finally be in a position to spell out the specific content of the first basic normative factor.

This last remark may need to be explained. As we noted at the start of this chapter (in 2.1), virtually everyone agrees that the goodness of an act's consequences is at least one morally relevant factor in determining the moral status of that act. But until this claim is combined with a theory of the good—a theory that enables us, at least in principle, to rank the goodness of the various possible outcomes—one cannot say very much about what this factor comes to. Once we are armed with a theory of the good, however, acts can be compared to see which one better promotes the good—that is, which act better promotes individual well-being, equality, fairness, and so on. Now obviously enough, those who differ as to the *correct* theory of the good will often disagree as to just which act it is that has the best consequences. But that, of course, is the very point: there simply cannot be any disagreements about the relative value of the outcomes of various acts until substantive theories of the good have been introduced. That is to say, it is only when combined with a particular theory of the good that this first normative factor takes on determinate content.

Since we have just spent the better part of a chapter discussing disagreements concerning which subfactors affect the intrinsic goodness of outcomes, it is obvious that the precise content of an adequate theory of the good is a matter of some controversy. However, even if we put questions about the precise nature of the good aside, there is still room for disagreement about our first factor. For while (as I have repeatedly emphasized) virtually everyone agrees that the goodness of an act's consequences is at least *one* morally relevant normative factor, some want to go much further and claim that goodness of outcomes is the *only* morally relevant factor in determining the status of a given act. This more extreme view is often called *consequentialism,* since it holds that, morally speaking, consequences are the only things that matter.

One way to understand the difference between consequentialism and the more common, more modest position is this. If we believe that consequences are not the only thing that can help determine the moral status of an act, then all we will say is: you should perform the act with the best consequences, *other things being equal.* This leaves open the possibility that there are other normative factors that may come into play so that, for example, in at least some situations the best act may not be the one with the best consequences. But if consequences are the *only* morally relevant factor, then the "other things being equal" clause no longer has any work to do and can be dropped. We can then simply say that you should perform the act with the best consequences, *period*. And this is exactly what consequentialism holds: in any given choice situation, the agent is morally required to perform the act with the best consequences.

Two points are worth emphasizing immediately about this view. First of all, according to consequentialism, the agent is morally required to perform the act with the *best* consequences. It is not sufficient that an act have "pretty good" consequences, that it produce more good than harm, or that it be better than average. Rather, the agent is required to perform the act with the very best outcome (compared to the alternatives); she is required to perform the *optimal* act, as it is sometimes called. Second, according to consequentialism, the agent is morally *required* to perform the act with the best consequences. The optimal act is the *only* act that is morally permissible; no other act is morally right. Thus the consequentialist is not making the considerably more modest claim that performing the act with the best consequences is—although generally not obligatory—the *nicest* or the most *praiseworthy* thing to do. Rather, performing the optimal act is morally *required*: anything else is morally forbidden. (On rare occasions two or more acts will be tied for first place, with equally good outcomes; any one of these optimal acts will then be permissible—but any other act will be forbidden.)

Consequentialism provides a very simple *theory of the right*: an act is morally right (or morally permissible) if and only if it produces the best consequences. Of course, as we have just seen, a claim like this still needs to be supplemented with a theory of the good; only then do we have a fully determinate normative theory. And in principle, almost any theory of the good could be incorporated into a consequentialist framework. Accordingly, there are as many different versions of consequentialism as there are theories of the good. All share the basic consequentialist claim that an act is right if and only if it best promotes the good, but they differ insofar as they incorporate different theories of the good.

The most famous consequentialist theory is *utilitarianism,* which is the result of combining consequentialism with welfarism. Since consequentialism holds that an act is right if and only if it leads to the best consequences, and welfarism holds that the goodness of an outcome is ultimately a matter of the amount of individual well-being, counting everyone equally, it follows that utilitarianism is the view that an act is right if and only if it leads to the greatest total amount of well-being. (Strictly speaking, since some reject the total view for the average view—recall the discussion in 2.3—there are both total utilitarians and average utilitarians. The former hold that an act is right when it leads to the greatest total amount of well-being; the latter, when it leads to the greatest average amount of well-being. Once more, however, little of what follows turns on this, since the two differ only in cases where the size of the population is at issue, and for simplicity I shall discuss only the total utilitarian view.)

Historically, many utilitarians have accepted hedonism (although this is probably a minority view among contemporary utilitarians), and so utilitarianism is sometimes known as the greatest happiness principle: the right act is the act that leads to the greatest total amount of happiness overall. Sometimes the utilitarian goal is said to be "the greatest happiness for the greatest number." Insofar as this expression is simply a way of reminding us that everyone's happiness is to be counted equally, it is unobjectionable. But sometimes this expression is thought to mean that "majority rules" or that the right act is the act that benefits the greatest number of people. As we have already seen (in 2.3), however, this is a mistake. Utilitarianism simply directs us to perform the act that will result in the outcome with the greatest total amount of well-being, and this might well be an outcome that benefits a few individuals a great deal, rather than many individuals very little each.

Unquestionably, utilitarianism is the best known consequentialist theory. But it is important to bear in mind the possibility of consequentialist theories based on more complex or more pluralistic theories of the good. For one might well find the basic consequentialist claim plausible while nonetheless rejecting welfarism as an inadequate theory of the good. Obviously enough, if welfarism is a flawed theory of the good, then utilitarianism will be flawed as well: it will inherit whatever shortcomings welfarism may have. Not surprisingly, then, many of the objections that are raised against utilitarianism turn on its acceptance of welfarism. (For example, it is sometimes argued that utilitarianism gives counterintuitive results in cases involving equality or desert or, alternatively, that it fails to provide an adequate account of the moral significance of these notions.) Now one may or may not find these objections persuasive (it will depend on whether or not one accepts welfarism), but at best such objections show that we should replace welfarism with a more pluralistic theory of the good—one that acknowledges other factors besides well-being as having a role in determining the goodness of outcomes. Thus, even if such objections are sound, it still might be that the correct normative theory is one that retains the acceptance of consequentialism but combines this with some other theory of the good. Such a theory will admittedly no longer be *utilitarian,* but it will still be consequentialist.

I do not at all mean to belittle the significance of such objections to utilitarianism. However, since we have already examined objections to welfarism in some detail (in 2.4 and 2.5), there is, I think, no need to repeat these arguments here. What we do still need to ask is whether there are any objections to the *consequentialist* component of utilitarianism. That is, what are we to make of the consequentialist's claim that you are always required to perform the act with the best consequences? Bracketing our disagreements over how the consequences are to be evaluated, what are we to make of the claim that goodness of consequences is the only morally relevant normative factor?

First, however, a bit more needs to be said about the meaning of the term "consequentialism." I have defined consequentialism as the view that an act is right if and only if it leads to the best consequences. Consider, then, the moral theory—usually called *egoism* or *ethical egoism*—that says that an act is right if and only if it leads to the best consequences *for the agent*. Rather implausibly, egoism holds that the effect of my actions on others simply has no moral relevance (unless it happens to affect my own well-being). But whether plausible or not, is this a version of consequentialism? It would certainly be natural to use the term "consequentialism" in this broad way: like the utilitarian, the egoist thinks that all that matters are the consequences; it is just that the utilitarian evaluates the consequences in terms of how they affect *everyone's* well-being, while the egoist evaluates them only in terms of how they affect the *agent's* well-being. We might call utilitarianism a version of *universalistic consequentialism*, while saying that egoism is a version of *individualistic consequentialism*. And, indeed, this is exactly the way that some people use the terms.

Nonetheless, in what is probably the more common practice, "consequentialism" is used more narrowly than this, so that it includes only the "universalistic" theories (like utilitarianism) and excludes egoism and other "individualistic" theories. Of course, this is all just a matter of terminology—we will still need a general label for the broader category that includes *all* those moral theories that require the agent to promote the good—both individualistic theories and universalistic theories. A common proposal is to call all such theories *teleological*. We can then say that not all teleological theories are consequentialist (egoism, for example, is not). A teleological theory will be consequentialist only if it evaluates the consequences from a universalistic rather than an individualistic perspective: only, that is, if it requires the agent to perform the act that leads to the best consequences *overall*. Following what I take to be the more common practice, I will be using "consequentialism" in this more narrow sense.

This means, of course, that consequentialism cannot literally be combined with *any* theory of the good at all: it can only be combined with universalistic theories, theories of the overall good. That's why I said—after introducing consequentialism—that "almost" any theory of the good could be incorporated into a consequentialist framework. What I meant was this: any *universalistic* theory of the good can be incorporated into a consequentialist framework. (I should perhaps point out that giving a precise definition of the distinction between individualistic and universalistic theories of the good is actually more difficult than meets the eye. But I will continue to rely on our intuitive grasp of the distinction.)

Strictly, then, before examining the plausibility of consequentialism, we should first consider the plausibility of individualistic teleological theories like egoism. But as I have already noted, egoism seems to be rather strikingly implausible as a theory of the morally relevant normative factors. It is quite difficult to believe that the only factor that is at all relevant to the moral status of my act is how my own well-being will be affected. Surely, if I murder someone, the harm to the victim is morally relevant in determining the moral status of my act! I propose, therefore, to turn our attention directly to universalistic teleological theories—that is, to consequentialist theories. (Despite its implausibility as a theory of the normative factors, however, egoism is a significant view for moral philosophy. Many find egoism much more plausible when it is recast as a theory of rationality, thus giving considerable force to the question "why be moral?" For related reasons, egoism may be worth reconsidering as a theory about the foundations of normative ethics. So we will return to it in 6.2.)

Perhaps the most common objection to consequentialism is this: it is impossible to know the future. This means that you can never be absolutely certain as to what all the consequences of your act will be. An act that looks like it will lead to the best results overall may turn out badly, since things often don't turn out the way you think they will: something extremely unlikely may happen, and an act that was overwhelmingly likely to lead to good results might—for reasons beyond your control—produce disaster. Or there may be long term bad effects from your act, side effects that were unforeseen and indeed unforeseeable. In fact, lacking a crystal ball, how can you possibly tell what *all* the effects of your act will be? So how can we tell which act will lead to the best results overall—counting *all* the results? This seems to mean that consequentialism will be unusable as a moral guide to action. All the evidence available at the time of acting may have pointed to the conclusion that a given act was the right act to perform—and yet it might still turn out that what you did had horrible results, and so in fact was morally wrong. Indeed, it will never be possible to say for sure that any given act was right or wrong, since any event can continue to have further unforeseen effects down through history. Yet if it is impossible to tell whether any act is morally right or wrong, how can consequentialism possibly be a correct moral theory?

The first thing to note about this objection is that, if it is sound, it threatens not only consequentialism, but indeed all plausible normative theories. For if it is in fact impossible to get a grip on the consequences of an act, then this problem will be inherited by all theories that give this factor any weight at all—and that will be virtually all theories. For as we have noted, all plausible theories agree that goodness of consequences is at least *one* factor relevant to the moral status of acts. (No plausible theory would hold, for example, that it was irrelevant whether an act would lead to disaster!)

Luckily, however, although the difficulty noted in the objection is real, the problem of uncertainty may not be incapacitating. After all, life is full of risks and uncertainties—not just in moral cases, but everywhere. Although we may lack crystal balls, we are not utterly in the dark as to what the effects of our actions are likely to be; we are able to make reasonable, educated guesses. And thus we can—and do—set ourselves goals and choose our acts with an eye toward how we are most likely to promote those goals. Uncertainty need not lead to paralysis. (Of course it remains true that there will always be a very small chance of some totally unforeseen disaster resulting from your act. But it seems equally true that there will be a corresponding very small chance of your act resulting in something fantastically wonderful, although totally unforeseen. If there is indeed no reason to expect either, then the two possibilities will cancel each other out as we try to decide how to act.)

But what, then, should we say, if someone does an act that *looks* like it will lead to the best results overall—all the best available evidence supports this belief—but in fact it leads to bad results overall? Did they do the right act, or didn't they? It seems that there are two basic approaches we can take in cases like this—that is, cases where the facts differ from what the agent takes them to be. We can maintain an *objective* account of rightness, holding that whether an act is right is a matter of the facts as they actually are; or we could adopt instead a *subjective* account of rightness, holding that whether an act is right is a matter of what the agent believes, or perhaps what a reasonable person would believe.

If we are objective consequentialists, we will say that the right act is the act that *in fact* leads to the best results. If, unfortunately, the act that looks like it will lead to the best results turns out not to be the optimal act after all, then it was not in fact the right act to do. Some other act—the act that was in fact optimal—was the right thing to do. Now this may seem a harsh verdict, but it need not be. For we can also point out that it was quite *rational* to perform the act that looked like it would lead to the best results, and we certainly won't want to *blame* the person who made this unavoidable mistake. Indeed, we will want to praise her, for trying her best to promote the good. (Encouraging people who are sincerely doing their best to promote the good will normally lead to good results; so from the consequentialist perspective this will be the right thing to do.) But—the objective consequentialist continues—although the mistake was a rational one, and the person's intentions should certainly be praised, the fact remains that she did not do the act with the best results, and so did not do the particular act that was best from the moral standpoint.

This may still seem an incorrect account of the case. Those who are attracted to subjective accounts of rightness will find it implausible to suggest that some act could be the right thing to do even though no one could possibly have known that this was so. Accordingly, if we are subjective consequentialists, we will say that if in fact all the available evidence supported the belief that the given act would have the best results—if this was the conclusion that any reasonable person would have reached—then this was indeed the right act for the person to choose. Admittedly, this was not the act that ended up having the best results, and this is unfortunate. But given that there was no way to know this, the right thing for the person to do was the act that looked like it would lead to the best results overall; it is this act that was best from the moral standpoint.

Whether one finds the objective account or the subjective account of rightness more plausible will turn on larger metaethical issues concerning the point and purpose of morality. Those who conceive of morality as fundamentally being a guide to decision making will be drawn to subjective accounts; those who conceive of morality as offering instead a standard for evaluating acts, which we may simply fail to get right, will be drawn to objective accounts. I will not try to settle this dispute here. The point to be emphasized, however, is this: any objection to consequentialism that turns on the uncertainty of the future actually has little or nothing to do with consequentialism per se; it points instead to the need to choose between objective and subjective accounts of rightness, and this choice must be made by *every* moral theory. For some, the ubiquity of uncertainty may motivate adoption of the subjective approach; others will feel that there are sufficient resources within the objective approach to deal adequately with cases of uncertainty and risk. But whatever your position here, once you have adopted a stance, you are likely to feel that the problem of uncertainty has been adequately answered. And since—as we have just seen—consequentialism can be offered as either an objective or a subjective theory, this first objection can, I think, be put aside. (For simplicity, in what follows I will continue to present consequentialism and other normative theories in objective terms; but those who prefer subjective accounts can easily keep the necessary modifications in mind.)

The second most popular objection to consequentialism follows quickly upon the heels of the first. If consequences are the only things that matter for determining the moral status of an act, then doesn't it follow that the agent will have to be forever calculating the consequences of his acts? Yet anyone who actually did that would never have the time to *do* anything, and so could hardly be performing the act with the best results. Thus consequentialism seems to place an impossible burden upon the agent (if it requires doing all the calculations and yet still having time to act)—or else it is self-defeating (if it allows the agent to constantly calculate, instead of acting).

Once more, however, it should be noted that were this objection sound, it would threaten virtually all normative theories, since all plausible theories include consequences as at least one relevant normative factor. The need for calculation seems to be based on the fact that we count consequences at all; it has nothing to do with the particular claim of consequentialists that consequences are indeed the only things that matter. (Admittedly, on certain nonconsequentialist views further factors might sometimes outweigh consequences so completely that there would be no need to calculate consequences at all; but even for such views there will be plenty of other cases in which the consequences *do* need to be taken into account, and so the calculation objection will arise for these views as well.)

It is fortunate, therefore, that this objection too seems to be misconceived. Consequentialism does *not* direct people to be forever calculating. What it requires people to do is to perform the act with the best results. Since it is obvious that someone who is forever calculating will not be bringing about the best results, such a person is not doing what consequentialism requires. Another way to grasp this point is to bear in mind that acts of calculation are indeed just one more kind of act—to be performed if and only if they will lead to the best results overall. Sometimes, perhaps, more calculation is called for, if the situation is complex, and the agent will not perform the optimal act without it. But in every situation, too *much* calculation is forbidden, since calculating on and on will never bring about the best results.

How, then, should the agent decide which act to perform? The simple answer, of course, is this: consequentialism holds that the agent should decide by whatever method yields the best results. And it is an *empirical* question just what method this is. In principle, it could turn out that flipping a coin is the optimal decision procedure, or perhaps doing the very first thing that comes into one's head. Of course in point of fact it seems extremely unlikely that either of these is the optimal method of deciding how to act. But in and of itself, consequentialism takes no stand at all on this empirical question.

Nonetheless, there is a method of decision making that has been favored by many consequentialists, and that seems plausible in its own right as well: appeal to ordinary moral rules, insofar as these can be derived from the more fundamental consequentialist principle. The basic idea here is that, except in extraordinary circumstances, certain *types* of acts tend to have good consequences overall, or bad consequences overall. For example, murdering someone almost always has bad consequences overall; keeping your promises, in contrast, generally has good consequences. (At least, this will be true if we are using a plausible theory of the good.) Starting with consequentialism, then, and using these empirical generalizations about the typical consequences of various kinds of acts, we can derive "subsidiary" or "secondary" moral rules: all other things being equal, keep your promises; all other things being equal, don't kill; and so on. Normally, then, all the agent needs to do is to see which of these derivative moral rules applies in the given situation and follow the rules; further calculation is unnecessary.

This basic account can easily be made more sophisticated. The secondary rules derived from consequentialism can be relatively simple—since they only say what to do "other things being equal"—but they need not be absurdly simpleminded. Consequentialism will frequently justify building various "exception clauses" into the rules. For example, the prohibition against killing is likely to have an exception clause for self-defense, since self-defense has a deterrent effect on would-be aggressors, and so typically leads to better results overall. Similarly, consequentialism can yield plausible "priority rules," rules that tell us what to do in cases where two or more secondary rules conflict. It tells us, for example, that the rule against telling lies will normally be outweighed by the rule requiring us to save lives—should one ever have to choose between the two—since the harm done by telling a lie is typically smaller than the good done by saving a life.

Armed with these slightly more complex (but correspondingly more plausible) rules, the agent typically has all she needs, to know what to do in normal situations. Of course, there will still be a place for calculation—in unusual circumstances where the rules conflict, and there is no familiar priority rule, or where something marks the situation as being atypical, and so the secondary rules may be misleading. But this will be the exception. Normally there will be no need for anything like a direct calculation of the consequences. Indeed, in many ordinary circumstances the agent will not even need to rehearse the secondary moral rules to herself: habit will make an appropriate response virtually automatic.

Thus the consequentialist has available a plausible response to the calculation objection. And in the course of developing it, an attractive feature of consequentialism has emerged as well: consequentialism offers a plausible account of the basis of the various ordinary moral rules of commonsense morality. These rules are not themselves ultimate, but instead are derived from the more fundamental consequentialist principle that agents are required to promote the good.

What's more, consequentialism offers a way to refine and evaluate these secondary moral rules. We have already seen how a consequentialist might argue that a general prohibition against killing should make an exception for self-defense. But this process of refinement can go further. For example, most of us believe that although self-defense is justified, my killing someone in self-defense is *not* justified if I am myself the aggressor, and the person trying to harm me is only defending himself from my unprovoked attack. Consequentialism can explain and justify this further view as well (since it will not lead to better results overall if aggressors defend themselves). In other cases, changed circumstances may call for alterations in the derivative moral rules, and consequentialism can guide the process of emendation and modification. And in still other cases, consequentialism may instruct us to altogether disregard rules that may have currency in common moral consciousness but which have no useful role in promoting the overall good. Thus we can use consequentialism to explore and articulate the precise borders and contents of our various secondary moral rules, fixing what needs fixing, rejecting what is without value, and justifying what remains. Consequentialism thus offers what appears to be a plausible account of the ordinary rules of commonsense morality, and a standard against which they can be evaluated.

But this is not to say that there are no significant objections to consequentialism. Consequentialism claims that there is one and only one factor that is of intrinsic significance in determining the moral status of an act—the goodness of the act's consequences as compared to those of the alternative acts available to the agent. But commonsense morality believes that there are many other factors that equally possess intrinsic normative significance. If commonsense morality is correct about this, then consequentialism is an inadequate normative theory.

Of course, as we have just seen, consequentialists have available a powerful and plausible account of the various other features of commonsense morality. But for all that, that account may yet be inadequate. For commonsense morality grants these other features a place and a significance not captured by the consequentialist account. In short, the truly telling objection to consequentialism amounts to the claim that there are other normative factors that cannot be adequately accounted for within a consequentialist framework. To assess the merits of *this* objection, however, we must turn to extended considerations of the various other normative factors that are endorsed by commonsense morality.

# 3

## DOING HARM

### 3.1 Deontology

Consequentialists accept a simple theory of the right. There is one and only one factor that has any intrinsic moral significance in determining the status of an act: the goodness of that act's consequences (as compared to the consequences of the alternative acts available to the agent). Of course, as we have also seen (in 2.6), consequentialists can find a place for the more familiar rules of commonsense morality as well—a requirement to keep one's promises, a prohibition against lying, and so on. These secondary rules pick out types of acts that generally have good or bad consequences, and so provide helpful guidance in normal deliberation. But whatever the usefulness of these more familiar rules, the fact remains that from the consequentialist point of view they have no intrinsic moral significance. The various factors identified by these rules (promise keeping, truth telling, and so on) may be instrumentally valuable in discovering which act *has* the best results; but in and of themselves they play no role in making it be the case that a given act has the moral status that it does. Ultimately, an act is right if and only if it will have the best results; morally speaking, nothing else matters.

So say the consequentialists. But many people find this a difficult position to accept. Intuitively, at least, it seems that many normative factors have a moral significance that is not exhausted by the good or bad results that they normally involve. Intuitively, that is, most of us believe that there are other factors that have intrinsic moral significance beyond that of goodness of outcomes. Of course, as I have repeatedly emphasized, virtually no one denies that goodness of outcomes is *one* of the intrinsically relevant factors; but the point to remember now is that one can accept this modest claim while still rejecting the consequentialist's considerably bolder claim that this is the *only* factor with intrinsic significance.

In opposition to consequentialism, most people believe that there are *several* normative factors with intrinsic moral significance. And the moral status of an act is determined by the interplay of all of these various factors—not good consequences alone. In principle, at least, this means that a given act might be morally forbidden even though it has the best results. For there may be a second normative factor that comes into play—a factor capable of "outweighing" or "overriding" the fact that the act will have the best possible results overall.

An example should make the point clear. Imagine that there are five patients, each of whom will soon die unless they receive an appropriate transplanted organ: one needs a heart, two need kidneys, one needs a liver, and the fifth needs new lungs. Unfortunately, due to tissue incompatibilities, none of the five can act as donor for the others. But here is Chuck, who is in the hospital for some fairly routine tests. The hospital computer reveals that his tissue is completely compatible with the five patients. You are a surgeon, and it now occurs to you that you could chop up Chuck and use his organs to save the five others. What should you do?

If you are a consequentialist, the answer depends only on the goodness of the results. Of course, until we specify a particular theory of the good, we can't say for sure which results would be better. But for simplicity, let's consider the answer of the utilitarian—the consequentialist who accepts a welfarist account of the good. (Other plausible theories of the good are likely to give the same answers in this case, so restricting our attention to utilitarianism shouldn't beg any questions against consequentialism. But see 6.4.)

Your choices are these: do nothing, in which case five people will die and one person will live; or chop up Chuck, in which case Chuck will obviously die but *five* people will live. From the utilitarian standpoint the results certainly seem to be better if you chop up Chuck. After all, if everyone counts equally, then it is simply a matter of five versus one. Obviously, it is a horrible result that Chuck will end up dead; but it would be an even worse result if *five* people end up dead. So the right thing to do—according to utilitarianism—is to kill Chuck.

But this seems absurd. Intuitively, at least, most of us have little doubt that it is morally forbidden to chop up an innocent person, even if this is the only way to save five other innocent people from death. Some acts are morally off-limits; they are forbidden, even if the results would be good. So there must be other factors that can play a role in determining the moral status of an act—beyond the goodness of that act's outcome. In the case at hand, it seems highly relevant that the admittedly good result of saving five people can only be brought about by an act that involves harming, indeed *killing,* an innocent person!

Here, it seems, we have identified a second relevant normative factor. The moral status of an act depends not only on the goodness of its results, but also on whether or not it involves doing harm to someone. (By itself, perhaps, this case cannot establish whether we care about harming per se, or only killing in particular; but similar examples would quickly support the former conclusion.) What's more, the organ transplant case suggests that most of us believe that this second factor straightforwardly outweighs the first factor, good results: even if harming someone is the only way to bring about the best results, it just can't be done. Morally, it is more important to avoid doing harm than it is to *save* people who need our help. This, at any rate, appears to be the view of commonsense morality.

It is important to be clear about what this view holds. It does *not* claim that it is morally irrelevant that five people are going to die. The possibility of saving five lives remains a significant factor in determining what we should do. Obviously, if there were some way to save the five without killing Chuck then we would be morally required to do so. But commonsense morality insists that the possibility of saving five lives—even though this is the best result overall—is not the only factor of intrinsic moral significance. It is also relevant that the only way to bring about the best results involves *doing* harm. And given a conflict between these two factors—given the necessity of either doing harm or failing to produce the best possible results—it is more important to avoid doing harm.

Now in principle, a moral theory could be *pluralistic*—recognizing more than one normative factor—without going so far as to hold that goodness of results can sometimes be *outweighed* by these other factors. (For example, a moral theory might claim that doing harm is intrinsically relevant but only as a tie breaker: according to such a theory, if two acts would have equally good results, it would be morally preferable to pick the act that does not involve doing harm; but if doing harm was necessary to bring about *better* results, it would still be permissible.) So it is important to stress that commonsense morality appears to do more than merely recognize the intrinsic significance of harm doing: it invests this factor with considerable weight—a force sufficient to outweigh good results. We are forbidden to do harm, even if this is the only way to bring about the best results overall. Indeed, the significance of harm doing is so great—according to commonsense moral intuition—that all other things being equal, if an act involves doing harm, it is simply forbidden.

We can express this point by saying that commonsense morality recognizes a *constraint* against doing harm. That is to say, there is a prohibition which rules out performing a certain type of act—in this case, doing harm—even when performing an act of that type is necessary to bring about the best results overall. Now obviously enough, consequentialist theories leave no room for moral constraints, since such theories hold that whatever act will lead to the best results is always permissible. But it is precisely at this point that commonsense morality diverges from consequentialism. Let us call any moral theory that does incorporate constraints *de-*

*ontological.* It appears, then, that commonsense morality is deontological, rather than consequentialist.

Unfortunately, although the term "deontology" is widely used in contemporary moral philosophy, there is nothing like a standard or received definition of the term. In defining deontology, I have appealed to the concept of a constraint: deontologists, unlike consequentialists, believe in the existence of constraints, which erect moral barriers to the promotion of the good. But why not take the more straightforward approach and simply say that deontologists are all those who reject consequentialism? This would make for a sharp contrast between deontology and consequentialism, but it would also be far too broad to capture anything like the contemporary philosophical use of the term "deontology." (A moral system in which every act is permissible would certainly not be consequentialist—but it would never be classified as deontological either.)

Similarly, if we hope to capture contemporary usage, it won't quite do to label as  deontologists all those who accept additional normative factors, beyond that of goodness of results: we must add the further stipulation that in at least some cases the effect of these additional factors is to make certain acts morally forbidden, even though these acts may lead to the best possible results overall. In short, we must say that deontologists are those who believe in additional normative factors that generate constraints.

This characterization of deontology—in terms of constraints—is by no means the most common one. I believe, however, that it comports reasonably well with contemporary use. (And, at the very least, it is probably sufficient for the purposes of recognizing typical deontological positions.) In any event, other common attempts to define deontology suffer from their own difficulties as well.

For example, it is sometimes suggested that in contrast to consequentialism—which assesses the moral status of an act solely in terms of its effects—deontological theories also assess an act in terms of its *intrinsic character.* But it is difficult to see how to come up with an account of "intrinsic character" so that this is necessarily true. (If I harm someone, generally it is not the *intrinsic* character of the act that makes it harm doing, but rather the fact that the act has a certain kind of result.) Similarly, it is sometimes suggested that deontologists, unlike consequentialists, believe in absolute rules. But this too is an inadequate way of drawing the contrast. As we will see, deontologists need not actually be absolutists about their rules; and, at any rate, consequentialists *are* absolutists: they are absolutists with regard to the requirement to do the act with the best results.

Another proposal is that deontologists—in contrast to consequentialists—believe in "the priority of the right over the good." The idea behind this expression is this. Consequentialists start with a theory of the good, and then "define" the right in terms of it: the right act is simply that act that leads to the best results. For consequentialists, then, the good is prior to the right. In contrast, deontologists believe that sometimes the right act is *not* the one that leads to the best results overall. Accordingly, the right cannot be simply defined in terms of the good or "reduced" to the good; it has some content independent of the good, and is in this sense "prior" to it. Understood in this way, the claim that deontologists believe in the priority of the right over the good is merely a shorthand way of expressing this thought: deontologists believe that goodness of results is not the only normative factor relevant to determining the moral status of an act; other factors are relevant as well, and these can have the effect of making it impermissible to perform the act with the best results. So understood, this is more or less equivalent to the way in which I have characterized deontology.

But the claim that deontologists—unlike consequentialists—accept "the priority of the right over the good" is potentially also a rather misleading one. For it may create the impression that somehow it is only deontologists who recognize the importance of doing the right thing—whereas the reality, of course, is that consequentialists believe in this as well. Talk of the priority of the right over the good may also create the impression that deontologists must *define* the good in terms of the right (just as consequentialists are said to "define" the right in terms of the good). But this certainly need not be the case: the deontologist need not believe that the right is *prior* to the good in any robust sense; it is simply that the deontologist—unlike the consequentialist—holds that considerations of goodness do not exhaust the considerations relevant to determining the act's rightness. In particular, certain factors may make it morally impermissible to perform an act, even though that act would have the best results. It is only in this sense that deontologists must believe that the right is "prior" to the good.

For all of these various reasons, then, I think it preferable to define deontology in the way that I did—that is, in terms of the acceptance of constraints. But however we define deontology, the important point is really this: commonsense morality does indeed accept constraints; and this is the reason why most of us find consequentialism an inadequate moral theory.

Here is another way to express the point. Admittedly, consequentialists can find *some* place in their theory for the rules of commonsense morality, including a rule against harming people. (After all, in *normal* situations harming an innocent person is hardly likely to bring about the best results.) But it doesn't follow that consequentialists can give these rules the same sort of weight that they have in ordinary moral thinking. And what the organ transplant case suggests is that consequentialists fail to give these rules sufficient weight; they permit breaking the rules in cases where the rules should not be broken.

For the consequentialist, the familiar rules of ordinary morality are merely "rules of thumb": they pick out acts that in normal circumstances tend to have good or bad results; the rules should therefore be followed *all other things being equal*. But in exceptional cases, in cases where obeying the rules would not actually lead to the best results overall, the rules have no further weight or significance—they are, after all, mere rules of thumb—and so the consequentialist thinks they should be broken. In contrast, what most of us believe is that these rules identify further factors that have a direct role to play in determining whether an act is right or wrong. And if these factors do have intrinsic weight—if they matter in their own right and not merely as indicators of good or bad results—then the mere fact that breaking some rule will lead to the best results overall will not necessarily be sufficient, in and of itself, to justify breaking the rule.

Other examples reinforce the point. Imagine that some horrible crime has been committed, and unless the guilty party is found soon, an angry mob will riot in the streets, killing several innocent people. You are the sheriff, and you cannot figure out who actually committed the crime. But it occurs to you that you are in a position to secretly fabricate evidence, framing an innocent person, thereby satisfying the mob and saving the lives of those who would otherwise be killed during the riots. What should you do? It certainly looks as though the consequentialist must classify this as another "exception"—a case in which the familiar rules of justice are to be violated. But intuitively, at least, most of us would find it morally unacceptable to knowingly frame an innocent man, even if this is the only way to save lives. So here too we find consequentialism endorsing the breaking of rules in a case where they should not be broken. (Presumably this is the thought that lay behind the attempt—noted above—to define deontology in terms of absolutism; I think it is a mistake, however, to focus on absolutism per se, rather than on the particular rules that the consequentialist is prepared to break.)

What the organ transplant case, the angry mob case, and similar examples seem to show is that consequentialism is inadequate as a moral theory. Because it accepts an inappropriately short list of normative factors, it permits acts that are not in fact morally permissible. It tells us to chop up Chuck, to frame the innocent man, and so on, even though these are clearly immoral acts. In short, consequentialism *permits too much*. At any rate, that's the objection offered by consequentialism's deontological critics.

There are, however, a number of ways in which consequentialists can try to resist this objection. Obviously enough, the objection gets its bite from the claim that in various cases consequentialism yields intuitively unacceptable results. Accordingly, one way to undermine the force of the objection is to deny that this is the case, that is, to deny that consequentialism actually supports performing the intuitively unacceptable acts.

In the organ transplant case, for example, the problem is that consequentialism appears to support chopping up Chuck, an act that certainly strikes us, intuitively, as morally impermissible. But the consequentialist could insist that—initial appearances to the contrary notwithstanding—killing Chuck isn't likely to have the best results. After all, organ transplants have a very high failure rate; if you chop up Chuck you could easily end up with *six* people dead rather than merely five. In light of the risks, it is far from obvious that killing Chuck will do more good than harm. Furthermore, it is important to remember that *all* the results have to be taken into account— not only the short term benefits but the long term costs as well. Consider, then, the likely effects of your act once it comes to light that a perfectly healthy person was killed during a routine visit to the hospital: people will start thinking twice about seeing doctors or going to hospitals, and in the long run the negative effects on public health will be horrible. The total outcome will thus be much worse if you kill Chuck than if you refuse to do it and simply let the five original patients die. But if chopping up Chuck isn't really the act with the best results, then consequentialism doesn't en- dorse performing that act, and so consequentialism hasn't been shown to be intuitively unacceptable.

A reply along these lines obviously relies on its various empirical claims, and so the critic of consequentialism might try to challenge them. But there is another possibility as well. The critic could simply alter the example, at- tempting to arrive at a version of the case in which it is undeniable that chopping up Chuck *would* have the best results overall. For example, we might be asked to imagine a time in which organ transplant procedures have been perfected, thus guaranteeing that the five will indeed be saved if only Chuck's organs become available. Similarly, to avoid the potential long term negative effects of your being open about having killed Chuck, we might be asked to imagine that you find a way to kill him secretly, mak- ing it look as though he died of a rare and unexpected medical complica- tion. Properly modified, it seems as though we will eventually arrive at a version of the organ case in which it is indeed true that killing Chuck so as to save the five patients will have the best results overall.

Some consequentialists will still deny this. They might claim that for no version of the story will it be true that killing Chuck has the best results overall. Of course, the more we add to the story—the more unrealistic we make it—the harder it is for the consequentialist to insist that the results of killing Chuck simply *cannot* be best. But this then points to a slightly differ- ent reply open to the consequentialist: he might agree that *eventually* we may be able to tell a version of the story in which killing Chuck has the best results; but he will insist that once we actually produce such an example— filling in the details so that it is clear that anything other than killing Chuck will have even worse results overall—we will no longer find it counterintu- itive to claim that (given all the bizarre circumstances of the case) killing Chuck is the right thing to do.

Other consequentialists may prefer a somewhat different tack. They might insist that for all *realistic* examples, consequentialism yields intu- itively acceptable results. They may concede that for sufficiently outlandish, "science fiction"–type cases, consequentialism may well support acts that seem intuitively unacceptable. But—they will insist—for such highly unrealistic cases there is simply no reason to *trust* our intuitions. After all, unless you believe (implausibly) that our moral intuitions have a direct pipeline to the truth, you have to worry about the reliability of those intuitions; and the more outlandish the case—the more it falls outside the range of normal human experience—the more reason we have to doubt what our intuitions tell us about that case. So even if there *are* cases where, intuitively, consequentialism seems to permit too much, there is no reason to give our intuitions about those cases very much weight.

(More radically still, some consequentialists simply insist that intuitions about specific cases should carry little or no weight *in general* in assessing moral theories. On this view, even if there is a completely realistic version of the organ case, and even if it is conceded that consequentialism endorses an act—killing Chuck—that seems quite unacceptable intuitively, this will still have little or no force as an objection to consequentialism.)

These, then, are some of the ways in which a consequentialist can respond to a proposed counterexample. He can concede that it would be unacceptable for a moral theory to endorse a given act but insist that consequentialism doesn't actually endorse that act; he can admit that consequentialism endorses the act in question but insist that the given act is not actually intuitively unacceptable (given the circumstances); or he can admit that consequentialism endorses an act that appears intuitively unacceptable but argue that intuition is not—in this case, at the very least—to be trusted. In actual practice, of course, consequentialists typically avail themselves of all of the various replies that I have been sketching, using different answers in response to different specific cases. In this way, they hope to disarm the array of intuitive counterexamples.

How successful is the consequentialist strategy? This is, of course, a matter of some controversy; and like the others considered in this book, I won't try to settle it here. Many find the various consequentialist maneuvers—whether singly, or in combination—sufficiently persuasive so that consequentialism remains a plausible theory of normative ethics. (The discussion from 1.3 should also be recalled: it may be that no theory fits all our intuitions perfectly; so if consequentialism is sufficiently attractive on other grounds, it may be that we are justified in accepting it despite its having counterintuitive implications in certain cases.) Others, however, find the intuitive objections to consequentialism sufficiently compelling that they are forced to conclude that it is inadequate as a normative theory. And if this is the conclusion that one accepts, then of course it is not difficult to find a plausible diagnosis of the source of consequentialism's flaws: consequentialism will seem implausible because of its insistence that goodness of outcomes is the only morally relevant normative factor. A more adequate moral theory will need to recognize the existence of constraints as well; it will need to be deontological.

But for those who do want to move beyond consequentialism, the question arises: what further normative factors are to be recognized? Note that it won't provide much guidance simply to say that we want to move to a deontological system. In principle, after all, deontological theories can differ considerably as to the precise constraints that they accept; so to say that a theory should be deontological just doesn't go very far toward specifying its content. But if the goal is, rather, that of trying to capture something like *commonsense morality* along deontological lines, then we are much further along. We can use the familiar rules of commonsense morality to identify further normative factors that intuitively seem to possess intrinsic moral significance.

In point of fact, we have already identified one further factor that, it seems, must be embraced if we hope to capture something like our ordinary moral intuitions: if an act involves *doing harm,* then this is a highly relevant fact about it, and it weighs in heavily against the moral permissibility of the act. Apparently, then, any normative theory that hopes to capture our ordinary moral intuitions will have to incorporate a constraint against doing harm. Obviously, this is not to say that, with this addition, the list of normative factors is now complete. There may well be other factors that need to be accepted as well—other constraints that must be recognized. The point is simply this: if we are going to move beyond consequentialism, then—whatever other factors we may want to add as well—at the very least we will want to add a constraint against doing harm.

(A final comment about terminology may be in order. Strictly speaking, normative factors are one thing, and the constraints based on them—if any—are another. After all, as we have already noted, a theory might recognize an extra normative factor—such as harm doing—without investing it with the weight and significance necessary to ground a constraint. And from a logical point of view, at any rate, even if a theory does incorporate constraints, it still seems appropriate to distinguish between the normative factor per se—which is the relevant feature that a given act might possess or lack—and the *constraint,* which is the prohibition against performing acts that possess the feature in question. Nonetheless, it doesn't seem seriously misleading to sometimes speak as though the constraint itself were the extra normative factor, or to say that a relevant factor in determining the status of an act is that it violates a given constraint. And so, unless context requires otherwise, I will often speak interchangeably of the constraint-generating normative factors and the constraints that these factors generate.)

## 3.2  Thresholds

As we have seen, many people believe on reflection that harm doing is a factor of intrinsic normative significance; the fact that an act involves doing harm provides a reason not to perform that act. But how much weight should this factor have? If in some case doing harm is the only way to produce the best results overall, which factor is more important—producing good results, or not doing harm?

It may seem as though we have already answered this question. After all, I have suggested that virtually everyone who accepts the intrinsic normative significance of harm doing gives this factor sufficient weight to override goodness of results in cases like that of the organ transplant. That is to say, they accept a *constraint* against doing harm: it is morally forbidden to kill one innocent person (for example, chopping up Chuck)—even if this is the only way to produce an even better result (saving four more lives overall). But there is still room for disagreement, for the question can be raised as to whether or not this constraint is absolute, or whether it too can be overridden when enough is at stake.

Suppose, for example, that killing an innocent person was necessary not merely to save five lives (as in the organ transplant case)—but a *hundred,* or a *thousand,* or a *million!* (Imagine that killing the one is the only way to prevent a nuclear war; or that the innocent person's body must be used to produce a serum that will provide a cure for a plague that will otherwise kill millions.) Is it still morally impermissible to kill the one innocent person—even with *so much* at stake? Even if this is the only way to prevent a catastrophe?

Some people find themselves still inclined to embrace the constraint, even in the face of such catastrophes. They are *absolutists* about the constraint against doing harm: harming an innocent person is morally forbidden, no matter how horrible the results will be otherwise, no matter how much good could be done. The importance of avoiding harm doing *always* outweighs the importance of producing good results (even when the "good results" include the prevention of bad results.)

Many other people, however, find this absolutist attitude toward the constraint unacceptable. They believe that the constraint against doing harm can itself be outweighed, if *enough* is at stake. Presumably, killing an innocent person is morally forbidden even if this is the only way to save five, ten, or maybe even a hundred or a thousand people—but at *some point,* when the amount of good that needs to be done is great enough, the constraint is overridden, and it is morally permissible to act.

Those who reject the absolutist attitude toward the constraint against harming are *moderate* deontologists. They believe that the constraint has a *threshold:* up to a certain point—the threshold point—it is forbidden to kill or harm an innocent person, even if greater good could be achieved by doing it; but if *enough* good is at stake—if the threshold has been reached or passed—then the constraint is no longer in force, and it is permissible to harm the person.

Should we say that in such a case it is permissible to *violate* the constraint? This way of putting it seems needlessly paradoxical, since talk of "violating" a rule normally suggests that one has acted impermissibly, whereas the idea here is that the act in question is in fact perfectly permissible, given the pressing circumstances. But we could say, perhaps, that the act *infringes* the constraint—since it is undeniably the kind of act that the constraint normally forbids. If we adopt this convention, then we can say that moderate deontologists believe that not all constraint infringements are forbidden. Normally, of course, it does violate the constraint to infringe it; but when enough is at stake—when the threshold has been met—infringing the constraint is morally justified.

Consequentialists sometimes argue that the attempt to accept deontology while rejecting absolutism is incoherent. After all—they claim—if you are prepared to infringe the constraint on the basis of the good that can be achieved by doing so, then you have in effect admitted that consequences are really the bottom line; and so, whether you realize it or not, you must be some kind of a consequentialist. Interestingly, this is a charge that is often seconded by deontological absolutists, who argue that if you recognize the intrinsic significance of the constraint against doing harm, then you cannot coherently be prepared to abandon or disregard that constraint merely because of the good that this might achieve. Sometimes, then, both sides insist that the only consistent positions are either consequentialism or deontological absolutism; moderate deontology, it is said, is a confused or incoherent position.

I think, however, that such arguments are mistaken. Moderate deontologists can plausibly insist that their position does not reveal itself to be "at bottom" consequentialist, even though they acknowledge that constraints can sometimes be outweighed by good consequences. Consequentialists, after all, believe that goodness of results is the *only* factor with intrinsic significance; it is, therefore, *always* permissible to perform the act that will lead to the best results. But moderate deontologists are *pluralists* who believe in the intrinsic significance of harm doing as well; and normally—that is, when the threshold for the constraint has not been met—it will be morally forbidden to harm someone, even if this will indeed bring about better results overall. Moderate deontology is thus a genuine alternative to consequentialism.

Nor is there anything necessarily incoherent in recognizing the existence of constraints but insisting that these constraints can, for all that, sometimes be outweighed by goodness of results. This is, after all, just what we might expect from a pluralistic view, one that accords intrinsic significance to both goodness of results *and* harm doing. For if there are two (or more) factors, then it shouldn't be surprising if in some cases the first factor outweighs the second, while in other cases the second outweighs the first. Since harm doing has a significant amount of weight in its own right, it will often outweigh goodness of results: this yields the constraint against harming. But as the amount at stake in any given case increases, the importance of this second factor will presumably increase as well—and this might well yield a *threshold* for that constraint. There is nothing at all incoherent in the suggestion that—despite the intrinsic significance of harm-doing—in some cases goodness of results can be great enough to outweigh the importance of avoiding doing harm, so that, on balance, it will be permissible to infringe the constraint. Moderate deontology is thus a perfectly coherent form of deontology. (But this is not to say that there is anything necessarily incoherent about absolutist deontology either: even if goodness of results has intrinsic normative significance, it might still be that it is *always* outweighed by the importance of not doing harm.)

For those who are attracted to moderate deontology, the question arises of where, exactly, the threshold for the constraint against harming should be located. How *much* must be at stake before it becomes permissible to infringe the constraint? In principle, it should be noted, the range of possible answers is tremendous. Of course, if the constraint is to have any force at all, the threshold must be set above zero. And if absolutism is to be avoided, the threshold must be set at a finite amount. Still, this obviously leaves a huge range of possibilities (an infinite range, in fact). A low threshold might permit killing one to save ten. (Indeed, an extremely low threshold might even permit killing one to save *two!*) A high threshold, in contrast, might only permit killing one to save millions, or billions.

Wherever the line is drawn, the moderate deontologist faces a further challenge (it can be raised by both consequentialists and deontological absolutists): why draw the line *there?* Since the threshold could always have been placed higher or lower, any specific location is bound to seem rather arbitrary. How can it possibly be defended? (By contrast, the consequentialist and the deontological absolutist have staked out the two end points of the continuum; whatever their other drawbacks, the two extremes at least seem less arbitrary.)

Most moderate deontologists, however, will not be greatly distressed by this objection. They will admit that, in some sense, any location for the threshold will seem arbitrary, since it could always have been higher or lower; but they will note that such an appearance of arbitrariness will be present *whenever* a theory needs to trade off two factors against each other. So long as there are two or more factors that need to be balanced, a trade-off schedule of some sort will be required. And in principle, the question can always be raised as to why one particular schedule should be accepted rather than another. But to ask this is to raise an epistemological question: what evidence supports a given schedule as opposed to some alternative? And the answer, presumably, might turn on any number of considerations, including, for example, the extent to which a given schedule fits our intuitions. Since there is no particular reason to think that such evidence cannot be marshaled to help locate the threshold for the constraint against doing harm, moderate deontology is—on the face of it—no worse off than any other form of pluralism.

Presumably, the precise location of the threshold is something that different moderate deontologists will differ over. But it does seem safe to say that if the moderate deontologist hopes to capture something like commonsense morality, then—whatever its exact location—the threshold will have to be fairly high. (It is, however, rather obscure as to exactly *how* high the threshold would have to be to capture our ordinary moral intuitions. It is also unclear how much *precision* is appropriate in specifying the threshold: should we, for example, expect that the threshold can be captured in a precise number, say, "exactly 100 lives"? Or will the threshold be fixed only roughly and imprecisely, "somewhere around 100" or "somewhere in the range of 75 to 125"? These are important issues; but I am going to put them aside.)

Asking for "the" location of the threshold against doing harm may create the impression that there is some single, fixed amount that must be at stake before the constraint can be infringed. On reflection, however, it is clear that this is rather implausible. Far more likely is that the level of the threshold depends on the size of the harm that needs to be done to bring about the good results. For it is important to note that harms do indeed come in different sizes and different kinds; and it is implausible to think that the same amount must be at stake, regardless of the particular harm involved. For example, as we have seen, many people have the intuition that one cannot *kill* an innocent person unless some rather large number of lives can be saved. But presumably most people believe it would take far less to justify inflicting some *minor* harm. It might well be permissible, say, to punch an innocent person in the nose, even if this would save "only" *one* life! Similarly, it seems as though a great deal must be at stake before it would be permissible to cause someone excruciating physical pain; but inflicting some mild discomfort would presumably involve a far lower threshold.

Accordingly, the moderate deontologist might well want to suggest that the level of the threshold in any given case is a function of the nature of the harm involved. On the most simple view of this sort, the level of the threshold is determined by multiplying the *size* of the harm by some fixed amount (so the level of the threshold will vary, but the "multiplier" will be constant). Obviously, however, more complicated functions are possible as well. In addition, the level of the threshold might well be sensitive not only to the size of the harm but also to the *kind* of harm involved. For example, perhaps the threshold is lower if the act merely involves damage to someone's property, rather than to their body. It is far from obvious what a plausible "threshold function" would look like; and it must be admitted, I think, that moderate deontologists have done little toward filling in the details.

There is a second way in which the need for thresholds for the constraint against harming can arise. Consider the fact that many of our actions involve the *risk* of harming someone else. Driving a car, for example, clearly runs some chance of killing a pedestrian; less obviously, so does riding a bicycle. Few acts, if any, are altogether risk free, although, obviously enough, the level of risk can vary tremendously from act to act. It is also true that few acts, if any, are absolutely guaranteed to cause harm; usually there is at least some chance, however small, that things will end up all right. Now what is a deontologist—any deontologist, absolutist or moderate—to say about these facts? How does the constraint against doing harm apply to cases that only involve the *risk* of doing harm?

One's answer here might well depend on whether one accepts an objective or a subjective account of rightness (see 2.6). An objective deontologist might choose to say that issues involving risk—the mere *chance* of doing harm—are simply irrelevant to the question of whether one has *in fact* violated morality. On this approach, you haven't violated the constraint unless you actually *do* harm. The mere fact that you ran the *risk* of violating the constraint doesn't mean that you actually violated it. (Of course, if the risk is high, you might well be morally blameworthy for taking this chance; but such an evaluation of the *person* shouldn't be confused with the distinct question of whether the act itself violates morality.)

Those attracted to subjective accounts of rightness are likely to prefer a different approach. Consider an act that has a very high risk of causing harm, but imagine that luckily—unexpectedly, and unforeseeably—the harm isn't actually produced. According to the objective deontologist, the agent hasn't actually done anything wrong: since no harm was done, the constraint wasn't violated. But the subjective deontologist finds this an implausible claim: whether the act is right or wrong cannot be a matter of whether or not the harm *happens* to occur; rather, it is a matter of what the agent *believes* (or what it would be reasonable to believe). On this approach, to knowingly perform an action that runs a high risk of causing harm is to act immorally. Thus, the constraint against harming must be understood as a constraint against imposing the *risk* of harm.

But this raises the question: how *great* a risk? That is, what *level* of risk of harm is ruled out by the constraint? It won't do to suggest that the constraint rules out imposing any kind of risk of harm at all: for as we have already noted, almost every act carries *some* risk of harming others. Nor does it seem plausible to claim that the constraint rules out only "high" or "significant" levels of risk. Aside from the vagueness of such labels, there is the deeper problem that risks can be arranged in a smooth continuum from low to high; and it is hard to believe that the constraint might oppose all acts at a given level of risk while remaining altogether indifferent to acts that are only slightly less risky.

This is the point at which an appeal to thresholds might again prove useful. We have already noted the possibility that the level of the threshold is, at least in part, a function of the size of the harm. Here we can note the further possibility that the level of the threshold might also be (in part) a function of the level of the *risk*. Perhaps acts that run a high risk of causing harm have a high threshold, while acts that run a low risk have a low threshold: other things being equal, the higher the risk, the higher the threshold.

An approach along these lines would explain why it is normally permissible to perform acts that carry only a slight risk of harming others: the risk is low, and so the threshold is low and easily met; such acts need only produce a little good in order to be justified. But acts with significant levels of risk will normally be forbidden: here the threshold will be high, and so it will only rarely be met. Such an approach avoids the need to introduce sharp and arbitrary discontinuities into the constraint. Running any kind of risk at all *infringes* the constraint; but since the level of the threshold varies with the level of risk, many ordinary acts will not violate the constraint.

Of course, this entire approach is only available to moderate deontologists. Absolutists reject the existence of thresholds for the constraint, and so must find some other solution to the problems of risk. They must either embrace the objective approach (according to which risk per se is irrelevant to the constraint), or—if they accept a subjective account of rightness—they must propose a principled and nonarbitrary way to distinguish between unacceptably high levels of risk and ordinary, acceptable levels.

## 3.3  The Scope of the Constraint

Despite their differences, moderate and absolutist deontologists are alike in believing that harm doing is a factor with intrinsic normative significance. It is only if this factor has normative weight in its own right that there can be any kind of constraint against doing harm (regardless of whether that constraint is absolute or not). That is to say, there can be a constraint against doing harm only because the very fact that an act involves the doing of harm weighs heavily against performing it.

Up to this point, however, we have done little by way of describing the content of this factor. To be sure, we have considered alternative views about the *weight* that this factor might have, but we haven't said very much about the nature of the factor itself. Given our previous purposes, we were able to get by through the use of examples that drew upon our intuitive understanding of harm doing. But it is time to examine the nature of this factor directly. What exactly is it that constitutes doing harm? Just what does the constraint against doing harm oppose?

A natural proposal is this: we harm someone when we act in such a way as to affect their interests adversely. That is to say, to harm someone is to bring about a lowering of their well-being relative to the level that they would have been at, but for our action. If someone is worse off as a result of our act, then we have harmed that person.

It is important to realize just how much gets classified as doing harm under this proposal. In ordinary usage, talk of someone's being "harmed" often suggests pain, physical injury, or death. And this might lead us to expect that "doing harm" to someone will necessarily involve *causing* them pain, injury, or death. But in fact, if we accept the proposal to construe harm in terms of acting in such a way as to leave a person less well off than they would have been otherwise, then doing harm will include far more than this. First of all, we need not actually *produce* anything intrinsically bad. It will also count as doing harm if we *interfere* with some process that would have *eliminated* some of these intrinsic bads. Thus, although giving someone a painful disease is certainly one way to harm them, it is equally true that you harm someone if you prevent her from getting cured. Furthermore, the relevant change in well-being need not actually involve any intrinsic bads at all: it will suffice if your act leaves the person with fewer intrinsic *goods*. If you "rob" someone of some of the pleasures that she would have had, but for your act, then this too is a way of harming her. Finally, it may be worth recalling that in most cases all we can directly alter is the distribution of *instrumental* goods or bads; but this too can constitute doing harm. We can certainly harm someone by directly causing her pain; but we can also harm her, indirectly, by destroying her property or taking her money.

It seems, then, that we can do harm to someone in all these ways: by adding something evil or bad to their life, or by removing something good; by interfering with the addition of something valuable, or by interfering with the removal of something bad. What's more, the value or disvalue of the goods or bads in question can be either intrinsic or instrumental. But even having said all this, it still may not be appreciated just how much is going to be counted as doing harm. If it is true that we have done harm to someone whenever our act has adversely affected their welfare, then apparently it doesn't matter what the particular causal connection is between our act and the change in their welfare; so long as they would have been better off but for our act, we have harmed them. And it also doesn't matter how *much* worse off the person is; so long as they would have been better off—no matter how slightly—we have done them harm and violated the constraint.

By this point many deontologists might begin to worry that the constraint against doing harm is being construed too broadly. Presumably it is uncontroversial that a constraint against doing harm will rule out killing someone, chopping off their leg or finger, or even punching them in the nose. But do we really want to say that the constraint is violated whenever we leave someone slightly sadder than he might otherwise have been? Do we really want to say that the constraint is violated whenever we damage a blade of our neighbor's grass? Or whenever the government imposes a tax, however minimal?

Uncomfortable with these results, the deontologist has various options open. Moderate deontologists can appeal, once again, to the existence of thresholds for the constraint against harming. Perhaps we should admit that the constraint truly is *infringed* in all the cases just mentioned, but insist that in many cases of this sort, at any rate, the constraint is not *vio-*

*lated,* because the relevant threshold has been met. (If the harm is small, little good needs to be accomplished before the act is justified; and if no good at all is going to be promoted, then perhaps it is indeed immoral to harm another, no matter how slightly.)

Deontological absolutists must take a different tack. One possibility, of course, is to embrace the implications of this "broad" reading of the constraint against doing harm. Perhaps we should admit that the constraint is indeed violated, even in cases involving such minimal harms. If this shows just how difficult it can be to live without violating morality, so be it.

Alternatively, the deontologist might try to find a more "narrow" reading of the constraint against doing harm—so that it rules out fewer types of acts. The difficulty, of course, is finding a plausible way of restricting the scope of the constraint. On some views, for example, only the use of *force* is ruled out by the constraint. But this seems too narrow to capture the full range of cases that the deontologist is likely to want to forbid. (If Captain Hook leaves a poisoned cake for the Lost Boys, and they find it, eat it, and die, this presumably violates the constraint against doing harm—even though no force has been used at all.) Other views interpret the constraint in such a way as to rule out only certain *kinds* of harms. (For example, causing death, pain, or physical injury would presumably be forbidden; but causing mere sorrow, inconvenience, or offense might not be.) But here too there is the danger that in at least some cases the deontologist will find the restricted constraint too narrow. And, at any rate, the deontologist may be hard pressed to offer a convincing explanation as to why the various "excluded" types of harm "don't count," as far as the constraint is concerned. Similar difficulties face other approaches. Clearly, none of this shows that a plausible narrow reading of the constraint cannot be provided; but it is, I think, far from obvious what it would look like.

A different question about the scope of the constraint arises if we consider the following case: suppose that George is trapped beneath a fallen tree, and will die unless we free him by cutting off his trapped leg. If we amputate, have we harmed him? And if so, have we violated the constraint?

We get two different answers to the first question, depending on how we interpret the proposal that we harm someone if we act in such a way as to leave him worse off than he would have been otherwise. Is the relevant test whether the person is worse off *overall* than he would have been otherwise? Or is it, rather, whether the person is worse off *in some regard* than he would have been otherwise?

On the first interpretation, we consider only the bottom line: we disregard the specific changes in the various components of well-being and simply ask whether *on balance* the person is worse off than he would have been otherwise. On such a *global* interpretation of doing harm, if we save George's life by amputating his leg, we have not harmed him. It is true, of course, that we have cut off his leg—but presumably it is better for him to lose a leg than to lose his life, which is what would have happened if we hadn't amputated. Overall, then, our act does not leave George worse off than he would have been otherwise; so we haven't harmed him.

On the second interpretation, we're not actually concerned with the bottom line at all—that is, where the person ends up *on balance*. Rather, we look at the various individual elements that contribute to changes in well-being (whether intrinsically or instrumentally), and we ask whether the person is worse off with respect to one or more of *them* than he would have been otherwise. On such a *local* interpretation of doing harm, if we cut off George's leg, we have harmed him. It is true, of course, that doing this saves his life and leaves him better off overall. But it is also true that the lack of a leg will adversely affect his future well-being; and so, in cutting off George's leg, we have harmed him.

Ordinary language, I think, finds itself somewhat torn between the local and the global interpretations of doing harm. On the one hand, it seems plausible to say, "I didn't *harm* George at all—I saved his life!" And this seems to support the global interpretation. On the other hand, it also seems plausible to say, "I wish I could have saved his life without harming him at all, but unfortunately I had to cut off his leg." And this seems to support the local interpretation. I suspect that the local interpretation fits common usage somewhat better than the global, but rather than try to resolve this question, let's consider the implications of each for the constraint against harming as applied to the case of George. If you do cut off George's leg, does this violate the constraint?

On the global approach, of course, it's obvious that the constraint hasn't been violated, since you haven't harmed George at all. Thus the only relevant factor is the good that can be done; and this justifies your amputating George's leg, since this is the only way to save his life. And the claim that amputation is justified is, I presume, a plausible one: intuitively, that is, it does seem permissible to act in this case. On the local approach, however, things are less clear. Cutting off George's leg harms him, and so this appears to violate the constraint against doing harm. But how then can we justify proceeding?

One possible answer is that the constraint should be interpreted in such a way that it only rules out doing "global" harm, that is, harming someone overall. After all, even if the local interpretation of "doing harm" better captures common usage, it still might be the case that the *constraint* against doing harm is concerned solely with harm that leaves the person worse off overall. If we adopted this approach, we could admit that cutting off George's leg harms him, yet still insist that there is no violation of the constraint, given that George is better off overall having his leg amputated. Yet even if this approach gives the right answer in this case, it remains rather puzzling as to why the constraint *should* be restricted in this way. If "local" harms are true and genuine harms, and if there is something especially significant about the doing of harm, then why should the constraint apply *only* in cases of "global" harm?

Moderate deontologists might try a different approach, appealing once again to the existence of thresholds. Perhaps we should admit that cutting off George's leg harms him, and thus falls under the scope of the constraint, but insist that this merely *infringes* the constraint—rather than violating it—since enough is at stake to justify the infringement. After all, doing harm in this case saves a life, so perhaps this is enough to meet the constraint's threshold. If so, then despite the infringement, it will be permissible to proceed.

On reflection, however, the moderate deontologist is unlikely to feel comfortable with the suggestion that the threshold has been met. For consider a different case, where cutting off someone's leg enables us to save someone *else's* life! (Suppose that if we cut off Harold's leg we can use it to make enough serum to save Maude's life.) Presumably the moderate deontologist believes that normally it is *impermissible* to cut off a person's leg—even if this is the only way to save someone else's life. So the moderate deontologist must hold that the constraint's threshold has not been met in such a case: saving a life is not *enough* of a good to override the constraint against cutting off a leg. But if this is so, then we still lack an explanation of what makes it permissible to proceed in the case of George.

There is, of course, another factor that seems highly relevant, one which we've yet to mention. It is George's *own life* that is saved if we cut off his leg, not that of some third party. Intuitively, it seems to matter whether the beneficiary is the very same person who is to be harmed (as with George) or some other person (as with Harold and Maude). But how, exactly, does this make a difference? One possibility is that the threshold is *lower* when the person being harmed is himself the beneficiary. This might allow us to cut off George's leg for his own sake, without permitting us to cut off his leg for the sake of someone else.

A different possibility is this. If George will die unless we amputate his leg, then presumably he will approve of our doing so. That is to say, he will give us his *permission;* he will *consent* to our action. Perhaps, then, it is the presence of George's consent that makes acting permissible. We might think of it like this: the constraint against harming protects the individual against being mistreated in various ways. It provides a moral safeguard against his being harmed *against his will*. But if the individual chooses to forego this protection—if for various reasons he *agrees* to being harmed—then the harm no longer constitutes *mistreatment*. In such cases, the protection that is normally in place disappears, and the constraint loses its force. Thus, given that George consents to our cutting off his leg, our act may well infringe the constraint, but it does not violate it.

A suggestion along these lines seems to accord fairly well with a wide range of ordinary moral judgments. For example, normally it would violate the constraint for you to punch me in the nose. But if we've agreed to a boxing match, then each of us has given the other permission, and your punching me seems permissible. (Note, incidentally, that I've only consented to *your* hitting me; if Martha comes along while we're sparring and hits me, this still violates the constraint. The constraint only loses its force against those who have my *permission*.) Similarly, normally it would violate the constraint for you to cut one of my rare, prize-winning orchids; but not if you ask me first, and I agree.

This view is not, however, without its own difficulties. If the constraint loses its force when the individual consents to our harming him, then what if the person consents for silly or stupid reasons? What if the person is insane, or irrational? What if he gives permission only because of some further belief which is—unbeknownst to him—simply false? Does the constraint lose its force in all these cases too? (Suppose Martha foolishly believes that if we cut off her toe she'll grow another one, and so consents to our taking it; is the constraint really without force in this case?)

Some of those sympathetic to the thesis that consent eliminates the force of the constraint are prepared to embrace this claim even when the person agrees for poor reasons, mistaken reasons, or no reasons at all. Others, however, attempt to narrow the scope of the thesis. Perhaps consent has its normal effect only when the person is rational, and only if the decision is informed by full and accurate knowledge of the facts. (In many institutional contexts there is a corresponding requirement that one get "informed consent.") Perhaps consent only has its normal effect if it is backed by good and sufficient reasons.

There is a further problem with the suggestion that it is the presence of George's consent that explains why it is permissible to amputate his leg. Suppose that George is trapped by the tree, as before, and that he will die unless we cut off his leg. But imagine now that George is unconscious and cannot be asked for his consent. Imagine, as well, that if we try to bring him to consciousness first, so as to obtain his consent, too much precious time will be lost, and it will be too late to save him. Can't we amputate his leg anyway—since this is the only way to save George's life—even though we're unable to get his permission first? But if this is permissible, then how is it to be justified?

Those committed to the belief that it is consent that is the key to explaining why the constraint lacks its normal force, may now have to *expand* their view. Since there is no *actual* consent in this case, they might appeal instead to a notion of *hypothetical consent*. Presumably George *would* agree to the amputation, if only he knew the facts and were able to decide for himself. Perhaps such hypothetical consent suffices to eliminate the force of the constraint. (It may be worth noting, if only in passing, how an appeal to mutual hypothetical consent might help explain why it is permissible for us to engage in the normal, everyday activities that subject others to low levels of risk: presumably it would be rational for us to agree to being subjected to such risks by others, in exchange for their permission to engage in such minimally risky actions ourselves.)

By this point, however, those critical of the relevance of consent might begin to wonder whether *consent* is still doing any real work. After all, we've already seen that the presence of consent may not be sufficient; it may need to be backed by good and sufficient reasons. And now we've seen that consent may not actually be necessary either. For despite its name, hypothetical consent is not really a form of consent at all: it simply points to the fact that it *would* be rational to consent, because there are good reasons for agreeing. But if consent only works in the presence of good reasons, and if good reasons are sufficient, even in the absence of consent—why not just drop the reference to consent altogether? Why not just say that the force of the constraint is eliminated by the various facts themselves—whatever they are—that would make it rational to agree? The consent itself would just drop out of the picture.

Of course, if we do take this more critical line, then we still need an account of exactly what sorts of facts suffice to eliminate the force of the constraint, and why. If consent is not the relevant factor, just what is? Furthermore, there may be cases where it is less easy to dismiss the relevance of consent: suppose that George is conscious but *refuses* to consent to our amputating his leg, arguing that he would rather be dead than a cripple. Many people will be less confident that we can still proceed in this case, even though everything is the same—everything, that is, *except* for the fact that George is withholding his permission. This seems to support the view that it is indeed the presence or absence of *consent* that is relevant to whether or not the constraint retains its normal force. Indeed, even those who think that it is still permissible to proceed, despite George's protests, will likely feel that the constraint has been *overridden* in this case, and not that its force has simply been eliminated; if the constraint is to literally lose its force, consent itself still seems necessary. (This last case may also cause problems for the global interpretation of doing harm: if—as the global interpretation insists—our cutting off George's leg to save his life doesn't actually harm him at all, why would it even be relevant whether or not he opposes our action?)

Let me turn now to one final question about the scope of the constraint against doing harm. Suppose that Agnes immorally attacks Victor, without provocation or other justification. Indeed, Agnes is about to kill Victor. Luckily, however, Victor can protect himself and avoid being harmed—but only if he harms, and indeed kills, Agnes first. Is it permissible for Victor to do this? Or would it violate the constraint against doing harm?

Most people think the answer is fairly obvious: it is morally permissible to kill in self-defense. This point is worth stressing. According to this common view, killing in self-defense is morally *justified*. This position therefore needs to be distinguished from another, according to which killing someone in self-defense may be something we should normally *excuse,* but it is, for all that, *wrong.* After all, it might be argued, a willingness to kill in self-defense is a natural—perhaps even instinctive—human reaction; accordingly, there might not be much point in *blaming* someone who killed another to defend himself. But none of this would show that such acts are in fact morally justified. I take it, however, that the common view is that killing in self-defense is not merely understandable, and perhaps excusable; rather, it is *permissible.* Provided that you have harmed someone only in self-defense, you have not acted immorally at all. (Actually, according to the common view, you need not literally be engaged in an act of *self*-defense; you're also permitted to defend *others.* For simplicity, however, I'll stick to the case of self-defense.)

Distinguishing, in this way, between these two views draws upon a distinction between excuses and justifications. Circumstances that *justify* are factors that alter the moral status of the act, so that—given all the relevant facts—the act in question is morally permissible. In contrast, circumstances that merely *excuse* don't affect the moral permissibility of the act; they merely alter our willingness to blame the agent should the forbidden act be performed anyway. The common view, I take it, is that self-defense provides a moral justification and not merely an excuse; indeed, since self-defense is justified, there is nothing to be excused.

Nonetheless, although belief in the permissibility of self-defense is widespread, it is not universal. *Pacifists* hold that it is morally forbidden to harm another, even if this is the only way to defend oneself from unjustified attack. After all, they argue, to harm someone else—even a deliberate aggressor—violates the *constraint* against doing harm. It is true, of course, that Agnes is herself bent on violating the constraint; she is about to harm Victor. But the fact that *Agnes* is trying to violate the constraint doesn't make it any less true that *Victor* will be violating the constraint if *he* harms *her* instead. As the old saying goes: two wrongs don't make a right.

Obviously enough, those who reject pacifism will deny that harming in self-defense violates the constraint. They'll claim, instead, that it merely infringes it. But how is this view to be defended?

An appeal to thresholds does not seem especially promising here, since any given act of self-defense may not do all that much more good than harm. If Victor kills Agnes, for example, one life is lost and one life is saved—a result no better than if he had simply let *her* kill *him* instead. So even a relatively low threshold might not be met. Things are improved somewhat, but not much, if we accept the view (considered in 2.5) that evil aggressors may deserve to suffer. On such a retributivist view, the harm to Agnes may actually count as a *good* result, rather than a bad, and so we will be that much closer to meeting the threshold. But as long as the threshold isn't very low, this isn't likely to take us far enough. We are somewhat further along—perhaps even considerably so—if we take into account the *deterrent effect* that an act of self-defense might have on other would-be aggressors (not to mention Agnes), who may be more hesitant about attacking others if they reasonably fear that they themselves might be harmed in the process. Perhaps all of this together would help us meet a low threshold, or even a moderate one. But, as we have seen, most people accept a rather *high* threshold for the constraint against doing harm; and it seems rather unlikely that *enough* good will be done by normal acts of self-defense to meet such a threshold.

More promising, and probably more intuitively compelling, is the suggestion that the constraint against doing harm simply doesn't *apply* to harming aggressors. On this view, the constraint doesn't actually oppose doing harm per se; it only opposes harming the *innocent*. Since Agnes is a deliberate aggressor, the use of harm against her does not fall within the scope of the constraint. Indeed, this view is so widely held that when I introduced the constraint (in 3.1 and 3.2) I often explicitly stipulated that the person being harmed was innocent; I did this because I wanted to make sure that the constraint would seem intuitively relevant.

But why *should* the constraint apply only to the innocent? The existence of pacifists, after all, shows us that it is far from self-evident that harming the guilty is morally permissible. Exactly why is it, then, that Agnes's *guilt* takes her beyond the moral protection normally afforded by the constraint?

Perhaps this is a question that can only be settled by appeal to one or another theory about the *foundations* of normative ethics (something we won't be turning to until 6.1). Maybe the best we can do at this stage is to note that, intuitively at least, most people do find it plausible to suggest that guilt versus innocence is itself a factor with intrinsic normative significance: there are indeed weighty moral reasons that oppose doing harm to someone, but these reasons only exist if the person is innocent; if someone is a deliberate aggressor, these reasons don't apply, or have no force.

Unfortunately, even this answer is inadequate, for it points us toward an overly simplistic account of self-defense. In reality, our beliefs about self-defense are surprisingly complex. For example, even if Agnes is a deliberate aggressor, most people don't believe that the protection normally afforded by the constraint simply disappears altogether. Roughly speaking, Victor must use the *minimal* amount of force necessary to defend himself against the attack. (If Victor knows he can save himself by shooting Agnes in the leg, rather than killing her, that's all he's permitted to do; and if merely brandishing his rifle would suffice to stop her, he can't simply go ahead and shoot her anyway.) Similarly, the harm imposed in self-defense must be *proportional* to the harm that the aggressor is trying to do. (A defender may not be restricted to imposing the *same* size harm as would be imposed by the aggressor, but nonetheless there is a limit: if all that Agnes is trying to do is to punch him in the nose, Victor isn't permitted to *kill* her—not even if there is no other way to stop her.) Yet if the constraint against doing harm simply didn't *apply* in cases where the person being harmed is a deliberate aggressor, then neither of these requirements would make any sense. Apparently, then, the constraint against doing harm must still be in force—although somehow altered or modified in various ways—even if the person being harmed isn't *innocent*.

What's more, the permissibility of self-defense also seems to extend to some cases where the person being harmed isn't a deliberate aggressor at all! Imagine that Malcolm is pointing a loaded gun directly at you and is about to shoot it—mistakenly believing that it is only a harmless toy. Malcolm is clearly not a deliberate aggressor. Yet many people believe it would still be permissible to harm him, were this the only way to prevent him from shooting the gun. Apparently, then, an appeal to self-defense can also justify harming *innocent threats,* and not only harming the guilty.

Of course, an innocent threat is still a *threat*—however unwittingly—so it is possible that accommodating these intuitions will require only a minor modification of the account of self-defense. Note, however, that the innocence or guilt of the threat seems to make a difference to how *much* harm we are permitted to impose in the course of defending ourselves; so, if anything, the account must grow more complicated still.

And there are still other cases where it seems permissible to harm someone who is not, in point of fact, a threat at all. If the only way to stop Abigail from running you and your family over with her tank is to blow the tank up, this still seems permissible to many people—even if this will also kill the baby that Abigail has wickedly strapped to the front of her tank. Thus *innocent shields* of threats can apparently be harmed as well, in the course of defending oneself.

Obviously enough, by this point we have gone far beyond the simplistic suggestion that self-defense can be accommodated by restricting the scope of the constraint so that it only rules out harming the innocent. An adequate account of self-defense, it seems, will be a rather complicated affair (assuming one can be provided at all). No simple appeal to guilt versus innocence is likely to capture the various subfactors that play a role—intuitively, if nothing else—in determining when one can infringe the constraint against doing harm for the sake of defending oneself. (It should also be noted that this increasingly complex account would grow even more complicated, were we to try to extend it to cover the permissibility of *punishment.* For in punishment, unlike normal cases of self-defense, we harm the guilty party only *after* the fact, that is, when it is too late to prevent the violation from occurring in the first place.)

One final question. If you do believe in the permissibility of self-defense, does this show that you are not an absolutist? This is presumably what pacifists would say, insisting—plausibly—that one can hardly be an absolutist about the constraint against doing harm if one is prepared to make an *exception* to that rule in cases of self-defense. Yet the permissibility of self-defense has been accepted by many self-styled absolutists. They would presumably argue that they do not literally accept a constraint against doing harm per se, but rather a more complex constraint, which can be roughly (and only roughly) summarized as being a constraint against doing harm to the innocent; and with regard to *this* constraint, they might insist, they *are* absolutists: no exceptions can be made to it (for example, it can't be infringed simply because of the good that might thereby be accomplished). This too seems a plausible response. Yet what then prevents the moderate deontologist, who accepts thresholds, from insisting that she too is an absolutist—an absolutist with regard to the even *more* complex constraint which can be summarized (again, only roughly) as being a constraint against doing harm to the innocent unless enough is at stake?

The moral, I suspect, is this: talk of "absolutism" reveals little, if anything, about a person's normative theory. There is simply no useful substitute for detailed knowledge concerning which normative factors a person accepts, and how those factors are thought to interact.

## 3.4  Doing and Allowing

Given the questions about scope raised in the previous section, it may be misleading in certain contexts to talk as though the deontologist accepts a simple constraint against "doing harm." In reality, as we have seen, the situation may be rather more complex than this: roughly speaking, the constraint may only oppose certain *ways* of harming someone; and (again, roughly) if the person isn't innocent, or if she consents to being harmed, the constraint may not oppose doing harm at all. Nonetheless, for many purposes we can put these qualifications aside. After all, in many "paradigm cases" of doing harm (for example, killing an innocent person against their will, where the person is neither a threat, nor a shield of a threat, and so on), these qualifications simply don't come into play. Accordingly—and if only for the sake of simplicity—it doesn't seem seriously misleading if we continue to talk of the deontologist's accepting a constraint against "doing harm." We can, of course, still bring in the various qualifications as needed.

Now as we noted at the start of this chapter (in 3.1), such a constraint cannot be accepted by the consequentialist. It is worth recalling precisely why this is so: it is due to the fact that—unlike the deontologist—the consequentialist rejects the intrinsic normative significance of *harm doing*. Of course, as we also saw, the mere acceptance of this factor does not, by itself, suffice to ground a *constraint;* that will result only if one goes on to invest this factor with sufficient weight. But the fact of the matter is that the consequentialist denies that harm doing per se has any intrinsic moral significance at all.

But how can this be? Surely the consequentialist recognizes that doing harm to someone can make the results worse overall. How then can the

consequentialist deny that this has moral significance? The consequentialist's answer, of course, is that doing harm does have moral significance, but
it has no *intrinsic* moral significance, in and of itself. That is to say, there is
nothing especially significant about your *doing* harm, as opposed to other
ways that you might fail to prevent or eliminate harm.

As far as the consequentialist is concerned, all that matters is that you act
in such a way that the overall results be as good as they can be. If your *doing* harm to someone is the only way to prevent or eliminate an even
greater amount of harm, then so be it: what is important is only that overall harm be minimized so far as this is possible; no particular significance
attaches to the question of whether you yourself have *produced* any of
those harms. Since all that matters is the results—and not how they come
about—if you have allowed a given harm (one that you could have prevented or eliminated) this is just as significant as if the harm were one you
had produced yourself. In short, for the consequentialist, harm doing has
no intrinsic normative significance, because there is no intrinsic moral significance to the distinction between *doing* and *allowing*.

For the deontologist, in contrast, it matters tremendously how a given
harm has been brought about—whether it is a harm that you yourself have
caused, or merely one that you have failed to prevent. According to the deontologist, there is something especially morally significant about *doing*
harm to a person, a significance which is lacking if you have not actually
brought about the harm but instead have merely *allowed* it to happen.
Something like this must be true if there is to be a constraint against doing
harm, since it is, after all, only the *doing* of harm which is prohibited by the
constraint; allowing harm is not similarly forbidden. Thus the deontologist
seems committed to the view that the distinction between doing and allowing has intrinsic normative significance.

This view should not be misunderstood. The suggestion is not being
made that the deontologist thinks it morally unimportant if, in a given case,
you have allowed harm. If there is some harm that you could have prevented, and you fail to do it, then this weighs heavily against the moral permissibility of your act—even though you have merely allowed the harm
and haven't brought it about yourself. All other things being equal, your
act is still forbidden.

Suppose, for example, that you are walking along the pier and see a man
drowning. You have a life preserver and can easily throw it to him, saving
his life. But you do nothing, and the man drowns. The deontologist will
certainly think your act (here, your "inaction") was morally impermissible.
Should you try to justify your inaction by noting that you did not literally
kill the drowning man, but merely allowed him to die, this will hardly get
you off the hook! It is, of course, quite true that you did not *kill* the man;
you merely allowed him to die. (It is not as though you pushed him into the
water or held his head under the waves.) And allowing harm does not bring

into play the *particularly* weighty reasons that arise in cases of doing harm. But none of this shows your action to be justified. On the contrary, there was obviously a great deal of good that could have been done, and no other factors come into play to offset this; thus you were morally *required* to throw the life preserver. Allowing harm may be *less* important than doing harm, but that doesn't show that it is *unimportant*.

The deontologist's position, then, is this: allowing harm is certainly morally important; it's just that doing harm is even more important.

One way to see the difference in moral significance is to compare similar cases that differ with regard to whether the agent has done harm or merely allowed it. Consider again the example of the drowning man: if you fail to throw the life preserver and let the man drown, you have ("merely") allowed harm. As I have just explained, the deontologist considers your action here impermissible; you have done something immoral. But your act would be even *worse,* morally speaking, if you had actually *killed* the person—if you had, for example, dragged him off the beach, tied him down with weights, and thrown him into the water. The first case is bad enough, but the second is even worse. And the difference—says the deontologist—is explained in terms of the moral significance of doing harm as opposed to merely allowing it. Similarly, it may well be morally objectionable if you fail to send money for famine relief, knowing full well that someone will die for the lack of food, whose life you could have saved; but however objectionable this may be, it would be even worse to *kill* someone by sending them poisoned "care" packages. It is one thing to allow someone to die; it is quite another to kill them yourself.

Now in the cases just considered, it is possible to avoid both doing harm and allowing harm: on the one hand, you can easily refrain from killing anyone (so that you will not have done any harm), and on the other hand, you can also take the steps—albeit somewhat less easily—to save the lives of the people in need (so that you will not have allowed any harm either). Consider, however, the possibility of a situation in which you cannot successfully avoid both: you must either do harm or allow it. If there could be such a situation, then—given the greater weight that applies to doing harm as opposed to merely allowing it—we would expect that in such a case it would be more important not to *do* harm to anyone. Indeed, if doing harm is sufficiently more weighty than allowing harm, then we would expect that it would be wrong to do harm to someone, even if this were the only way to avoid allowing a *much greater* amount of harm. That is to say, it would be forbidden to do harm, even if this would have better results overall. In short, there would be a *constraint* against doing harm.

We have, of course, already considered cases of just this sort, cases where one must choose between doing harm and allowing it. Not surprisingly, I used an example of exactly this kind—the organ transplant case—when I wanted to introduce and motivate the constraint against doing harm. Recall how the story goes (see 3.1): five patients will die for lack of the relevant organs, unless you chop up an otherwise healthy sixth individual, Chuck, and use his organs to save the others. If killing Chuck is to be forbidden and if, as seems plausible, this is to be explained in terms of a constraint against doing harm, then the distinction between doing harm and allowing it must be of intrinsic moral significance. For if you do not kill Chuck, five people will die, people whom you *could* have saved. Thus, it seems, you *allow* the deaths of the five. And, as we have seen, allowing preventable deaths is not something that the deontologist considers morally unimportant; it is, on the contrary, a morally weighty matter. If, despite all this, you are forbidden to chop up Chuck, then apparently it must be because killing Chuck would be *doing* harm to him, and doing harm is a considerably weightier matter than merely allowing it. Indeed, it is more important not to *do* harm to one than it is to *save* five.

Thus we can see how the constraint against doing harm presupposes the intrinsic moral relevance of the distinction between doing and allowing. In the light of this, it is not surprising that the distinction between doing and allowing has been subjected to considerable scrutiny—both by those who endorse the intrinsic relevance of the distinction, and by those who deny it. (Actually, much of the debate takes place in terms of the distinction between "killing" and "letting die"; and since the relevant arguments are similar, I'll continue to use both sets of locutions. For the record, however, the distinction between doing and allowing appears to be the more fundamental one.)

In thinking about this issue, we need to distinguish between two questions. First, how exactly shall we characterize the distinction between doing and allowing? Second, is this distinction, so characterized, indeed of genuine moral relevance? Obviously, our answers to these two questions will be connected. Whether we consider a given distinction relevant will always depend, in part, on what exactly we take the distinction to come to. But even someone who thinks it obvious that the distinction matters may be uncertain as to how best to characterize it. This is true, even for defenders of the distinction between doing and allowing.

Consider, for example, a patient dying of a painful and incurable disease, who is being kept alive on an artificial respirator. If, at the patient's request, we turn off the life-support equipment, is this a case of *killing,* or is it rather—as is often said—a case of *letting die* ("allowing nature to take its course")? The simple fact of the matter, I believe, is that people disagree. Some think the former, some the latter, and many are unsure. It seems, then, that if we are to settle cases like this, the deontologist will have to move beyond a brute appeal to our intuitive understanding of the distinction between doing and allowing (or between killing and letting die). We'll need an explicit analysis of the distinction, in the light of which such controversial cases can be classified.

.In principle, it should be noted, such investigations might be of interest even to those who deny the moral relevance of the distinction between doing and allowing. At the very least, one might simply be intellectually curious about the best way to classify cases like that of turning off the artificial respirator, even if ultimately one thought the matter of no moral significance. (Denying that a distinction *matters*, morally speaking, is not the same thing as denying that the distinction is *real;* differences in skin color, for example, are perfectly real, even if morally unimportant.) More ambitiously, a critic might hope that, ultimately, adequate analyses of the distinction will make it easier to recognize the *irrelevance* of the distinction: once the "inner nature" of the distinction between doing and allowing is understood, it may be intuitively obvious that such a distinction could not possess any intrinsic moral significance.

Nonetheless, finding an adequate analysis of the distinction may not be a pressing task for those who deny its relevance. The crucial point (for such critics) is to argue that, despite the initial plausibility of thinking the distinction relevant, on reflection we cannot accept this. And although one way to argue for this conclusion involves critical analysis of the nature of the distinction itself, this may not be the only way.

Recall the deontologist's suggestion that the significance of the distinction between doing and allowing can be shown by comparing similar cases that differ only insofar as one involves doing harm and the other involves allowing harm. It was suggested, for example, that allowing a man to drown, however morally objectionable, was less objectionable than deliberately drowning the man yourself. This seemed to show that the distinction between doing and allowing has intrinsic moral significance: how else can we explain our different reactions to the two cases? But critics of the do/allow distinction might well object that this example provides an inadequate test: too many things differ in the two cases, and not only whether one has done harm or merely allowed it. For example, your motive in the second case is likely to be much worse than your motive in the first (outright hostility to the person as opposed to mere indifference). Perhaps, then, our reaction is due to the difference in motives and *not* the difference between doing and allowing per se. For a truly adequate test we must really keep everything else the *same*. And when we do—the critics argue—we no longer find ourselves reacting differently to cases of doing harm and cases of allowing harm.

Suppose, for example, that if your six-year-old cousin dies, you will inherit the family fortune. The two of you are alone in the house, and he is taking a bath. You creep upstairs to the bathroom and hold his head under the water, killing him. Obviously, you have done something morally horrendous. Now compare this to a second case, exactly like the first, except that when you enter the bathroom you discover, to your joy, that your cousin has slipped in the tub and is now drowning. You could easily pull him out, saving his life, but instead you stand there, watching him drown. You are, indeed, ready to push him back under the water should he manage to get out, but "luckily" you never need to do this. Obviously enough, you have, once again, done something morally horrendous. Indeed, your action (or inaction) in the second case seems quite as objectionable as your action in the first case.

Yet in the first case you have *done* harm to your cousin—you have killed him—while in the second case you have merely *allowed* the harm to happen; you have only *let* him die. And so, if doing harm were genuinely worse than allowing harm—in and of itself—your action in the first case would have to be worse than your action in the second case. Intuitively, however, that's not our reaction to the two cases at all. What you do in the one case seems just as bad as what you do in the other, despite the fact that one case involves doing harm and the other "merely" allowing it. Thus we can see that, in and of itself, the distinction between doing harm and allowing harm actually has no moral significance. (If we are sometimes tempted to think otherwise, this is because in many normal cases other factors that *do* matter come into play as well, and we are accidentally misled by our reactions to these other factors.)

Many find this a persuasive argument. But advocates of the distinction are not without possible replies. One possible response is this: perhaps the difference between doing and allowing *does* make a difference, even in cases like that of the drowning cousin. If we fail to notice this, it may be because the evil motive in the story is so overwhelming that our intuition fails us, and we are unable to detect the fact that although both acts are morally horrendous, drowning your cousin is indeed even *worse* than deliberately letting him drown. (It may be easier to notice the difference if we ask ourselves what sorts of *punishments* would be appropriate in the two cases: if, as seems intuitively plausible, the first case deserves greater punishment than the second, what can explain this except the fact that one case involves doing harm, while the other does not?)

A second possible response concedes that the do/allow distinction may make no difference in *this* pair of cases, but insists that it might still make a difference in *other* cases. Perhaps the distinction between doing and allowing only makes a difference in the right *context*—a context that is somehow missing in the case of the drowning cousin, but which is normally present in more typical cases. Now it does seem true that if our theory of the normative factors is sufficiently complex, it will allow for the possibility that a given factor will make one kind of difference in one context while making quite a different difference in another context (including, perhaps, making no difference at all). Nonetheless, it must be admitted that until this more complicated theory is proposed, this second answer is nothing more than a promissory note.

Perhaps one or another of these replies can be spelled out in a convincing manner. If so, then the distinction between doing and allowing may still have intrinsic moral significance. But if no such reply can be made plausible—or if other attacks on the relevance of the distinction are successful—then it is not just the significance of the distinction between doing and allowing that will be called into question. The very possibility of accepting a constraint against doing harm will be threatened as well.

## 3.5  Intending Harm

Attacks on the relevance of the distinction between doing and allowing can come from different sources. Not surprisingly, they are often offered by consequentialists who—as we've seen—think it morally unimportant how a given harm comes about, since all that matters is reducing the overall amount of harm so far as this is possible. What may well be surprising, however, is that criticism of the do/allow distinction can also be offered by *deontologists,* including deontologists interested in capturing our ordinary moral intuitions.

How can this be? Haven't we seen throughout this chapter that commonsense morality endorses a constraint against doing harm? Yet such a constraint presupposes the relevance of the do/allow distinction. How, then, can a deontologist sympathetic to ordinary morality reject the distinction as lacking in moral significance?

The fact of the matter, however, is that it might well not be a constraint against *doing* harm that best fits our ordinary moral intuitions (not even if the scope of that constraint is restricted, as discussed in 3.3). The suggestion that such a constraint best captures the commonsense moral outlook is only a hypothesis, or a conjecture. It is, obviously enough, a pretty plausible conjecture; it clearly fits a large number of common intuitions fairly comfortably. But it is, for all that, only a conjecture. It is conceivable that there is some other constraint—similar to, but not quite identical with, the constraint against doing harm—which fits common intuitions even better.

Consider this case. Imagine that there is a runaway trolley car, careening down the track. The brakes have failed, and there is no way to stop the train. If it continues on its present path, it will hit—and kill—five innocent schoolchildren, who cannot be gotten off the track in time. Luckily, there is a switch that you can throw (you are standing next to the track), which will divert the trolley onto a side track well before it hits the five children. Unfortunately, however, this side track is not empty either: there is a sixth child on it, who will inevitably be hit and killed by the train if you throw the switch. What should you do?

Many people—perhaps even most people—who think about this case conclude that it is morally permissible to throw the switch, saving the five children. But if there is indeed a constraint against *doing* harm, it is difficult to see how this can be so. Surely, whatever the precise analysis of the do/allow distinction, it is undeniable that if you throw the switch you have done harm to the sixth child: aiming a runaway trolley at someone is certainly one way to harm them! In contrast, if you refrain from throwing the switch you have not *harmed* the five children at all, even though they die: you merely *allow* them to be killed by the train. So if doing harm is morally more significant than allowing harm—if there is a *constraint* against doing harm—then it seems that we will have to say that it is forbidden to throw the switch.

Some deontologists are quite prepared to accept this conclusion. They need not be bothered by the trolley problem at all. But other deontologists want to permit throwing the switch—and it is hard to see how this can possibly be reconciled with a constraint against doing harm.

Note that an appeal to thresholds isn't likely to be of much use here. Even if there is a threshold for the constraint, if it is set so low that it is permissible to kill the one child to save the other five, then this will have the unpalatable result that it is also permissible to kill *Chuck*, using his organs to save the five patients. Yet virtually no one believes that *that* is permissible! But if the threshold is high enough to rule out killing Chuck, it will also be high enough to rule out turning the trolley away from the five.

The challenge, then, is this: is there some way to identify a morally relevant difference between the trolley case and the organ transplant case—a difference that will allow the deontologist to say that throwing the switch is permissible, although chopping up Chuck is not? Some deontologists retain the hope that a factor can be identified that will allow us to restrict the scope of the constraint against doing harm once again. Properly qualified— the hope goes—the constraint will still forbid normal cases of doing harm, but it will not apply in cases like the trolley problem.

Other deontologists draw a more radical conclusion: if a constraint against doing harm forbids throwing the switch—and it certainly seems to—then the constraint against doing harm should be *rejected;* it fails to provide an adequate fit with our ordinary moral intuitions. Of course, deontologists who draw this more radical conclusion still need to propose an alternative constraint to govern cases involving harm. After all, if they are to avoid consequentialism, it will hardly do to simply jettison the constraint against doing harm without offering a replacement: a constraint of some sort is still needed to block the permissibility of chopping up Chuck. But what should this new constraint look like?

Various proposals have been made. Let me mention only one. Perhaps instead of a constraint against *doing* harm, the deontologist should accept a constraint against *intending* harm. Such a constraint is based not on the distinction between doing harm and allowing it, but rather on the distinction between intending harm (as a means or as an end) and foreseeing harm (as a mere side effect).

This new distinction is far less familiar than the one it is intended to replace. Furthermore, the terminology, although fairly standard in the contemporary philosophical literature, is potentially quite misleading. The problem is that in ordinary language we are generally prepared to say that someone "intended" a given harm whenever she realized that her act would result in the harm and she deliberately performed the act anyway. It must be emphasized that this common use is *not* the one relevant to talk of a constraint against "intending harm." On the contrary, many such cases will be classified as merely *foreseeing* the harm as an inevitable side effect of one's act. As far as the constraint against intending harm is concerned, the agent intends the harm (in the relevant, technical sense of this term) only in certain quite specific circumstances: if the occurrence of the harm is itself among the agent's ultimate goals, then she intends it as an *end*; and if—as is more common—the harm itself helps the agent to achieve one of her ultimate goals, and this is the reason the agent permits the harm, then she intends it as a *means*. In all other cases, the harm is a mere *side effect* of the agent's act. This is true even if the agent foresees the harm: unless the harm itself is one of her goals, or is a means to achieving one of her goals, and unless this is the *reason* why the agent countenances the harm, the harm is a mere foreseen side effect of her act.

A few examples should make these notions somewhat easier to use. If I am a sadist, and that is why I cause you pain or allow your suffering to continue, then I intend harm to you as an end. Usually, however, it is fairly rare to intend harm to another as an end. Far more common is to intend harm to another as a means. For example, if I murder my rich aunt as a way of inheriting her money, it's not likely that the harm to my aunt is among my *goals;* I might well wish there were some way to get the money without hurting her. Nonetheless, I have harmed her as a *means:* the death of my aunt helps me achieve my goal of becoming wealthy, and this is the reason why I kill her. So I still intend the harm (as a means). In most cases, on the other hand, even if I knowingly bring about a harm, I do not intend it at all, in the relevant sense. For example, if you're behind me in line, and I buy the last ticket to the concert, I may know full well that this will cause you distress and disappointment. But I don't intend the harm, neither as an end nor as a means; your suffering is a mere *side effect* of my action. (It's not an end, since I don't wish you ill; and it's not a means, either, since your being inconvenienced and disappointed doesn't do anything to help me achieve my goal of getting into the concert.)

The suggestion being made, then, is that we go wrong in thinking that there is something morally significant about the distinction between doing and allowing. On the contrary, the morally relevant distinction is that between harm that is intended—whether as an end or as a means—and harm that is merely foreseen as an unintended side effect. If this proposal is correct, then what is especially objectionable from the moral point of view is not doing harm per se, but rather intending harm. In short, instead of a constraint against doing harm, we should have a constraint against *intend-*

*ing* harm. (Traditionally, this position is sometimes known as the *doctrine of double effect*: roughly, it may be permissible to perform an act with both a good effect and a bad effect, provided that the bad effect is a mere side effect; if it is either your goal or a means to your goal, the act is forbidden. This is equivalent to a constraint against intending harm.)

Of course, in many cases a constraint against intending harm yields the same verdict as a constraint against doing harm. Consider, for example, the organ transplant case: *both* constraints rule out killing Chuck. We already know that this is true of the constraint against doing harm, but it is easy to see that it is true of the constraint against intending harm as well. For if I chop up Chuck, my reason for doing this is obviously that it is a means of achieving my goal of saving the five patients; thus, I harm Chuck as a means, in violation of the constraint against intending harm. On the other hand, if I save money for my college education rather than giving it to charity, *neither* constraint rules this out: the harm that I fail to prevent is a mere side effect of my act (since it doesn't help me achieve my goal of getting an education), and it is also harm that I merely allow. So neither constraint forbids my action. (The parallel continues even further: if I fail to throw a drowning man a life preserver, my act is still immoral, even though his death is a mere side effect of my inaction. Harm that is "merely" foreseen is still important, even if it is *less* important than harm that is intended.)

There is, then, considerable overlap between the two constraints. This shouldn't surprise us, since both attempt to capture commonsense views governing harm. Nonetheless, the two constraints are not identical; there are cases where their verdicts diverge. For example, it is possible to intend harm, even though the harm is merely *allowed*. In such cases, of course, one violates the constraint against intending harm, but not the constraint against doing harm.

To see this, consider the following variation on the organ transplant case. Suppose that Chuck is in the grips of a seizure that will soon kill him. You have the medication that would end the seizure, and normally, of course, you would readily give it to him. But it occurs to you that if you *refrain* from helping him he will die, and then his organs can be used to save the five other patients.

Many people feel it would be immoral to refuse to help Chuck, even though this would have a better result overall. And a constraint against intending harm easily supports this view. For as far as such a constraint is concerned, it is simply irrelevant that, in this version of the case, the harm to Chuck is not something that you yourself bring about but merely something that you allow. What is important, rather, is that if you allow Chuck to die, you do this as a means of achieving your goal of saving the five. So you still intend harm as a means, in violation of the constraint. In contrast, a constraint against doing harm is of no use in defending the judgment that it is immoral to let Chuck die. Since withholding the medicine is merely a case of allowing harm, the constraint against *doing* harm is simply irrelevant. (Of course, advocates of the constraint against doing harm might still hope to point to some *other* factor to explain why letting Chuck die is immoral—despite the fact that this has better results overall. Nothing at all rules this out. Here the point is simply that the two constraints *diverge:* one forbids, where the other remains, at best, neutral.)

A second area where the two constraints yield different verdicts is this: cases where the agent does harm, but it is a mere side effect. In such cases, obviously enough, the constraint against doing harm may well forbid the act, but the constraint against intending harm will not. For example, a pilot during the war may bomb a munitions factory, knowing full well that the explosion will inevitably kill a certain number of innocent civilians who live nearby. This is clearly a case of doing harm. (Is it, accordingly, forbidden by the constraint against doing harm? Some think so. But others claim, instead, that this is a case of justified infringement. Perhaps the relevant threshold has been met, or the civilians should be classified as innocent shields of threats. But either way, it is clear that killing the civilians constitutes doing harm.) However, even though dropping the bomb does harm the civilians, this harm is a mere side effect of the pilot's act. Assuming the pilot bears no ill will toward the civilians, he does not intend their deaths as an end; and he doesn't intend them as a means either, since what helps the pilot achieve his goal of winning the war is the destruction of the munitions factory—not the deaths of the civilians. (Matters would be quite different if the pilot deliberately bombed, say, an orphanage, hoping thereby to destroy the country's will to fight on. Here the harm would indeed be intended as a means.)

The situation, then, is this. The constraint against intending harm agrees, to a considerable extent, with the judgments generated by a constraint against doing harm. But the two constraints are not identical; in a variety of cases the judgments supported by the two constraints diverge. Thus the constraint against intending harm is a genuine *alternative* to the constraint against doing harm. And it is, accordingly, an important question which better fits our various moral intuitions. On reflection, the deontologist may find that she does not actually want to endorse a constraint against doing harm at all; she may prefer to embrace a constraint against intending harm.

The trolley car case may provide some support for this position. As we have already observed, it is difficult to see how to reconcile a constraint against doing harm with the intuition that it is permissible to throw the switch, saving the five. For throwing the switch kills the one, and this certainly seems to violate a constraint against doing harm. In contrast, a constraint against *intending* harm does not oppose throwing the switch at all, for the death of the one, although horrible, is unintended. (What saves the five is throwing the switch and diverting the train, not the harm to the one; *that* contributes nothing at all toward saving the five.) Thus, although it is tragic, the death of the one is "merely" an unintended side effect of saving the five.

Apparently, then, if the deontologist wants to permit throwing the switch, she may have reason to embrace a constraint against intending harm.

Of course, any such decision will need to be based on examination of a large number of cases, not just the trolley car case. We have already considered a few that seem relevant; but there are many, many others. (Here is one more: suppose that if you operate to save the lives of five patients, this will inevitably release some poisonous gas that will kill a sixth person who cannot be moved out of harm's way. Many think it would be impermissible to operate under these conditions, and the constraint against doing harm has a ready account of why this is so. But a constraint against intending harm offers nothing to support such a judgment, since the death of the one would be a mere unintended side effect.)

Which constraint would seem most attractive if we systematically compared their implications? The answer is not at all obvious. Each constraint has its advocates and its critics. Indeed, some deontologists think that an adequate normative theory will need to incorporate both constraints, although it is far from clear how this is to be done. (Many others simply fail to distinguish between the two.) Furthermore, although the two constraints we've discussed are the most common proposals made for governing cases involving harm, they do not exhaust the field. Other—even more exotic—constraints have been proposed for this area as well.

We have, then, yet another controversy that cannot be settled here. Despite the apparent naturalness of the suggestion that commonsense morality incorporates a constraint against *doing* harm, it may be that an adequate normative theory would actually incorporate a constraint with somewhat different content. Nonetheless, for the sake of simplicity, in what follows I shall write as though it is indeed settled that it is a constraint against *doing* harm that is to be accepted. The constraint against doing harm is by far the most familiar of the relevant alternatives, and acceptance of this constraint is by far the most common opinion.

# 4

# OTHER
# CONSTRAINTS

## 4.1 Lying

Given a general constraint against doing harm (suitably qualified), we can derive a large number of more specific constraints—one for each way of doing harm. Which of these more narrow constraints we choose to identify with a special label will largely be a matter of convenience. Thus, depending upon our purposes, in some cases it might be useful to talk of a constraint against killing another, or a constraint against chopping off someone's leg, or even a constraint against punching someone in the nose, and so on. On the other hand, at other times and for other purposes it might be more helpful to subsume these three under a somewhat more general category; we might, for example, prefer to talk of a constraint against doing bodily damage.

So far as I can see, nothing significant turns on the question of which of these more specific constraints we isolate and identify in this way. Philosophically, the important point is simply that there are various ways of doing harm, so that if there is a constraint against doing harm, then there is a constraint against doing harm in each of these particular ways.

Of course, it may be helpful to remind ourselves of just how *many* ways there are to do harm. Not only can we inflict harm by doing bodily damage, we can also harm someone simply by causing them pain—even if there is no ensuing damage to their body. Thus we can cause someone physical pain or mental anguish, humiliation, embarrassment, or offense. Similarly, we can harm others by interfering with their liberty, by enslaving them, confining them, or otherwise interfering with their autonomy—their ability to control their own lives. And we can harm others by damaging or taking their resources, thus reducing their ability to promote their well-being.

Even this list does not exhaust the possible ways of harming another, but it may be long enough to impress upon us how many of the familiar constraints of commonsense morality can be justified in terms of the more basic, underlying constraint against doing harm.

Indeed, once one notices just how many specific constraints can be justified in terms of the general constraint against doing harm, the question arises as to whether there are any plausible constraints that *cannot* be justified in this way. That is, might it be the case that *all* plausible constraints can be viewed as specific versions of the constraint against doing harm? Obviously, nothing in logic alone requires that this be so; but for all that, it might be that the only constraints that we find intuitively plausible are those that can be reduced to some form of the constraint against doing harm. If so, then once we have a constraint against doing harm, we will have sufficient normative resources to derive all of the familiar constraints of commonsense morality. Whether or not this is so, it is, at the very least, a testimony to the breadth of the constraint against doing harm that it is far from obvious whether we need to add any other basic constraints beyond this one.

Consider, for example, a prohibition against lying. Now obviously enough, a consequentialist can easily find a place for such a prohibition, since telling lies typically does more harm than it does good. But for reasons that are by now familiar, the consequentialist will view any such prohibition as a mere rule of thumb (see 3.1); there is no objection to telling a lie if the results of doing so would truly be better. Yet from the standpoint of ordinary morality, such an account seems inadequate; intuitively, it seems, the fact that a given act would involve telling a lie is a morally significant normative factor in its own right. And it is a factor capable of outweighing goodness of results. That is, it is wrong to tell a lie, even if doing so might bring about better results overall. In short, commonsense morality seems committed to there being a *constraint* against lying.

Of course, the consequentialist will presumably argue that it is a mistake to let the prohibition against lying take the form of a constraint rather than a rule of thumb. He might argue that cases where telling a lie would truly have better results overall are quite unusual. Perhaps if we spelled out such a case, and then carefully reflected upon the details, we would find ourselves prepared to judge that telling a lie in such a case is intuitively acceptable after all. Or perhaps we should hesitate to place much weight upon our intuitions about such unusual cases. In fact, in attacking a constraint against lying, the consequentialist could avail himself of suitably modified versions of all of the strategies he used previously to attack the suggestion that there is a constraint against doing harm (see, especially, 3.1 and 3.4). I won't repeat all these arguments here, nor judge their persuasiveness. But it seems safe to say that just as many felt that it was a *constraint* against doing harm that was called for (and not a mere rule of thumb), many will feel that we similarly need a constraint against lying.

But is this an *additional* constraint? That is, does a constraint against lying add anything to the general constraint against doing harm? Does it go beyond it? Or, alternatively, is lying simply one more way of harming someone—so that the constraint against lying is just one more specific version of the more general, underlying constraint against doing harm?

We certainly know that in the *typical* case telling a lie is harmful. (That's why the consequentialist endorses a rule of thumb against it.) Knowing the truth is an extraordinarily valuable means of achieving one's goals. When you tell a lie, you virtually always rob someone of a crucial ingredient—information—that they need to accomplish whatever it is that they wanted to accomplish (that, after all, is presumably your reason for telling the lie in the first place). Sooner or later, the person is likely to act on the misinformation you've given them, or fail to act when they should have acted, and the result will typically be frustration and disappointment, pain or anger. In the normal case, then, telling a lie to someone is a way of harming them. So if we already have a constraint against doing harm, we can easily derive from it a constraint against telling lies.

Is such a derivation the whole story? Does the moral significance of lying simply boil down to the significance of harm doing? Not all those who believe in the constraint against lying accept this suggestion. They claim, instead, that lying is a normative factor with intrinsic moral significance *in its own right* and not merely derivatively as a way of doing harm.

How might we test this claim? How can we tell whether lying has any intrinsic significance beyond its capacity for doing harm? The most natural suggestion is to consider cases where a lie has been told, but no *harm* has been done to the person lied to. If no harm has been done in a given case, then clearly the constraint against doing harm is irrelevant. If, nonetheless, we still feel that it was immoral to tell the lie, then this will support the claim that lying is an intrinsically significant normative factor in its own right. On the other hand, if we decide that it was not immoral to tell the lie in this case, given that no harm was done, then this will support the claim that lying has no moral significance in and of itself, but rather only when—and insofar as—it is a way of doing harm.

Suppose, then, that we try to imagine a case in which a lie is told, but no harm is done. First of all, we will have to assume that the *content* of the lie is not particularly unpleasant; that is, it is not especially distressing or painful to be told this particular lie. Second, we must imagine that the person lied to never *finds out* about the lie, never discovers the truth in some painful or unpleasant way. Finally, we will also have to assume that the person never suffers anything painful or unpleasant as a *consequence* of having been lied to.

Presumably, friends of the view that lying is a distinct normative factor in its own right will hold that if we imagine cases of this sort we will still believe the act of lying is wrong, even though no harm is done. Of course, not everyone will share that intuition. But those who do think it wrong to lie even in a case of the kind we are imagining may well take this to show that lying is indeed a normative factor with intrinsic significance in its own right.

One difficulty with this line of argument is this. Examples of the kind we are imagining only establish the intrinsic significance of lying if it is truly the case that no harm has been done to the person lied to. But on reflection it is far from obvious that cases of the kind we have described involve no harm at all. We have of course stipulated that the person suffers no pain from being told the lie; but this does not guarantee that the person has not been harmed. Perhaps, for example, she was lied to about the nature of some wonderful opportunity she faced. If not for being misled by the lie, she would have taken advantage of the opportunity and would have had various pleasurable and rewarding experiences. In such a case, even though the woman hasn't suffered any pain, she has still been harmed. But if the woman has indeed been harmed, then for all we know the constraint against doing harm may fully explain the wrongness of telling the lie.

Obviously, this objection could be put to rest by making sure that we are considering a case in which a lie is told but no harm whatsoever is done to the person. But as we have just seen, it may be more difficult to construct such a case than meets the eye. This point will be especially important once we bear in mind that what constitutes harm will depend in part on the correct theory of well-being. Even if we imagine a case in which all of the person's various mental states are identical to (or better than!) those she would have had if she had been told the truth, we still cannot assume that no harm has been done to her—*unless* we are adopting a mental state theory of well-being.

In this context it may be helpful to recall the example of the deceived businessman (from 2.2). This man is lied to by his family and acquaintances, but so successful is the deception that he feels loved and respected. Now *if* we accept a mental state theory of well-being, then presumably we will want to maintain that this man has not been harmed by the various lies told to him. And so, if we do believe nonetheless that telling those lies was wrong, this will indeed support the claim that lying is a basic normative factor, with intrinsic moral significance. But for those who reject a mental state theory of well-being, there will be no reason to grant that the man has not been harmed.

For example, on a preference theory of well-being—according to which a person is well off to the extent that his desires are actually satisfied—lies can still harm someone even if they do not adversely affect his mental states. The lies told to the deceived businessman, for example, get in the way of his achieving what he actually wants to accomplish with his life (to be successful, loved, and respected); they interfere with and frustrate his ability to satisfy his desires. Thus, lying to the deceived businessman harms him. And indeed, this will almost always be the case on a preference theory of well-being: lying to someone will interfere with their ability to satisfy their various desires; and, if nothing else, it will frustrate their desire *to know the truth* about the matter at hand. Accordingly, given a preference theory of well-being, it will be extraordinarily difficult—and perhaps impossible—to describe a case in which a lie is told but no harm is done.

The same thing will be true for many objective theories of well-being. For example, according to perfectionism the constituents of well-being are the various goods that would make up an ideal or perfect human life. If I interfere with someone's attaining any of these objective goods, I harm them (regardless of whether they happen to have a preference for them). Since it is plausible to think that knowledge and accomplishment would be included on such a list of objective goods, this means that a person will be harmed by any actions that interfere with their ability to accomplish their goals or that undermine their knowledge. Thus, lying to someone will harm them—regardless of their desires, and regardless of the effect on their mental states. So here too, it seems, it will be difficult, and perhaps impossible, to describe a case in which a lie is told but no harm is done.

What about a case of the following sort? Suppose you know that I am a habitual liar, and so you don't believe what I tell you. You thus avoid being harmed by my lie. But presumably it was still wrong for me to tell the lie, and so—it seems—the wrongness of lying cannot be based on the wrongness of doing harm.

Even here, however, it is not obvious that no harm has been done. Most of us desire to be in honest and open relationships with others; this preference is directly thwarted when others lie to us, even if we realize they are lying. Similarly, a perfectionist theory might say that the existence of such honest and open relationships is an objective good; yet my lying undermines the possibility of such a relationship obtaining between us. And in any event, the very realization on your part that I am prepared to lie to you may be a painful one. So whatever our theory of well-being, we might still want to say that my lie harms you even if you don't believe me.

But suppose otherwise. Suppose, that is, that if you don't believe me, no harm is done. Even here we cannot assume that the significance of lying goes beyond that of doing harm. For on a subjective account of rightness (see 2.6), the following argument seems possible. Although I haven't actually harmed you (since you didn't believe me), this is irrelevant to the question of whether I have acted wrongly. What matters is not whether harm actually occurs, but rather whether it was reasonable for me to *believe* that harm would occur. Since I *expected* you to believe me (otherwise, why did I lie?), it would have been reasonable for me to expect that you would end up being harmed in one or another of the ways we've discussed. In short, the wrongness of lying, even when you don't believe me, can be explained, given a subjective reading of the constraint against doing harm.

Of course, this particular explanation is not available to those who would prefer an objective account of rightness (at least as far as the constraint against harm doing is concerned). But here a slightly different argument is possible (it was introduced in 3.3 during the discussion of risk). Strictly, perhaps, my telling the lie was *not* wrong, since no harm was done. But I can certainly be *blamed* for telling the lie, since I ran the risk of harming you, and indeed expected this to happen. Perhaps, then, when our intuitions tell us that something is still amiss in the case where I tell you a lie that you don't believe, all we are responding to is the undeniable fact that I am morally at fault and deserve to be blamed.

In sum, it is a surprisingly difficult matter to determine whether or not lying is a basic normative factor in its own right, or whether its moral significance is simply a function of the constraint against doing harm. And this, it will be recalled, was the point I was trying to make when I introduced the topic of lying. It seems fairly clear that any adequate account of common-sense morality will have to include a constraint against lying. But it is far from obvious whether or not doing this involves going beyond the constraint against doing harm.

Even if we were to conclude that the normative significance of lying cannot be reduced to that of harm doing, there might still be some *third* factor, not yet identified, from which the normative significance of lying *is* derivable. One popular suggestion along these lines is that lying violates the *autonomy* of the person lied to. Perhaps it is this violation of autonomy that explains and justifies the constraint against lying. If so, then the new normative factor that should be introduced at this point is not lying per se, but rather—and more generally—autonomy.

Now the notion of autonomy is a complex and controversial one, but one basic idea seems to be something like this. To have autonomy is to have the various aspects of one's life under one's control. Typically, if I have autonomy over some aspect of my life (whether my career, my hair color, or how I spend this Thursday afternoon), then I can deliberate concerning how I want that aspect of my life to go, choose among the various alternatives open to me, and act so as to make my life the way I want it to be in that regard. But lies misinform me about how my life is going and what my options are; they distort my sense of what I can achieve and what needs attending to. The suggestion, then, is that being lied to interferes with my autonomy, by reducing my control over my own life. Accordingly, lying to someone is wrong because it violates their autonomy.

One difficulty with this view is that it is not altogether clear that lying really does interfere in this way with another's autonomy. After all, even if you lie to Rebecca, it is still the case that *she* is the one who is in control of her life, in the sense that she is still making decisions about how she wants her life to go, and she is still free to implement those decisions to the best of her ability. It is true that, given the misinformation, Rebecca may do a less *effective* job of having her life go the way she wants. But for all that—it might be argued—her *control* over her life is not diminished. Against this, however, it might be suggested that true autonomy involves not only the mere *fact* of control but also a significant degree of effectiveness of control. And if this is right, then perhaps lying does interfere with autonomy after all (at least in the typical case).

On the other hand, even if we grant that lying violates autonomy this, will only point in the direction of a new normative factor, if having one's autonomy violated is not simply another way of being harmed. Unfortunately, in the typical case at least, reduction in autonomy *does* seem to be a kind of harm (in fact, a very significant one). And what this means, of course, is that explaining the wrongness of lying in terms of the importance of autonomy may simply be a roundabout way of reducing the wrongness of lying to the wrongness of doing harm.

It would not, I think, be particularly plausible to deny that interfering with someone's autonomy can harm them. Admittedly, for mental state theories, interference with autonomy won't in and of itself constitute a reduction in well-being. Nonetheless, given that for all practical purposes the possession of autonomy is a necessary means of achieving the best possible mental states, even mental state theories are likely to classify violating another's autonomy as a way of harming them. And for other theories of well-being, the connection is even tighter. Perfectionist theories, for example, are likely to include autonomy among the objective goods that make for the best kind of life. And preference theories are likely to note that normally we have an intense desire to live autonomously. So for either of these theories, interfering with autonomy directly reduces well-being, and is thus straightforwardly a way of doing harm.

Of course, even granting all of this, autonomy might still have normative significance in its own right, above and beyond its significance for well-being. This too is a popular suggestion, and it might be thought to gain support from the common view that it can be wrong to interfere with another's autonomy, even if doing so leaves the person better off overall. (Prohibitions against *paternalism* rule out interfering with another's autonomy in such cases—for example, forcing someone to do what's best for himself.) Given a global reading of the constraint against doing harm (see 3.3), it might be argued that if the person is truly left better off overall, interfering with their autonomy does not actually *harm* them. Accordingly, if interfering with another's autonomy is still forbidden—even in cases like this—then the significance of autonomy cannot be reduced to the significance of harm; we will need to recognize an independent constraint against interfering with autonomy.

Perhaps, however, the constraint against doing harm should be given a *local* reading instead (again, see 3.3). If so, then the constraint against doing harm *has* been violated, whenever autonomy has been interfered with, even if the person has been left better off overall. And this means that there will be no reason to view interference with autonomy as a basic normative factor in its own right; the constraint against interfering with another's autonomy will simply derive from the more general constraint against doing harm. But this, of course, leaves us back where we began: uncertain as to whether or not all plausible constraints—including the constraint against lying—can be derived from a more basic constraint against doing harm.

At this point, I propose that we put aside the question of whether or not lying is a basic normative factor with intrinsic moral significance in its own right, or whether, alternatively, its significance derives wholly from that of autonomy, or some other factor or factors. Up until now, we have been assuming that whatever its ultimate basis, the nature of the constraint against lying is relatively clear and unproblematic. In fact, however, there are various complications here as well, and it may be helpful to indicate a few of them, however briefly.

First of all, it is not altogether uncontroversial just what telling a lie comes to. Initially, I think, many people might offer something like the following definition: to tell a lie is to say something that's not true. One implication of this definition is that if you accidentally say something untrue (perhaps you have yourself been misinformed) you have still told a lie. On reflection, however, most people are not willing to call this a lie, and so the definition needs to be modified. We might try: to tell a lie is to say something you take to be false. This avoids the first difficulty but may introduce another. For on the modified definition it is possible to tell a lie while saying something *true* (so long as you mistakenly believe it to be false). Is this implication acceptable? Here, I think, intuitions will differ more widely. Some may find this a welcome result. But at least some people will want to distinguish between the mere unsuccessful attempt to deceive, and actually having told a lie. Accordingly, those who believe that one cannot lie without saying something false may need to modify the definition again. Perhaps telling a lie requires saying something you take to be false which is also, in point of fact, false. Or perhaps—building even more into the definition— you have to *know* that what you are saying is false. (I should note that— here, as elsewhere—the choice between these different alternatives might well be influenced and complicated by the distinction between objective and subjective accounts of rightness. But I won't attempt to spell out the various possibilities.)

Furthermore, merely *saying* something you take to be false (even if you know it is false) may not suffice for telling a lie. For actors on the stage seem to do this routinely, yet almost no one wants to classify acting as lying. Of course, whether or not this is truly a difficulty for the definition depends on what exactly we mean by *saying* something. But the important point, in any event, is this. Merely uttering the relevant string of phonemes doesn't suffice for lying; rather, lying requires *asserting* the claim in question, where this seems to involve, among other things, the intention to mislead the listener. Actors may recite their lines, but they don't assert them (in this sense); so they're not telling lies.

Whatever the precise definition of lying, this much seems clear: the constraint against lying should not be confused with a requirement to tell the truth. There is no requirement to *tell* the truth, since in most situations there is no obligation to say anything at all. Keeping your opinions to yourself does not violate the constraint against lying. To do that, you have to say something.

Of course, sometimes silence can be misleading, or deceptive. And the same thing is obviously possible with regard to telling the truth. (A judicious selection of truths can create a very misleading impression.) In short, one can deliberately and effectively deceive another without telling any lies at all. This raises anew the question of whether lying has any distinct moral status. Should we embrace, perhaps, a general constraint against deception (with lying simply being a particular method of deceiving)? Or is lying somehow unique among the various forms of deception—and if so, why?

Although commonsense morality certainly finds deception in general to be morally objectionable, I think many people are inclined to consider lying to be especially pernicious. It is not clear to me whether this is the majority view or not, and it is even less clear whether or not distinguishing in this way between lying and other forms of deception can be adequately justified. Admittedly, there is some pull to the thought that the particular abuse of language involved in lying marks it as deserving a special moral status. But a comparable abuse of language seems to be involved in deliberately selecting truths so as to mislead; and it is difficult to see whether there is any good reason to treat the first of these abuses as worse than the second.

Assuming that we do identify lying as a normative factor with distinct, intrinsic moral significance, the question will still remain as to just how much weight this factor possesses. The fact that some act would involve telling a lie will be a reason not to perform that act. But how strong a reason will it be?

I have, of course, already suggested—and I have been assuming for some time—that from the standpoint of commonsense morality, at least, the significance of lying is sufficiently great that it is capable of outweighing goodness of results. That is to say, the mere fact that the results would be better overall will not typically be sufficient to justify telling a lie. In short, what most of us believe is that there is a *constraint* against telling lies.

But it is a distinct question, one we have not yet addressed, as to whether this constraint is absolute or not. Must we never tell lies, no matter how much good might be achieved by lying? That's exactly the position of those deontologists who are absolutists with regard to the constraint against lying. But we should also recall the possibility of being a *moderate* deontologist (see 3.2). One can perfectly well accept the reality of a given constraint while still maintaining that it has a threshold. Normally, that is, it is forbidden to perform the given type of act, even if doing so would produce a greater amount of good overall; but when *enough* good is at stake, it is permissible to perform the act that would otherwise be forbidden. In such cases, says the moderate, it is permissible to "infringe" the constraint.

Accordingly, one might be a moderate deontologist with regard to the constraint against lying. One might hold, for example, that although one cannot normally tell lies, even for good causes, it is perfectly permissible to tell a lie if this is the only way to prevent a war or some other catastrophe. In point of fact, the threshold for telling a lie might be fairly low. Perhaps it is permissible to tell a lie if this is the only way to save even one life. Indeed, it might be permissible to lie if this is the only way to prevent a loss of limb, or to save someone from excruciating pain. Obviously, the lower the threshold, the smaller the barrier to the promotion of the good that is erected by the constraint against lying. But as long as this barrier hasn't disappeared altogether, the prohibition against lying is still taking the form of a constraint.

If the constraint against lying does, in fact, have a threshold, then it seems plausible to think that the level of that threshold might not be the same in all cases. Some lies are harder to justify in this way than others. But what then accounts for the difference? One obvious suggestion is that the level of the threshold reflects the amount of *harm* done by the lie: the more harmful the lie, the more good that needs to be at stake before it can be justified. Of course, a view of this sort seems most plausible if the constraint against lying really does just boil down to the constraint against doing harm. But even if the moral significance of lying is not exhausted by the fact that it is harmful, it is certainly obvious that the harm done by the lie matters; and so it will still be plausible to think that the level of the threshold for telling a given lie will be influenced by the amount of harm that would be done by that lie.

Beyond these issues about the threshold, there are also questions about the *scope* of the constraint, similar to those that we considered (in 3.3) for the constraint against doing harm. Again, this is hardly surprising, if the constraint against lying is simply a particular version of the latter constraint. But even if it isn't, it doesn't seem implausible to suggest that similar issues of scope might arise quite generally for different constraints.

For example, does the guilt or innocence of the person being lied to make a difference to the permissibility of telling a lie? Does it matter if the lie is necessary to *defend* oneself, or another, from attack? Suppose, for example, that a would-be murderer has come to your door, looking for his intended victim—who is hiding in your basement. Is it permissible to lie, denying knowledge of the victim's whereabouts?

Obviously, an absolutist concerning the constraint against lying might insist that the fact that it is a would-be murderer to whom you would be telling a lie is simply irrelevant; it is still forbidden to tell the lie. Alternatively, a moderate deontologist might claim that it is permissible to tell the lie (since the possibility of saving a life is a great enough good to justify infringing the constraint); and yet, for all that, the moderate might agree with the absolutist that the guilt or innocence of the person being lied to is unimportant.

But many people would find it plausible to suggest that the guilt of the person being lied to is quite significant indeed, and that the constraint against lying simply does not apply to lying to an *evil aggressor*. And it should be noted that a view of this sort is available not only to those who think the constraint against lying has a low threshold but also to those who think that the threshold for lying is fairly high, or even those who think that lying lacks a finite threshold altogether. That is to say, it is perfectly consistent to think that no amount of good whatsoever could justify telling a lie to an innocent person, but that it is permissible to tell a lie to a would-be aggressor. Like killing in self-defense, lying in self-defense (or in defense of another) may simply fall outside the scope of the constraint.

Finally, it may also be worth mentioning the possible impact that *consent* might have on the permissibility of telling a lie. Intuitively, it seems, it makes a great deal of difference if the person you are lying to has previously agreed to your doing this. (Might this provide a better account of the example of actors in the theater? Has the audience given its tacit consent to being lied to?) And if mere *hypothetical* consent has force as well, this might also go some way toward justifying certain "white lies." (For example, we might know that someone *would* have agreed to being lied to, for the sake of being thrown a surprise party.)

## 4.2 Promises

Another factor relevant for determining the moral status of an act, at least from the standpoint of commonsense morality, is whether the act in question involves keeping or breaking a promise. Other things being equal, the fact that I have promised to perform a given act provides a weighty reason for doing it.

Now the practice of making and keeping promises is an extremely valuable one. Here's why. Very often I can achieve some goal only through the cooperation of others; for example, I may need someone else to perform an act which I am incapable of performing myself. Now if I have reason to believe that the other person will perform the necessary action, I may well be prepared to take the various other steps needed to bring about the desired outcome. But often it will only be sensible for me to take these steps *if* I can be reassured that the other person will indeed do her part. My own efforts in isolation might be much less effective or, worse still, lead to disaster. And I may well have grounds for worrying that the other person will not in fact do what I need her to do. In such cases, what is needed is a way that the other person can reliably reassure me that she will indeed perform the act in question. Unfortunately, mere statements from the woman as to her current intentions may not be enough; even if they are sincere, I may reasonably worry that she will change her mind and fail to carry through.

Luckily, the practice of promising provides a way out of this impasse. For if the woman *promises* me that she will perform the required act, I may now be reassured that I can count on her cooperation: given that she has made the promise, and given her recognition of the fact that having made a promise provides her with a morally weighty reason to perform the promised act, I can be justifiably confident that she will act in the way that she has promised.

Often, this need for reliable reassurance is mutual. For example, each of the two of us might need the help of the other to achieve our own distinct goals (I might need your help plowing my fields, while you need my help picking your crops). Each of us might be willing to help the other, but only given adequate reassurance that the other person will return the favor. Promises make such reassurances possible, allowing both of us to better achieve our own personal goals. And even with a common goal, neither party may be confident that the other will do their part. I may justifiably worry that you will not do your part, because I realize that you are justifiably worried that I will not do my part, because I am justifiably worried that you will not do your part—and so on. But if each of us makes a promise to the other, confidence can be restored, and the common goal can be achieved.

(Sometimes, instead of promising to *do* something, one promises another that a specified statement is *true*. Although no further action is called for, here, too, promising functions as a method of providing reassurance. Since such promises are not to be made lightly, you are reassuring the other person that they can justifiably rely on your authority as to the matter in question. Some of the discussion that follows would need to be modified slightly so as to explicitly include promises of this second kind as well; but for simplicity, I won't consider them further.)

Obviously enough, the making of promises is only useful if people generally *keep* their promises; otherwise there is no reason for anyone to be reassured. Accordingly, the consequentialist will endorse a general requirement to keep one's promises. As usual, however, such a principle of promise keeping will only be a rule of thumb. It will be perfectly permissible to break your promise whenever doing so will produce a better outcome overall. The mere fact that you have made the promise will not, in and of itself, have any moral significance. (Of course, breaking a promise may harm the person who has relied on your word, and this is a bad outcome that needs to be taken into account in assessing the overall results. But the mere fact that a *promise* has been made is of no particular moral significance.)

Against this, what most people believe is that the prohibition against breaking your promises is no mere rule of thumb, but rather a *constraint*:

you are required to keep your promises, even if better results overall might come about by breaking them. This is, of course, simply another example of the general debate between consequentialists and deontologists. Consequentialists argue that most of the familiar principles of commonsense morality should indeed be embraced, but not—they insist—in the form of constraints. Deontologists, on the other hand, insist that it is this very failure to recognize the existence of constraints that marks consequentialism as an inadequate moral theory. Now with each new constraint endorsed by the deontologist (whether against doing harm, telling lies, breaking promises, or what have you) a new supply of relevant examples, counterexamples, and moral intuitions is opened up. However, since the basic issues remain the ones that we have already discussed, there is no need for us to rehearse once again the volley of charges and countercharges. But I do think it fair to suggest that many people will indeed conclude that the requirement to keep your promises should take the form of a constraint.

It may be worth observing, however, that as with the constraint against telling lies, it is far from obvious whether or not a constraint against breaking your promises goes beyond the constraint against doing harm or whether, alternatively, the former is simply a specific version of the latter. For it does seem plausible to think that in the typical case, at the very least, if you break a promise you will end up harming the person to whom the promise has been made. Relying on your promise, the person may have put himself out in one way or another (or failed to make alternative arrangements); if you fail to carry through, expectations are dashed, and the results can range from disappointment and lost opportunity to danger, wasted resources, or death.

Of course, even though breaking a promise typically harms the person to whom the promise was made, this fact—though important—might not exhaust the moral significance of promise breaking. Perhaps the fact that an act involves keeping or breaking a promise is a basic normative factor with intrinsic moral significance in its own right. Taking our lead from the discussion of the constraint against lying, we might try to settle the question by constructing cases in which a promise is broken, but no harm is done. But as we saw in that earlier discussion, it can be much more difficult to construct the requisite cases than meets the eye, and the results may be inconclusive.

Suppose, for example, that you make a promise to a friend while he is on his deathbed. He dies immediately thereafter, and no one else even knows the promise has been made. If you fail to carry through, breaking your promise, have you harmed your friend?

On a mental state view, your friend can't be harmed by your breaking the promise. Since the future cannot affect the past, your later actions—whether you break your promise or keep it—cannot affect the mental states that were previously had by your (now dead) friend while he was alive. So *if* it is wrong to break the promise, this cannot be by virtue of its involving a violation of the constraint against doing harm—for there is no such violation. Accordingly, if it is indeed wrong to break the promise, it may be that promise breaking has a normative significance that goes beyond the harm it may do. (Of course, some may feel it perfectly permissible to break the deathbed promise. For those who accept the mental state view, this will support the suggestion that the wrong of promise breaking is simply a matter of the harm involved.)

For other theories of well-being, however, we cannot conclude so confidently that breaking the promise does not harm the dead. Consider, first, a preference theory of well-being. Presumably, your friend had a desire that you perform the act in question (that's why he made you promise to do it); for example, he may have valued some outcome that he knew you could bring about. If you fail to keep your promise, then your friend's desire is never satisfied, and so to that extent, at least, his life has indeed gone less well than it might otherwise have gone. (Of course, your friend will never know either way; but this is not the decisive point it is sometimes taken to be, once we move beyond mental state theories.) Similarly, on an objective theory, your future action or inaction may affect the degree to which your friend's life was successful in its various endeavors, or the extent to which his reputation is secured, and so on. If these are among the objective goods, then breaking your promise might well harm your friend after all.

Of course, even if it could be shown that the moral significance of promise keeping does not simply reduce to the avoidance of harm, there might still be some third normative factor to which it *can* be reduced. If this is right, then obviously there is still no need to add promise keeping to the list of basic normative factors.

One common suggestion along these lines is that the requirement to keep one's promises can be derived from the more general requirement not to tell lies. The idea, roughly, is that if you break your promise, your initial assertion is made untrue—and you have told a kind of lie. (Hence, to avoid lying, you must keep your promises.) Although this is an intriguing suggestion, it faces a number of obvious problems. Admittedly, if you make a promise that you simply have no intention of keeping, this does seem tantamount to telling a lie. But what if at the time of making the promise you are sincere? Provided you don't decide to break the promise until later, it is not at all clear that breaking the promise makes it be the case that earlier you told a lie. Earlier you said something that (as it turned out) was untrue; but if telling a lie requires saying something that (at the time you say it) you *take* to be untrue, then you haven't told a lie.

Perhaps such a "veracity" account of the obligation to keep one's promises can be developed so as to answer this, and similar, objections. Of course, even if it can, it might still be the case that the importance of keeping one's promises derives, ultimately, from the importance of not doing harm. For as we have seen, it might well be that the constraint against lying is *itself* simply a particular version of the more general constraint against harm doing. If it is, then it will turn out that the obligation to keep one's promises is based on the constraint against doing harm after all; we will merely have shown this in a more roundabout way.

On the other hand, ultimately we might come to a very different conclusion: perhaps, despite the various connections to doing harm and lying, neither of these factors exhausts the moral significance of promise keeping. If so, then promise keeping might well deserve to be considered a basic normative factor in its own right.

Let us now put this particular debate aside. For whatever conclusions we may reach about the basis of the constraint against breaking your promises, there are also a number of other controversies concerning the constraint as well. One such puzzle concerns the existence of what is sometimes called the *uptake requirement*. Must the person to whom the promise is made say or do something for the promise to be binding? If so, what exactly must the person do?

Suppose the person verbally acknowledges and accepts the promise, and then—believing the promisor to be sincere—goes on to act in a way that relies upon the promise in some manner. Pretty clearly, this will satisfy any plausible account of the necessary "uptake," and the promise will be binding. But which of these elements, if any, are actually necessary?

Presumably, if acknowledgment of the promise is required for it to be binding, this acknowledgment need not be verbal—a nod or a smile might suffice. But must the promise be outwardly acknowledged at all? Perhaps it suffices if the person understands the promise made and adjusts his expectations accordingly. On the other hand, it also seems fairly plausible to suggest that the promise will still be binding even if it is not actually believed; after all, even if you don't expect me to keep some promise, surely this cannot, all by itself, release me from the obligation to keep it. Is mere acknowledgment, then, sufficient? Some think so. Others, however, deny this, holding that a promise is only binding if there has been some further act of reliance on the part of the recipient. Obviously, it would take some time to sort through all the possible positions here; but we should also at least mention one further possibility—that *all* promises are binding, regardless of what the recipient says or does. That is to say, perhaps there is no uptake requirement at all. (Must the recipient at least understand that a promise has been made?)

If a promise has been made, and the relevant uptake conditions (if any) have been met, then the person who has made the promise is now required, other things being equal, to keep that promise. Intuitively, however, other things are *not* equal if the recipient *releases* the promisor from his promise. If I tell you that you need no longer keep your promise to me, then the promise becomes void; it is no longer a factor in determining what you should do. Similarly, if I refuse to accept the promise in the first place—when it is first made—you never have any obligation at all. (This suggests the following minimal uptake condition: a promise isn't binding if the recipient immediately rejects it.) This appears to be another case where the presence of consent makes a difference as to what constitutes a violation of a given constraint. As with the constraint against doing harm, an act that would normally violate the constraint (here, failure to keep the promise) may become permissible if it is done with the permission of the "victim." Of course, a full account of these matters would also need to explore the question of whether consent always releases the promisor from his obligation (or whether, alternatively, the promise might still be binding, if the decision to release was not a reasonable one). It would also need to examine the significance—if any—of hypothetical consent. But let us leave these further complications aside as well.

Now when a promise is made, it is common for there to be one or more conditions incorporated explicitly into the promise. I might, for example, promise to take Ari to the park this afternoon—provided that it's not raining. Or I might promise to pick up Rebecca from school—if my meeting finishes on time. In such cases I promise to perform a given act, but only if certain particular conditions are met. If, happily, the specified conditions are indeed met, then—straightforwardly enough—keeping my promise requires me to perform the relevant act. Suppose, however, that the various conditions are not met. (It's raining, or the meeting runs late, or what have you.) What then? Since I only promised to perform the given act if the relevant conditions are met, and they are *not* met, clearly I have no obligation to perform the particular act in question. If, accordingly, I refrain from doing it, what should we say? Have I *kept* my promise? That seems wrong. It seems more natural to say that—under the circumstances—I didn't have to keep my promise. Have I then *broken* my promise? That seems worse (even if we add: and I am justified in doing so). Perhaps we should say that the promise has been nullified or made *void,* so that the question of keeping it or breaking it no longer arises.

Beyond whatever particular conditions I choose to explicitly incorporate into my promise, it seems plausible to suppose that there is also a larger and somewhat open-ended set of conditions that are understood as being included as well, even though they are not explicitly stated. We might think of these as constituting the normal background conditions for the promise. For example, if I promise to meet you for lunch, we will both understand the promise to be conditional: I will meet you for lunch—provided that I don't suffer a stroke, provided that my car doesn't break down, provided that war doesn't break out unexpectedly, and so on. Normally, it would be tedious and pointless to try to state all the background conditions that are typically left unexpressed. Instead, commonsense and shared understanding provide the best guides here. In certain cases, however, where a great deal is at stake, we may grow much more explicit about what the relevant conditions are, perhaps developing a standard list that will be presumed operative unless we explicitly note otherwise. (Contracts can be understood as formalized promises of this sort.)

In the light of these points, consider this example. Suppose that I have promised to meet you for lunch, but as I am going to meet you I come across the victim of a car accident. Help is on its way, but unless I stop to administer first aid, the person will likely die. If I do stop to help, however, I will be unable to make it to our lunch appointment as I promised. So what should I do?

Logically, of course, one might claim that I should keep the promise, regardless of the fact that, if I do, the accident victim will die. But this position is absurd. Far more plausible is the view that it is permissible to break the promise so as to save the life. Fair enough. But what exactly explains why doing this is permissible?

One possible approach would be that of the moderate deontologist. Perhaps the requirement to keep your promises has a threshold, so that if enough is at stake it is permissible to infringe the constraint and break the promise. Promises may matter; but they are not all that matters. When a life is at stake—as in this case—the threshold is met, and the constraint is overridden.

This first approach seems plausible (at least, to those already attracted to moderate deontology), but there is a second possibility as well. Perhaps this is a case in which the background conditions that normally remain unexpressed come into play. I may have promised to meet you for lunch, but presumably both of us understood this to include a tacit qualification: I would meet you for lunch—*provided* that I was not (unexpectedly) needed elsewhere to avert a tragedy. Given that a tacit condition of the promise has not been met (since I *am* needed), I may simply have no obligation to meet you. (This second approach, it should be noted, makes no appeal to the existence of a threshold for the constraint; unlike the first, therefore, it is available not only to moderate deontologists but also to absolutists.)

Although these two approaches agree that it is permissible to aid the victim, even though this means I will miss the promised lunch date, and they even agree that it is the very possibility of saving a life that explains why this is permissible, nonetheless they still disagree concerning the correct moral description of the case. On the first approach, the promise is in force, but it is overridden by a second factor, distinct and external to it. On the second approach, in contrast, the promise is not overridden at all; rather, given that one of the conditions internal to a complete specification of the promise has not been met, the promise is simply null and void. How, then, should we decide between these two rival accounts?

One possible argument to help us decide appeals to a general principle concerning compensation. As we know, moderate deontologists believe that it can be permissible to override a constraint when the threshold of that constraint has been met. But typically, they also believe that in such cases we still owe compensation to the person who has been harmed—even though infringing the constraint is justified. For example, if I break into an empty cabin, so as to save my life in an unexpected winter storm, and I damage the cabin in the process, I owe the owner more than an explanation; I need to pay him for the damage done. That is, even though infringing his property rights is justified here by the good that is at stake, I still need to compensate him for the harm that is done. Applying this general principle about compensation to the particular case of promises, it follows that if breaking a promise is justified by the fact that some threshold has been met, compensation will still be owed. (We'll return to the topic of compensation in 4.3.)

In contrast, if a conditional promise has been made—but the conditions haven't been met—then normally we don't owe anything more than an explanation. For example, if I promise to meet you unless it rains, and it does rain so I don't come, then later I owe you an explanation, but nothing more (not even if you end up losing money because of the fact that the meeting didn't take place). So now we can ask, in the original case where I break the promise so as to save the life, what exactly do I owe you? If I owe you compensation, then it seems plausible to suggest that a threshold has been met, and the constraint has been overridden. But if all I owe is an explanation, then it seems more plausible to appeal to an implicit condition of the promise that has simply gone unmet.

So which is it? Suppose you lose some money as a result of my not keeping our lunch appointment. Must I compensate you for your expenses, or is an explanation (telling you about the accident victim) sufficient? Perhaps intuitions will differ here as well, but most people, I imagine, will think that an explanation is in fact all that I owe you. If so, then in *this* case, at least, there is no need to claim that the promise was overridden, and indeed no reason to think the constraint even has a threshold. Of course, there might be *other* cases, with a similar structure, where intuition favors the other answer: as the harm I do to you by breaking the promise increases, and the good to be achieved by breaking the promise gets smaller, do we come across a range of cases where infringing the promise is still justified (because there is still enough good at stake), but now compensation is owed? If so, then the constraint may have a threshold after all. If, on the other hand, we move immediately from cases where infringing the constraint is justified, and an explanation suffices, to cases where infringing is simply unjustified—then there may be no reason to ascribe a threshold to the constraint at all.

Here is a completely different way to try to settle the choice between the threshold and the implicit condition accounts. Normally, it is a simple matter to explicitly *exclude* any conditions we don't want to incorporate into our promise: for example, I can promise Ari to take him to the park this afternoon even if it rains. In such a case, obviously enough, even if it does rain, the promise is still binding. But can I do this in the case of the lunch date and the accident victim? That is, suppose I promise to meet you for lunch even if I'm needed to help avert some disaster. And now, on my way through town, I come across the accident. Am I now obligated to keep my promise, and let the accident victim die? That seems very hard to believe. Yet if the best explanation of the original version of the case was in terms of an implicit condition of the promise, then it seems that in this modified version of the case—where I have explicitly excluded the relevant condition—the promise should still be binding.

In fact, however, even in this modified version of the case, it still seems perfectly permissible to infringe the promise and help the accident victim. And it is difficult to see how this can be explained on the implicit condition account. (Why did my attempt to exclude this condition fail?) In contrast, the moderate deontologist has no difficulty with this case at all: despite my attempt to exclude the condition, the constraint still has a threshold, and the threshold has been met. Thus, regardless of what conditions the promise may include or exclude, the constraint has simply been overridden—outweighed by another factor. That is why it remains permissible to break the promise.

Let's put this latest controversy aside as well, and turn to another. The existence of a promise—we are assuming—is a factor that can help determine the moral status of an act. Occasionally, it merely reinforces the mandatory nature of an already required act. More commonly, however, prior to my having made the promise, I am under no obligation to do the given act: doing it is permissible, but so is refraining. In the typical case, therefore, making a promise shifts the moral status of the promised act from optional to mandatory. But is there a third possibility? Can a promise make mandatory an act that was previously *forbidden*?

It might seem that this is an incoherent possibility. If a given act is immoral, then, obviously enough, it is immoral to do it; one cannot be morally *required* to perform an act that is morally forbidden. And so—trivially—you cannot be morally required to perform forbidden acts, *even* if you have promised to do them. Far from making forbidden acts mandatory, a promise to perform an immoral act is simply without moral force altogether.

But this argument moves too quickly. Admittedly, there can be no requirement to perform an act that is forbidden *all things considered*. But it is perfectly coherent to say of a given act that it *would* be forbidden—were it not for the presence of some particular factor that is in fact at work. (For example: it would be forbidden to kill her, were this not a case of self-defense.) So it remains a possibility that there might be cases in which a given act would be forbidden *but for* my having promised to do that act; so that, all things considered (once we take into account the existence of the promise) the act is actually permitted, and indeed required. In short, a promise to perform an immoral act—more accurately, an act that would be immoral but for the existence of the promise itself—might possess moral force after all.

However, that is not to say that such promises do possess any force. Suppose I promise you that I will kill your business partner. Surely, even though I have promised, I am still forbidden to kill her. So in this case, at least, my promise cannot shift the moral status of my act from forbidden to mandatory (or even optional). Are all "immoral" promises like this, or are there other cases where the immorality of the promised act is milder, so that the force of the promise is enough to shift the balance? (What if I promise to tell a lie so as to save you some undeserved embarrassment?) I suspect that intuitions will differ on this question.

At the very least, it does seem uncontroversial that, despite my promise, I cannot kill your business partner. Once again, however, it is not altogether obvious how this is best explained. Clearly, the constraint against doing harm weighs heavily—and indeed decisively—against killing the partner. But what about the constraint requiring one to keep one's promises? Is this a relevant factor at all, albeit one that is outweighed? On one possible account, my promise does indeed have a certain amount of weight, however slight. On this view, although the constraint against doing harm is undeniably more significant, the fact that I have made a promise is not completely irrelevant. (A view of this sort would fit quite naturally with the position that in rare cases, where the immorality of the promised act is slight, a promise can indeed succeed in making the forbidden mandatory.) On a second possible account, however, the promise to kill the innocent person simply has no weight whatsoever. On this view, we might say, promises made to perform immoral acts simply fall outside of the *scope* of the constraint; they have no force at all.

Finally, let me mention a controversy concerning the force of promises that are extracted coercively. Suppose you are kidnapped by pirates, who release you only after you have promised to send them a ransom once you get home. Safe at home, must you still keep your promise? Some people think so, claiming that despite the immorality of the pirates, "a promise is still a promise." Others, however, think the situation analogous to justifiably harming an evil aggressor in self-defense (or, perhaps more accurately, punishing one after the fact). Only promises freely made are binding, they claim; promises obtained through the use of violence or threats fall outside the scope of the constraint.

## 4.3  Special Obligations

The constraints that we have considered so far—against doing harm, lying, or breaking promises—are all *general* in the following sense: they represent obligations that everyone has to everyone else. Each of us is required to refrain from harming anyone else, each of us is required to refrain from lying to anyone else, and each of us is required to keep all our promises, regardless of who we have made them to.

Perhaps, stated this baldly, this claim is not quite accurate. For as we have seen, on many views it may be permissible to harm someone in self-defense, or if you have their consent, or if enough good is at stake to override the constraint; and similar exceptions may exist for the other constraints as well. Still, these exceptions are just that—exceptions caused by special circumstances that don't normally arise. Thus, it still seems helpful to think of these constraints as being general: they represent obligations that everyone has to everyone else—special circumstances aside, or in the absence of special conditions.

In contrast to this kind of generality, other obligations seem more restricted, in terms of who owes what to whom. For example, intuitively at least, I seem to have certain *special obligations* to my children, or to my students, or to my friends. No doubt, others often have similar obligations: you to your children, say, or Linda to hers. But my obligation is to *my* children, while yours is to *yours*. Thus *who* we have the obligations to varies from person to person. (I don't have the same obligations to your children that you do.) Similarly, in many cases, *which* special obligations we have varies from person to person as well. Rhonda is a doctor, and so has special obligations to her patients; I am not a doctor, and so have no special medical obligations at all. I am, however, a teacher and a parent, and so have special obligations to my students and my children; but Ari is neither a teacher nor a parent, and so does not have any of the relevant parental or academic obligations.

Thus, unlike general obligations which (special circumstances aside) everyone owes equally to everyone else, these special obligations are owed only by certain specific individuals to certain other specific individuals. In effect, for a general obligation each person has the relevant obligation to every other person—*unless* special circumstances have cancelled or overridden that obligation. In contrast, for the various special obligations, a given person has the relevant obligation to another given person *only if* special circumstances have created or generated it.

Perhaps it will be helpful to state these points even more abstractly. Whether a given agent has a particular special obligation to a given person depends on whether the relevant special circumstances obtain with regard to that given agent and that given person, that is, whether the agent stands in the relevant special relationship to the person (where this isn't true in general). Since (typically) the agent won't stand in the relevant relationship to all other people, she won't have the particular special obligation in question toward all others, but only to some specific individuals at best, and perhaps to none at all. Similarly, since it won't (typically) be the case for any given person that all agents stand in the relevant relationship to that person, not everyone will owe the person the particular special treatment in question; at best only certain specific agents will owe it to him, and perhaps no one will owe it at all. Put still another way: if a given agent has a particular special obligation to a given person, this will be an "exception" from the norm; other agents won't necessarily be similarly obligated to the person in question (indeed, they may not be similarly obligated to anyone else at all), and other people won't have similar treatment owed to them by the given agent (indeed, there may be no one at all who has a similar obligation toward them).

(A further point of clarification: since a general obligation is one owed by everyone to everyone, it's appropriate to classify as a special obligation anything more restricted than this. So in principle, there might be a special obligation which some particular agent owes to everyone else (even though most agents are not under any such obligation), or one where some particular individual is owed special treatment by everyone (even though most individuals are not). Generally, however, the special obligations that we are likely to find plausible are significantly more restricted than this. Indeed, in the typical case, the numbers involved are fairly small. A parent, for example, has special parental obligations only to the few children that are his or her own; and a given child is owed this special treatment only by his or her own parents. Still, it should be noted, in some cases the numbers involved are quite large. For example, if—as many believe—there are special obligations toward one's fellow citizens, then hundreds of millions of Americans owe them equally to hundreds of millions of their fellow Americans. Nonetheless these obligations are still special rather than general: I owe them only to my fellow Americans, not to all the billions of inhabitants of the earth; and only other Americans owe them to me.)

Where do special obligations come from? Some of them, at least, derive from familiar general constraints. Consider, for example, the requirement to keep one's promises. This constraint is, of course, a general one, since everyone must keep their promises to everyone else. But focus now on some particular case of promising. Suppose that Gina has promised Elana to take her to the beach. Given the general constraint (and given normal circumstances), it follows that Gina now has an *obligation* to take Elana to the beach. Note, however, that this is a *special* obligation: It is only *Elana* whom Gina is obligated to take to the beach; she needn't do the same for others (to whom she hasn't made a similar promise). And it is only *Gina* who is now obligated to take Elana to the beach; no one else is obligated to do so (assuming that no one else has made a similar promise). In short, the general obligation to keep one's promises yields—given the special circumstances under which promises are generated—a special obligation, whose particular content is fixed by the content of the promise. None of this is problematic. And in a similar fashion, of course, other acts of promising generate other specific special obligations.

Can all special obligations be derived from general constraints in this way? In a trivial sense, at least, this does seem possible. For each person is required (special circumstances aside) to fulfill whatever special obligations he may be under. Thus we can, if we like, speak of a *general* constraint requiring everyone to fulfill their special obligations. Of course, a constraint of this trivial sort will be of no help in justifying or deriving claims about particular special obligations. But we can do somewhat better. For each basic *type* of special obligation, we can introduce a corresponding constraint: each person will be required by that constraint to fulfill whatever special obligations of that type he may be under. (Compare the constraint requiring each of us to keep whatever promises he may have made.) These obligation-specific constraints will still be general, since everyone will have an obligation to everyone else to conform to them. And once we have "created" these general constraints, we can derive all the particular cases of one individual having a special obligation to another.

Presumably, therefore, the interesting question is really this: can all special obligations be derived from the *familiar* general constraints, in particular the ones that we have already examined? Unfortunately, the correct answer to this new question is far less obvious.

Consider, for example, the requirement to *compensate* those that we have harmed. Normally, if I have harmed you then I have a special obligation to compensate you, to pay for the damage I have done. Intuitively, this is indeed a special obligation, for I have particular reason to aid *you* (rather than all the other needy individuals I might help), and *I* have more reason to help you than the others do (that is, those who could help, but who haven't harmed you). Of course, as we have just seen, there corresponds to this special obligation a general constraint—a general requirement to compensate those one has harmed. But does this constraint itself derive from one of the others that we have examined? Obviously enough, it wouldn't be plausible to suggest that a requirement to compensate derives from the constraint against lying; nor does it seem to derive from the constraint against breaking your promises (who, after all, has promised to compensate those he harms?). But what about the constraint against *doing* harm? Does the constraint against doing harm somehow entail a requirement to compensate those whom one has harmed?

At first glance, this doesn't seem especially plausible either. Failure to compensate may well be forbidden; it may even violate a constraint. But failure to compensate doesn't seem by itself to violate the constraint against doing harm. Of course, the initial harmful act presumably did violate (or at least infringe) the constraint against doing harm. And with that initial violation in place, one becomes *liable*—that is, obligated to provide compensation. So, clearly, the requirement to compensate *depends* upon the existence of the constraint against doing harm: were there no prohibition against doing harm, there would be no requirement to compensate when the prohibition is violated. But none of this shows that failure to compensate is itself a way of doing harm. So none of it shows that the requirement to compensate is itself simply an instance of the more general constraint against doing harm.

On the other hand, the following argument is possible. If I compensate you for the harm that I have done, then I minimize the damage that I do to you. You suffer a temporary setback, rather than an on-going one. So compensation is a way of minimizing the extent to which I have violated the constraint against doing harm. And it does not seem at all implausible to suggest that the constraint against doing harm directly entails a requirement to do as little harm as possible. Accordingly, a requirement to compensate may indeed be derivable from the constraint against doing harm.

Although this argument is attractive, it is not completely clear whether it is successful. In some cases of compensation, it seems more natural to say that the original harm remains untouched, but compensatory goods are offered in an effort to *balance* the harm done, so that the victim is left no worse off *overall*. In such cases, it doesn't seem appropriate to view compensation as a matter of literally minimizing the harm or undoing the damage. (Of course, what we say here may depend in part on whether we adopt a global or a local interpretation of harm (see 3.3).)

Now if the obligation to compensate cannot in fact be derived in this (or some other) way from the constraint against doing harm, then we will have to expand our basic list of normative factors once more. And, obviously, it will follow that there are at least some special obligations which cannot be derived from any of our familiar, general constraints. On the other hand, even if we *can* derive the obligation to compensate in this way, it still might not be true that *all* special obligations can be similarly derived.

But before we go on to consider any other special obligations, it may be useful to say a bit more about the requirement to compensate. The first point to make is that, as with the other principles of commonsense morality that we have examined, the consequentialist is likely to endorse some form of the requirement. (If those who cause harm take themselves to have a special obligation to pay for the damage, this is likely to minimize the extent to which we harm others.) But as usual, this requirement will only be a rule of thumb. Upon reflection, however—or so I have been assuming—most people will believe the requirement should take the form of a constraint. After all, if I have an obligation to compensate you for the harm I have done to you, then I must indeed compensate you—even if more good could be done by spending the money in some other way.

The second point to make is by now familiar as well: even if we agree that there is a *constraint* against failing to compensate, it is a distinct question whether that constraint is absolute, or whether instead it has a threshold, permitting the constraint to be infringed when enough good is at stake.

Our next point, however, is somewhat less obvious. An obligation to compensate can arise not only in those cases where you have acted unjustifiably in harming another—but also in many cases where you have harmed another *permissibly.* That is to say, it does not require a *violation* of the constraint against doing harm to generate a requirement to compensate; even if the constraint has been infringed justifiably, you may still have an obligation to provide compensation for any harm that you have done. Actually, we already noted this fact in the previous section, and illustrated it with the example of breaking into an empty cabin while hiking so as to save yourself from a deadly winter storm. Presumably your act is justified—it is more important to save your life than to avoid damaging the cabin—and yet, for all that, you will later have an obligation to compensate the owner of the cabin for any damage you may have done to it. This point is worth emphasizing, since it is natural enough to assume that one can only become obligated to compensate another if one was somehow at *fault* in harming the other. But what the example of the cabin shows is that even if you were completely justified—and not at all at fault—in harming another, you may still owe them compensation.

When do we owe compensation, then? Are we obligated to compensate *whenever* we have harmed another? That seems wrong too. If you attack me without provocation, and I harm you in self-defense (assuming that we have a case where this is permissible), it seems, intuitively, that I don't owe you *anything* for the harm I do to you. I am not liable. Similarly, if I harm you with your permission (again, assuming that we have a permissible case of this), I don't owe you compensation either (unless, of course, I promised to repay you). On the other hand, as we have just seen, if I harm you in order to achieve some great good, then—even if my act is justified—it seems that I do owe you compensation. This suggests the following principle: compensation is due whenever the constraint against doing harm has been *overridden* (whenever, that is, infringement is justified by the fact that the constraint's threshold has been met); but in those cases where the act in question falls outside of the *scope* of the constraint, no compensation is owed.

Absolutists concerning the constraint against doing harm will obviously have none of this. They may insist that liability can only arise if one has acted impermissibly; if someone gains a duty to compensate after harming another for the sake of some greater good, that just goes to show that there was no threshold, and the original harmful act was simply a *violation* of the constraint. Against this, however, moderate deontologists can put forward a more complex picture. On this alternative view, a given normative factor can be outweighed, even though it has genuine weight. And if (in some particular case) it is indeed outweighed, it will then be permissible—all things considered—to act against or "infringe" that factor. Yet even when the factor is outweighed, it does not vanish without a trace; it can still alter the configuration of what is, and what is not, required. In particular, then, even when the constraint against doing harm has been outweighed by other considerations, so that it is permissibly infringed, the factor may still play a role in generating a requirement to provide compensation. (In contrast—it might be suggested—when an act falls outside the *scope* of the constraint there is a sense in which the factor isn't really present at all; in such cases, then, it can have no similar "residual" influence.)

One final remark about the requirement to compensate. Fulfilling an obligation to compensate requires *doing* something. In particular, of course, it requires paying compensation; but at the moment I want to focus on the more general fact that meeting this obligation requires you to *do* something in the literal sense, to perform some kind of act. For this reason, a requirement to compensate is sometimes called a *positive duty*. In this regard, a requirement to compensate differs from the constraint against lying, which can be completely met by doing nothing at all. (Recall that the constraint against lying does not literally entail an obligation to tell the truth, since you can always keep your opinions to yourself.) No positive acts are required by the prohibition against lying; it suffices to refrain from performing any acts of the forbidden sort. For this reason, the constraint against lying is an example of a *negative duty*.

Now this distinction—between positive and negative duties—initially seems quite clear and robust. Positive duties *require* some kind of action, while negative duties merely *forbid* the wrong kind of action. And intuitively, at least, we typically have little difficulty classifying obligations as being of one type or the other. The constraint against killing, for example, is a negative duty, as is the constraint against inflicting pain. Similarly, if I promise to lend you my car, I now have a positive duty—to lend you my car.

In at least some cases, however, we find ourselves more puzzled. Consider the general requirement to keep your promises. At first glance, this may strike us as being a positive duty: to satisfy it you must *do* something, *keep* your promises. But our intuitions shift if we redescribe this very same requirement in the language of constraints. For now we have a constraint against *breaking* your promises, and this makes it sounds like a negative duty. So which is it? If the distinction between positive and negative duties is going to be of any significance, it had better be more than a momentary artifact of the language we happen to pick to describe our obligations.

More careful reflection upon the requirement to keep your promises suggests the following. The *particular* obligations that we find ourselves under, thanks to the specific promises that we have made, are often positive duties. Thus, promising can generate positive duties—to lend you my car, to meet you after work, or what have you. For the same reason, any particular promise made may well constitute a positive duty. But the *general* requirement to keep one's promises is actually—despite initial appearances—a *negative* duty. One can meet this obligation perfectly well without doing anything at all (provided that you make no promises), and this is the mark of a negative duty. Like all true negative duties, the requirement to keep your promises only forbids you to perform a certain kind of act (in this case, the complex act of making and then breaking a promise).

What the example of promising shows is that under the right circumstances a general negative duty can yield a particular positive duty. And once we put the point this way, we can see that the same thing is true for compensation and liability. There is a general requirement to compensate those one has harmed. Despite the "positive-sounding" nature of this language, however, this is actually a negative duty. (You can meet it perfectly well by doing nothing at all—that is, by not harming anyone.) But under the right circumstances (namely, harming someone), this negative duty can generate particular special obligations—to compensate this person or that person for the harm you have done them. And these particular obligations, as we have seen, are positive duties.

Notice, however, that for both compensation and promising, the specific positive duties can only be generated under the right circumstances. In particular, the positive duties can only be generated if you have performed the right kind of "triggering" act. (You have to have made a promise first, or harmed someone.) Is this true in general? Is it impossible to have a *positive* duty except in those cases where the agent has first triggered the obligation by performing some earlier act?

Many people find a view of this sort rather attractive. If it is correct, then it follows that one can avoid positive duties by taking care to avoid performing the relevant triggering actions. (In contrast, it should be noted, virtually no one is attracted to the view that *negative* duties have to be triggered in this way.) Some people go even further, claiming that positive duties can only be triggered by actions that are under one's voluntary control.

Is this last claim true? Consider a case where I have harmed someone, but I haven't done this deliberately (it was an accident). Does the requirement to compensate extend to cases like this as well? If it does—and I suspect that this is the majority view—then the relevant triggering act need not be a voluntary one, and the more ambitious claim is false. But the original, more modest suggestion might still be true: perhaps all positive duties must be triggered by *some* earlier act of the agent (whether voluntary or not).

It might be argued that even this more modest suggestion is shown to be false once we remember the first basic normative factor we identified—goodness of results. For we agreed long ago that one factor relevant to determining the moral status of an act was the good that would result from the act. Suppose, then, that I can do some good. To keep things simple, let us also assume that I can bring about this good result without violating any constraints. For example, suppose (as is indeed the case) that I could save the life of some child dying for lack of adequate nutrition by sending ten dollars to a famine relief organization. If no other factors are relevant to this case (I haven't promised the money to anyone else, I don't need it for medicine for my own children, and so on), aren't I morally required to contribute the money? And won't this constitute a *positive* duty (since I can't satisfy this obligation by doing nothing at all)? Yet my obligation here is generated by the mere fact that I have more money than I need, and others are starving through no fault of their own. That is, no prior triggering act on my part seems necessary for the existence of this positive duty. So positive duties don't always require earlier triggering acts on the part of the agent.

I must say that I find this argument rather compelling. But I realize that not everyone will. I take it to be reasonably uncontroversial that a requirement to contribute to famine relief—if there is such a requirement—will constitute a positive duty; I also assume that the requirement as I have described it is not triggered by any particular earlier act on my part. So the key question comes down to this: is there really a requirement to contribute in cases like this? More generally, can we legitimately talk of a *requirement* to promote the overall good? (When the focus is on helping others—as in our current example—those who accept such a requirement sometimes refer to it as a *duty of beneficence*.)

Not everyone is willing to accept such a requirement. And it should be noted that one can consistently deny the existence of such a requirement at the same time that one *affirms* that goodness of results is a genuine normative factor. For, as we have seen, factors can have other roles to play in determining the moral status of acts besides that of generating requirements. In particular, it seems possible to maintain that goodness of results can make an act morally commendable without making it morally required. And this might be what someone wants to say about giving the money to charity. (Similarly, moderate deontologists can hold that when enough good is at stake, this fact can make it permissible to infringe a given constraint; but they need not hold that it makes doing so obligatory.)

But can one plausibly maintain that one is never simply required to promote the good? Suppose I see a child drowning, and I have a spare life preserver in my hands. Surely I am required to throw it. And what explanation can we offer for this, except to say that in this case, at the very least, goodness of results has generated a requirement to act? It seems as though anyone hoping to capture our commonsense moral intuitions will have to concede this point.

There is, however, an alternative explanation. It might be suggested that what we have at work in the case of the drowning child is not mere goodness of results but rather a new factor altogether—the ability to directly *rescue* someone in immediate danger. Now, obviously, cases of rescue involve the opportunity to do good. But according to this alternative view, the mere fact that some act will have good results typically provides at best relatively weak reasons for doing that act. In contrast, in those special cases where we have the opportunity to directly rescue someone near to us in immediate need, we have extremely strong moral reason to do so. That some such distinction strikes us as intuitively plausible is revealed in the fact, already noted, that we normally take ourselves to be under no obligation to contribute to famine relief, whereas we would take ourselves to be under a weighty obligation to save the drowning child. Similarly, as a society we feel ourselves obligated to spend a considerable amount of money *rescuing* people (for example, miners in a collapsed mine, or infants born prematurely) even though we take ourselves to be under little or no obligation to spend significant amounts of money on *prevention* (increased mine safety, say, or prenatal care for pregnant women).

Thus, intuitively at least, rescuing appears to be a normative factor distinct from mere goodness of results—and a weightier one, to boot. Indeed, in cases where the two factors conflict, rescuing someone often seems more important than bringing about the best results. That is, if someone needs to be rescued, we often take ourselves to be obligated to expend what may end up being a considerable amount of money to save them; and we feel obligated to spend that money on the *rescue*—even if it could do far more good were it spent in other ways. In short, from the point of view of capturing certain common moral intuitions, it seems plausible to suggest that the requirement to rescue takes the form of a *constraint*.

Nonetheless, to say of such a constraint that it captures some of our common moral intuitions is not at all to say that it is easily justified. And on the face of it, it seems as though finding an adequate defense for such a constraint will be rather difficult. For if a requirement to rescue is indeed to be defended as something distinct from (and potentially opposed to) mere goodness of results, then we must find morally relevant distinctions between cases of rescue and other cases which are merely those of bringing about good results. Yet included in the latter will be cases of preventing deaths and tragedies every bit as horrible as those prevented in cases of rescue. Apparently, then, a defense of a special obligation to rescue will need to affirm the moral relevance of distinctions such as these: (1) the difference between those in need here and now and those merely in need elsewhere or in the future; (2) the difference between those victims whose identities are known to me and those who remain (for the time being, at least) mere faceless statistics; or (3) the difference between those who can be aided directly and immediately by my action and those who will be helped only indirectly and eventually.

Unfortunately, none of these distinctions seem especially plausible when stated so baldly; it is difficult to believe that any of them have much intrinsic moral significance, if any at all. But if distinctions of this sort cannot be defended, then we will have to conclude that a constraint based on these distinctions cannot be defended either. Accordingly, we may have to conclude that cases that we are intuitively inclined to classify as being instances of a special duty to rescue are nothing more than striking examples of a more general duty to promote the good, differing at best in terms of our emotional response.

Luckily, we need not try to settle this question here. For it will be recalled that the topic originally under investigation was whether all positive duties need to be triggered by earlier acts on the part of the agent. And this question, it seems, can safely be answered in the negative—at least by those who concede that there is some kind of duty to save the drowning child, however this duty is to be explained. Whether it is simply an instance of a general requirement to promote the good, or whether it is instead an instance of a more narrowly defined duty to rescue, either way it is a *positive* duty, and one that does not require any previous triggering act by the agent. So some positive duties, it seems, are "pure" (as we might put it) or "unconditional," in the sense that the existence of these duties is not conditional upon earlier actions of the agent. Apparently, sometimes being in the right place at the right time (or the wrong place at the wrong time?) may be enough.

Are there other examples of "pure" positive duties? Well, if there are special obligations of *gratitude,* then sometimes these may be pure in this way as well. Unfortunately, the nature of our obligations here is rather obscure. Suppose you freely bestow some good upon me, do me a favor, where this isn't the result of some obligation on your part, or the result of being coerced. Then I seem to be under a "debt of gratitude" to you. But what exactly do I owe you? At the very least, no doubt, I owe you a certain kind of positive regard, a feeling of appreciation and thanks. But many people feel that obligations of gratitude go beyond this, that there is also a requirement that I *return the favor.* Of course, I may not be able to literally duplicate the act, but there may be some other good that I can bestow upon you, where this seems a fitting repayment. Am I indeed obligated to do this?

It may be helpful to distinguish two types of case. In the first, I previously *asked* you to do me the favor. In the second, I made no such request; you acted, rather, on your own initiative. Of course, for either type of case, if repayment (rather than mere appreciation) is called for, the duties will be *positive,* in a robust sense, since specific types of acts will be required. But only in the second type of case would the duties be *pure* positive duties, for only there would the obligations be generated without having been triggered in any way by my own earlier actions. (In thinking about the first of these cases, it is important to bear in mind that I can ask for a favor without promising to pay it back. Thus so-called debts of gratitude should not be confused with more typical cases of debt, such as when I have promised to repay a loan.)

Many people have felt that there are such obligations of gratitude—even of the second sort. Indeed, it has often been suggested that such a general duty of gratitude may be the source of a number of other commonly accepted special obligations. For example, grown children may owe their parents support in their old age, out of gratitude for the love and support their parents gave them as children. Similarly, citizens may owe their society loyalty and obedience, in repayment for the education, protection, and other benefits that society has provided them. If gratitude can indeed generate these, or similar obligations, then we seem to have another class of pure positive duties. (Not that these particular derivations are unproblematic. Don't parents and societies themselves have *obligations* to provide these goods? If so, doesn't *gratitude* seem somewhat misplaced?)

It is, however, far from clear whether there is in fact any such requirement to repay favors. No doubt, grateful appreciation is always appropriate toward those who have done you some favor; but it is not at all clear whether more than this is normally called for. And it is particularly controversial whether there is a requirement to repay favors that were not requested. (Indeed, much of the skepticism is due to the very fact that such obligations would *not* be conditional upon one's own previous actions.) If nothing else, it is striking that belief in such a requirement is far less common nowadays than it was in other eras. Whereas previously gratitude might have been prominent on a list of normative factors, today its status is at best peripheral, and many, I think, would be skeptical of the existence of any such requirement at all.

Let me return now to a question we raised at the very beginning of this chapter, namely, whether all constraints are simply particular instances of the more general constraint against doing harm. We are now in a position to see just why it is so difficult to decisively settle this matter. Consider, first, constraints that represent *negative* duties—that is, duties which forbid you to perform a particular kind of act (either a simple act, such as lying, or a complex act, such as making and then breaking a promise). You violate such a duty by *doing* something, by performing the morally objectionable act. What we've seen, however, is that with sufficient ingenuity virtually any objectionable act can be shown to have a harmful aspect. And this then raises the possibility that it is the harmful nature of the act in question that explains and justifies the prohibition against performing acts of that kind. In short, for any negative duty, it will be difficult to decisively rule out the claim that the given duty derives from the general constraint against doing harm.

Thus, if we want to find a clear counterexample to the claim that all constraints derive from the constraint against doing harm, we have to focus on *positive* duties. But not all positive duties will do the trick either. For if the positive duty is conditional upon some earlier act on the part of the agent which helps to trigger that duty, then violation of that duty will still involve an objectionable action on the part of the agent—in particular, the *complex* act that consists of performing the triggering action and then *not* performing the requisite duty. But this complex act (commission followed by omission) may itself be harmful (think again about the complex act of making and then breaking a promise). And so, once again, it will be difficult to rule out the possibility that the specific duty in question is ultimately to be derived from the constraint against doing harm.

Suppose, however, that there were a positive duty that was not at all conditional upon an earlier triggering act on the part of the agent. If there were
such a duty, then—at last!—failure to meet it could not plausibly be construed as a case of doing harm. For the agent could fail to meet the duty
without having *done* anything at all. In sum, if we are to find a clear counterexample to the claim that all constraints derive from the constraint
against doing harm, we will need to point to cases of *pure* positive duties.

Now we have, in fact, identified three possible cases of pure positive duties: a duty to rescue, an obligation to repay unrequested favors, and a general requirement to promote the overall good. Obviously enough, the last
of these is irrelevant for our present purposes. Even if there is a requirement
to promote the good, since it clearly won't take the form of a constraint, it
might still be true that all *constraints* derive from the constraint against doing harm. That leaves us with just the first two duties (both of which, intuitively at least, do take the form of constraints). We can therefore say: *if*
there is indeed a special duty to rescue, or a duty of gratitude to repay unrequested favors, this will provide us with clear counterexamples to the claim
in question; *some* constraints will be distinct from the constraint against
doing harm. Unfortunately, as we have seen, it is controversial and uncertain whether either of these two constraints represents a genuine moral requirement. And what this means, of course, is that it is controversial and
uncertain whether there are indeed any constraints that cannot be derived
from the general constraint against doing harm. For the time being, at least,
the matter remains unsettled.

## 4.4  Conventions

As we have seen, special obligations (and the obligation-specific constraints
from which they can be derived) form a wide-ranging and varied group.
But that is not to say that we cannot generalize at all about them. On the
contrary, as we have also seen, many special obligations seem to be a function of the particular *roles* that the agent plays. I am a father, a teacher, and
a citizen, and as such I may have the various special obligations that go
along with having those roles. Other roles (nurse, judge, sibling) generate
other *role obligations*.

Are all special obligations role based in this way? The answer depends on
how broadly we are prepared to construe the notion of a "role." I suggested that all special obligations depend upon the agent's standing in the
relevant particular relationship to one or more specific individuals. If we
are prepared to talk of a *role* corresponding to each such relationship, then
indeed all special obligations are role based. If we do take this line, we will
have not only familiar roles of the kinds just mentioned—familial, occupa-
tional, and political roles—but other, potentially less familiar cases as well:
there will be the role of promisor, and the role of harm doer, and perhaps

the role of potential rescuer or the role of debtor for favors done, to mention just a few. For some of these it may be natural enough to think of the situation in terms of there being a role filled by the particular agent; for others this may seem to stretch the notion of "role" beyond its normal boundaries. But in principle there seems to be no reason why we couldn't think of all special obligations as being role obligations.

On the other hand, we might find it preferable to restrict talk of roles to cases where the specific obligations assigned seem to be largely a matter of *convention*. The contrast I have in mind is this. In some cases, the fact that an agent's standing in a given relationship to some individual generates the particular special obligations that it does seems a "natural" reflection of the relationship in question. This seems to be the case, for example, with the obligation to compensate another for the harm you have done them, or (if there is such an obligation) the duty to rescue. Here it seems appropriate to speak of a *natural duty*. In many other cases, however, it seems somewhat "arbitrary" or "artificial" which particular obligations are assigned to which relationships. This is clearly the case for a number of special obligations based on occupation. Consider, for example, the specific duties of being a nurse rather than a doctor, or being a lawyer rather than a judge. Within any given area, no doubt, some assignment of duties may be necessary and appropriate (and so the matter is not altogether arbitrary), but the particular assignment made seems largely a matter of convention. (Think of all the other ways that responsibilities could be divided up between doctors and nurses, say.) Accordingly, in such cases it seems appropriate to think of these duties as (largely being) *conventional*.

Although common usage hardly settles the matter, there is, I think, some tendency to restrict talk of "roles" to those cases where the particular special obligations attached to the role are conventional, at least to a significant degree. That may be the reason why it seems more natural to talk of the role of nurse, or teacher, or lifeguard than it is to talk of the role of potential rescuer, or debtor for favors done. Political roles seem similarly conventional (think of the different ways that duties of citizenship can be, and have been, assigned). Family roles make an interesting test case. To the extent that we think of parental obligations, say, as being natural, it seems correspondingly strained to talk of being a parent as a ("mere") role. But we may begin to think of the particular obligations assigned to some family position—say, that of being a mother—as largely a matter of convention (and perhaps in need of reform); if we do, it will seem more natural to talk in terms of family roles. Similar uncertainty may arise in other cases as well, where there is disagreement concerning the extent to which the assignment of duties is conventional (as in, for example, the case of promising, or friendship).

Obviously, it is not an especially pressing issue whether or not we adopt the proposal to restrict talk of roles (and role based obligations) to cases where the assignment of duties is largely conventional. But regardless of our decision, the distinction between natural and conventional duties seems an important one, and it prompts an obvious question: why do conventional duties have any moral force at all? What is the basis of their moral significance?

If we try to raise the corresponding question about some natural duty, the answer, presumably, is to be found through careful reflection upon the precise nature of the particular relationship upon which the natural duty is founded; the whole point of characterizing the duty as *natural* is to suggest that there is some essential connection between the grounding relationship and the ensuing duty. But when we are considering conventional duties there is no such essential connection; the assignment of particular duties to particular relationships is to a significant degree "arbitrary," a mere convention of a given society or group. Accordingly, if these duties truly have any moral force, the explanation of this force will largely have to appeal to the existence of these very conventions. But why should such conventions have any moral force at all?

Part of the answer, of course—and a significant part—is that well-designed conventions can be extraordinarily helpful in bringing about the best possible results. The point is probably obvious, but it is worth belaboring. First of all, by assigning particular duties to particular roles, a division of moral labor is achieved. Specific individuals can become specialists, learning to fulfill particular duties with a skill and efficiency that would otherwise be impossible. Division of moral labor can also promote a kind of coordination that would otherwise elude us. Each of us can devote special attention to the particular tasks assigned us, without worrying that other—equally significant—tasks are going unmet. The value of all of this can hardly be exaggerated. More generally, conventions generate stable and predictable patterns of behavior, allowing people to make informed plans, and permitting efficient interaction and coordination among independent individuals.

(Of course, not every logically possible convention would do the job well. Some conventions will be better suited than others. To this extent, it can be rather misleading to speak of the choice of conventions as *arbitrary.* But often enough, and to a significant degree, more than one pattern of behavior would work well, perhaps even equally well. Among these well-suited candidates it matters less *which* pattern is adopted than that *one* of them be adopted and generally conformed to. (The standard example here involves our conventions concerning which side of the street to drive on.) Often it is a matter of historical accident, or contingencies of the particular society or group, that determines which particular pattern is adopted. It is only to the extent that this is so, that it is appropriate to think of the obtaining of that pattern in the given society or group as *conventional.)*

By conforming to the particular conventions extant in our society—meeting our various role based obligations, and pressuring others to do the same—we do our part in sustaining these conventions, and thus help to bring about the various and sundry goods that these conventions contribute in the production of. In short, meeting our conventional duties is one way in which we can help bring about better results overall. Thus, to the extent that we have moral reason to promote the good, we have reason—other things being equal—to act on our conventional duties.

The argument just given appeals to consequences: conventions are mechanisms for achieving good results through coordination and division of labor. As such, it is available to all those who give moral weight to the promotion of the good. It should be noted, however, that this argument can only provide conventional duties with the status of being rules of thumb. All other things being equal, meeting our conventional duties will normally bring about better results overall; but other things are not always equal, and when even better results can be obtained by violating our conventional duties, the appeal to consequences will give no reason not to do this. Consequentialists, of course, will think that this is just as it should be. But deontologists are likely to believe that even conventional duties typically have the force of constraints. If so, further moral foundation for these conventional duties must be found.

Progress in this direction can be made by appeal to the constraint against breaking your promises. It can be argued, plausibly, that when you take on a well-articulated role in a society, you promise—whether explicitly, or implicitly—to fulfill the various special obligations conventionally assigned to that role. Provided that there is a clear understanding of the duties that come with the role—and in the absence of an explicit disclaimer—in signing on for the role you have promised to meet the various role based obligations that have been assigned to it. You have, in effect, promised to meet the conventions; and so, of course, the mere fact that the assignment of particular obligations to particular roles is indeed conventional does nothing to diminish the force of that promise. Given the assumption that the prohibition against promise breaking is indeed a constraint, this means that the various role based duties are constraints as well.

Clearly, the success of this argument depends upon the extent to which it is plausible to claim that a given agent has promised to fulfill the various duties conventionally assigned to her various roles. In some cases, obviously, the suggestion seems quite plausible indeed—the agent might, for example, take an oath of office, explicitly stating her agreement to meet a specified list of duties. In other cases, however, a person taking on a role may not at first appreciate or grasp all the relevant duties. Or there may not be anything recognizably like an act of promising when the role is entered into. In such cases, unfortunately, a promise-based account of conventional duties seems less plausible.

There is another moral principle—one that we've not yet considered—that may have a role in grounding conventional duties as well, *the principle of fair play.* The idea here is this. Often we are participants in a group practice of some sort, a practice from which we have received and are continuing to receive benefits, and from which the other members of the group benefit as well. Maintaining the practice, keeping it going, typically requires contributions of some sort on the part of the members of the group. Suppose that others have been making their contributions, and now—according to the rules of the practice—it is your turn. The principle of fair play holds that you are indeed required to make the relevant contribution, to do your fair share toward maintaining the mutually beneficial practice.

For example, you might be a member of a discussion group, which meets monthly. Each month, a different member of the group brings refreshments. Suppose that this has been going on for several months, and each month you have happily eaten the food provided by others. Now it is your turn. According to the principle of fair play, you have an obligation—owed to the other members of the group—to do your fair share, and provide refreshments. Note, however, that no suggestion is being made that you have *promised* to take your turn. The claim, rather, is that it is only *fair* for you to do so, given that you have knowingly participated up to this point (and given that there is no particular reason why you should be exempted, and so on).

In the example just given, the practice in question was quite simple and relevant only for a small group. But in principle there is no reason why considerations of fair play should not be relevant for quite complex practices as well—with different responsibilities assigned to different individuals. And there is no reason why the relevant group might not be rather large, extending perhaps to an entire society. In this way, it might be suggested, the principle of fair play can help to explain the moral force of conventional duties. We can think of the entire set of conventional duties as forming part of an elaborate moral practice from which we all benefit. Provided that others have been doing their share—meeting their conventionally assigned duties— and you have been receiving the benefits from all of this, considerations of fair play require you to do your share as well, that is, to meet your own conventionally assigned duties. Finally, if we assume that the principle of fair play is indeed a constraint (since you are required to do your part when it is your turn, even if more good might be attainable otherwise), then we have again provided a deontological basis for conventional duties.

Some indeed might want to take this line of argument even further. For why should it be only conventional duties that get defended in this way? Perhaps all duties—indeed all other moral principles altogether—should be justified by appeal to the principle of fair play. That is, perhaps we should think of *all* of morality as a mutually beneficial practice in which we are continuously participating. And so, given that others are doing their fair share in keeping the practice going—meeting their various duties—each of us is in turn obligated by considerations of fairness to obey the various moral principles as well.

If we do take this extreme view, then in effect there will only be one basic normative factor: fair play. The moral significance of all other normative factors will derive from this single one. The view will thus be a form of normative *monism*—like consequentialism in this regard, and unlike the more pluralistic deontological views that we have been considering, in which there is more than one basic normative factor. Unlike consequentialism, however, the current view would be a version of *deontological* monism.

I won't try to evaluate the various strengths and weaknesses of deontic monism based on fair play. I only want to note that one can resist going this far, while still embracing the more modest proposal to justify all conventional duties in terms of fair play. That is, even if one is a normative pluralist, endorsing the existence of several distinct basic normative factors, it might still be the case that all conventional duties ultimately do derive their force from the principle of fair play. More modestly still, perhaps certain conventional duties can be justified in this way, even if not all of them can.

It should be borne in mind, however, that the possibility of deriving any duties at all from the principle of fair play ultimately depends upon whether the principle of fair play is itself plausible. A judgment on this question depends in turn on how exactly the principle is to be stated. Surely not any practice whatsoever is sufficient to generate a moral requirement to make whatever contribution may happen to be stipulated by that practice. The basic idea, of course, is that the practice must rather be a *fair* one.

At the very least—or so advocates of the principle normally assume—this means that the practice must be mutually beneficial. That is, all those being asked to make a contribution toward maintaining the practice must benefit from the existence of that practice. But this condition does not yet seem sufficient. The distribution of benefits must itself be fair; if some get more than others, there must be good reason for this. Similarly, the distribution of burdens under the practice must be fair as well; if some are asked to contribute more than others, there must be good reason for this too. Nor is it obvious that this is yet enough. It is often suggested, for example, that it is only fair to require an individual to contribute to a practice if she has *already* benefited from that practice, if she freely accepted that benefit, and if she did so *knowing* that under the rules of the practice she would be obligated to make the contribution to the practice. Unless benefits have been freely and knowingly accepted in this way, fair play may not generate any kind of requirement at all. (Note that in the absence of such qualifications, the principle of fair play would have been able to generate pure positive duties; with these qualifications in place, however, there must first be something like a triggering act on the part of the agent.)

With these qualifications in place, should the principle of fair play now be accepted? The matter remains controversial. Some think that further qualifications must be added as well but that a sound version of the principle of fair play can nonetheless be articulated. Others claim, however, that no robust version of the principle of fair play will stand up to critical scrutiny. I won't try to settle this debate here, but I do want to make two further points. First, the more we move in the direction of requiring that benefits first be freely and knowingly accepted, the more plausible it becomes to view the agent as having made an implicit *promise* to obey the rules governing the practice. Thus, even if there is a sound version of the principle of fair play, despite initial appearances it may not actually point to a normative factor distinct from that of promising. Second, and independently of the first point, the more we qualify the principle of fair play—the more conditions that must be met before it can generate a requirement—the more difficult it will be to bring that principle to bear in any given case. Accordingly, the suggestion that all conventional duties can be defended by appeal to fair play becomes increasingly more difficult to maintain. Even if there is a sound version of the principle of fair play—and even if it is distinct from the requirement to keep your promises—it seems likely that in at least some cases, for the conventional duties of some individuals, the relevant conditions will not all be met.

How, then, are conventional duties to be defended? Perhaps instead of having a single basis, the situation is more like that of a patchwork quilt. Different conventional duties may have different bases. We have already noted the possible relevance of consequences, of promising, and of fair play. In any given case, one or more of these may be at work—and no doubt other factors may be relevant as well. (For example, some would argue that one has an obligation to obey the conventions of one's society out of gratitude for benefits received.)

Before leaving the topic of conventional duties, it may be useful to make some brief remarks about *property*. A *property regime* can be thought of as consisting of a set of rules. These rules govern: (1) the acquisition of previously unowned objects; (2) the transfer of ownership from one person to another; and (3) the treatment of objects that are owned. Among other things, these rules assign various special obligations and duties. The most familiar such duties will involve obligations on the part of those who do *not* own a given object not to *use* that object in various ways (not to move it, for example, or not to consume it). But, although they come to mind less readily, there might also be special duties incumbent upon the *owner* (for example, to preserve or to enhance the object, or to transfer it to some other individual). Different property regimes can be distinguished in terms of the details of these rules and the different duties that they entail.

As usual, consequentialists will view these duties as mere rules of thumb—extremely useful for coordinating the efficient use of resources, but lacking any normative force beyond that. And, also as usual, deontologists will view the duties instead as having the force of constraints. But the point I want to make here is a different one, namely, that the rules (and ensuing duties) do indeed vary widely from one possible property regime to the next—in terms of who can own what, and what they can do with it, and what others may and may not do, and so forth. (Just to scratch the surface, consider regimes with private property versus collective ownership, or differences over whether ownership of land is in perpetuity, or questions about the possibility of owning "ideas.") It has seemed to many people, intuitively, that within quite a wide range, any number of distinct property regimes would be morally permissible. And this has suggested, in turn, that the duties arising from property are themselves *conventional;* that is, what particular property-related obligations we have depends, in large part, on the particular property regime that has been adopted by our society.

Although this is a common view, it is by no means the only possible view. Many have held that property-related obligations are actually *natural* duties. The most common view of this sort holds that, under the right conditions, ownership of external objects ("second property") follows logically from ownership of one's own body and labor ("first property"); and it does seem plausible to suggest that ownership of oneself is a natural moral fact, rather than being merely conventional.

Of course, even if it is conceded that first property is owned naturally rather than conventionally, it is not at all obvious that we can derive rules governing second property from those governing first property. That is to say, even if we "naturally" own our own bodies, ownership of external objects might still be conventional. Unfortunately, the various arguments relevant to this issue are quite complex, and we cannot pursue them further here. But it should be noted that, to the extent that one finds it plausible that a *range* of property regimes would all be morally acceptable, it is almost inevitable that convention will play at least some role in determining our actual property-related obligations.

In any event, it is also important to emphasize that adopting a conventionalist approach to property does not at all mean that *every* property regime is morally acceptable (provided only that it has been adopted by the society). To take the obvious example, property regimes that permit the owning of slaves are unacceptable. And—to take a far more controversial example—it has often been argued that capitalist property regimes are morally unacceptable as well.

How can this be? If the relevant property-related obligations are conventional, doesn't anything go? But it is important to bear in mind that we are not interested in the empirical question of what kinds of conventions have been or can be adopted by society. We are investigating, rather, when (if ever) those conventions have any moral force. And our tentative answer has been that conventional duties have moral force *when they do* by virtue of the good consequences of those conventions, promises made to obey them, considerations of fair play, and so on. Clearly enough, none of these potential justifications will support a property regime that permits slavery. (To state the obvious: slaves have not promised to be slaves, benefits and burdens are not fairly distributed among slaves and slave owners, and societies with slaves hardly maximize the good, counting everyone equally.) Thus, despite the fact that a society may have adopted a regime that permits slavery, none of the conventionally assigned duties relevant to the ownership of slaves will have any moral force.

This point is, of course, a general one. It covers not only property regimes (assuming, for the sake of argument, that these are indeed conventional) but all conventional duties whatsoever. The mere existence of a convention does not in and of itself guarantee that the duties assigned by that convention have any moral force. Conventionally assigned duties only have moral force when this can be derived from something else—consequences, fairness, promising, and so on. If one or more of these factors supports the convention, then to that extent the duties assigned by that convention will indeed be genuine moral duties. Often enough this is just what happens. But it does not always happen. Some conventional duties have no moral force at all.

It should be noted, finally, that even if a convention does succeed in generating some genuine moral duties, this is no reason to assume that the convention is therefore impervious to moral critique. Perhaps only certain aspects of the convention are morally legitimate. If so, only some of the duties assigned by that convention will have force. Or perhaps the convention—despite being fair and beneficial on the whole—could be improved. Then we must work to improve it. To say that a convention has moral legitimacy—and that its duties are real—is not to say that the convention is morally perfect. Conventional duties can often be improved upon.

## 4.5 Duties to Oneself

There is one further class of special obligations that warrants particular attention: duties to oneself. Are there any such duties? The issue is surprisingly controversial. Traditionally, I think, there would have been nothing especially contentious about the suggestion that there are moral restrictions on how I may treat myself. Nowadays, however, many find the notion of moral duties owed to *oneself* somehow suspect.

It is sometimes claimed that talk of duties to oneself simply makes no sense, since such duties would have nothing to do with the basic point of morality, which is to govern our treatment of *others*. Morality, it might be suggested, is a matter of counting others equally, not harming them, not lying to them, and so forth; in a word, the essential outlook of morality is *other-regarding*. In contrast, duties to oneself, if there were any such thing, would be *self-regarding*, and as such they fall outside the scope of morality altogether. In short, the only genuinely moral duties concern how we behave toward others; given the very nature of morality, there are—and can be—no duties to oneself.

Of course, given the existence of duties to others, we might well have *derivative* duties concerning ourselves. For example, I might have a duty to keep myself fit, so as to be able to meet my obligations to my children. But these would not be duties I owe to *myself*. Duties that are truly duties to oneself make no sense. Or so the claim goes.

Clearly, whether a position of this sort is right depends on a number of metaethical issues concerning the purpose and extent of morality. Given a conception of the nature of morality as essentially other-regarding, duties to oneself will simply be impossible. But there are other metaethical conceptions which take a broader view of morality than this. According to one such broader conception, although the moral point of view certainly includes other-regarding concerns, it is not necessarily exhausted by them; there may be a place for self-regarding considerations as well. If so, the possibility of duties to oneself cannot be ruled out. (There are, of course, still other metaethical conceptions, including some for which self-regarding considerations are absolutely central to the moral enterprise.)

Given the limited scope of the present book, we cannot undertake to adjudicate between these rival metaethical positions. For the sake of argument, therefore, let's tentatively adopt the more tolerant point of view. That is, let's assume that the possibility of duties to oneself cannot be ruled out by metaethical considerations alone. That doesn't yet give us any reason to believe that there *are* any moral duties to oneself; it simply leaves the possibility open.

Where, then, should we look to find plausible duties to oneself? A natural place to start is by considering the implications of the various normative factors that we have already identified. Of course, up to this point, when exploring the different normative factors, I have cast the discussion in terms of the treatment of others: I've talked about harming others, for example, or keeping the promises you have made to them, or compensating them for harm you have done to them, and so forth. No doubt, doing things this way has implicitly suggested that the factors have a restricted scope—that they only apply to my treatment of everyone *else*. But despite this, it does seem possible (at least, until we discover otherwise) to view the factors as actually having a very wide scope, so that they govern my treatment of absolutely *everyone*—not just my treatment of others, but my treatment of myself as well. Thus, if we make the tentative assumption that the factors are truly universal in this way, we will want to investigate the possibility and moral implications of harming myself, lying to myself, making promises to myself, and so on for all the other normative factors as well.

Now for some of these factors, it is fairly simple to think of cases to which they apply that involve only me. For example, I am certainly capable of harming myself. Similarly, I am also capable of benefiting myself—promoting my own well-being and thereby promoting the overall good. Of course, this is not yet to say that these factors have any genuine moral

weight in cases where they apply; it is merely to make the *logical* point that
it is at least possible to do these sorts of things to myself.

With some of the other factors, however, things are much less straightforward. As soon as we try to apply them to cases involving only me, we seem
to run up against logical difficulties. It is puzzling whether it even makes
sense to try to imagine an act of the relevant kind. For example, it is not at
all obvious whether it is possible for me to rescue myself, or to lie to myself,
or to compensate myself. Here too, the question is not the moral one—
should these factors have any moral weight in these cases?—but rather a
logical one: can the factors in question even so much as apply? Is it even
possible to *do* these sorts of things to myself?

In principle, it certainly seems possible that there might be certain types
of acts that I can do to others which I simply cannot do to myself. If so,
then rules governing these acts will never have any relevance in cases involving only me. And this may well be the situation for some of our normative factors. In other cases, however, even though it seems strange to apply
the normative factor, it is not literally *impossible* to behave in the relevant
way toward myself. Perhaps in these cases the difficulty is actually more
like this: on any plausible construal of the factor in question, that factor
will only be relevant when certain conditions are met; and it may be impossible to meet some of those conditions in cases involving only me.

But even if we restrict our attention to factors where these logical difficulties don't arise, once we turn to the moral question of whether these factors should be given any weight in those cases where they do apply, a perfectly general problem crops up. For if what is in question is only my
treatment of myself, it is obvious that I will always be acting with the *consent* of the person I am affecting. And as we have previously noted, on
many views consent robs a constraint of its normal force. Consider, for example, the constraint against doing harm. Normally, it is impermissible to
perform an act if it would involve harming someone. But not, as we have
seen, if you have the permission of the person you are harming; consent of
the victim removes the act from the scope of the constraint. Yet isn't it clear
that if I deliberately harm myself, I have my own permission to do so? If so,
then at best this will be a case of my permissibly infringing the constraint,
rather than my violating it. More generally, whatever the constraint, if consent removes an act from the scope of that constraint, then I always act permissibly in my treatment of myself. Given the force of consent, and given
the necessity of there being consent (when "victim" equals agent), there
simply cannot be any duties to myself.

Obviously enough, this argument can be resisted by those who deny the
relevance of consent. But less obviously, it can also be resisted by those who
do accept the relevance of consent—provided that they believe that the
force of consent is restricted. Recall the possibility (noted in 3.3) that consent may only work in those cases where the agent has good reasons for

giving that consent. If a view like this is correct, then the mere fact that I necessarily act with my own permission may not be enough to remove my actions from the scope of the various relevant constraints. To return to the earlier example, if I harm myself—and lack adequate reason for doing so—this may well constitute a violation of the constraint against doing harm. At the very least, the mere fact that I consented to my having harmed myself will not be sufficient to show that I have acted permissibly. In short, even if the presence of consent is morally relevant, it won't necessarily follow that anything goes in my treatment of myself.

(A view of this more circumscribed sort seems especially plausible in those cases where my current action affects me, but only much later. Here, it seems more natural to think of the relationship between my present self and my future self as more like that obtaining between two different individuals. All that my current act guarantees is the consent of my present self. But it may well be the consent of my future self that is relevant for waiving the protection of the constraint; and when the time comes, it may be lacking.)

If we assume—if only for the sake of argument—that the force of consent is not unlimited, the possibility of duties to oneself now seems a live one. For if some normative factors can appear even in cases involving only me, and if my consent does not automatically guarantee the permissibility of my action, then in at least some cases my behavior may well involve violating obligations that govern my treatment of myself.

Accordingly, let's review the different normative factors in systematic fashion, beginning with the constraint against doing harm. As we have already observed, I am certainly capable of harming myself. Is it wrong to do so? Not, it seems, if I have good reasons for doing this. I might for example, sacrifice my life so as to save that of my friends or loved ones. Or, more commonly still, I might *risk* harm to myself for the sake of some valuable goal. But it is also obvious that I am capable of harming myself in situations where I lack adequate reasons for doing this. I might, for example, ingest poison on a dare, or cut off my nose to spite my face. Here, it seems, we might well want to claim that such acts violate a moral duty not to harm myself.

Certainly the most familiar duty of this sort is the commonly accepted prohibition against committing suicide. Often, this prohibition is thought to be absolute. But if the prohibition against suicide derives from the constraint against doing harm, and if consent can undermine the force of that constraint, then it is likely that this absolutism must be rejected. Obviously, those who think the force of consent is unlimited will simply dismiss a prohibition against suicide altogether. But even if consent is only effective in those cases where the person has good reasons to consent, suicide will still sometimes be permissible—provided that in some cases one can have good reason to kill oneself. And it seems clear that one can have such reasons. For example, you might be suffering from a painful and untreatable illness, or you may have become so incapacitated that your future holds no possibility of the goods that make life worthwhile. (In cases like this, is it still accurate to say that in killing yourself you are *harming* yourself? On a global view of harm, perhaps not (see 3.3); but on a local conception of harm it will be.) Of course, to say that suicide is not always wrong is not the same as saying that it is never wrong. If you lack good reasons, then killing yourself will be immoral.

Obviously, the absolutist concerning suicide will think that such a moderate position does not go far enough. It is, however, difficult to see how to avoid some kind of moderate position here. For it is important to bear in mind that in at least some cases people kill themselves as a way of *saving* the lives of *others*. Such acts of self-sacrifice are almost universally praised—but it is unclear how they can even be *permissible* if there is an absolute prohibition against killing oneself. It is only if we assume that consent (backed by good reasons) eliminates the force of the constraint against doing harm that the permissibility of self-sacrifice becomes explicable. But if consent can have this effect when our goal is to help others, there is no reason to think that it cannot have this effect when our goal is instead to minimize our own future suffering, as in more typical cases of suicide.

In any event, as this discussion makes clear, it does not seem altogether implausible to think that one or more normative factors may indeed generate duties to oneself. At the very least, this seems to be a plausible position with regard to the constraint against doing harm.

What about the requirement to keep your promises? The situation here is somewhat more obscure, but it is not obviously impossible to make a promise to myself. If I do, must I keep it? As usual, consent seems relevant—since I can be released from a promise by the person to whom I have made the promise. But it is at least arguable that such a release isn't effective if it is given without good reason. So suppose that I have promised myself to do something, and have no good reason to release myself from my vow. Perhaps in such a case there is indeed a special obligation to keep the promise that I have made. If so, then we have a second possible source of duties to oneself.

For other constraints, however, the attempt to derive such duties seems much less straightforward. Consider, for example, the constraint against lying. As we have previously noted, it is not at all clear that it is even so much as possible to tell a lie to myself. I can certainly say something that I don't believe; but I may not be able to do this with the intention of deceiving myself. If this is right, then the prohibition against telling lies may have no possible relevance in cases involving only me. (On the other hand, we do talk about the possibility of self-deception, and we normally take this to involve some kind of moral shortcoming. Is this a simple application of a more general prohibition against being deceptive? That seems wrong; but the issues are too complicated to pursue here.)

Or consider the obligation to compensate those we have harmed. If I harm myself—do I then owe myself compensation? One possible complication, of course, is that compensation may not be owed when one has the consent of the person harmed. On the other hand, even with consent, compensation might be owed anyway, if the person consented without good reason. So suppose that I have indeed harmed myself without adequate reason: must I now compensate myself for this? Obviously, however, it is rather difficult to get a grip on what compensation would come to in a situation like this. I can hardly transfer resources from myself to myself in an effort to make myself whole. So this constraint too may have no implications in cases involving only me. (Am I perhaps obligated to *use* the resources I already have—so as to undo the damage I have done to myself?)

An obligation to rescue seems equally unpromising as a source of duties to myself. No doubt, I can sometimes rescue myself from danger. But even if we assume that there is indeed an obligation to rescue those in danger, presumably the obligation only extends to those cases where the people in danger are incapable of saving *themselves*. So if I am *capable* of rescuing myself from some danger I find myself in, a relevant background condition won't have been met; the special obligation to rescue simply won't become engaged. Similarly for the principle of fair play: presumably if all the members of some practice choose to stop that practice, they are not being unfair to one another; so in "practices" involving only me, fair play won't be violated if I decide against carrying on. And a similar point seems true—finally—for gratitude. Even if there are obligations to repay favors, such an obligation is discharged once the recipient of the favor has done something comparable for the benefactor. But in cases where I do something for myself, the recipient *has* already benefited the benefactor (since the recipient is the benefactor), and so there can be no further debt.

This leaves us with just one further factor (of those already identified): goodness of results. Presumably my own well-being is a component of the overall good. Furthermore, I am obviously in a position to affect it. At the very least then, if my action will benefit me in some way, it seems plausible to think that this is a factor that will be relevant in determining morally what I should do. (For example, it seems permissible to count my own good in determining whether the threshold for some constraint has been met; I need not limit myself to considering the good that is at stake for others.) But can there be a *duty* to benefit myself? As we saw, it is somewhat controversial whether there can ever be a requirement to promote the good. But if there can be such a requirement, then why shouldn't my own good count too? Perhaps, then, there is a duty to benefit myself, to promote my own well-being. This is sometimes called a duty of *prudence* (although this often suggests an element of exaggerated cautiousness or frugality that is not relevant to our present concern).

Nowadays, it is more typical to think of the requirement to promote one's own well-being as a requirement of *rationality* rather than of *morality*. But we began this section by putting aside the metaethical assumption that moral requirements can only be based on other-regarding considerations. And once we have done this, it is not at all clear why a requirement to promote my own overall well-being or happiness should not be considered one of my moral duties. Of course, it might be suggested that talk of a *duty* in this context makes no sense, since each person will inevitably do what he can to promote his own happiness. However, a moment's reflection shows that this is unduly optimistic: people often fail to have sufficient regard for their future.

The argument that I have just given for a duty to promote one's own well-being derives that duty from the more general requirement to promote the good. Defended in this way, the duty is only a rule of thumb. If even more good could be done overall by benefiting others, rather than by nurturing my own future well-being, there is no objection to my doing this. But some may think this casts the duty in too weak a form. It might be suggested that it is wrong for me to sacrifice my own well-being even if this leads to a net *gain* in the overall good—at least, it's wrong if the incremental overall gain is slight. Doing this is "selling" myself "too cheaply." That is to say, perhaps there is a *constraint* against forgoing my own future well-being, even if doing so would lead to some modest increase in the overall good. Such a constraint certainly need not be absolute. When the gain to others is *significant,* it may well be permissible to sacrifice my own welfare. The point is simply that it may not be permissible to do this when the net gain is minimal.

Note that if there were such a constraint, it would be a pure positive duty: I would be required to promote my own well-being, and this requirement would not have been triggered by any earlier action on my part. Furthermore, it does not seem possible to derive this constraint from any of our earlier examples of pure positive duties. On the one hand, a requirement to promote my own well-being does not seem explicable in terms of a duty to rescue or in terms of obligations of gratitude. And on the other hand, as we have just seen, if the requirement to promote my own well-being is indeed to have the force of a constraint (rather than being a mere rule of thumb), it cannot be derived from a requirement to promote the overall good. Therefore, if there is such a constraint, we will have identified a new basic normative factor—albeit one that only concerns my treatment of myself.

However, it is not at all clear that there is any such constraint. Put aside the obvious point that the consequentialist will reject it (since the consequentialist rejects all constraints). Even deontologists are likely to find the constraint we are considering problematic. For it should be noted that if there were such a constraint, it would go well beyond saying that everyone is to count equally. It does not merely require you to view your own well-being as no less important than that of everyone else (our original rule of thumb did that). Nor does it even stop with saying that you are sometimes *permitted* to count your own well-being more heavily than that of others (a possibility to be considered in the next chapter). Rather, the constraint says that you are morally *required* to give your own well-being more weight than that of others. And it is difficult to believe that any such requirement could be mandated from the *moral* point of view.

In any event, it is important not to confuse the constraint we are considering with the more modest duty of *self-respect*. To respect yourself is to recognize your own worth and value (and to act upon this recognition). So a duty of self-respect might plausibly be thought to have several components. First, you are required to count your own well-being as no less important than that of others. Second, you are required to "make something of yourself"—to develop your talents in such a way as to promote your own well-being, as well as contribute to the overall good. Third, recognizing that you have the same moral value as others, you are required to "stand up for your rights"—to protest and defend yourself against mistreatment at the hands of others. All three of these more specific duties can be readily embraced without endorsing a constraint requiring you to promote your own well-being even when greater good can be done for others. Of course, one might try to argue that such a constraint is in fact a fourth component of the duty of self-respect. But this fourth component seems much more controversial than the first three; and at any rate, it does not seem especially plausible to suggest that I fail to show adequate self-respect if I make a sacrifice so that others may gain even more.

Are there any other special obligations that I owe to myself? It might be noted that all the suggestions we have been examining concern natural duties, so perhaps we should end by considering the possibility of *conventional* duties to oneself. In principle, it must be admitted, it does seem possible that a society might conventionally assign each of its members a set of duties governing each person's treatment of himself. In terms of their *content,* then, such duties would be self-regarding. Assuming, however, that these conventions derive their moral force in the normal way—that is, via promises, fair play, or overall consequences—the *source* of the moral force of such duties would actually be other-regarding. Thus, allegiance to any such conventional duties would be owed primarily to others. Despite appearances, then, even if there are duties of this sort, it does not seem especially helpful to think of them as being duties owed *to oneself.*

# 5

# FURTHER
# FACTORS

## 5.1 Demanding Too Much

In the last three chapters we have examined a number of different norma-tive factors. I have not attempted an exhaustive survey of all the normative factors that have ever been endorsed, nor even all those that have been en-dorsed in the name of commonsense morality. But I have, I believe, at least touched upon most of the significant factors recognized by our common moral intuitions (although it must be admitted that, for the most part, con-ventional duties were only discussed as a class). Each of these factors, as we saw, is surrounded by controversy. In some cases, it is controversial whether the factor truly has any significance at all from the moral point of view. In other cases, it is unclear whether the factor matters in its own right—that is, whether it belongs on a list of *basic* normative factors—or whether, alternatively, it derives its significance from some other, more fun-damental factor. And in every case there were questions of detail concern-ing the precise content of the factor or its scope.

But despite these controversies, and despite the apparent diversity of the factors in question, there is a common theme that emerges. Or rather, it emerges once we include one or more factors beyond our first, goodness of consequences. That common theme consists in an attack on consequential-ism. More particularly, it consists in the objection that consequentialism *per-mits too much,* that is, that consequentialism is inadequate as a moral theory because it permits actions that are not, in fact, morally permissible (see 3.1).

Obviously enough, this is a claim that is denied by consequentialists; but it is the acceptance of this claim that unites deontologists, all of whom fault consequentialism for failing to incorporate one or another constraint. In-deed, from the intuitive point of view (if nothing else), virtually all of the factors that we identified in the last two chapters provide support for the objection that consequentialism permits too much. Harm doing, promises, lies, liability, fair play, and so forth—each of these, intuitively, takes the form of a constraint. That is to say, from the point of view of commonsense morality each factor is capable of outweighing the good, not necessarily in every case, but in at least many cases. Thus, even if an act would have the best possible results, it might still be forbidden to perform that act, once *all* the morally relevant factors are taken into account. If consequentialists don't see this (so the objection goes), that's because they fail to recognize the intrinsic normative significance of these other factors. The result, of course, is that consequentialism permits any number of acts that are actually morally forbidden. Consequentialism permits too much.

But this objection—significant though it may be—is not the only way in which consequentialism gives what is intuitively the wrong answer. Consequentialism also *demands* too much. Or at least, so it is often claimed. According to this second objection, consequentialism requires the agent to make sacrifices that go beyond what morality actually requires. It requires acts that, although permissible, are not in fact mandatory; it is simply too demanding.

To see this—and to see that this is indeed a different objection from the complaint that consequentialism permits too much—let's consider a case where there is some good to be done, and let's also assume that the good can be achieved without violating (or infringing) any constraints. Building on an example introduced earlier (in 4.3), suppose (as is indeed the case) that by sending ten dollars to a suitable charity you could save the life of a child who would otherwise die. Imagine, then, that you are about to spend this much to see a movie. But as you approach the ticket office, someone collecting for the charity asks you to skip the movie and make a contribution of the money instead. Clearly you are *permitted* to do this; normally, after all, one has no special obligation to see a movie. But are you morally *required* to make the contribution?

From the consequentialist perspective, answering the question requires comparing two possible outcomes. On the one hand, you could go to the movie and enjoy yourself for a few hours; on the other hand, you could forgo the movie, and save a child's life. Now on any plausible theory of the good, the pleasure you get from seeing the movie will count for *something*—but saving the life of the child will count for much, much more. So in terms of outcomes, the results will be much better *overall* (that is, counting everyone equally) if you give the money to the charity rather than spending it on the movie. But consequentialism says that you are required to perform the act that will have the best results overall. And so (assuming that there is no third act available to you right now that would have even better results) you are indeed required to make the contribution. Going to the movie is morally *forbidden*.

I suspect, however, that the most common response to this case would be rather different. I take it that a more typical view would maintain that although it would be morally *meritorious* for you to make this sacrifice, you are certainly not morally *required* to make it. Sacrificing your personal pleasure in this way is above and beyond the call of duty; it is *supererogatory* (a term traditionally used to mark acts that, although meritorious, are not obligatory). Matters would no doubt be quite different if it were somehow your fault that the child was in need; then you might well have a special obligation to provide aid. But in the situation we are imagining, where you are not at all responsible for the plight of the child, making the sacrifice is doing more than morality requires of you.

Of course, not everyone will accept this less demanding judgment concerning our case. Intuitions differ here, and some will find it more plausible to maintain that you are indeed required to contribute your ten dollars, rather than going in to see the movie. So it is important to see how easily the demands of consequentialism get extended. Let's continue our story. Suppose that you agree to make the contribution, rather than see the movie. You place the money in the can of the woman collecting for the charity, and you go home. Next weekend, however, you are once again looking for something to do, and so you head off again to the movie. But the woman is there again too, and she makes the same request. When you point out that you gave last week, she points out that there are, of course, many other children still in need. And so you face the same choice that you faced last week: a few hours pleasure, or saving the life of an innocent child.

From the standpoint of consequentialism, the answer is again straightforward: you are morally required to make the contribution. But even those who believe that you were required to do this the first week may be less confident that you are similarly obligated the second time around. In any event, we can imagine the same thing happening, week after week. Eventually, the woman points out that since there are literally millions of children who die each year, each of whom could be saved with a few dollars, it is unlikely that you will ever be justified in going to see a movie. You might as well go home and write one big check to the charity covering all the money you would have spent on movies for the coming year. According to consequentialism, it seems, this too is required.

By now, far fewer people will be prepared to embrace the judgment of consequentialism. Almost everyone will think that consequentialism has gone too far, demanded too much. Although it might well be morally praiseworthy to give up on movies altogether, so as to spend the money saved on others, doing so is supererogatory. Making such a sacrifice goes beyond what morality genuinely requires of us.

In fact, however, we have barely begun to scratch the surface of the demands of consequentialism. For it is obvious that there is nothing special about the movies to make them unusually vulnerable to consequentialist considerations. You are on your way to buy a stereo, when it occurs to you that the hundreds of dollars could do far more good were they sent instead to an appropriate charity. You are on your way out to eat, when it occurs to you that you could eat at home far more cheaply, and the extra money could be sent to charity as well. Similar thoughts occur to you as you set out to purchase expensive gifts for your friends, a luxury automobile, or comfortable furniture. In each case there is some "bare bones" alternative available to you, and the savings could be sent to charity. Again, the claim of the consequentialist is not that the sacrifices you might make do not count—your own well-being and that of your family and friends certainly need to be counted along with that of everyone else. But given that far *more* good would be done if you made the various sacrifices, this is what you are morally required to do. In short, if consequentialism is to be believed, a huge percentage of your income must be devoted to promoting the greater good. To fail to do this is to live in a manner forbidden by morality.

(Exactly how much would you have to give? Up to that point where giving any more reduces your net contribution to the overall good. For example, further sacrifice on your part might damage your ability to hold down your job—you might need a car to get to work, say—and without a job your ability to contribute to the greater good will obviously be impaired. Or it might be that in some case a particular sacrifice would damage your own well-being more than it will contribute to that of others. And so on. It may be difficult to know exactly how large a sacrifice would be involved in your greatest possible contribution to the overall good; but it does seem clear that it would be tremendously larger than the sacrifices most of us make, or that most of us believe we are required to make.)

Nor do the demands of consequentialism stop here. For the only sacrifices that have been considered so far are sacrifices of money (and the things that money can buy). However, similar sacrifices of time and effort can be required as well. Having forsworn movies, you may find yourself spending more time at home watching television. But it is not difficult to think of things that you could do with your time that would produce more good overall. You might visit the sick or the elderly, record books for the blind, or tutor people with reading disabilities. The point is, of course, perfectly general: whatever it is you are doing with your free time, unless you are devoting that time to making your greatest possible contribution to the overall good, consequentialism will condemn your act as morally forbidden. And the consequentialist argument extends to your choice of career as well. For example, if you have the right kind of talent, you could decide to become a doctor and devote yourself to treating indigent patients in the inner city. Perhaps such a career holds little appeal for you—you would rather study philosophy. But if, as seems plausible, you would do far more good as a doctor, then this is the choice you are required to make. (An unhappy doctor will doubtless be less effective than a happy one; but even an unhappy one, assuming she is reasonably conscientious, can do a tremendous amount of good—far more than most philosophers, even happy ones.)

And the demands of consequentialism go even further. In some cases you might be required to sacrifice life or limb. For example, suppose that there are six people, each of whom will die unless they receive some of the medicine which is rightfully in your possession. Five of these people need only a fifth of what you have, while the sixth needs all of it. It is therefore a case of five lives versus one. And so, barring some unusual circumstance (for example, the sixth is about to find the cure for cancer), more good will be done by dividing the medicine among the five, rather than giving all of it to the sixth. This is, therefore, what consequentialism says you are required to do. But let us now add one more detail to the story: *you* are the sixth person, the one who needs all of the medicine!

As far as consequentialism is concerned, however, this does nothing to change your obligations; you are still morally required to give the medicine to the five. You are required to sacrifice your life for the sake of helping others. It is worth emphasizing what is being claimed here. It is not that it would be nice of you to make such a sacrifice, praiseworthy but not obligatory. Rather, making such a sacrifice is what you are *required* to do. (Similarly, recall the organ transplant case, from 3.1, and imagine that you are Chuck. According to consequentialism, you must *volunteer* for the operation, sacrificing your own life to save the lives of the five other patients.)

In sum, there is simply no limit to the sacrifices that might be asked of us by consequentialism. You might be asked to give up anything at all, provided only that doing so would be part of your making your greatest possible contribution to the overall good. This is what consequentialism demands of us.

Intuitively, almost all of us find this impossible to believe. Even those of us who accept some kind of requirement to promote the good, and who are willing to embrace some of the initial, more modest sacrifices as obligatory, are likely to think that consequentialism goes too far in its endorsement of such a wide-ranging and demanding version of this requirement. Note, however, that the cases we have been discussing need not involve the violation of any constraints. Rather, we have been imagining cases in which your promoting the good has required significant sacrifices—but it has not involved your telling any lies, breaking any promises, harming others, or failing to meet your various special obligations. In some of the examples, admittedly, it may be correct to say that you have done harm to yourself; but given the tremendous amount of good that you thereby accomplish, you can hardly be accused of "selling yourself too cheaply." So even if there is a duty not to harm yourself (see 4.5), these will presumably be cases where that duty is permissibly infringed. Thus, if consequentialism errs in holding that these sacrifices are obligatory, the problem is not that consequentialism *permits* too much; on the contrary, making the various sacrifices is permissible. Rather, consequentialism errs here by *demanding* too much: it says of various actions that they are morally required, when in fact they are morally *optional*. At least, that seems to be the verdict of commonsense morality.

Not surprisingly, consequentialists will deny the charge that consequentialism demands too much. One possible strategy for resisting the objection is to maintain that the actual implications of consequentialism are far less demanding than they appear to be. That is, it might be suggested that although it is certainly true that consequentialism requires you to make your greatest possible contribution to the overall good, a number of empirical considerations work together to limit the onerousness of doing this.

First of all, it is difficult to be confident that contributions made to charity actually do as much good as we might like to think. For example, newspapers often tell stories of aid supplies rotting on foreign docks while local authorities squabble about their distribution, or report how aid intended for the needy ends up in the pockets of corrupt foreign governments or warring soldiers, and so on. And even if the aid does make it to the intended recipients, often little or nothing is done to alter the on-going conditions of poverty; in the long run, therefore, short term aid may actually do nothing more than extend the period of misery and suffering.

Perhaps in some cases problems like these can be overcome. But given the significant risk that when one attempts to do good on the global stage one will actually end up making things worse, the consequentialist might argue that we are likely to do more good if we focus our attentions instead on helping those near and dear to us, where we can be reasonably confident of success. This suggestion is reinforced by the thought that we know our own needs and that of our family and friends far better than that of strangers. Furthermore, helping those to whom we are attached by personal ties results in an increase in our own well-being as well, multiplying the payoff. Finally—and on a somewhat different track—in order to maintain our ability to do good, we must periodically rest and "recharge our batteries." For this reason too, therefore, promoting the good will often support "indulging" ourselves in a number of ways. Once one puts these and similar considerations together—some consequentialists argue—it is fairly rare for promoting the good to require very much by way of personal sacrifice.

The strength of this first reply depends, of course, upon the plausibility of the various empirical assumptions underlying it. And although there is certainly something to the points just made, it might be argued that their force should not be exaggerated. For example, even if it is difficult to be confident of success when acting on the global stage, in many cases we may know enough to justify the risk, given the tremendous amount of good that is at stake. And, in any event, even if it is conceded that we can be more confident of success if we turn our attention closer to home, the fact remains that there are likely to be significant unmet needs in one's own town or neighborhood. Accordingly, making one's greatest possible contribution to the overall good can still involve tremendous sacrifices, even if those sacrifices are to be made on the local level. Similarly, although it is certainly true that one must periodically rest and "indulge oneself" so as to maintain one's ability to do good, it does not seem especially likely that this consideration will come close to justifying the tremendous amounts of time that most of us squander, or the tremendous expenditures on luxuries that we typically bestow upon ourselves.

Of course, the consequentialists who favor the first sort of reply might counter with further empirical arguments. And these, in turn, would need to be examined as well. We might, therefore, try to sidestep this debate by pressing the logical point that *in principle* there is no limit to the sacrifices that consequentialism might ask of an agent. We might appeal to an imaginary case, like that of the six people who need the same medicine. Here we can simply *stipulate* that more good will be done if you donate your medicine to the five others, thereby sacrificing your own life.

At this point, however, some consequentialists may be prepared to offer a second reply. They might concede the *logical* possibility of constructing a case in which making one's greatest possible contribution to the overall good would involve a tremendous personal sacrifice. But they might insist that if we reflect carefully upon such cases we will find, intuitively, that *these* sacrifices do indeed seem obligatory. And if we don't see this immediately, this may be a function of the difficulty of keeping the details of the case firmly in mind and taking them seriously as givens.

Still other consequentialists might concede—and this is a third possible reply—that it may be possible to construct cases in which consequentialism gives what is *intuitively* the wrong answer. (Indeed, the medicine example may well be such a case.) But these consequentialists will deny that this fact should have much force as evidence against consequentialism. Perhaps our moral intuitions should be given little or no weight in general. Or perhaps—less radically—there is particular reason to be skeptical about their reliability when it comes to questions about the demandingness of morality. After all, it might be noted, people tend to be rather distressingly self-centered: if we have intuitions that consequentialism is too demanding, perhaps this is simply our selfishness talking, rather than our understanding of the moral point of view. Indeed, one of our firmest moral beliefs is that from the moral point of view everyone counts *equally,* and it is obviously rather difficult to see how to reconcile this belief with a rejection of the demands of consequentialism. This then supports the suspicion that if we do have intuitions that consequentialism demands too much, these particular intuitions should not be trusted.

(It may be worth commenting on the similarities between these replies and the ones offered previously (in 3.1) to the objection that consequentialism permits too much. The replies are similar because—in principle, at least—the same basic logical possibilities are available *whenever* a given normative theory is claimed to be counterintuitive in some regard: one can deny that the given theory actually has the counterintuitive implications in question; one can deny that the implications that it does have are all that counterintuitive; or one can deny the evidential force of the relevant intuitions. And, of course, one can try a mixture of these three strategies as well.)

Are these replies—or some combination of them—adequate? Do they succeed in rebutting the objection that consequentialism demands too much? Some will conclude that this is indeed the case. But many others, I think, will find these replies unconvincing. They will continue to maintain that consequentialism is flawed in its endorsement of such an overwhelming requirement to promote the good.

Note, however, that if this is indeed a valid objection to consequentialism, no progress is made toward answering it by adding constraints to our moral theory. Consequentialists, of course, believe that any act at all is permissible, provided that it will lead to the greatest good overall. By adding constraints, therefore, we do manage to qualify the requirement to promote the good, but only in the following way: certain *methods* of promoting the good are forbidden (namely, those that would involve violating the constraints). But even with this qualification in place, the requirement to promote the good can still be extremely demanding. In effect, if all we do is add constraints, we are still left with a requirement to do all we can to promote the good, provided we act within the *confines* of those constraints. But as we have already observed, it seems quite possible to make tremendous personal sacrifices while promoting the good, without violating any constraints at all. So even if we adopt a pluralistic deontological theory—that is, one that includes constraints as well—the requirement to promote the good might still be unacceptably demanding.

Apparently, then, if we are to avoid the feature of consequentialism that makes it too demanding, we must add a new kind of element to our normative theory. From the point of view of commonsense morality, we need not be forever promoting the good (not even if we restrict ourselves to permissible means). Although promotion of the good is permissible (at least, within the confines of constraints), it is not typically required. Rather, in the normal situation, promotion of the good is *optional*—neither required nor forbidden. Intuitively, it seems, it is permissible for people to pursue their various interests and projects instead of the greater good. They have the option of choosing to promote the good, of course, but they also have the option of refusing to do this. In short, commonsense morality includes *options* as well as constraints.

Like constraints, options serve to qualify the force of the requirement to promote the good. Unlike constraints, however, options don't restrict the range of our morally acceptable choices; rather, options *increase* the range of our morally acceptable choices. Where constraints forbid doing acts (of the wrong kind), even if promoting the good would require them, options give *permission* to do acts (of the right kind), even if promoting the good would rule them out. Thus, if consequentialism demands too much, this is not because it fails to include constraints, but because it fails to incorporate any options—permissions to perform less than optimal acts. And this means, accordingly, that any deontological theory that fails to include options will demand too much as well. Apparently, then, options merit further investigation.

## 5.2  Options

As we have seen, most of us believe that we are not forever required to be promoting the good. In typical situations, it seems, rather than giving everyone's well-being equal weight in our deliberations, we are permitted to favor ourselves or our friends or our families; similarly, we can devote ourselves to promoting the various projects and goals that we happen to care about, even though other projects and other goals might contribute more to the good overall. In short, thanks to the existence of *options,* we are permitted to pursue our various personal interests, even though doing so fails to make our greatest possible contribution to the overall good.

But what explains the existence of options? Why *isn't* there a constant requirement to promote the good (within the limits of constraints)? The answer would be simple, of course, if goodness of results were not a normative factor relevant to determining the moral status of actions. If it simply didn't matter from the moral point of view what the results of your action were—or if nobody's well-being mattered but your own—then it would hardly be surprising if there were no general requirement to promote the good. But as we have seen, virtually everyone agrees that overall goodness of outcomes is indeed one of the factors relevant to determining the moral status of our acts. It may not be the only such factor, but it is certainly one of them. So in those cases where more good would be done by performing a given act—and no constraints would be violated—why doesn't this fact automatically generate a requirement to do the act in question?

It might be suggested that although goodness of outcomes is indeed a morally relevant factor, it is not itself capable of generating moral *requirements*. After all, not all factors work the same way. Consider, for example, my giving you permission to break your promise to me. The presence of my permission is certainly relevant to the moral status of your later failure to do what you earlier promised. But this factor does not create new requirements—rather, it cancels them. Indeed, permission, in and of itself, simply seems incapable of creating requirements. This is not at all to suggest that goodness of outcomes works exactly in the same way that permission does; obviously that is not the case. But it does point to the possibility that, like

permission, it might be a factor that is incapable of generating requirements. If so, then the existence of options would again be a straightforward
matter. There would be no general, constant requirement to promote the
good, because there could be no requirement to promote the good at all.

Although a view of this sort certainly seems to be a logical possibility,
and there are some people who appear to hold it (as noted in 4.3), it is not,
I think, a view that many of us can accept. For as just mentioned, this view
has the implication that one can *never* be morally required to perform an
act simply by virtue of the fact that the results would be good—no matter
*how* much good was at stake. Thus, even if I could prevent some horrible
catastrophe, at no risk or cost to myself, I would have no moral obligation
to do so (provided that no other factors come into play). But this is very
difficult to believe. From the point of view of commonsense morality, at
any rate, it seems clear that I *would* be morally required to act in a case of
the kind I have just described. And what this means, of course, is that goodness of outcomes is capable of generating requirements (at least, it seems to
be from the standpoint of commonsense morality). But if it is capable of
doing this in principle—and if, indeed, it does so sometimes in fact—then
we still need an explanation of why it does not do so all the time. (Could
one argue that the requirement to avert the catastrophe is to be explained
in terms of a duty to rescue, rather than a requirement to promote the
good? But the catastrophe might be one threatening distant strangers, and
perhaps only sometime in the future—in which case it wouldn't fall comfortably under the duty of rescue as that is normally construed.)

A different suggestion is that goodness of outcomes is capable of generating requirements, but only when *enough* good is at stake. If the amount of
good is too small, then even though a given act might lead to some slight increase in the overall good, there will be no requirement to perform that act.
Requirements are only generated when the net increase is sufficiently large.

This new view does seem to have a certain amount of plausibility to it (although it is not altogether obvious why small increases in the good shouldn't
be enough to yield a requirement to act). If it's right, then this will explain the
existence of a certain class of options. For example, in cases involving small
favors—like telling someone the time—not very much is at stake. Accordingly, even though somewhat more good might be done by doing the favor,
there will be no *requirement* to do this. Rather, doing the favor will be optional, something you are permitted to do but not required to do.

Unfortunately, even though an approach of this sort may explain the existence of some options, it won't go very far. For in the kinds of cases with
which we began this chapter, the amount of good that is at stake is tremendous. (We were, after all, considering cases in which one or more lives were
at stake.) And even when the sacrifices necessary to bring about the best results were significant, the net gain in terms of the overall good was always
quite substantial. In cases like these, it doesn't seem at all plausible to sug-

gest that the potential net increase is still "too small" to enter the range in which requirements can be generated. Thus if—as we are assuming—these cases are governed by options as well, we still need an account of where these options come from. If the good is capable of generating requirements, and a great deal of good is at stake, why doesn't this automatically generate a requirement to act?

Perhaps the answer can be found by identifying yet another morally relevant factor, a factor capable of outweighing or overriding the overall goodness of results. What we need, apparently, is an additional normative factor that comes into play in those cases where people have options even though a significant amount of good is at stake. On an approach of this kind, it would be the presence of this further factor that prevents the goodness of outcomes from generating a requirement. If a factor of the right sort could be found, then we might be on our way to a sufficiently general account of options.

Once we think of explaining options in this way, an obvious and plausible candidate suggests itself, namely, the *cost to the agent* of promoting the good. That is, perhaps the cost to the agent is relevant in determining whether the agent is in fact required to do the act with the best consequences. In particular, when the cost is high, this may prevent the goodness of the results from generating a requirement. This is, indeed, the obvious suggestion to make, for—intuitively—what seemed objectionable about a constant requirement to promote the good was the fact that there was no limit to the sacrifices that one might be required to make in the course of fulfilling that requirement. But if the cost to the agent is itself a factor capable of outweighing the good, the mere fact that some act would lead to better results overall will not suffice to guarantee that the act is required; if the sacrifice involved would be too large, this will block the generation of the requirement.

Note that a view of this sort is able to capture our belief that, despite the existence of options, in some situations there *is* a requirement to promote the good. To begin with, if promoting the good literally wouldn't cost the agent anything at all, then (as long as constraints aren't involved, and a reasonable amount of good is at stake) there is nothing to prevent the creation of a requirement to promote the good. Of course, in any kind of realistic case promoting the good will cost the agent *something*, even if only a trivial amount. But it does not seem especially plausible to suggest that cost to the agent is capable of outweighing the good no matter *how slight* the cost involved. It seems far more plausible to suggest that whether or not there is a requirement will depend on the *size* of the sacrifice required, as well as on the *amount of good* that is at stake. Thus, even if promoting the good would involve some cost to the agent, this might still be required, if the amount of good at stake is sufficiently large. But as the cost to the agent grows larger, it takes more and more good to generate a requirement. In many cases, therefore—in particular, in at least some of the cases with which we began—the cost to the agent will be too great, relative to the amount of good that is at stake, and no requirement will be created.

Some of these points can be usefully expressed in the language of thresholds. On the view being considered, options exist because cost to the agent is sometimes capable of overriding goodness of results. But if it is also true that goodness of results is sometimes capable of outweighing cost to the agent, then it follows that our options have *thresholds*. That is, when *enough* good is at stake, the option "gives out," and we are indeed required to promote the good. Furthermore, the precise level of the threshold does not seem to be fixed across the board. Rather, how much good is "enough" is itself a function of the size of the sacrifice involved in performing the act in question; the greater the sacrifice, the higher the threshold.

Depending on how high or low the threshold is set—for a given cost to the agent—the option will be either more or less significant. Clearly, if very little cost to the agent is enough to outweigh a very large payoff in terms of the overall good, then our options are quite extensive, and we will rarely be faced with a requirement to promote the good. On the other hand, if it doesn't take much of a net increase in the overall good to outweigh even a fairly significant sacrifice on the part of the agent, then our options are quite limited in their extent, and we will face requirements to promote the good rather frequently. So it is important to ask: how high are the thresholds?

Unfortunately, this is a matter where intuitions differ rather widely. Although few are willing to go so far as to say that we have no options at all, a somewhat larger number may be quite satisfied embracing rather limited options. Similarly, although few are willing to go so far as to say that our options are completely unlimited (so that we never have a requirement to promote the good), a rather larger number may be prepared to embrace options with extremely high thresholds (so that requirements to promote the good, although possible, are quite rare indeed). No doubt, most people think the line needs to be drawn somewhere in the *middle*. But this is, of course, a very large area, and not many people, I suspect, have determinate views beyond this. (On the other hand, given how little most people sacrifice to promote the greater good, it might plausibly be suggested that most of us must implicitly accept options whose thresholds are rather high indeed.)

A second, related question about the thresholds is this. Although it does seem plausible to suggest that for "modest" sacrifices, if a sufficiently large amount of good is at stake, one might well be required to make the sacrifice after all, it is not at all obvious whether there is *always* a threshold for the option. That is, it might be that some sacrifices are *so* large that *no* amount of good would be enough to generate a requirement to make a sacrifice of that kind. For example, it might be suggested that you could never be morally required to sacrifice your life (special obligations aside)—no matter *how* many lives could be saved by your doing this. Indeed, it might even be suggested that you could never be required to make a sacrifice of an arm or a leg. On the other hand, others might prefer to argue that, in principle, any sacrifice at all could be required, but the amounts of good that would have to be at stake are so incredibly enormous, that in all but the most extreme of cases there simply won't be enough good at stake to generate the requirement. That is, even if every option has a threshold, it might well be that for some sacrifices the threshold is so high that no real-life case can come close to meeting it.

However these issues about the precise levels of the thresholds are resolved, it seems clear that this kind of appeal to the cost to the agent of promoting the good provides a promising approach to explaining the existence of options. More particularly, if cost to the agent is indeed a normative factor capable of outweighing or overriding goodness of results, this seems to yield most of the options accepted by commonsense morality.

Nonetheless, there are still some complications in working out the details of such an account. Let me briefly mention a few. First of all, it is important to bear in mind that when our action is covered by an option, although we are not required to promote the good, we are nonetheless permitted to do this, if we choose. Intuitively, after all, we not only have the option of pursuing our various personal interests; we also have the option of sacrificing those interests, for the sake of the greater good. (Indeed, such sacrifices are typically thought to be praiseworthy.) Thus, in any given case, we will not have succeeded in creating an *option* if we end up replacing a requirement to promote the good with a different requirement—a requirement not to sacrifice our interests. That is, even if the cost of promoting the good would be significant, this had better not result in a prohibition against making the sacrifice. What this means, of course, is that if cost to the agent is truly going to help produce options, this must be a factor that can *block* the generation of requirements, but cannot typically *create* any. More precisely, it had better not be the case that cost to the agent automatically generates a prohibition against making sacrifices in all those cases where cost is enough to override the good. Otherwise, there won't be any options. (It may not be problematic if in extreme cases cost does generate a prohibition against sacrificing oneself; some would find such a prohibition plausible.)

Second, it is not completely clear how the notion of the *cost* to the agent is to be understood and measured. What should count as a sacrifice? It might be suggested, narrowly, that the only things that are relevant are changes in the agent's well-being. Or perhaps, more broadly, we should count anything at all that has the potential to adversely effect the agent's well-being, whether or not it actually does. (In effect, this is asking whether or not a sacrifice must involve the loss of well-being itself, or whether the mere loss of resources valuable as a means to well-being counts as well.) Alternatively, perhaps we should count anything at all that the agent takes an interest in, or is personally concerned about, whether or not that state of affairs has any direct implications for the agent's own well-being. (On some preference theories of well-being, of course, this won't truly be a distinct alternative; but on other theories of well-being it might well be.) More broadly still, perhaps we should count as a sacrifice anything at all that restricts the agent's choices and alternatives, whether or not this affects anything the agent cares about. Clearly, the broader our conception of what is to count as a sacrifice, the more far ranging the options that will be generated.

A related issue is whether all sacrifices (of the relevant sort) should count, regardless of size. As we have seen, it seems plausible to hold that small sacrifices generate options with lower thresholds than large sacrifices do. But is it indeed the case that all sacrifices are protected by options of some sort, no matter how small or trivial the sacrifice? This is indeed one possibility. But it might be, rather, that the sacrifice involved must be of a certain minimum size before any option is generated at all.

Next, it should be pointed out that commonsense morality recognizes what seem to be two rather different types of options. The options that we have been considering so far are those in which you are permitted to favor yourself or some personal project or goal at the expense of the greater good. We might (somewhat misleadingly) refer to these as *agent-favoring* options. (The label isn't perfect, given that some of the goals that the agent promotes under "agent-favoring" options may have nothing in particular to do with the agent's own well-being.) But commonsense morality also recognizes the existence of an option to *sacrifice* your own well-being for the sake of others, even in cases where the good that you are doing for them is less than the cost to yourself. We might refer to options of this second sort as *agent-sacrificing* options. (They are genuine options, since they permit you to act in a particular way—sacrificing your own interests—even though this leads to a net decrease in the overall good.)

Although, as we have seen, appeal to the cost to the agent of promoting the good seems a promising way of explaining the existence of agent-favoring options, it is less clear how successful this approach will be for agent-sacrificing options. After all, if you sacrifice your own well-being (so as to bring about a lesser gain for others), the permissibility of your doing so does not seem easily explicable in terms of the *cost* to you of acting in a manner that would have better promoted the overall good. For in cases of self-sacrifice, it might be suggested, it is not promoting the good, but refraining from doing so, that is costly to the agent.

Nonetheless, despite this apparent difficulty, we might still be able to explain agent-sacrificing options in terms of cost to the agent, if we embrace a suitably encompassing conception of cost. For if the agent is forbidden to sacrifice his own well-being for the sake of lesser gains for others, this will indeed impose certain kinds of costs upon him, in terms of restricted choices and inability to promote some of the things he cares about. Perhaps we can explain why options should protect him from these kinds of costs as well, even if acting on these options will leave the agent worse off overall. Assuming that we can, in fact, provide the relevant explanation, then the appeal to cost will indeed support agent-sacrificing options after all.

In any event, a similar explanation is necessary even for *agent-favoring* options, at least for those cases where the agent promotes some favored goal (rather than the overall good) in a way that involves some cost to the agent in terms of personal well-being. If a defense of these options is to appeal to the cost to the agent of being required to promote the good, then we again need to explain why options should protect the agent from the costs of being unable to promote the given goal, even when acting on the options will leave the agent at a lower level of well-being. It is not obvious what this further explanation will look like, but it seems likely that the same explanation—if it can be found—will do the job for both agent-favoring and agent-sacrificing options.

Assuming that these various complications can be resolved, the basic thought behind this account of options remains this: when the cost to the agent would be sufficiently great, this fact is capable of blocking the creation of a requirement that the agent act; in particular, cost to the agent can block or override what would otherwise be a requirement to promote the good. But this raises an obvious question: can cost to the agent block or override *other* requirements? Think of all the various constraints that we have identified in previous chapters. Should we say that agents are required to meet these constraints—*unless* the cost to the agent of doing so would be too high?

For some constraints, it actually seems fairly plausible to suggest that when the cost to the agent would be significant, this may indeed free the agent from the requirement to meet the constraint. For example, even if there is a duty to rescue, it seems unlikely that one must save others regardless of the cost to oneself. If cost to the agent would be high enough, therefore, this may well generate an option to refrain from undertaking the rescue. The same thing may be true for some of the special obligations we may have toward members of our family. Even if, say, I must make significant sacrifices to safeguard and protect the well-being of my children, it is not at all clear that there is *no* limit to the sacrifices I may be required to make for their sake. So for *some* constraints, at least, it does not seem implausible to hold that when the cost to the agent is high enough it can generate an option, blocking or overriding the requirement to satisfy the constraint in question. What is less clear is whether this is a plausible position to take with regard to *all* constraints.

Consider, for example, the constraint against doing harm. Normally, of course, I am forbidden to harm others. But what if the cost to me of meeting this requirement would be significant? Can I kill someone—say, my business rival—if this is the only way I can avoid a substantial personal loss? Intuitively, of course, the answer is clear. I am forbidden to kill, despite the cost to me of my refraining. But how is this to be explained?

What we want to say, obviously, is that there is a *constraint* against doing harm and that killing my rival violates that constraint. But we have been assuming that when the cost to the agent is great, this fact can block or override the creation of a requirement that might otherwise be in place. So why not here too? Perhaps we should embrace an option to kill, when the cost of not killing would be too great. More generally, perhaps there is an option to *do* harm, and not merely an option to *allow* harm. (Similarly, perhaps there are options to break promises, tell lies, and so on—when the cost of not doing so is too great. But for simplicity, let's stick to the generic case of doing harm.)

Looking back, it is likely that the sorts of options we have been imagining before now have all been options to *allow* harm. That is, we have been considering cases in which the agent pursues her own personal projects, rather than the overall good (or some special obligation). In doing this—by failing to make her greatest possible contribution to the good—it is almost inevitable that the agent will often allow harm that she could have prevented. But as long as the agent pursues her projects in the normal ways, she need not necessarily *harm* anyone. In short, in freeing the agent from the requirement to promote the good, we presumably intended to give permission to *allow* harm, but not to *do* harm.

But now, it seems, in the course of defending options to allow harm we have unwittingly opened the door to options to do harm as well. Is this an acceptable result? How should we respond to the possibility of options to do harm?

One possible response, of course, is to embrace them. We may not have set out to endorse options to do harm, but if the only promising defense of options to allow harm also entails the existence of options to do harm, then apparently we will have to choose between having both sorts of options and having neither. Admittedly, some people (for example, consequentialists) may be happy enough to do without any kinds of options at all. But others may decide that the inclusion of options to do harm is a price worth paying, if this is indeed the only way to retain options to allow harm.

Of course, the plausibility of this first response will depend in large part on just how intuitively unacceptable options to do harm really are. And it might be suggested that these options are not as unattractive as they might at first appear to be. For even if real, options to do harm might be much more limited in their extent than options to allow harm. First of all, the sacrifices involved in not doing harm will typically be small, unlike the sacrifices involved in not allowing harm. (Promoting the good is costly; refraining from doing harm normally is not.) So options to do harm would normally have rather low thresholds; it won't take very much harm before the permission to cause that harm "gives out."

Second—and more importantly—in the case of options to do harm, cost to the agent is opposed by more than one factor. Unlike typical options to allow harm, where cost to the agent only needs to outweigh goodness of outcomes, in cases involving options to do harm, cost to the agent must outweigh both goodness of outcomes and the *further* fact that harm is being done. In effect, cost must outweigh not only the good but also the constraint against doing harm. Clearly, the combined force of these two factors is greater than that of the good by itself. So even if we assume that cost does weigh in against constraints, it will take a far greater cost to the agent before the combined force of the constraint and the good is overcome. In short, options to do harm will be quite weak and limited. Only when the cost to the agent is severe, and the harm to be done is minimal, will an option to do harm be generated. And it is not at all obvious that options to do harm of this weak kind are not in fact intuitively plausible.

Of course, some will find the prospect of options to do harm utterly unacceptable, even if the options are weak and limited in this way. But rather than abandoning options altogether—including options to allow harm—it might be insisted that cost to the agent is simply incapable of outweighing factors other than goodness of results. Perhaps the various factors that underlie constraints cannot be outweighed by considerations of cost, no matter how great the cost and how minor the infraction of the constraint. If, for example, the constraint against doing harm automatically outweighs cost, then there simply cannot be any options to *do* harm at all. And the same thing may be true for options to violate the various other constraints. (Somewhat more complicatedly, perhaps cost can outweigh *certain* constraints—like the duty to rescue—but not others, such as the constraint against doing harm.)

Obviously, a view of this sort will most readily appeal to absolutists concerning constraints, since they are used to thinking of constraints as being incapable of being outweighed by other factors. But it seems possible that this position might be attractive to many moderate deontologists as well. That is to say, the moderate deontologist might insist that even though certain constraints can in principle be outweighed by the *good,* they can never be outweighed by cost to the agent. (On the other hand, if cost can outweigh the good, which is how we explain the existence of options, and if the good can outweigh some particular constraint, which is, according to the moderate deontologist, how we explain the constraint's having a threshold, then by transitivity we would expect that cost *would* be able to outweigh the given constraint, contrary to the view being suggested here. Is it objectionable for the moderate deontologist to violate transitivity in this way?)

Finally, it should be noted that even if it provides the basis for a promising explanation of options, there remains something puzzling about the suggestion that cost to the agent is a distinct normative factor which matters in its own right. After all, judgments concerning the overall good already take *everyone* into account, including the agent. Thus, to say that cost to the agent can outweigh or override the good is to say, in effect, that the agent can give extra weight to his own interests, tipping the scales in his own favor. And it is difficult to see how to reconcile this with the thought that from the moral point of view everyone is to count equally.

Nonetheless, it must be admitted that we do seem to give this kind of weight to cost to the agent. Intuitively, at least, it does seem relevant to ask whether promoting the good in any given case would involve a significant sacrifice on the part of the agent, and if it would, this seems to militate against the existence of a requirement to promote the good. So in terms of our common moral intuitions, if nothing more, it does seem appropriate to identify cost to the agent as a further normative factor, one that is relevant to determining the moral status of our actions.

## 5.3  Rights

Our survey of basic normative factors is now complete. With the addition of cost to the agent, I believe we have at least touched upon all the most important factors recognized by commonsense morality. But this may seem a peculiar claim to make, in the face of what appears to be a significant and obvious omission. For up to this point there has been no discussion of moral *rights*. Yet talk of rights figures prominently in almost all contemporary moral debates. How then can our survey be complete, if we haven't yet introduced one of the most central elements in normative ethics?

The answer, of course—at least in part—is that we *have* been talking about rights, even though we haven't been using the term. As we will see, pretty much everything that people normally want to say in the language of rights can be expressed in terms of the various normative factors and distinctions that we have identified. For the most part, then, the omission has been apparent, rather than real.

But if this is so, then why have I been at such pains until now to avoid the language of rights? The reason is that talk of rights, although perfectly legitimate, is horrendously *ambiguous*. The simple fact of the matter is that people mean a large number of different things when they talk about rights. As a result, an unadorned claim about rights can rarely stand on its own; unless we know which particular concept of right is intended, it is impossible to know what exactly is being claimed. Indeed, often enough (although certainly not always) people end up speaking past each other, failing to recognize their confusion because the various claims have all been couched in the misleadingly simple language of rights. If we are to avoid such confusion, we need to get clear about the different sorts of things people can mean when they ascribe rights.

In what is probably the broadest sense of the term, to say of something that it has moral rights is only to say that it has moral standing—that it *counts* from the moral point of view. In this sense, most of us believe that people and animals have rights of some sort, but books and rocks do not.

That is to say, we think that people and animals matter, morally speaking, in their *own* right (unlike books and rocks). Put another way, if something has rights in this broad sense of the term, our treatment of it is not morally irrelevant, nor is it of mere derivative significance (due, perhaps, to possible effects on other things that do count in their own right).

Clearly, ascribing rights in this broad sense imparts limited information about the object in question. It does not yet say anything in particular about *how* the thing must be treated; rather, it marks the very fact that by virtue of its moral standing, it makes *sense* to worry about whether it is being mistreated. Nonetheless, this broad concept of rights does have an important role—in debates about which things, exactly, *do* have moral standing. Historically, for example, when those who opposed slavery claimed that slaves too had moral rights, whatever else they may have been saying they were making the significant claim that enslaved people *mattered* from the moral point of view, that they had moral standing (even though this standing was not recognized by the law). And when contemporary debates about abortion are expressed in terms of whether or not fetuses have rights, a large part of what is being debated is whether fetuses *count* from the moral point of view. Similarly, much of the debate concerning the existence of animal rights comes down to disagreement over whether or not animals truly have moral standing in their own right. In all of these debates, the question who or what counts is logically prior to asking how, exactly, the things that count are to be treated. Put another way: asking who or what *has* rights is prior to asking what *kinds* of rights they have.

In this broad sense of the term, therefore, *every* normative theory believes in the existence of rights. Theories may differ over which kinds of things have rights, and what kinds of rights these things have, but presumably every moral theory thinks that *something* has moral standing, so every theory believes in the existence of rights of some sort. The point is worth emphasizing, because it is often suggested that consequentialists, and in particular utilitarians (consequentialists who accept a welfarist theory of the good), deny the existence of rights. But in the broadest sense of the term, this is certainly false. (Utilitarians, for example, typically believe that all sentient creatures have rights, while nonsentient beings lack them.)

This is not at all to deny that in *some* sense of the word, consequentialists do reject rights (the ambiguity of rights talk, after all, is precisely my point). In addition to the very broad concept of rights that I have just been describing, there are a number of narrower conceptions—and some of these are indeed rejected by consequentialists. But it is important to be clear that not *all* conceptions of rights are rejected by consequentialists, not even all of the narrower ones.

If something has moral standing, then there are moral considerations that directly govern and limit our treatment of that thing. From the point of view of any given agent, there are moral requirements (of *some* sort) on how the thing is to be treated, interacted with, or behaved toward. The same idea can be expressed from the standpoint of the thing with moral standing, by saying that it has a *claim* against the agent to be treated in the appropriate ways (whatever those might be). Thus to say of someone or something that they have rights (in the broadest sense of the term), is simply to say that they have some sort of claim against us to be treated appropriately; it is not yet to say anything about the content or the force of the claim.

In using the language of rights and claims we shift the focus of our attention from the agent (and what she is required to do) to the right holder (and how she has a right to be treated). Is there more going on here than a mere shift of emphasis? Some think that the shift in focus may point us in the direction of an important insight, namely, that those things with moral standing possess that standing by virtue of facts about *them,* facts about their natures or activities. Many others, however, think the shift of focus from agent to right holder is only that—a shift of emphasis, marking nothing deeper. (In any event, note that some right holders, such as infants or animals, may not be able to *assert* their claims; others will need to do this for them. Having a claim doesn't necessarily entail being able to literally *make* the claim.)

By distinguishing between different types of claims, we can introduce into the language of rights distinctions corresponding to those we drew between different types of duties. For example, some rights are general—giving each person a claim against all others. But other rights are special: perhaps only certain individuals (rather than everyone) can make a particular kind of claim, or the claim may only be binding against particular agents. Similarly, we can distinguish between positive rights, where someone has a claim against one or more agents that they perform a particular type of act, and negative rights, where the claim against one or more agents is that they *refrain* from performing a particular type of act. (Negative rights can, in principle, be respected by others' doing nothing at all; positive rights, in contrast, require that the relevant parties *do* something.) Or—in a similar fashion—we might distinguish between natural rights and conventional ones.

Now when it is suggested that consequentialists deny the existence of rights, a particular *kind* of right is intended. These are rights that correspond to the existence of *constraints*. Bearing in mind our ability to redescribe the requirements facing an agent from the standpoint of the person who has the right in question, we can say that if there is a constraint of some sort governing how agents are permitted to treat a given person, then that person has a *right* not to be treated in that way. The person has a claim against us not to be treated in a way that would violate the constraint. For obvious reasons, we might call rights of this sort *deontological* rights. Thus, if there is a constraint against doing harm, then people have a right— a deontological right—not to be harmed. If there is a constraint requiring the payment of compensation to those one has harmed, then people have a right to compensation. If there is a constraint against telling lies, then people have a right not to be lied to. And so on, in like fashion, for each of the various other constraints.

Clearly, since consequentialists deny the existence of constraints, they necessarily deny the existence of deontological rights. For if someone is protected by a deontological right, certain ways of behaving toward that person are forbidden—even if more good could be done overall by treating the person in the forbidden manner. In effect, deontological rights protect the person against being "sacrificed" to the greater good.

Note, however, that this is not the same thing as saying that deontological rights are *absolute*—ruling out the various forbidden types of behavior, no matter how much good is at stake. Of course, one certainly can adopt an absolutist position with regard to any given deontological right. But it is equally true that one can be a moderate about the right instead, believing that when enough good is at stake, the right can be permissibly infringed. (Obviously enough, the issues here are exactly the same as those surrounding absolutism concerning constraints; a given deontological right will be absolute if and only if its corresponding constraint is as well.) In any event, even if a deontological right has a finite threshold, it still represents a barrier to the promotion of the good: assuming that the threshold has not been met, one cannot infringe the right, not even if more good would result overall. Thus consequentialists must reject the existence of deontological rights—all of them—even in their nonabsolute form.

Some theorists think that only deontological rights are worthy of the name. Although they may well be prepared to entertain the possibility that something might have moral standing—thus making moral claims upon us—while lacking deontological rights, they want to reserve talk of *rights* to those cases where the claims correspond to constraints. Luckily, there is no need for us to try to settle this issue here. For our purposes it suffices to point out that anyone who does restrict talk of rights in this way is using the term more narrowly than those who use it in the broad sense with which we began. If nothing else, confusion is likely to result, unless care is taken to specify the precise notion of rights that one is employing.

Given the correspondence between constraints and deontological rights, each of the controversies concerning the scope of a given constraint finds expression in the language of rights as well. For example, as we saw previously, despite the existence of a constraint against doing harm, many think it permissible to harm an aggressor in self-defense. In the language of rights, we might say that although each of us has a right not to be harmed, if I unjustifiably attack another I *forfeit* my right. Here is another example: as we have also seen, many people are attracted to the thought that consent eliminates the force of a constraint. Thus, although harming another is normally forbidden, it may be permissible if you have the permission of the person you are harming. In the language of rights, we can say that the right holder has the ability to *waive* the protection afforded by the right. By virtue of the significance of consent, the right holder has a special kind of moral control over how it is permissible for others to treat him.

Some theorists want to make this feature part of the very definition of having a right. That is, on this new view, having a claim will only count as having a *right* if the claim holder is able to waive that claim. Assuming, then, that I can release you from your promises to me, give you permission to tell me lies, or free you from your obligation to compensate me, we can correctly speak of my having rights in these matters. But if in some area, or in some particular case, I cannot waive the right—if, that is, the purported right is *inalienable*—then it is improper to say that I have a right at all.

Once again, we need not try to settle the question of how well this further restriction agrees with ordinary usage. As before, the important point for our purposes is to note how this introduces yet another possible meaning for rights talk, multiplying the opportunities for confusion unless care is taken.

Indeed, some want to restrict talk of rights further still—so that it covers only those cases in which it is permissible to *enforce* the relevant claims. Consider your right not to be harmed. If I am trying to violate that right, is it permissible for you to use force to try to stop me? This is, of course, the question of the justifiability of self-defense. If we believe self-defense legitimate—and more generally, if we believe it permissible for third parties to use force in the defense of others—then we are saying that it is permissible (for you, and for others acting on your behalf) to enforce your claim against me that I not harm you. Similar questions can be raised about the enforcement of other claims: if I owe you compensation, but refuse to pay, may you (or others, acting on your behalf) use force to extract it from me? If I try to steal your property, may you use force to stop me? If I fail to carry through on a promise I have made, may you enforce my compliance? On the view being proposed, it is only appropriate to speak of your having a *right* in any of these cases if it is permissible to enforce the relevant claim. Rights are claims that are justifiably backed up with force.

Another feature that many theorists want to build into the concept of a right is the existence of an *option* on the part of the right holder to perform the various acts protected by the right. According to this view, for example, if I have a right to go the movies, then I have an option giving me permission to perform (or to refrain from performing) all the sundry acts that going to the movies involves: I am permitted to go to the movie theater (that is, to physically relocate myself), to spend my money purchasing a ticket, to enter and take a seat, to spend my time watching the screen, and so on. My having the option of doing all these things is part of what we mean—according to this latest proposal—when we say that I have a right to go to the movies.

On this view, therefore, rights include more than claims concerning the behavior of others. They also include options—permissions to act as I choose within the sphere demarcated by the right. Admittedly, identifying the relevant option is not always a trivial matter. Things are relatively straightforward when (as in the movie example) the right is articulated as a right to *do* something. Here, presumably, I have a claim against others that they not interfere with my doing the given activity, and the corresponding option is an option to perform the activity in question. Unfortunately, identifying the relevant option isn't always as simple as this. (For example, if I have a right not to be told lies, what option is it exactly that I am thought to possess?) Often, however, if we can get clear about the precise nature of the claim involved in the right, it isn't too difficult to find a plausible proposal for a corresponding option. Thus, if I have a right not to be harmed by being deprived of some good, presumably the corresponding option permits me to retain that good (that is to say, I am not required to give it up). At any rate, the proposal is not that whenever we have a right the content of the relevant option is always obvious (after all, the precise content of the relevant claim is not always clear either); the suggestion is simply that where there is a right, there must be an option as well.

Now were we to accept all of the restrictions on rights talk that we have been considering, it would be appropriate to ascribe a right only when a large number of features came together. It would not suffice for someone to have a claim on the behavior of others: the claim would have to correspond to a constraint, and it would have to be waivable, and enforceable, and there would also have to be an option corresponding to the claim. If any of these features were missing, talk of a *right* would simply be out of place. Of course, as we have seen, it is also possible to offer various accounts of rights that are more modest—building some, but not all, of these features into the very definition of a right.

In point of fact, although I have introduced the different accounts as members of a series, each of which builds on and adds to the requirements of the earlier definitions, the different features are actually logically independent of one another. So there are other possible definitions as well, definitions which incorporate some of the later features without requiring certain of the earlier ones. Thus, for example, one might hold that one has a right only if the claim is waivable, or enforceable, or both, without requiring that the claim correspond to a constraint. And there are, of course, many other possible definitions as well.

All of this should serve to reinforce my main point: although the language of rights is in itself perfectly legitimate, the use of the term varies significantly. If someone simply ascribes a right, without taking some care to specify what conception of rights they are working with, it will be difficult to understand—let alone evaluate—their claims.

It should also be noted that one might resist the attempt to build these various features into the *definition* of a right, while still believing that in many (or perhaps even most) cases the features tend to be found together.

That is, regardless of whether or not one is prepared to talk of there being a right in some situation where one or another of these features is lacking, one might still believe that as a matter of moral fact the various features typically go together (in a "bundle," as it were). After all, it might be suggested that typically the various features won't have much "point" unless the others are present as well. For example, as we have seen, claims corresponding to constraints can be viewed as protecting the right holder from being sacrificed against her will—even for the greater good. But, it might be argued, what is the point of having such protection, if the right holder is herself required to make the very same sacrifice? Thus, the claim may not serve much purpose unless it is accompanied by the corresponding option. Similarly, it might be suggested that a claim won't have much point unless it is permissible to enforce that claim against those who would otherwise fail to respect it. And in the same vein, it might be noted that the protection afforded by a claim will not necessarily be an unqualified benefit to the right holder, unless that protection can be waived when doing so better suits the right holder's purposes.

For these and other reasons, then, it may not be implausible to suggest that, for a wide range of cases, if some of these features are present, all of them are. But whatever the plausibility of this suggestion as a broad generalization, it is important to bear in mind that it does seem possible to have some of these features in place without the others. For example, I might have an option permitting me to perform some act—even though I have no claim whatsoever against others with regard to my performing the act in question. (Perhaps I have the option of parking my car at a certain location on the street, although I have no claim against others to help me or even to refrain from interfering by parking there first!) Sometimes, in fact, people say that they have a *right* to perform a given act, where it is not clear that they mean to be ascribing to themselves anything more than the relevant option. If this is indeed a proper use of the term, then there may be rights that do not include any kind of claims at all; if so, then even our "broad" account of rights—the one with which we began—may not be broad enough to include all of the uses to which the term is put.

Before leaving the discussion of rights, it may be helpful to say a few words about the idea of *justice*, for justice is often thought to be essentially a matter of respecting rights. We might begin by noting that it certainly seems relevant, when assessing the moral status of an action, to ask whether the act is unjust, or whether it treats anyone unjustly. It might seem, therefore, that justice is yet another basic normative factor, one that we have previously overlooked. I suspect, however, that as with rights talk itself, talk of justice is another case in which no new factors are introduced beyond those we have already considered.

On what is probably the most common general account, justice is a matter of giving each person "their due." Obviously enough, on such an approach, the question immediately becomes one of determining what exactly any given person is due. And a natural enough proposal is that this comes to whatever it is that they have a right to. Suppose, then, that we understand talk of rights in our broad sense, so that it includes all claims, whatever their precise content or force. Then acting justly is simply a matter of recognizing and giving due weight to each person's claims. And this, in turn, can be further specified in terms of the various factors and distinctions we have already identified.

On this broad reading, then, acting justly is more or less equivalent to acting morally, meeting the various requirements governing our treatment of others. Sometimes, however, justice is construed more narrowly: giving each person their due is still understood as a matter of respecting their rights, but talk of rights is now restricted in one of the ways that we have already considered. For example, justice might be thought to be concerned only with respect for *deontological* rights, rather than all moral claims whatsoever. On such a reading, obviously, acting justly will not necessarily exhaust one's moral duties; but in any event, concern for justice will not *add* anything to the factors we have already identified.

Finally, it should be noted that different types of justice are often distinguished, depending on the particular subject matter of the claims in question. For example, *distributive* justice is particularly concerned with the legitimate distribution of benefits and burdens, especially material goods. *Retributive* justice concerns legitimacy in punishment. And *corrective* justice involves correcting past wrongs through compensation. Each of these specific types of justice remains concerned with giving each person their due, within the relevant domain. But as far as I can see, talk of justice does not, in and of itself, add anything. Determining what each person is due remains a matter of clarifying the interplay of the relevant normative factors.

## 5.4   Interaction

The moral status of a given act is jointly determined by the various normative factors that are relevant in the case in question. No doubt, in the simplest kinds of cases imaginable, only a single instance of a single type of factor would come into play. If such cases are truly possible, then that single relevant factor would—all by itself—determine the status of the alternative actions available to the agent. But in most cases, and perhaps all realistic ones, more than one factor comes into play, or there is more than one instance of a given factor (for example, there may be more than one promise to be kept). In such cases, the various relevant factors *jointly* determine the moral status of the available acts. Put another way, the status of any given available act is determined by the *interaction* of the different relevant factors.

We have, of course, been concerned with questions about the interaction of the different normative factors throughout our investigation. Early on, for example (in 2.4), questions were raised about trade-offs between well-being and equality in determining the overall goodness of an outcome. And constraints were introduced (in 3.1) to represent the common view that goodness of outcomes could itself be outweighed by various other factors. The possibility of thresholds for these constraints was raised in turn (most fully in 3.2) as a way of capturing the still more complex view that the various constraint-generating factors could themselves be outweighed if enough good was at stake. And it was noted (for example, in 3.3) that still other factors, such as consent, may be capable of eliminating the force of constraints altogether. In these, and other ways, then, the topic of the interaction of the various factors has never been far from our attention.

Nonetheless, it is obvious that we have barely scratched the surface in this matter. For one thing, for most of the factors we have discussed, we have done little more than raise some of the most basic questions concerning the factor's precise contours and content. Numerous subfactors have been noted with little or no discussion, and many potentially relevant subfactors have not been noted at all. Given that the listing and characterizing of factors is incomplete, it follows trivially that we have not exhaustively surveyed all the different possible interactions of the various normative factors. Second, even for those cases where questions about possible conflicts and interaction have been explicitly raised, we have not tried to settle these questions. Typically we have done little more than distinguish between the various possible positions. Admittedly, intuitive strengths or weaknesses of a given position have often been noted; but in all cases, far more could be said on behalf of one or another position, and many more arguments would need to be considered before decisively settling for a particular view. Furthermore, most of the interactions that we have considered have been fairly simple ones, involving at most two or three factors. But the possible combinations grow quite complex indeed, and this brings in its wake the need to address these more complicated interactions.

A few examples should make these points obvious. Recall one of our earliest examples (introduced in 1.4), in which you can save a drowning woman by rowing out to her in a boat. Normally, of course, saving someone's life will bring about a better result than letting her die—so there is at least one factor that speaks in favor of saving her. If there is a duty to rescue, then this will be a second relevant factor, one that supports the same course of action. If these are the only relevant factors, then it seems plausible to think that saving the woman is morally required. But suppose that saving the woman is not altogether free of risk. The water is choppy, and there is some slight chance that the boat might capsize; since you cannot swim, there is a chance that you might drown in a rescue attempt. This introduces a third factor—cost to the agent—one which works against there being a requirement. Is the cost great enough to outweigh the factors that would otherwise generate a requirement? We can imagine the risk growing substantial; at some point we may prefer to say that saving the drowning woman is optional, rather than being required. But what point is this?

Imagine now that the woman is not a stranger. She is your wife. This may introduce a fourth factor—a special obligation to your spouse. This factor presumably supports the existence of a requirement to save. Is it enough, in combination with the first two factors—goodness of results and rescue—to outweigh cost to the agent, so that on balance you are required to save your wife, despite the risk? If cost can still block the existence of a requirement when it is great enough (suppose it is very likely you will save her, but you'll drown in the process), does the presence of the special obligation at least raise the level at which the requirement to save becomes merely optional?

Or suppose that the only available boat isn't yours. This introduces a fifth factor, the property rights of the owner. If the owner is not around, so that you cannot ask for his permission, borrowing the boat will infringe his property rights. This seems to speak against the permissibility of the proposed course of action. Perhaps, however, this is a case in which the constraint is outweighed by the other factors—so that on balance it remains permissible to borrow the boat and rescue your wife. Or, alternatively, perhaps this case is better construed in terms of the hypothetical consent of the owner (a possible sixth factor). That is, perhaps the owner would consent were we only able to ask him in time, and this explains why it is permissible to infringe the property rights. If so, then what should we say about a case in which the owner can be asked, but he refuses to give permission? Is borrowing the boat still permissible? What if the boat is likely to be damaged, and you cannot conceivably afford to compensate the owner? Clearly, as the number of relevant normative factors increases, questions about the overall interaction of these factors grow ever more complex.

As a second illustration, consider once again the organ transplant case (from 3.1): by chopping up Chuck and distributing his vital organs, you can save the lives of five other patients. Intuitively, despite the better results overall (one relevant factor), there is a second relevant factor—that you would be doing harm—that also comes into play, opposes this first factor, and outweighs it. So you are forbidden to kill Chuck. (Should the chance to save the five be construed as a case of rescue? If so, there may be a third factor at work, presumably outweighed as well by the constraint against doing harm.) Suppose, however, that Chuck has volunteered for the operation. This introduces another factor, which would normally serve to weaken or eliminate the force of the constraint against doing harm. Does it have this effect here? (If it does, does performing the operation become obligatory, or is it merely optional?) If consent does have its customary effect here, would the force of the consent itself be weakened if Chuck were a family man, with special obligations to look after his children? Or suppose that Chuck is *responsible* for the fact that the five are dying (perhaps he deliberately poisoned them, causing the different cases of organ failure). This may bring in two other factors, self-defense and compensation. Should killing Chuck be viewed as a form of defending innocents against an aggressor (where killing him and using his organs is the only available way to prevent him from killing his innocent victims)? Or is it, perhaps, a legitimate form of enforcing compensation for the harm Chuck has done? Once again, obviously, the more complex the case becomes, the more complicated the interactions between the various normative factors.

As these examples make clear, interactions between factors can take on a number of different forms. Factors can be mutually reinforcing, supporting one and the same action, or opposing the very same requirement. Or the relationship between factors can be transformative, one of them undermining or eliminating or otherwise modifying the force of the other, or restricting its scope. Or two factors might *conflict,* supporting rival (incompatible) actions. In this last type of case in particular, it will seem especially natural to think in terms of *trade-offs* between the conflicting factors, of one factor outweighing or overriding another.

Talk of factors as conflicting should not be misunderstood. As our examples show, the fact that two factors conflict does not mean that there is some kind of logical—or moral—impossibility in having both at play in a single case. On the contrary, it is obviously quite possible for a single case to involve several conflicting factors, each "pulling" in a different direction. Often enough, one or another of these conflicting factors will outweigh the others, generating a requirement to perform the particular act it supports. But in all cases, whatever the details, what exactly it is right to do depends on the balance, interplay, and interaction among all of the normative factors at play in the given situation.

There seems to be nothing especially problematic about the notion of conflicting factors. But what about the possibility of conflicting *duties?* Could the interplay of the various factors yield not just one, but two or more duties, and might these conflict as well? Certainly there is nothing problematic in the thought that in some situation a given set of factors might generate two or more duties. (For example, in a variant of the case of the drowning woman, perhaps there is both a requirement to save the woman by borrowing the boat, even though it belongs to another, *and* a requirement to later explain and apologize to the owner.) But what if it is impossible for the agent to fulfill all of the duties generated? If duties can conflict in this sense, then it will be impossible for an agent to meet all of her obligations. And isn't this an unacceptable state of affairs?

Not necessarily. We can distinguish between *prima facie* duties, or duties other things being equal, and duties *all things considered.* To say that something is your duty all things considered is to say that you are required to do it given *all* of the factors that are relevant to the case at hand. In contrast, to say of something that it is a prima facie duty is only to note the presence of one or more factors that *would* generate an all things considered duty—

in the *absence* of conflicting factors. In some cases, of course, a prima facie duty will in fact be your duty all things considered as well. (Perhaps there simply are no other conflicting factors, or if there are, they are outweighed.) But in other cases, conflicting factors will indeed outweigh those factors underlying the prima facie duty, thus preventing them from generating a duty all things considered.

(It may be worth remarking that the *label* "prima facie duty" is somewhat unfortunate, suggesting as it does that what is intended is an epistemological notion—something that *appears* to be a duty but may not be. In fact, however, what is intended here is a "metaphysical" notion: to say that there is a prima facie duty is to say that there are factors that *would generate* an all things considered duty, under the proper circumstances. In any event, for better or for worse, the use of the term is now standard philosophical practice. I should also note that, for obvious reasons, it would be rather cumbersome to be forever qualifying talk of duties with the phrases "prima facie" or "all things considered". For the most part, therefore, I have elsewhere let context suggest the relevant qualification.)

Accordingly, if in some situation the set of relevant factors yields conflicting duties, so long as these duties are only prima facie duties, there is still nothing especially problematic. It is of course true that, given the conflict of duties, it will be impossible for the agent to meet all of her obligations. But this only means that she will necessarily fail to meet one (or more) of her *prima facie* duties, and this won't be objectionable if the prima facie duties that she fails to meet are not in fact duties all things considered. So long as the agent fulfills those duties which are duties all things considered, then even though she fails to meet one of her prima facie duties, she will be able to justify her failure by pointing out how the prima facie duty in question was outweighed by conflicting factors, so that all things considered, she had no requirement to meet it.

But what about the possibility of conflicts of duties in a stronger sense? Could the interaction of the various relevant factors yield two (or more) conflicting duties where both duties are duties all things considered? Think about what it would mean for such a situation to arise. The agent would be required to perform some act, and would be required to perform some second act as well, and would be incapable of performing both. (Alternatively, the agent might be required to perform some act, and also be required to refrain from performing that very act.) Inevitably, the agent would fail to meet one or the other of these requirements. And there would be no justification for doing so, since each requirement would be a duty all things considered. That is, the agent could not justify her failure to meet either requirement by pointing to the conflicting factors that supported the other requirement. For by hypothesis, each was a duty *all things considered*, that is, despite the presence of the conflicting factors. Thus, if there can be conflicts of duties all things considered, the agent will inevitably fail to meet some duty where there is simply no justification for doing this (not even the inevitability of the failure).

In the philosophical literature, conflicts of this extreme sort are sometimes called *moral dilemmas*. It is important to bear in mind that this differs from the common use of the term, according to which an agent is said to face a moral dilemma whenever she faces a difficult moral choice, particularly one with conflicting factors. For as we have seen, situations can be characterized by complex patterns of conflicting normative factors and conflicting prima facie duties—thus making for a difficult and perhaps even tragic moral choice—without yet being a moral dilemma in the technical sense of the term. Our question, then, is this: can there be moral dilemmas in this technical sense, that is, can there be cases in which the agent is faced with conflicting duties, two or more of which are duties all things considered?

Many people find the notion of a moral dilemma (in this strong, technical sense) bordering on the incoherent. They argue that it violates one or another principle of logic to claim that an agent is faced with two conflicting duties all things considered. (The part of logic particularly concerned with moral principles is called *deontic logic*. The suggestion, then, is that the existence of moral dilemmas can be ruled out on grounds of deontic logic alone.) Others find the notion of a moral dilemma *logically* coherent, but think that the existence of such dilemmas would be morally unacceptable. Such people may want to argue against the possibility of moral dilemmas on *moral* grounds (for example, it might seem unacceptably *unfair* if an agent could find herself in a situation in which it is inevitable that she will fail to meet one of her duties all things considered); they may suggest, accordingly, that one important test of an adequate moral theory is that it be impossible for that theory to generate moral dilemmas. Still others find the existence of moral dilemmas perfectly acceptable, provided that the *only* way that an agent can find herself in such a dilemma is if she has *already* acted immorally, in some earlier situation where doing so was not inevitable. (They argue, in effect, that if it is her *fault* that she is in the present dilemma, then it is not unfair that she will inevitably compound her moral failings.) On such a view, the relevant test for adequate normative theories is not that it be impossible for the theory to generate dilemmas at all, but that it be impossible to face such a dilemma if one has never acted immorally. Finally, there are still others who think that moral dilemmas can face even the innocent. They argue, in effect, that the world is a tragic and conflict-ridden place, and that in principle anyone at all might find themselves in a situation in which, inevitably and unjustifiably, they will do wrong.

I will not try to adjudicate between these rival positions concerning the possibility of moral dilemmas. I only want to note that even if such dilemmas are possible, this does not threaten the general view that the moral status of any given act is determined by the interaction of the various normative factors at play in the situation. We might think of moral dilemmas as limiting cases of interaction, where conflict results in a *standoff* of sorts, without one side outweighing (or even neutralizing) the other. One subset of factors generates a requirement to perform some act, and another subset generates a requirement to perform an incompatible act; together the factors jointly determine that whatever the agent does, she will act immorally. Thus, even in the case of dilemmas, it remains true that the various factors at work jointly determine the moral status of the relevant acts.

In light of the ubiquity of factoral interaction, it is obvious that a complete normative theory must include more than a *list* of normative factors. It will also have to include what we might call *interaction principles*—that is, principles specifying how the various factors interact so as to determine the moral status of particular acts. (We can think of these principles as analogous to the principles of chemistry or physics. The outcome of a given chemical process is a function of the various chemical factors at work in that process; the principles of chemistry describe that function, specifying how different chemical compounds interact under differing conditions. Similarly, then, interaction principles for normative ethics specify how different normative factors interact so as to yield the particular moral outcomes that they do.) Even if two normative theories share the same list of basic normative factors, they can still differ—and differ crucially—insofar as they accept distinct interaction principles. Thus, without a statement of its interaction principles, the specification of a given normative theory is incomplete.

It might be thought, however, that interaction principles are only necessary for *pluralistic* theories—that is, theories that accept more than one basic normative factor. After all, if there is, in point of fact, only one single normative factor with intrinsic moral significance, then it is clearly impossible for more than one (genuine) factor to come into play. So questions of "interaction" can't even arise. Or so it might seem. But despite the initial plausibility of this suggestion, conflict is in fact still possible even for monistic theories. For there might be more than one *instance* of the single factor in a given case, and these distinct instantiations of the factor might conflict. Suppose, for example, that the only basic normative factor were that of promise keeping; since a person might make two promises and then find himself unable to keep both of them, the need for an interaction principle to govern such cases would not be eliminated. Indeed, even for a consequentialist theory with the simplest possible theory of the good, there will still be cases in which the agent must choose between two specific goods (for example, which of two pleasures to promote). Presumably, of course, the relevant interaction principle here is quite simple: given a conflict, the right thing to do is to promote the *greater* good. But being able to get by with fairly simple principles is not the same thing as being able to get by without any such principles at all. As far as I can see, *all* normative theories must include interaction principles.

Of course, to repeat a point made earlier, it is hardly as though we have neglected interaction principles up until now (even if we haven't called them by this name). The various normative factors were never introduced in isolation; questions of interaction have been with us throughout. But, as we have also observed, our discussion of interaction principles has been abbreviated and incomplete. In principle, it seems, a fully specified normative theory would include fully specified interaction principles. And this is something we have not tried to produce.

Is it truly possible to have such fully specified principles? Or must we remain content with truncated and imprecise principles of the kinds that we have examined? In answering these questions, it is important to distinguish between metaphysical and epistemological claims. It might well be the case that we could never *describe* a set of interaction principles that would strike us as both plausible and complete. Perhaps whatever principles we articulate, we will always find omissions and exceptions. This might be true for practical reasons (perhaps complete principles would be hopelessly unwieldy). Or our inability to articulate complete principles might go deeper than this. Perhaps we simply lack the epistemic resources needed to *discover* fully specified interaction principles, or lack the linguistic and conceptual resources needed to *state* them. These are clearly troubling possibilities, and we would need to undertake complex investigations in metaethics to try to settle them. I won't try to do that here.

But such broadly epistemological concerns need to be distinguished from the metaphysical thesis that no such principles *exist,* whether or not we can adequately discover and articulate them. Even if one accepts some of the epistemological worries, there might still be good reason to reject the metaphysical thesis. For if the moral status of any given act is indeed determined by the various normative factors at play, then it seems that there must be some principles or laws—governing the interaction of those factors—by virtue of which this particular combination of factors results in the particular moral outcome that it does. (Analogously, we may be incapable of discovering or articulating the basic principles of chemistry; but presumably such principles must exist, governing the outcomes of chemical interactions. Admittedly, however, the legitimacy of this analogy is itself a metaethical question, one which we cannot pursue.)

However, to insist that complete interaction principles must exist (whether or not we can state them) is not yet to say anything about how *general* these principles are. One could hold the view that in each specific case there is a correct or best answer concerning the moral status of any given act, while still maintaining that there are no interesting generalizations to be had—not even in theory—subsuming different cases. That is to say, one might be a *particularist* about moral cases. Each particular configuration of features might yield a determinate moral outcome. And, no doubt, any two cases that were *exactly* alike in every single aspect would be identical in terms of the moral status of the corresponding acts. But for all this there might be no generalizations whatsoever linking cases that differ in any way. Each type of case would be governed by its own unique principle, relevant only to that precise configuration of features. No principles more general than this would exist, not even in theory. (Of course, if there is a right answer in each case, then one could—at least in theory—string all of these together, into one hopelessly long, and perhaps infinite, principle. The question really is whether any generalizations exist other than this philosophically *uninteresting* one.)

The most radical version of particularism would not even accept the existence of a finite and fixed list of basic normative factors. On such a view, any feature at all might be morally relevant in the right circumstances—without deriving its moral force (in those circumstances) from some more basic normative factor. Features that made a difference in one case might never make any kind of difference again (except in cases literally identical to the first), and the very attempt to identify a list of basic normative factors would therefore be ill founded and illegitimate.

In point of fact, of course, many particularists are less radical than this. They accept the existence of a fixed number of basic normative factors, from which all other morally relevant features derive their significance. But they will deny that there are any general principles to be discovered governing the interaction of these factors. Each particular combination of factors remains governed by its own unique principle.

Some particularists are more moderate still. They are prepared to accept the existence of *generalizations*—provided that it is understood that these generalizations never take the form of principles that are exceptionless and universal. There may, for example, be statistical generalizations to the effect that a given factor typically outweighs another, or that some third factor normally loses its force in the presence of a fourth. But despite the truth of these generalizations, there will be no *complete* set of interaction principles; any set of true principles will fail to cover certain possible cases, or will be subject to exceptions. In theory, it should be noted, this type of particularism is compatible with belief in the existence of interaction principles with a quite significant degree of generality: large numbers of distinct cases might be subsumed under a few general principles. Obviously, a position like this last one is rather removed from the spirit of *radical* particularism; but it remains particularist insofar as it shares the basic claim that there is no complete set of exceptionless interaction principles (except, of course, for the trivial solution of listing all the right answers).

We can call those who reject particularism, even in its most modest form, *universalists*. Obviously enough, universalism is the view that there exists— at least in theory—a complete set of interaction principles. The principles are complete and exceptionless, insofar as they govern all possible combinations of normative factors; for each such possible configuration, the principles correctly assign a determinate moral status to the relevant actions on the basis of the factors at play. (Once again, if we are to avoid having universalism be true trivially, we will have to disallow making an infinite list that simply combines the right answer for each distinct case.)

It is worth emphasizing the point that universalists are only committed to the *existence* of such a complete set of interaction principles. They need not believe that we can discover these principles or articulate them. And they certainly need not believe that exceptionless interaction principles will have any role in practical moral deliberation.

They *need* not believe these things; but for all that, they *might* believe them. That is, universalists might in fact be fairly optimistic about our ability to discover, articulate, and make use of the interaction principles. After all, the number of *basic* normative factors might be relatively small, and the interaction of these factors might be governed by a limited number of reasonably straightforward principles. Admittedly, the possible combinations of normative factors may be able to grow ever more complex. But this does not, in and of itself, give reason to assume that the principles governing those interactions are themselves complex or beyond our grasp.

Whether such optimism is justified depends, again, on a number of metaethical issues that we cannot here explore. But universalists may prefer to defend their optimism by *vindicating* it. After all, the most persuasive demonstration of the existence of complete interaction principles would be to display them (of course, the accuracy of the principles would have to be established as well; mere assertion will hardly suffice). Accordingly, universalists often engage in the attempt to discover and state the various principles governing the interaction of the basic normative factors.

Such an investigation, however, is not at all limited to those who share the optimistic belief in our ability to discover complete interaction principles. Even if the only principles we are able to discover (and perhaps the only ones that exist) are limited and incomplete, we may still gain by articulating them—both in terms of theoretical understanding and in terms of practical deliberation. Virtually everyone—everyone, that is, except for the most radical of particularists—thinks that we are likely to gain at least *something* of value through the careful investigation of normative factors and their interaction.

We have, of course, been engaged in the beginnings of such an investigation throughout this book. But, as we have repeatedly seen, we have only taken some first few steps, and many difficult questions remain. The investigation of normative factors and their interaction is an on-going process. I think it fair to say that it comprises a large part of the contemporary discipline of normative ethics.

**Part Two**

# FOUNDATIONS

# 6

# TELEOLOGICAL
# FOUNDATIONS

## 6.1 Foundational Theories

Although the investigation of the various normative factors and their inter-action makes up a large part of normative ethics, it does not exhaust the field. For even if we had an adequate account of these matters, questions would still remain concerning the *foundations* of normative ethics (recall the distinction between factors and foundations drawn in 1.4). It is, after all, one thing to say which factors possess genuine moral significance; it is quite another thing to say what grounds or explains the moral significance of those factors.

Of course, whether a given factor is relevant in a *particular* case depends on the specific facts of that case. But what explains why a given basic nor-mative factor ever makes any difference at all to the moral status of our ac-tions? Why do the basic normative factors have the moral relevance that they do? Foundational theories in normative ethics try to answer these questions. They offer rival accounts concerning the grounding or basis of the normative factors. Similarly, they try to explain why the basic norma-tive factors have the precise contours and contents that they do, and why the various factors interact in the precise ways that they do.

It is perhaps worth noting explicitly that in calling such theories "foun-dational" I do not mean to be claiming that they are basic or primary in an epistemological sense. That is, I am not claiming that our knowledge of the foundations of normative ethics is somehow uniquely "prior" to, or more secure than, our knowledge of the normative factors themselves (though this is, to be sure, one possible view). Of course, as I have noted previously (in 1.4), it does seem likely that commitment to one or another theory at the foundational level will sometimes lead us to embrace particular views at the factoral level (helping us to settle factoral disputes that we cannot oth- erwise resolve). But it also seems likely that our commitments at the fac- toral level will themselves sometimes lead us to embrace particular founda- tional theories (namely, those theories capable of generating what we independently take to be plausible views at the factoral level). Thus, from the *epistemological* point of view, it might well be that neither level is more fundamental than the other.

But there is still a sense in which theories at this new "lower" level are in- deed more fundamental than theories at the factoral level, in that these the- ories purport to *explain* the various facts concerning the basic normative factors. That is, these new theories attempt to explain what it is *by virtue of which* the relevant factors are indeed relevant (and what makes it be the case that one factor outweighs another, and so forth); they offer accounts of the basis or *grounding* of the normative factors. It is to this feature that I mean to be drawing attention, then, in calling such theories *foundational*.

Of course it should be noted, right from the start, that one possible "foundational" theory simply *denies* that there is any deeper explanation to be had concerning what gives the basic normative factors their moral sig- nificance. No doubt certain ("secondary") factors can be derived from other, more basic factors (as, for example, many specific constraints can be derived from the more basic constraint against doing harm). But—or so this view holds—once we reach the list of basic normative factors, there is nothing more to be said. Each such factor possesses intrinsic moral signifi- cance, and there is simply no explanation at all as to why these factors (and not others) do possess moral significance in this way. Nothing grounds, or explains, the moral relevance of the basic normative factors. Similarly, there is no explanation to be had concerning why the various basic factors inter- act in the particular ways that they do. According to the *nonfoundational- ist*, then, the quest for a more substantial foundational theory is misguided.

Now it must be admitted that nonfoundationalism might very well be the truth. But, at the very least, it would be premature to conclude this before examining several of the most significant (substantive) foundational theo- ries that have been offered. For if we can indeed find a foundational theory that provides a plausible unified account of the basic normative factors— especially if that account seems independently attractive—then nonfounda- tionalism will have little to recommend it. So the claims of the nonfounda- tionalist must be kept in abeyance, until we have surveyed some of the more substantial foundational alternatives.

Unfortunately, I am not aware of any truly satisfactory scheme for classi- fying and ordering the various rival foundational theories. (In part, this is because the most plausible and familiar foundational theories tend to bor- row elements from one another.) But it is common to divide foundational accounts into two groups: *teleological* and *deontological*. I will follow this common practice, although it is important not to be misled by these labels, since they have already been put to (different) use in classifying factoral theories.

At the *factoral* level, as we know (see 2.6), a teleological theory is one that holds that the only basic normative factor is the good—whether the individual good (as in ethical egoism) or the overall good (as in consequentialism). Note that, in and of itself, teleology at the factoral level takes no stand whatsoever as to what it is that grounds or explains the relevance of this single factor. But one might, of course, accept the *foundational* view that the relevance of the basic normative factors (whatever they are) is ultimately to be explained in terms of the significance of some good or group of goods. This is to accept teleology at the foundational level. (It would also be natural enough, at this point, to make the still further assumption that whoever accepts teleology at the factoral level accepts it at the foundational level, and vice versa. But in fact, as we shall eventually see, this natural assumption is mistaken.)

Returning to the factoral level, *deontology* accepts the existence of normative factors capable of outweighing the good; that is to say, factoral deontologists accept *constraints.* Once again, however, a factoral view of this sort takes no stand in and of itself concerning what it is that grounds or explains the relevance of the various basic normative factors. In particular, factoral deontology in and of itself doesn't offer an explanation of why it is that certain factors are capable of outweighing the good. That is just to say that factoral deontology is not a foundational view. What, then, should we mean by calling certain *foundational* views deontological? Unfortunately, there is no completely satisfying suggestion to make at this point.

One possible line of thought begins by noting that in the case of teleology, the same concept—namely, the good—is central at both the factoral and the foundational level (hence the appropriateness of referring to both levels by the same qualifying label—"teleological"). Analogously, then, we might try suggesting that given that the central concept of factoral deontology is that of *constraints,* the central explanatory concept of foundational deontology must be that of constraints as well. That is, it might be suggested that foundational deontological views are those that hold that the relevance of the basic normative factors (whatever they are) is ultimately to be explained in terms of the significance of constraints. However, it is not at all clear how a foundational theory would proceed along these lines (that is, trying to explain the relevance and contents of the basic normative factors in terms of constraints). And, in any event, such a definition would be far too narrow to include most (if not all) of the foundational theories that are normally thought of as being deontological.

Alternatively, we might decide to call a foundational theory deontological provided that it *grounds* constraints at the factoral level. That is, any foundational theory that yields a deontological theory at the factoral level will itself, by virtue of that very fact, be labeled deontological. Unfortunately, although this seems a harmless enough suggestion, it threatens to undermine the very distinction between teleological and deontological foundational theories. For it presupposes that teleological foundational theories cannot generate deontological factoral theories, and this assumption (although an initially plausible one) is, as we shall see, false.

Perhaps we should simply understand deontological foundational theories to be those that are not teleological. Given our characterization of teleological foundational theories as those that explain the relevance of the basic normative factors (whatever they are) in terms of the significance of the good (or goods), we could then say that deontological foundational theories are those that do *not* hold that the relevance of the basic normative factors can be ultimately explained solely in terms of such an appeal to the good.

Such an approach may suffice, provided that we emphasize the point that a deontological foundational theory need not forgo appeal to notions of the good altogether. For in fact (once more, as we shall see), many theories typically characterized as deontological do make use of one or another concept of the good at some point. Rather, the idea is that teleological theories appeal *solely* to the significance of the good, whereas deontological theories make use of further fundamental concepts as well. (Analogously, deontological factoral theories need not deny that the good is *one* of the morally relevant normative factors; they differ from teleological factoral theories insofar as the latter think that the good is the *only* morally relevant normative factor.)

No doubt, drawing the contrast in this way is still something of an idealization, since *no* foundationally teleological theory actually gets by making use of *only* the concept of the good. Still, this approach rightly highlights the fact that teleological foundational theories emphasize and give priority to explaining things in terms of the good, while those foundational theories typically thought of as deontological do not similarly give notions of the good such exclusive priority.

One further proposal is worth considering as well. It is sometimes suggested that the defining characteristic of deontological foundational theories is that they recognize "the priority of the right over the good" (a corresponding suggestion for defining deontology at the factoral level was considered in 3.1). But such a suggestion is ambiguous. If it means that a foundational theory is deontological whenever it generates a factoral theory according to which the right has "priority" over the good—that is, whenever it generates a factoral theory that includes constraints—then this is simply duplicating the natural but mistaken assumption that teleological foundational theories cannot yield constraints at the factoral level. On the other hand, if the suggestion is that foundationally deontological theories are those that appeal to the priority of the right over the good as part of the *explanation* of the normative factors (whatever they are), then such talk seems to me unhelpful and confusing. At best, it may simply be an alternative (and potentially misleading) way of stating the point that the explanations offered by deontological foundational theories do not focus exclusively, nor even primarily, upon the significance of the good.

If this is the proper way to understand the proposal, then I obviously have no serious quarrel with it, since this is the very suggestion that I have endorsed. But talk of the priority of the *right* over the good seems to me unhelpful in this context, since even if deontological foundational accounts do appeal to other concepts beyond that of the good, there is no particular reason to think that these further concepts are necessarily characterizable in any helpful way as being concepts of "the right." (Indeed, we should never lose sight of the fact that *all* foundational theories—teleological as well as deontological—are attempts to explain or ground accounts of the right.)

For all these reasons, then, I think it preferable to define the notion of a deontological foundational theory in the way that I have: a foundational theory is deontological if it is not teleological. Although this way of drawing the distinction is hardly beyond reproach, I know of none better. At any rate, this approach does have the virtue of pointing toward a plausible way of organizing our survey of foundational theories. We can begin (in this chapter) with teleological theories, theories that attempt to explain the relevance of the normative factors in terms of the significance of some notion of the good. We can then move on (in the final chapter) to consider deontological foundational theories, theories that appeal to a broader (or alternative) explanatory basis.

Before beginning that survey, however, it may be worth repeating a warning I made at the start of the book (in 1.3): everything that follows is sketchy and incomplete. Only what I take to be the most important foundational theories will be considered (rather than all those that have been proposed). And even for those theories that I do discuss, there will be nothing like a thorough presentation: I will only identify some of the most important features of any given theory, and I'll typically do nothing more than briefly indicate some of the different ways that the details of that theory might be filled in. Finally, it must be borne in mind that although I will try to indicate some of the most significant advantages and disadvantages of a given theory, there is always more that could be said in response to any particular argument. I only hope to say enough to illustrate what I take to be some of the most interesting and difficult questions surrounding each foundational theory.

A warning of a rather different sort may be in order here as well. The discussion that follows is considerably more abstract than that found in Part One. Since the primary aim of the various foundational theories is to explain and to justify the content of the factoral level, rather than to *describe* that content, discussions of foundational theories tend to be relatively removed from the familiar features of everyday moral experience and deliberation (at least, in comparison to discussions of the normative factors themselves). What's more—perhaps in part by virtue of being so much more abstract—even the most important foundational views are considerably less familiar than the various factoral views that we considered in Part One. The result of all of this, I fear, is that some may find the ensuing discussion of foundational theories rather more difficult to master. The situation is unfortunate, but I see no way around it: without an examination of the possible bases or groundings of the basic normative factors, our understanding of normative ethics would remain incomplete.

## 6.2   Egoism

Foundational theories of normative ethics attempt to explain why the various features of the factoral level are the way they are. *Teleological* foundational theories share the basic thought that, ultimately, the explanation of the factoral level turns on the significance of the good. But different teleological theories diverge from one another insofar as they appeal to different notions of the good. In particular, it is worth recalling that an account of the good might be individualistic or universalistic (see 2.6); that is, talk of what is good might be limited to a personal or subjective point of view—what is good *for the agent,* say—or it might be concerned, rather, with the overall good, what is good from an impersonal or impartial point of view (see 2.3).

Suppose we begin, then, with teleological theories that focus on individualistic notions of the good, in particular on what is good for the individual agent. This is *egoism* (or ethical egoism). We have already considered ethical egoism, quite briefly, as a possible view at the factoral level (it was officially introduced at 2.6; but see 2.3 as well). As a *factoral* theory, egoism holds that there is one and only one factor with intrinsic moral significance—the outcome for the given agent. According to egoism as a factoral theory, a given agent's act is morally right if and only if it has the best possible results for that very agent; no one else's well-being matters at all (except insofar as it happens to affect the agent's own well-being). No other factors possess any intrinsic moral significance.

When discussing this view previously, I suggested that as a theory about which factors matter in determining the *moral* status of an act, egoism seemed a rather implausible view. Morally speaking, it seems, many things may matter besides the agent's own well-being.

Does egoism do any better as a *foundational* view? Interestingly, I think it may. (In point of fact, I think that whatever appeal egoism has at the factoral level is largely to be explained in terms of the considerable appeal of egoism at the foundational level. Some people, attracted to foundational egoism, are willing to embrace factoral egoism—*despite* its intuitive drawbacks—since they assume that factoral egoism is the inevitable outcome of foundational egoism. Whether this assumption is correct is a point to which we shall turn shortly.)

As a foundational theory, egoism holds that the ultimate justification for the normative factors (*whatever* they might be) is to be grounded in terms of an appeal to what is good for the individual agent. After all—the foundational egoist might suggest—it is the individual agent who, in any given case, must decide how to act. More generally, it is the individual agent who must decide *how to live*. Ultimately, then, morality must point to, or connect to, or be grounded in, considerations of the best kind of life to live. And what this seems to mean is that morality must be grounded in considerations of what is the best kind of life to *have*—that is, what kind of life constitutes the greatest benefit to the individual whose life it is. Accordingly, those normative factors (whatever they are) that possess genuine moral significance, do so by virtue of their connection to providing (or being a part of) a life that is the best possible life for the agent. Put another way, moral justification must ultimately be grounded in terms of what is best for the agent, in terms of the individual agent's well-being or self-interest.

Furthermore—the egoist might continue—it would be difficult to accept an account of morality according to which morality and rationality could conflict. That is, it seems implausible to believe that an adequate account of morality could be such that a given act could be one that is both *required* by morality and yet *irrational* to perform. So whatever the ultimate foundations of normative ethics, an adequate foundational theory must appeal to the sorts of considerations that it is rational to act upon. But as far as theories of rationality go—the egoist claims—we have independent reason to accept the doctrine of *rational egoism,* the view that rationality is a matter of promoting the individual agent's self-interest or well-being. Accordingly, we have further reason to accept *ethical* egoism as the appropriate foundation for normative ethics: the relevance of the normative factors with genuine moral significance must ultimately be grounded in terms of the connection of those factors to the individual agent's well-being.

Although this line of thought is one that many people find attractive, it can be resisted. For even if it is true that morality must connect to an account of the best kind of life to live, it does not necessarily follow that the best kind of life to live must be one that is best *for* the agent, that is, one that provides (or constitutes) the greatest possible *benefit* to the agent. Similarly, even if we were to grant that it must be rational for the agent to perform any act morally required of her, it would not necessarily follow that morality must be grounded in the agent's self-interest. For we might also reject egoism as an account of *rationality* (thus allowing for the possibility that it may be rational to give weight to considerations other than those that promote your own individual self-interest).

Obviously enough, to evaluate these various claims and counterclaims would require an extended metaethical discussion concerning the nature and purpose of morality; we would also need to draw upon the on-going philosophical debate about the nature of rationality. I won't try to do any of that here. So let me simply point out that although the ideas underlying ethical egoism as a foundational theory can be resisted, they are certainly ones that many people find attractive, even compelling. Accordingly, it is well worth our while to ask just what sort of theory would be generated at the *factoral* level were we to adopt egoism at the *foundational* level.

Of course, a natural and plausible thought to have at this point is that the particular factoral theory that is generated by foundational egoism is *factoral* egoism. After all, if moral justification must ultimately be a matter of what is best for the agent—what best promotes the agent's well-being— then it certainly seems plausible to conclude that at the factoral level the only normative factor with intrinsic moral significance will be that of the goodness of the outcome for the agent. Thus, it seems, foundational egoism supports factoral egoism. (That's why, as I've already noted, acceptance of the former might lead one to accept the latter, even if, in and of itself, fac- toral egoism seems implausible.)

Now if egoism is indeed the correct account at the factoral level, then the goodness of the outcome for the agent is the *only* normative factor with in- trinsic moral significance. That is, the moral status of a given act turns solely on the nature of the contribution made by that act to the agent's well-being. In any situation at all, the morally right act for a given agent to perform is that act (of those available to the agent) that best promotes the overall well- being of the agent. No other factor has any intrinsic moral significance.

But this is not to say that no other factors possess any kind of moral sig- nificance whatsoever. The egoist can certainly argue plausibly that most (and perhaps all) of the normative factors recognized by commonsense morality do have a kind of moral significance, insofar as conforming to the rules of ordinary morality tends to promote the individual agent's self-interest.

The basic point here is a simple one (familiar from the consequentialist's use of essentially the same strategy—albeit with a different fundamental principle—in 2.6). The fundamental principle of factoral egoism says that the right act is the act that leads to the best results for the agent. But if, as a matter of empirical fact, certain types of acts tend to have good conse- quences overall for the agent, the egoist can derive "subsidiary" or "sec- ondary" rules: all other things being equal, the agent should perform acts of those specified types. Similarly, all other things being equal, the agent should *avoid* performing any specific types of acts that (as a matter of em- pirical fact) tend to have *bad* consequences overall for the agent.

The mere logical possibility of deriving secondary rules from egoism in this way is fairly straightforward. What is interesting, and striking, is the egoist's further suggestion that—as a matter of empirical fact—it is the fa- miliar rules of commonsense morality that can be justified in just this way.

Let's consider a few examples. We are all acquainted with the old saying that "honesty is the best policy." Presumably, this slogan represents the common viewpoint that telling the truth—and more particularly, not telling lies—tends to redound to the greatest possible benefit to the individual. If this empirical claim is correct, then even the *egoist* has reason, all other things being equal, to avoid telling lies. And it does not seem implausible to suggest that it *is* correct. After all, when one tells a lie, one often runs a significant risk of eventually being found out. And others may then refuse to cooperate or to do business with those they take to be liars. In the long run, then, the short term gains from lying may be outweighed by the overall negative consequences.

Similarly, it doesn't seem implausible for the egoist to claim that agents typically do better if they avoid harming others (who might, after all, retaliate), if they keep their promises (earning the trust of others), if they abide by the principle of fair play (gaining access to beneficial group practices), and so forth. The general empirical point, of course, is this: we live in a world with other individuals who are capable of harming us in various ways, and whose positive cooperation we need if we are to achieve our various individual goals. It seems fair to suggest that, on the whole, the best way to get along with others—earning their trust and cooperation, and avoiding their wrath—is to conform to the rules of commonsense morality. No doubt, from the point of view of the individual agent, conforming to these rules will sometimes have its costs; normally, however, these will be more than outweighed by the various benefits.

In this way, many of the factors recognized by commonsense morality can be given a place within the egoist framework. Of course which factors, precisely, can be given such a defense—and how much weight, precisely, these factors will have against one another—will depend on the details of the relevant empirical generalizations (a matter we cannot consider further here).

It is also worth noting that it may matter as well which particular account of well-being is incorporated into the egoist's overall theory. After all, egoists may agree that the agent's well-being is all that matters; but they still need to supplement this claim with some favored account of well-being. And different accounts of well-being may well support significantly different types of action and, therefore, different rules. For example, although there will, no doubt, be considerable overlap, the specific types of acts that tend to produce *pleasure* for the agent, say, may not be exactly the same as the specific acts that tend to satisfy the agent's *preferences;* and the divergence may be even more significant for those theories incorporating *perfectionist* accounts of well-being. Accordingly, how good a job the egoist does of supporting the various rules of commonsense morality may depend upon the particular account of well-being adopted.

Nonetheless, however effective a job the egoist does of defending the rules of commonsense morality in this way, a difficulty remains. An approach along the lines we have just sketched inevitably ends up treating the familiar rules of commonsense morality as mere *rules of thumb*. Doubtless, honesty is typically the best policy, but what about cases in which lying would in fact produce an even greater benefit? If, as the egoist has it, the morally right act is the one that will produce the greatest overall good for the agent, then in such a case lying will be the morally right thing to do. Indeed, the agent will be morally *required* to lie—regardless of whatever harm may befall the person lied to—provided that there is no other way for the agent to reap a comparable benefit. The situation is exactly the same for cases involving the rules against harming others, breaking promises, acts of ingratitude, and so on. In each case, the agent will be morally required to break the ordinary rule, *whenever* such an act will lead to the best possible results for the agent. Nothing else matters.

Obviously, most of us find this all extremely difficult to believe (after all, these are supposed to be claims about what the agent is *morally* required to do). The difficulty, of course, is this. The factoral egoist holds that the goodness of the outcome for the agent is the only factor with any intrinsic moral significance. Other factors—as we have seen—can be given a kind of derivative practical significance, but they have no moral significance in and of themselves, and so have no weight *whatsoever* when they conflict with the agent's individual well-being. Egoism at the factoral level can do nothing more than view the rules of commonsense morality as rules of thumb. On reflection, most will find this an unacceptable implication.

(None of this should surprise us, since a similar objection was made at length—beginning in 3.1—with regard to the consequentialist's structurally similar attempt to justify the rules of commonsense morality. Of course, as we noted previously, the consequentialist also has a number of possible replies to this objection. Corresponding replies are available to the egoist as well, though I won't try to rehearse them here. It may be worth noting, however, that in at least one regard, despite the structural similarities, egoism may have an intuitively worse time of it than consequentialism: for consequentialism only permits my violating the familiar rules of thumb when doing so leads to better results overall, counting everyone equally; egoism, in contrast, condones my violating the rules whenever doing so benefits *me*—let others be damned! This seems considerably less plausible.)

Given the intuitive implausibility of factoral egoism, many will conclude that it is necessary to reject foundational egoism (despite whatever appeal it may have for them). But this assumes, of course, that factoral egoism is the inevitable outcome of foundational egoism. And this assumption may not be correct. For foundational egoism per se is simply committed to the view that the basic normative factors (whatever they are) find their ultimate justification in terms of their connection to the agent's well-being. Despite what we might assume, this view does not entail—in and of itself—that the goodness of the outcome for the agent is the only basic normative factor.

In effect, we have been assuming, up to this point, that the right way (and the only way) to generate a factoral view from foundational egoism is this: take the evaluative standpoint provided by foundational egoism—the question of what benefits the agent—and use it to directly evaluate the various *actions* open to the agent. Let's call this approach *act egoism*. Plausibly enough, if this is our approach, the only permissible actions will be those that best promote the agent's overall well-being. And if we then ask, accordingly, what *features* help to make permissible actions permissible, there will be one and only one factor with this kind of significance—the goodness of the outcome for the agent. Thus, it seems, act egoism leads to factoral egoism, with its single, basic, normative factor (all other factors being reduced to at best secondary significance).

But suppose that we take the evaluative standpoint provided by foundational egoism, and rather than using it directly to evaluate actions, we use it instead to directly evaluate alternative moral *rules*. Suppose, that is, that we first ask ourselves what moral rules are such that conformity to these rules on the part of the agent will be of the greatest benefit to the agent. Armed, then, with the optimal set of rules (as evaluated from the standpoint of foundational egoism), we can then go on to evaluate actions in terms of their *conformity* to those rules. That is, we can hold that a right act is one that conforms to the optimal set of rules. This is the approach of *rule egoism*.

(Since act egoists evaluate acts directly, while rule egoists do so only indirectly, the former are sometimes called *direct* egoists, while the latter are called *indirect* egoists. But these labels may reflect a bias in favor of acts. After all, even though rule egoists are admittedly indirect with regard to the evaluation of acts, they are nonetheless direct with regard to the evaluation of rules. Indeed, from the point of view of those who favor *rules* as the direct target of evaluation, it is the *act* egoist who might well be thought to deserve the label "indirect egoist"—since act egoists typically evaluate rules only indirectly, for example, in terms of which rules best promote performing the acts with the best results. In any event, as we shall see, rule egoism is, at best, only one *type* of indirect egoism (in this sense), rather than exhausting the class. Eventually, at the end of 6.5, I'll suggest a different use for the label "direct.")

Now on an approach of this second kind, there is no reason to assume that there will be one and only one basic normative factor. On the contrary, if the right act is the act that conforms to the set of optimal moral rules, then what we should expect is that there will be at least as many factors relevant to determining the moral status of an act as there are distinct moral rules (perhaps even more, since any given rule might be concerned with more than one feature of the situation). And since there is no reason to assume (in the absence of further argument) that there will be one and only one rule in the optimal set, it might well turn out that *several* factors will help to determine an action's moral status. In short, there might be several basic normative factors.

Thus there is no reason to assume that *rule* egoism will lead to *factoral* egoism. Yet rule egoism can still be seen as one possible way of working out the details of *foundational* egoism, given that the rules themselves are to be evaluated in terms of the benefit to the agent of acting upon these rules. Admittedly, rule egoism does not evaluate individual actions directly in terms of the agent's well-being. But it does do so *indirectly*: it evaluates actions in terms of their conformity to the optimal rules, and it evaluate the *rules* in terms of their impact on the agent's well-being. Thus rule egoism remains faithful to the foundational egoist thought that the normative factors (whatever they are) must *ultimately* be grounded in considerations of the agent's well-being. But it manages to do this in a way that avoids *factoral* egoism.

This last point is worth stressing. Our initial approach to foundational egoism—act egoism—led to factoral egoism, according to which goodness of outcome for the agent is the only normative factor with intrinsic moral significance. Thus, an act is permissible if and only if it leads to the best possible results for the agent. But it seems that nothing like this will be true for the second approach, that of the rule egoist. For *it* holds that an act is permissible if and only if it conforms to the optimal rules. So unless the optimal rules simply say "do the act that leads to the best possible results for yourself," some of the acts that are permitted by factoral egoism may well be forbidden by rule egoism.

We need to ask, therefore, what sorts of rules *would* be embraced by a rule egoist. That is, we need to ask what sorts of rules are such that, on the whole, acting on those rules would be best for the agent. But, in point of fact, that's a question we have already considered, when we noted how a factoral egoist might be led to the familiar rules of commonsense morality. Given various plausible empirical generalizations, it was suggested, acting on the rules of commonsense morality would normally have better results for the agent than disregarding those rules. But if this is right, then these would be among the rules endorsed by the rule egoist as well. In short, if we ask ourselves what set of rules would be selected as best (from the evaluative standpoint of foundational egoism), the answer might well be that the optimal set of rules will include the familiar rules of commonsense morality.

Obviously enough, our two different approaches to deriving a factoral theory from foundational egoism have much in common. Both start with foundational egoism, and both eventually arrive at the familiar moral rules. Indeed, both embrace those rules on the very same ground, namely, that conformity to those rules is, on the whole, likely to be best for the agent. But the *status* of those rules is quite different for the two approaches. According to the *act* egoist, the rules are mere rules of thumb, to be violated whenever doing so leads to better results overall for the agent. According to the *rule* egoist, however, the rules are not mere rules of thumb. On the contrary, since the right act is the act that *conforms* to those rules, violating the rules is morally *forbidden*.

(But what if the rules *conflict*? That is, what if any action open to the agent would violate one or another of the rules? Obviously enough, the possibility of such a case wouldn't pose any particular difficulty for an *act* egoist—who considers the rules to be mere rules of thumb—since violating a rule of thumb has no intrinsic moral significance. Therefore, in cases of conflict, as indeed in all cases, the right thing to do is whichever act has the best results for the agent. But according to the *rule* egoist, a given act is permissible by virtue of its *conformity* to the optimal rules. So what should be said about cases in which it is *impossible* for the agent to conform to all the rules? Some rule egoists may be willing to accept the possibility of such cases, viewing them as the source of intractable moral dilemmas (see 5.4). Others, however, may want to deny the possibility of such dilemmas. One approach would be to construe many of the ordinary familiar moral rules as statements of merely prima facie duties. These would then need to be supplemented with "priority rules" indicating which prima facie duties outrank others in generating duties all things considered (again, see 5.4). Presumably, these priority rules would then themselves be evaluated on the basis of their overall contribution to the agent's well-being. In what follows, I'll leave these complications aside.)

It is important to be clear about the status of the optimal rules under rule egoism. According to the rule egoist, since the right thing to do is to conform to the rules, violating those rules is simply forbidden—*even if* breaking the rules would lead to better results (in this particular case) for the agent. For rule egoism doesn't evaluate an individual act directly in terms of *its* consequences for the agent; and the mere fact that some act might have better results does not suffice to make that act permissible. Rather, rule egoism evaluates the individual acts only in terms of whether or not they conform to the optimal set of rules, and it is the *rules* that are evaluated in terms of their overall consequences for the agent. If a rule is truly a member of the optimal set, then the right thing for the agent to do is to conform to that rule, whatever the results in some particular case. Clearly, then, for the rule egoist, the optimal rules are far more than mere rules of thumb.

(How *could* a rule be a member of the optimal set of rules, if breaking it would be better for the agent? Perhaps the circumstances in which breaking the rule is beneficial are highly unusual, while in the more typical case conformity to the rule is quite advantageous. If so, then, *on the whole*, the agent might do better if she generally conforms to the rule. Thus despite the fact that in exceptional circumstances breaking the rule would—in that particular case—lead to better results for the agent, the rule might still be a member of the optimal set.)

So what, exactly, does rule egoism lead to at the factoral level? As we have seen, although the matter is controversial (and depends on empirical claims we cannot investigate here), it seems plausible to suggest that rule egoism supports a *pluralistic* view at the factoral level, according to which each of the optimal rules (or, more precisely, the various normative factors identified by those rules) has intrinsic normative significance. Furthermore, it seems plausible to suggest that the optimal rules will include many of the familiar rules of commonsense morality.

But a further point is worth noting as well. As we have observed in previous chapters, many of the rules of commonsense morality seem to take the form of *constraints* (ruling out various actions even if greater good would result from the impersonal point of view). It seems likely, therefore, that many of the optimal egoistic rules will take the form of constraints as well. And this means that rule egoism at the foundational level will generate *deontology* at the factoral level. This last point is worth emphasizing, since, as we have seen, it is natural to think that theories that are teleological at the foundational level cannot generate deontological theories at the factoral level. In sum, rule egoism may provide a possible foundation for something like commonsense deontology.

Of course, all of this is rather rough and conjectural, and many of the details are unclear. For example, assuming that rule egoism does indeed support factoral deontology, is it a moderate or an absolutist version of deontology? That is, will the optimal rules have thresholds, or not? But rather than pursuing these details any further, I want to return to the contrast between rule egoism and act egoism.

As we have noted, rule egoism and act egoism are *both* versions of foundational egoism; they share the foundational egoist thought that the basic normative factors (whatever they are) are ultimately grounded in questions concerning what benefits the agent. They both use benefit to the agent as the method of evaluating their favored objects of evaluation, whether acts or rules. But they differ in their choice of *primary* evaluative focal point. Rule egoists have *rules* as their primary evaluative focal point; it is the various possible moral rules that are evaluated directly in terms of their benefit to the agent. Of course, rule egoists do then go on to evaluate acts as well, but only in a secondary, or derivative, way, in terms of (conformity to) the directly evaluated rules. In contrast, act egoists select *acts* as their primary evaluative focal point, evaluating them directly. The act egoist does, of course, eventually go on to evaluate alternative moral rules as well. But this is, again, a secondary matter.

As we have also seen, this difference in choice of primary evaluative focal points seems to have significant implications at the factoral level, with act egoism leading to factoral egoism, while rule egoism leads to commonsense deontology. What all this means, of course, is that the mere allegiance to foundational egoism is not in and of itself sufficient to settle the issue of which normative factors possess intrinsic moral significance: we must also choose among potential primary evaluative focal points. Clearly, then, the choice of primary evaluative focal point is a weighty matter.

But just what is there to guide us in our choice between the act and the rule versions of egoism? One thing we can do, of course, is to trace out the various factoral implications of these two theories, in the way that we have been doing. Many people find it intuitively implausible to treat the familiar rules of commonsense morality as mere rules of thumb—as the act egoist does—to be violated whenever this is advantageous to the agent. This may then provide some reason to prefer rule egoism, which seems to give the rules of commonsense morality the same force they have intuitively. (Of course, those who think that such intuitions shouldn't be given much weight won't find this a compelling argument.)

Are there *other* grounds for choosing between rule and act egoism? Sometimes the charge is made that the rule egoist is irrational. After all, how can it be rational to conform to the rules even when you know that you would be better off breaking them in this particular case? The rule egoist seems guilty of "rule worship." One possible reply to this objection admits that it may be *irrational* to conform to the rules in such cases, but insists that conformity might nonetheless be *morally* required. But this reply doesn't seem an especially promising one for an *egoist* to make, given that much of the appeal of foundational egoism lies in its apparent ability to reconcile morality and rationality.

A more intriguing reply would be for the rule egoist to insist that conformity to the optimal rules can *never* be irrational—not even when you know that breaking them would leave you better off. After all, why should we assume that the rationality of an act is evaluated directly in terms of the benefits of that very act? Perhaps, instead, the rationality of individual actions should be evaluated indirectly, in terms of the act's conformity to the most beneficial rules. In effect, the objection assumes that the correct theory of rationality is act egoistic rather than rule egoistic. But assuming—without argument—that rationality takes the form of act egoism may simply beg the question against *rule* egoism (both as a moral theory and as a theory of rationality).

Even if we put aside such issues about the nature of rationality, the charge of rule worship might still seem to have force. After all, if—as foundational egoists believe—benefit to the agent provides the ultimate moral grounding for our normative theory, how can it make sense from the *moral* point of view to require conformity to rules in those cases where breaking the rules would provide greater benefit? But once again, this may just beg the question, by assuming that the *primary* evaluative focal point should be actions rather than rules. The rule egoist *agrees* with the act egoist that benefit to the agent provides the ultimate basis for normative ethics. But as we have seen, this point of agreement does not—in and of itself—settle the choice between rule and act egoism.

Perhaps there are more theoretical, metaethical grounds for choosing between rules and acts. For example, according to some people the very concept of a morality is that of a system of universal moral rules. On this conception, it will seem very natural indeed to select rules as the primary evaluative focal point. Others, however, may find it more plausible to suggest that central to the very concept of morality is the idea of evaluating actions. If so, then it may seem natural to insist that the *primary* evaluative focal point must be actions, rather than rules. No doubt, still other metaethical considerations may be relevant to this choice as well. Unfortunately, here, as elsewhere, sustained examination of such metaethical conceptions lies beyond the scope of this book.

## 6.3  Virtues

As we have seen, foundational egoists face a choice between evaluative focal points: some make acts the primary focal point, while others make rules primary. To state the obvious, however, rules and acts are not the only types of things that can be the focal point of moral evaluation. For example, to name just a few more, one can also evaluate motives, institutions, behavioral norms, or character traits. Clearly, there are many other possibilities as well. For each such focal point, there is a corresponding version of foundational egoism, one that makes direct evaluations of items of the preferred type, while evaluating the other kinds of focal points only indirectly, in terms of the primary set of evaluations. Thus we can have *motive egoism*, which first asks what types of motives would be most beneficial to the agent, and then holds that an act is permissible if and only if someone with the optimal motives could be motivated to do it. Or we could have *institution egoism,* which first asks what type of social institutions would be most beneficial to the agent. (There are various ways such a view might produce evaluations of the other focal points. For example, it might hold that an *act* is permissible if and only if it conforms to the various *rules* that would be promulgated by the optimal set of social *institutions*.) Similar possibilities arise for the other types of evaluative focal points as well.

There is no space here to consider each of these different focal points along with the corresponding versions of foundational egoism. But it would, I think, be helpful to consider more carefully the category of character traits. Obviously enough, one topic of central interest from the moral point of view is what people should be like, that is, what kind of character (or characters) we would like people to have. Thus, one important evaluative question is what types of characters are best from the moral point of view. The first point to note, however, is that although our ultimate concern here is with evaluating "complete" personalities, or "whole" character types, in thinking about this question it is often helpful to focus on specific character *traits*: what we want to know, in effect, is which specific traits of character are desirable and which are undesirable. The desirable traits are called *virtues;* the undesirable ones, *vices.*

Now it certainly seems that we could combine a commitment to foundational egoism with an acceptance of character traits as the *primary* evaluative focal point. The basic idea, obviously, would be this. First, we would use the evaluative standpoint provided by foundational egoism to choose between alternative possible character traits (honesty, craftiness, diligence, laziness, and so forth). That is, we would ask which character traits it would be most beneficial to the agent to have. These desirable traits are the ones that foundational egoism would consider to be virtues. (Correspondingly, those traits it would be harmful to the agent to possess would be considered vices. But for simplicity, in what follows, I will focus on the virtues and neglect the vices.) An approach of this kind makes evaluation of character its *primary* concern, but obviously it can still go on to evaluate other focal points (such as actions, or rules) in a derivative, secondary fashion. Let's call a view of this kind *virtue egoism* (though it might, with equal justice, be called *character egoism,* or *character trait egoism*).

Before turning to detailed consideration of virtue egoism, it may be helpful to say something more about the general notion of a character trait (and the corresponding notion of a virtue). In offering these remarks, I am doing something that didn't seem necessary when we considered our earlier evaluative focal points—rules and acts. I assumed then that the concepts of an action and of a rule were sufficiently familiar that there was no need to preface our discussions with general accounts of these notions. Perhaps this was an unwarranted assumption. But in any event, it seems that the concept of a character trait is sufficiently complex to justify a few general remarks.

Very roughly, and as a first approximation, we can say that a character trait is a disposition to act in certain ways (for example, to tell the truth, to lie when embarrassed, to help those in need, or to run away from danger).

One way that this rough and ready account of character traits is too simple is this. In principle, it seems possible that a mere disposition to act might be momentary or fleeting. In contrast, to many people it seems that talk of a character trait necessarily involves something settled and lasting, rather than momentary. This is not to suggest that one's character traits must be permanent—never altering. But they must be relatively stable, at least somewhat resistant to fluctuation. Thus, character traits must represent *standing* dispositions to act. (Can't one be compassionate for a single moment? Perhaps, but note that we would typically say that such momentary compassion was *uncharacteristic.*)

Second, it seems possible, at least in principle, that one might be prepared to talk of a disposition to act in a certain way, where the relevant sort of action was never actually performed. (Similarly, a cube of sugar might be said to have a chemical disposition to dissolve in water, although it might never do so, if it is never actually placed in water.) In contrast, many people have thought that talk of a *character trait* is only appropriate if the corresponding behavior is at least occasionally displayed. (For example, would it really make sense to talk of someone as brave, if they never faced danger, and so never acted bravely?)

But perhaps more important than either of these first two points is this. Mere dispositions to *act* (even if settled, and sometimes actualized) are too narrow. Character traits typically involve far more than this. Generally speaking, character traits also involve dispositions to *notice* the right sorts of things, and to give them a certain *weight* in one's deliberations (whether consciously or not), perhaps by *not* giving any weight to various other considerations, or not even noticing those other things. For example, compassion is in part a matter of noticing the needs of others (it won't suffice to be disposed to help those one sees to be in need, if one never notices the need). And honesty is perhaps in part a matter of not even thinking of lying as an option (even if one ultimately rejects it). Finally, character traits often involve emotional aspects, not merely cognitive and behavioral ones (for example, one *feels* compassion).

These various complications are important, but for many purposes it doesn't seem to be too seriously misleading if—having noted them—we sometimes revert to the original account and talk of character traits simply as dispositions to act (albeit of a special kind). For at the very least it does seem that identifying the relevant disposition to act is often central to giving an account of a given character trait. Thus we can say that honesty is (at its central core) a disposition to refrain from lying and deceit, trustworthiness involves (among other things) a disposition to keep one's promises, generosity is a disposition to bestow benefits, and so forth.

In picking these examples, I have, of course, chosen character traits which intuitively qualify as virtues. That is, most of us intuitively take these traits to be desirable from the moral point of view. Note, further, how these various virtues can be viewed as dispositions to give the appropriate kind of weight to one or another of the normative factors that have previously been discussed. For example, most people believe that the fact that an act is the telling of a lie adversely affects its moral status; accordingly, there is a corresponding virtue—honesty—which consists in the disposition to avoid telling lies. Similarly, the fact that an act involves keeping a promise is normally thought to ground its being required; accordingly, there is a corresponding virtue—trustworthiness—which consists (in part) in the disposition to keep one's promises. And the fact that an act would promote the well-being of some individual is a factor that would normally support performing that act; so there is a corresponding virtue—generosity—which consists in the disposition to benefit others.

Although it does seem plausible to suggest that there is a virtue corresponding to each of the normative factors we've previously discussed, it must be admitted that this correspondence is hardly a tidy one. On the one hand, at the very least, in many cases there is no obvious English term for the relevant disposition. Thus, some hold there is a special obligation to rescue (recall 4.3); if so, then it does seem appropriate to think of a disposition to undertake such rescue as a virtue. But there doesn't seem to be any familiar term for this virtue (if indeed it is one). Similarly, there doesn't seem to be any familiar term for the virtue (if it is one) that would consist in the disposition to repay debts of gratitude. On the other hand, in many cases there is something like an embarrassment of riches, with several similar but not quite identical virtues corresponding to what is more or less the same factor. Thus, compassion, kindness, generosity, and beneficence all differ from one another in various subtle ways, yet each corresponds to the same basic factor: promoting the well-being of another. And in still other cases (for example, trustworthiness), the familiar language of virtues seems to carve up the moral terrain in a way distinct from (even if it is compatible with) that suggested by the commonsense list of normative factors.

Perhaps the explanation of this lack of a tidy correspondence between the commonsense list of normative factors and the commonsense list of virtues lies in the very fact that virtues are *character* traits, and as such closely reflect facts about human psychology. That is, brute empirical facts about human psychology (for example, what sorts of things can we discriminate between, and what do we naturally group together? what must we notice? where are emotional responses inevitably going to differ?) may constrain us in various ways in the demarcation of distinct traits of character. If something like this is right, then it points to at least one way in which the selection of virtues as the primary evaluative focal point (rather than rules, or acts) may have significant implications at the factoral level.

It is also worth noting that at least some familiar virtues don't seem to correspond to specific normative factors at all. Instead, they might be better thought of as desirable second-order traits of moral agency. For example, there is general *attentiveness* to the various first-order normative factors, *practical wisdom* to deliberate well concerning the implications of the relevant factors in the case at hand, *resolve* to act appropriately in the light of one's deliberations, and so on.

One final, general point is this: if we label *all* desirable character traits as virtues, then we must recognize that the class of virtues per se will be considerably broader than what we intuitively think of as *moral* virtues. Intelligence, for example, is a virtue in this broad sense (that is, it is a desirable character trait), though we wouldn't typically consider it to be a moral virtue. We might try to demarcate the narrower class—the class of specifically moral virtues—in various ways, but I know of no approach that is completely satisfactory. For example, one natural proposal would be that the specifically moral virtues are those character traits desirable from the *moral* point of view. But this still seems too broad (after all, morality presumably does favor intelligence). To correct for this, one might suggest that moral virtues are those morally desirable character traits under voluntary control. Unfortunately, it is far from clear that all ordinary moral virtues

*are* under such voluntary control (consider, for example, compassion).
Other proposals have their own, attendant problems as well. However,
having noted the difficulty, let's put it aside, and continue to think of moral
virtues as (more or less) those character traits that are desirable from the
moral point of view.

In discussing the notion of a virtue, I have, of course, been helping myself
to familiar, commonsense examples, and commonsense views concerning
which character traits are indeed morally desirable. Obviously, however,
given that our particular concern is to think about virtues in the context of
a commitment to foundational egoism, the question becomes exactly which
character traits are desirable from the point of view of the *egoist*. That is to
say, we need to ask which particular character traits are such that the possession of those traits would benefit the agent.

Of course, it does seem plausible to think that many of the familiar, commonsense virtues will be endorsed from the point of view of egoism. This
should hardly surprise us, given the argument (made in 6.2) that certain
plausible empirical claims support the thought that the agent does best if he
has a general regard for ordinary morality. Although that earlier argument
was made specifically with regard to the familiar moral rules, it seems to go
through equally well for at least most of the commonsense virtues. Thus,
for example, honesty will be a virtue from the point of view of the egoist,
since agents disposed to be honest will be trusted by others, thus gaining
the fruits of cooperation. And the same thing will be true for many other
commonly accepted virtues as well. Of course, as before, much turns on the
details of complex empirical claims that we cannot consider (let alone evaluate) here. Still, it doesn't seem implausible to suggest that once the empirical evidence is in, the egoist's list of virtues will be fairly similar to that endorsed by common moral intuition.

Armed with the precise list of optimal character traits (whatever that
turns out to be), the virtue egoist goes on to suggest that character traits
should be the *primary* evaluative focal point. This particular claim is, of
course, highly controversial, and other foundational egoists will reject it. It
is important to see, however, that until this claim is made, there is nothing
in the discussion of virtues (whether in general, or as seen from the standpoint of egoism) that cannot be readily accepted by all egoists, including
those who reject virtue egoism. The act egoist, for example, can certainly
take a lively interest in the virtues, favoring those character traits that are
most likely to lead the agent to perform the acts that provide the greatest
benefit. Similarly, the rule egoist can be interested in knowing which character traits are most likely to lead the agent to conform to the optimal rules.
Although the precise yardstick used to evaluate character traits varies for
each of these theories (since the virtue egoist evaluates traits directly from
the standpoint of egoism, while the rule and act egoists evaluate traits only
indirectly, in terms of their favored primary focal points), the fact of the

matter is that the endorsed list of virtues is likely to be quite similar from theory to theory. That is, the very same character traits are likely to emerge *as* virtues regardless of which version of foundational egoism we select.

Where virtue egoists crucially differ from other foundational egoists is not so much in terms of the *list* of virtues, but rather in terms of the normative force that these virtues are taken to have. For virtue egoists (and only virtue egoists) make character traits the *primary* evaluative focal point, and as such, judgments concerning the other focal points depend upon those concerning character. In particular, judgments concerning the permissibility of action are derived from the relevant claims about virtue.

How is this done? One standard approach along these lines is to suggest that a given act is permissible if and only if a virtuous individual would perform it. (Perhaps we should say "might perform" rather than "would perform," to allow for the possibility that more than one act available to the agent is compatible with virtue.) Strictly speaking, this first approach is *causal* in that it asks which particular acts virtuous dispositions would lead the agent to perform. A slightly different approach would hold that an act is permissible if and only if it *conforms* to the virtues. (Since virtues are dispositions to perform acts of certain kinds under relevant conditions, we can say that a given act conforms to a given virtue provided that either the act is of the right kind, or the relevant conditions don't obtain.) Although there are interesting differences between the "causal" account of permissibility and this second, "conformity" account, these differences need not concern us here. Simplifying somewhat, we can say that for the virtue egoist, *violating* virtue is never permissible. (If specific virtues can conflict, then things are somewhat more complicated. Violating a particular virtue may be permissible if this is done in the service of an overriding virtue.)

Thus, for the virtue egoist, the virtues have intrinsic normative significance. And this is, of course, a claim that act and rule egoists reject. The *act* egoist, for example, thinks of virtues as having a merely instrumental status, similar to that of the optimal moral rules. According to the act egoist, even the best moral rules are mere rules of thumb—permissibly violated whenever doing so would lead to better results for the agent. Similarly, then, even the best character traits lack intrinsic normative significance (they are mere "traits of thumb," as it were): if, in some particular case, violating virtue would lead to better results for the agent, then this—says the act egoist—is exactly what the agent should do. In contrast, the virtue egoist insists that virtue *cannot* be permissibly violated—not even if doing so (in some particular case) would leave the agent better off. Thus, despite the fact that the virtue egoist and the act egoist share a commitment to foundational egoism, and despite the fact that both approaches lead to similar lists of virtues, the difference in choice of primary evaluative focal point results in potentially significant differences with regard to which particular acts are morally permissible.

Something similar holds for the *rule* egoist. Of course, as we know, the rule egoist rejects the act egoist's description of moral *rules* as being mere rules of thumb. But she certainly shares the judgment that *virtues* lack intrinsic significance: if, in some particular case, violating virtue is necessary to conform to the optimal rules, then this—says the rule egoist—is precisely what the agent should do. (As we can see, the rule egoist and the act egoist differ slightly as to the precise conditions under which virtues are to be violated; but they are in perfect agreement on the basic point—that virtues altogether lack intrinsic normative significance.) In contrast, the virtue egoist insists that virtue cannot be permissibly violated—not even if doing so is necessary to conform to the optimal moral rules.

Despite this theoretical difference, it remains possible that from a practical point of view not much may turn on the choice between virtue egoism and rule egoism. For in principle, the two approaches might well result in quite similar evaluations of the various acts open to the agent. It all depends on how *close* the correspondence turns out to be between the optimal set of moral rules and the optimal set of character traits. If the correspondence turns out to be very tight indeed (with a virtue corresponding to each optimal rule, and vice versa), then despite the rule egoist's willingness to violate virtue for the sake of the rules, such cases of conflict between the rules and the virtues may arise only rarely, if ever. On the other hand, if the correspondence is only a loose one, then we should expect such cases of conflict to arise more frequently, and so significant practical differences may well emerge here as well. (We have, of course, already noted some reasons to suspect that a closely related correspondence—that between virtues and commonsense normative factors—is, although genuine, not perfect; and these considerations are relevant in the present case as well. But, as usual, a great deal turns on the details of complicated empirical claims that we cannot evaluate here.)

Are there any other significant differences between virtue egoism and the other versions of foundational egoism? Interestingly, it seems that many virtue egoists are particularists; they deny the existence of universal interaction principles (see 5.4). Admittedly, for the most part they are not *radical* particularists, since they generally believe in the existence of a finite and fixed list of basic normative factors—to wit, those features that are the concerns of the virtues. Furthermore, most virtue egoists believe in the existence of various kinds of generalizations, to the effect that a given virtue typically takes precedence over another (if such conflicts are possible at all). Still, the fact of the matter is that many virtue egoists deny the existence of *universal* interaction principles: they hold that there is no complete set of exceptionless principles that is capable of determining for all cases what virtue requires.

As a result of this particularism, many virtue egoists accept a striking epistemological claim—that there is no way to *tell* what the right thing to do is, in any given case, except by *looking* to see what a virtuous person would do. But whatever the merits of this particular epistemological thesis, it should be noted that virtue egoists *need* not accept it. For the virtue egoist need not be any kind of particularist at all. Even if a virtue egoist holds the causal account of permissibility—where an act is permissible if and only if a virtuous person would *perform* it—indeed, even if the virtue egoist explicitly affirms that an act's permissibility is *based* on the very fact that it would be performed by someone with good character, this is all quite compatible with believing that in principle we are capable of arriving at a complete moral theory, a theory capable of telling us for any given case exactly what a virtuous individual would do. (We might, for example, be able to derive such conclusions from our knowledge of the *content* of the virtues.)

Thus, even a virtue egoist can believe in the existence of universal interaction principles, governing the interplay of the virtues, and even a virtue egoist can believe that in principle we have the epistemic ability to discover these principles. Of course, the virtue egoist need not believe either of these things; but there is nothing in virtue egoism in and of itself that rules any of this out.

(Even if a virtue egoist need not be a particularist, is it at least true that a particularist cannot be a rule egoist? Not necessarily. Presumably, since the rule egoist thinks that the moral status of any given act depends on whether it conforms to the optimal rules, *if* the rule egoist also believes that in each specific case there is a correct answer as to the moral status of any given act, then the rule egoist must also believe in the *existence* of an optimal rule governing that case. But in principle, it seems, the rule egoist could still be a radical particularist, holding that each specific type of case is governed by its own unique rule. Less radically, the rule egoist might believe that although many cases are straightforwardly governed by first-order rules, there is always the possibility of ever more complex cases where the first-order rules conflict, and where the conflict is resolved by a second-order rule unique to this or that particular type of conflict. Thus the rule egoist need not accept the existence of a complete set of universal interaction principles. It may well be true—as a matter of brute fact—that most rule egoists are universalists; but nothing in rule egoism per se seems to require this.)

Before leaving the discussion of virtue egoism, it is worth considering one possible objection. Just as the act egoist accused the rule egoist of "rule worship" (given the rule egoist's commitment to conforming to the optimal rules, even when violating them in some particular case might benefit the agent), the act egoist will similarly accuse the virtue egoist of "virtue worship": for the virtue egoist insists that virtue is never to be violated, not even if doing so in some particular case might leave the agent better off. How can such a commitment to virtue be reconciled with the foundational egoist thought that justification in normative ethics is ultimately a matter of benefit to the agent?

Once again, however, the best answer may be that the objection simply begs the question. The charge of rule worship failed to take seriously the suggestion that rules (rather than acts, or some other focal point) deserved to be the primary evaluative focal point. Similarly, then, the charge of *virtue* worship fails to take seriously the suggestion that virtues (rather than acts—or, for that matter, rules) should be primary. Like the act egoist and the rule egoist, the virtue egoist does indeed accept foundational egoism. But it seems that the commitment to foundational egoism does not in and of itself dictate whether the primary evaluative focal point should be acts, rules, virtues, or something altogether different. *That* choice, it appears, must be made on other grounds.

What grounds? As always, one might choose between the various foundational theories in terms of their diverging implications at the factoral level. As we have seen, it seems quite likely that virtue egoism and act egoism will give different assessments of many particular acts. In contrast, rule egoism and virtue egoism are probably closer for most cases; but even here the possibility of disagreement remains. Of course, to be worth taking seriously, all such comparisons require that the factoral implications of the various theories be worked out in far greater detail, and with far greater care, than we have done here. But in principle, at least, this may provide one possible ground for choice.

Similarly, one might appeal to various metaethical considerations in arguing for or against the choice of virtues as the primary evaluative focal point. On some conceptions of ethics, for example, morality is primarily a matter of what kind of *person* one should be. Not surprisingly, views of this sort may well support the suggestion that the primary focal point of moral evaluation should be character and the virtues. But there are, of course, alternative metaethical conceptions as well, and many of these point in the direction of other focal points. Ultimately, then, these (and other) questions in normative ethics may depend on settling substantive disagreements in metaethics. Unfortunately, as usual, to pursue these metaethical questions further lies beyond the scope of this book.

## 6.4  Act Consequentialism

All versions of foundational egoism start with the thought that the ultimate justification for the basic normative factors lies in an appeal to the good of the individual agent. Of course, as we have seen, despite this narrow focus on the agent's own particular good, at least some versions of foundational egoism may be able to generate a theory at the *factoral* level that captures something similar to (perhaps even identical to) our ordinary moral regard for the rights and well-being of others. Nonetheless, the very suggestion that at its *foundation* morality is concerned solely with the good of the individual agent is one that many people will find quite implausible. Surely—

it might be argued—morality is concerned at its heart with the well-being of all, with *overall good,* and not merely with the good of the particular agent.

Those who find this objection compelling may want to reject all versions of foundational egoism, and consider instead the possibility of a foundational theory that holds that the ultimate justification for the genuine normative factors (whatever they turn out to be) lies in an appeal to the overall good, to what is good from an impersonal or impartial point of view. This is *foundational consequentialism.* Like foundational egoism, an approach of this kind will still be teleological at the foundational level, given that it agrees that the ultimate justification for the normative factors lies in the significance of the good. But unlike foundational egoism, which appeals to an individualistic concept of the good, the relevant notion of the good here is a universalistic one, for foundational consequentialism appeals to an account of what is good overall.

We have, of course, already considered consequentialism at the factoral level (see especially 2.6). As a *factoral* theory, consequentialism holds that goodness of overall consequences is the one and only normative factor with intrinsic moral significance. Note that—in and of itself—factoral consequentialism is not committed to any particular view concerning the foundation or basis of normative ethics. Similarly, *foundational* consequentialism—in and of itself—does not take any particular stand concerning the *factoral* level. Obviously, however, one could certainly combine the two. That is to say, one might hold that the relevance of the basic normative factors (whatever they are) is ultimately to be explained in terms of an appeal to the moral significance of the overall good; and one might then also hold the further view that it is consequentialism at the factoral level which is generated by such foundational consequentialism.

Not only are foundational and factoral consequentialism compatible in this way, it is natural to assume that the partnership is a necessary one. That is, it is natural to think that foundational consequentialism necessarily leads to factoral consequentialism. And it is also natural to think that factoral consequentialism is necessarily grounded in foundational consequentialism.

In fact, however, there is reason to be suspicious of both of these assumptions. As our examination of the various versions of foundational egoism revealed, the choice of primary evaluative focal point can have significant and surprising implications at the factoral level. Arguably, for example, rule egoism can support commonsense deontology at the factoral level; foundational egoism, it seems, *need* not support factoral egoism. Similarly, then, even if it is true that some versions of foundational consequentialism do support factoral consequentialism, there might well be other versions of foundational consequentialism that yield nonconsequentialist, perhaps even deontological, results at the factoral level. So we should not assume that foundational consequentialism necessarily leads to factoral consequentialism.

Nor should we be so quick to assume that foundational consequentialism provides the only possible basis for factoral consequentialism. Even if it is true—as certainly seems likely—that there are indeed versions of foundational consequentialism which do generate consequentialism at the factoral level, it might still be possible to ground factoral consequentialism in quite different ways as well. (What might such a theory look like? Well, consider the possibility of a rule egoist who holds that the optimal set of rules actually consists of a single requirement—to promote the overall good. No doubt, the empirical claim presupposed by this position—namely, that of all possible sets of rules, the one that would most benefit the agent would simply require promoting the overall good—will strike most of us as rather implausible. But, at the very least, the example should suffice to demonstrate the *logical* possibility of combining factoral consequentialism with foundational views that are not themselves consequentialist. Further examples must await the introduction of other types of foundational views.)

Is it at least the case that we are right to assume that some versions of foundational consequentialism do indeed support factoral consequentialism? In thinking about this question, we do best to begin by recognizing the fact that foundational consequentialism, like foundational egoism, faces a choice between primary evaluative focal points. Indeed, this choice is faced by each basic type of foundational theory. For whatever our foundational theory, we must still decide what *sorts* of things should be the primary focus of our moral evaluations (whether rules, acts, motives, character traits, institutions, or what have you).

Foundational consequentialists share the belief that, ultimately, the appropriate evaluative standpoint is that of contribution to the overall good. But it seems that accepting this standpoint does not, in and of itself, commit you to any particular view concerning what the primary evaluative focal point should be. Accordingly, just as foundational egoists face a choice between act egoism, rule egoism, virtue egoism, and so forth, foundational consequentialists face a corresponding choice between *act consequentialism, rule consequentialism, virtue consequentialism,* and the like.

This being the case, we can take a further clue from the discussion of foundational egoism as well. Recall that it was *act* egoism at the foundational level which seemed to most straightforwardly support *factoral* egoism. Similarly, then, we might conjecture that among the various versions of foundational consequentialism, it is act consequentialism which most straightforwardly supports consequentialism at the factoral level as well.

In the light of all this, let's consider how the argument for factoral consequentialism might go. As we have seen, the foundational *egoist* begins with the thought that each of us easily recognizes the significance of our own individual good and is readily and appropriately moved to promote it. In fact, however (or so the foundational *consequentialist* insists), this exclusive concern with one's own good is *inappropriate* from the moral point of view. For morality is essentially impartial, equally concerned with the good of all. No doubt, it must be admitted that typically I am much more easily moved to promote my own good than the good of others. Still, from the point of view of morality, it seems that *all* genuine good is appropriately promoted, not just my own. While it may be tempting to think of my own good as having some special status, morally speaking this temptation cannot be endorsed. In effect, morality provides a standpoint from which *other* goods can be seen to possess intrinsic significance as well, and from this point of view—that is, from the point of view of morality—it is the overall good that ought to be promoted, rather than simply the good of the individual agent.

Suppose, then, that we take this more impartial evaluative standpoint and use it to evaluate individual *actions*. We can rank the various alternatives open to the agent in terms of their overall results, and then ask—in particular—which available act would do the most to promote the overall good. Thus, at the factoral level, there would be one and only one factor with intrinsic normative significance: goodness of overall results. But this, of course, is factoral consequentialism. In short, act consequentialism at the foundational level does indeed appear to generate consequentialism at the factoral level.

(Of course, factoral consequentialism only takes on determinate content when combined with a particular theory of the overall good. But the same thing seems true for foundational consequentialist theories as well: there is a sense in which they are incomplete, until they are combined with some particular account of the good. And it does seem plausible to think that once the choice of a theory of the good is made at the foundational level, it will be reflected at the factoral level as well. For example, one might combine act consequentialism with a welfarist theory of the good. This would be the foundational theory *act utilitarianism,* and it appears to support *factoral* utilitarianism, that is, the combination of factoral consequentialism and welfarism. Presumably, incorporating more pluralistic theories of the good into the act consequentialist framework would yield correspondingly more pluralistic versions of factoral consequentialism as well. But more on this in a moment.)

Various elements in this act consequentialist defense of factoral consequentialism can be resisted. Most obviously, one might reject foundational consequentialism, preferring instead the evaluative standpoint of foundational egoism or some other foundational view. Alternatively, one might accept the starting point of foundational consequentialism, but reject the assumption that actions provide the appropriate primary evaluative focal point (a position to be considered in the next section).

But there are less obvious possibilities as well. For—despite appearances—it seems that in principle one might accept both foundational consequentialism *and* the choice of actions as the appropriate focal point, while still resisting the claim that this combination of views necessarily generates consequentialism at the factoral level.

It is sometimes suggested, for example, that even if we do accept act consequentialism, so long as we go on to adopt an appropriately rich theory of the good at the foundational level, what emerges at the factoral level is not consequentialism at all, but rather deontology. That is (or so the claim goes), provided that our foundational *value* theory—our foundational theory of the good—includes the right sorts of elements, when this is combined with act consequentialism this will generate *constraints* at the factoral level.

As an illustration of this point, recall the organ transplant case (from 3.1), in which you, the surgeon, consider the possibility of chopping up the innocent (and currently healthy) Chuck so as to save five patients who will otherwise die. When considering this example previously, it was natural to assume that the only aspects of the good relevant to the case concerned *well-being*—that is, the well-being of Chuck, of the five patients, and perhaps of various other members of the society who might somehow be affected in the long run. Note, however, that if you do chop up Chuck, a *murder* occurs—the killing of an innocent—whereas if the five patients are allowed to die, no such murder is involved. Suppose, then, that at the foundational level we adopt a pluralistic theory of the good which gives weight not only to well-being but also to the occurrence of acts of murder. That is, suppose that the very existence of an act of murder is itself a factor in its own right, one that makes the *outcome* worse (above and beyond its various implications for well-being). Finally, suppose that the badness involved in the occurrence of acts of murder is very great, indeed weighty enough to outweigh well-being in most or all cases.

Armed with a value theory of this sort, the act consequentialist will *not* conclude that it is better to chop up Chuck (not even if we put aside consideration of long-term side effects). For the choice is no longer appropriately viewed simply as one dead versus five. That description only takes into account the well-being of the six. But we are currently assuming that the existence of acts of murder has intrinsic significance for the value of outcomes. Thus the choice is better described as being between one dead, where a murder has occurred, and five dead, where no murder has occurred. And if we then recall the further assumption that murder is sufficiently bad to outweigh well-being (at least when this is a matter of "only" five lives), then the fact is that the outcome will be *worse* if you kill Chuck than if you let the five die. Thus, it seems, armed with an appropriately "sophisticated" theory of the good, even the act consequentialist will disapprove of killing Chuck. In short, given the right value theory at the foundational level, at the *factoral* level we'll have constraints.

Now the first thing to notice about this argument is that, strictly speaking, its final step—which moves from the prohibition on killing Chuck, to the existence of constraints—appears to be an error. Strictly, it is not at all clear that what emerges at the factoral level are genuine *constraints*. For constraints, it will be recalled (see 3.1), were defined in terms of providing barriers to the promotion of the overall good. And nothing like that seems to be going on in the current case. Rather, in light of the nonstandard value theory that is being assumed—according to which the occurrence of a murder has significantly greater weight than the mere occurrence of several deaths—it simply turns out to be false that killing Chuck results in the better outcome overall. There are no *constraints* on performing those acts that truly lead to better results overall; there are simply nonstandard ways of evaluating the overall goodness of results. Thus what emerges at the factoral level is still *consequentialism*. The agent is still required to perform the act which best promotes the overall good; it is simply that the overall good is being measured in some unusual ways.

But perhaps this technical point should be put aside. Even if what emerges at the factoral level is still consequentialism, strictly speaking, rather than deontology, perhaps all that is really important is that we have at least arrived at a version of factoral consequentialism that successfully *mimics* the constraints endorsed by commonsense morality. After all, in ruling out the killing of Chuck, this "sophisticated consequentialism" gives the same answer, and thus serves the same purpose, as the commonsense deontological constraint against murder. Similarly, then, a suitably sophisticated value theory could be used to mimic the various other commonsense constraints as well. (Presumably it would do this by giving direct and significant weight to acts of harm doing, acts of lying, acts of promise breaking, and so forth. But unlike deontology, which views these factors as potentially opposing the good, thereby grounding constraints, the sophisticated value theory would view each of these as *subfactors* of the good, intrinsically affecting the overall goodness of the outcome, but with far more weight than mere well-being.) Loosely speaking, we might say that sophisticated consequentialism successfully mimics constraints, without actually endorsing them, by incorporating constraint violations directly into its theory of the good.

But this claim too is based on error. In point of fact, accepting sophisticated consequentialism is not at all the moral equivalent of accepting constraints. The simulation is at best a limited success. Admittedly, embracing the nonstandard value theory does have the desired effect of ruling out killing Chuck so as to save the five other patients. But even a sophisticated consequentialism cannot mimic the desired deontological judgment in every case.

To see this, let's modify the example. As before, suppose that killing Chuck is the only way to save five others. But this time, let's assume that the five are about to be *murdered*, rather than dying from natural causes. Despite this change, of course, our ordinary moral intuitions still forbid killing Chuck (assuming that he is not himself the aggressor, or a shield to the threat, and so forth). And this is the judgment supported by the deontological constraint against killing. But now the sophisticated consequentialist has *no* ground for opposing killing Chuck—not even with the nonstandard value theory in place. For in this new case, we no longer face a choice between one murder (and death) and five "mere" deaths. Rather, the choice is between one murder (and death) and *five* murders (and deaths). In a case like this, it really doesn't matter *how* much greater weight the nonstandard value theory gives to murders as opposed to mere death, the fact remains that five murders will be worse than one murder—and so the results will be better overall if you kill Chuck.

In sum, if we really want to rule out killing Chuck, we must appeal to a *constraint* against killing. The appeal to sophisticated consequentialism simply can't do the trick. (The corresponding point holds for other constraints as well, as can easily be seen by appropriately modifying the example.)

Furthermore, it should be noted that—considered in its own right—the requisite nonstandard theory of the good seems rather implausible. For example, if the outcome were truly significantly worse when an act of murder occurs than when five die by natural causes, then it seems that if you had to choose between *preventing* the murder of one person by someone else and preventing the accidental deaths of five others, it would be far preferable to prevent the murder, leaving the five to die. Many people, however, would find this judgment difficult to accept. (Obviously, this is not to say that *all* of the novel elements of the nonstandard value theory are implausible.)

No doubt, sophisticated consequentialism—with its nonstandard theory of the good—does a somewhat better job at mimicking constraints than consequentialism ordinarily does (when combined with more standard theories of the good). But from an intuitive point of view, it is not at all clear that the minimal extra gains are worth the extra cost.

For our purposes, then, the appeal to sophisticated consequentialism turns out to be rather unhelpful. Even if we embrace the relevant nonstandard value theory, at best this yields a rather limited ability to mimic ordinary constraints. And technically, of course, what emerges at the factoral level does not include genuine constraints, properly speaking, at all: it is simply factoral consequentialism with an unusual theory of the good.

Should we conclude, accordingly, that factoral consequentialism is indeed the inevitable outcome of act consequentialism at the foundational level? Must those who wish to avoid factoral consequentialism reject act consequentialism as well?

Not necessarily. As we have seen, act consequentialism provides us with an evaluative standpoint according to which the various actions available to the agent are to be ranked as better or worse according to their contribution to the overall good. Note, however, that factoral consequentialism makes use of this ranking in a *particular* way: it insists that a given act is permissible if and only if it makes a greater contribution to the overall good than any available alternative. That is, according to factoral consequentialism, an act is permissible only if it has the *highest* possible ranking (available to that agent in that situation). Thus, factoral consequentialism presupposes a *maximizing* attitude toward the good.

But it is not at all clear that this maximizing attitude is entailed by anything in act consequentialism per se. After all, it seems that you could accept the foundational consequentialist thought that *all* goods are appropriate objects of moral concern, and indeed that all goods are to be ranked impartially (without special regard for your own individual good)—without thereby committing yourself to the further claim that this overall good must be *maximally* promoted. Of course, it would be peculiar to suggest that *indifference* to the good could ever be appropriate, morally speaking. But in and of itself, this does not show that the only appropriate attitude to the good is to strive to produce as *much* of it as possible. Perhaps, at a certain point, *enough* good has been done—even if there is still more good that *could* be done. The basic idea here could be put this way: an appropriate concern for the good certainly requires that a *satisfactory* level of good be achieved; but there is no reason to assume that the only satisfactory level is the *maximal* one.

If this is right, then it seems that a maximizing approach is not the only one compatible with act consequentialism. We need to allow as well for the possibility of a *satisficing* approach to the good. Thus, we will need to distinguish between maximizing act consequentialism and satisficing act consequentialism. It may well be that if we adopt act consequentialism in its maximizing version, factoral consequentialism is indeed the inevitable result. But there is no reason to assume that factoral consequentialism will be supported by the satisficing version of act consequentialism as well.

Very well, then, what exactly would emerge at the factoral level from satisficing act consequentialism? Presumably, goodness of overall results would remain at least *one* of the factors with intrinsic normative significance. For even a satisficing act consequentialist rejects those acts that fail to do *enough* to promote the good. Thus *one* factor relevant to determining the moral status of an act will be the goodness of its results (as compared to the alternatives).

But given a satisficing approach to the promotion of the good, some acts may well be morally acceptable, even if still more good could be done by performing some alternative act. In at least some cases, therefore, a given act might be permissible even if it is not the act that would do the *greatest* amount of good. However, even though the agent would be *permitted* to perform this less than optimal act, presumably she wouldn't be *required* to perform it (since other acts, including at the very least the optimal one, will be "good enough" as well). Thus, among the various acts that are good enough, the agent is free to do as she chooses. In short, the factoral level would include *options*.

What would these options be like? Will they be similar to the options recognized by commonsense morality (considered in 5.1 and 5.2)? It is difficult to say, without knowing much more about how the line that marks the satisfactory level is specified. That is to say, we need to know more about what constitutes *enough* good. For example, is this simply a function of the total overall level of good in the world, or is it relative to the amount of good at stake in a given situation? Similarly, is what's "good enough" in a given case simply a function of how much good the agent has already done, or is it relative to how much *more* the agent could do? And does it depend on the difficulty or cost to the agent of doing more good, or is the line the same for all agents, regardless of the ease with which they could do more? Presumably, different satisficing theories will answer these questions in different ways, thus setting the line in different ways. And this, in turn, will generate different kinds of options.

But even if some version of satisficing act consequentialism would generate options similar to those recognized by commonsense morality, it should be noted that *no* version generates anything like commonsense *deontology*. For there is nothing in the satisficing approach to support *constraints*. After all, the idea behind satisficing is that you only need to do enough good; you need not do all the good you possibly can. But nothing in this idea *opposes* your doing more good than the minimal satisfactory level; in particular, maximizing the good remains permissible. In short, there is nothing in the idea of satisficing to support the deontological thought that sometimes it is forbidden to perform the act that would lead to the greatest amount of good. Satisficing act consequentialism will support *options* at the factoral level, but it will not generate constraints.

Nonetheless, even though satisficing act consequentialism does not generate deontology at the factoral level (since it doesn't support constraints), it remains the case that the result at the factoral level isn't consequentialist either (given the presence of options). And so we see that, despite the temptation to assume otherwise, factoral consequentialism is *not* the inevitable outcome of act consequentialism at the foundational level. It is only *maximizing* act consequentialism that supports factoral consequentialism.

Of course, maximizers may well want to object at this point that a satisficing approach to the good is somehow incompatible with a genuine commitment to foundational consequentialism. After all (they might complain), if the ultimate basis for the normative factors is the good—and nothing but the good—then how can anything other than a maximizing attitude to the good be appropriate? Surely, more good is better than less.

But this objection may simply beg the question. The satisficer can insist that at the foundational level she recognizes the significance of nothing but the good. And she can readily admit, as well, that more good is better than less. But she also insists that the mere fact that something is better does not entail that one *must* choose it. So long as you achieve enough good, that suffices.

To the maximizer, of course, this reply borders on the incoherent. And if maximizing is indeed the only acceptable attitude to the good, then all *coherent* versions of act consequentialism will generate factoral consequentialism. Unfortunately, this debate—between maximizers and satisficers—is yet one more issue that we cannot try to resolve here.

(It should be noted that the distinction between maximizing and satisficing has implications for the discussion of foundational *egoism* as well. It is only *maximizing* act egoism that would generate factoral egoism, with its requirement that the agent do *all* he can to promote his own good. In contrast, satisficing act egoism would generate *options* at the factoral level: the agent would always be free to promote his overall good, but so long as he had already done *enough* in this regard, he would not be required to do more. Similarly, a satisficing version of *rule* egoism might have an easier time generating options than would a maximizing version; or, at the very least, it might generate different kinds of options.)

If we suppose that satisficing does represent an acceptable attitude toward the good, then, as we have seen, act consequentialism at the foundational level is compatible with options at the factoral level. But as we have also seen, not even satisficing act consequentialism is capable of generating constraints. However, it may be worth noting that there are still other approaches to the good, representing even more radical alternatives to maximizing—and it may be that one or another of these more radical approaches may succeed in generating constraints out of an act consequentialist foundation.

Consider, for example, the fact that both satisficing and maximizing share the thought that it is always legitimate to sacrifice any given good for the sake of achieving a greater overall balance of good. Unlike maximizers, of course, satisficers will not always *require* such sacrifices (not if enough good has already been achieved)—but even satisficers will always at least *permit* them. But it might be suggested that this willingness to sacrifice any good for the sake of more good reveals an inappropriate attitude to the good—it bespeaks an inappropriate lack of *respect* for the good being sacrificed. Perhaps the appropriate way to respect the value of individual goods is to "honor" them, by refusing to *violate* them, refusing to sacrifice them—not even for the sake of achieving a greater overall balance of goods. Accordingly, instead of maximizing or satisficing the good, one might approach the good with *respect*. (Of course, maximizers and satisficers will properly insist that it would simply beg the question to assume without argument that it is indeed this latest attitude that shows the most respect for the good. But for now, the point is simply to find a reasonably helpful label for this third possible approach.)

Suppose, then, that one adopts this kind of respect attitude toward the good and combines it with act consequentialism. Individual acts will be evaluated in terms of whether or not they properly respect the various individual goods at stake in a given situation. Acts that manifest disrespect for specific goods by violating those goods will be rejected as morally impermissible. Thus certain acts—those acts that sacrifice, destroy, or otherwise violate goods—will be forbidden, even if performing such acts is the only way to lead to an even greater overall balance of good. In short, at the factoral level, there will be *constraints*—constraints against performing the various types of good-destroying acts.

Of course, it will be impossible to say much more about what kinds of constraints will emerge, until we know more about the specific theory of the good which is to be incorporated into the foundational approach we are describing. At the very least, presumably, individual well-being will be taken to be a good. And so, at the very least, there is likely to be a constraint against harm. But until we know what further goods, if any, are recognized by the theory (or, for that matter, until we know what elements are taken to be constitutive of individual well-being), we won't be able to say anything more concerning which specific constraints would emerge from such an approach.

Still other approaches to the good are possible as well. Or it may be possible to *combine* elements of the satisficing and respect approaches. For example, it might be suggested that a proper attitude toward the good requires only that one achieve enough good, so long as specific goods are never violated. If this complex attitude toward the good were incorporated into an act consequentialist foundation, the result at the *factoral* level might well be something like commonsense deontology, with a modest requirement to promote the good, tempered by both options and constraints. (A quite different kind of mixed theory should be noted as well: perhaps different attitudes are appropriate for different *types* of goods.)

It must be admitted that these various nonmaximizing versions of act consequentialism are fairly exotic, and to date they have received little attention from moral philosophers. (They certainly deserve further investigation.) It should also be noted that to the limited extent that such theories have been discussed, it has typically (although not always) been in terms rather different from the ones we have been using. In part, this has been because of the common failure to distinguish between factoral and foundational consequentialism. And in part, it has been because of the common (but mistaken) assumption that foundational consequentialism must assume a maximizing form. But as we have seen, foundational consequentialism, even act consequentialism, can be combined with nonmaximizing attitudes toward the good—at least, this seems possible in principle—and when this is done, what emerges at the factoral level can be something quite different from factoral consequentialism.

Of course, this is not to say that each of the attitudes toward the good that I have been discussing is plausible, or even coherent. It is certainly possible that only one approach represents an intelligible attitude toward the good. If—as many have thought—maximizing is indeed the only coherent attitude to take toward the good, then (as we have previously noted) the only coherent version of act consequentialism will be maximizing act consequentialism.

Historically, at any rate, the fact remains that act consequentialists have almost always been maximizers. And here (as we have also previously noted) it does seem correct to say that the outcome of such foundational consequentialism must be consequentialism at the factoral level as well—possessing neither options nor constraints.

And so the main conclusions of this section still stand. I have not tried to resolve whether or not there really are plausible nonmaximizing attitudes to the good. If there are, then even act consequentialism, when combined with such attitudes, may lead to nonconsequentialist results at the factoral level. But whether or not such alternative approaches are possible, if it is indeed *maximizing* act consequentialism with which we start, then what emerges at the factoral level will be consequentialist as well.

## 6.5 Rules

Even if maximizing were the only plausible attitude to take toward the good, it still would not follow that foundational consequentialists must be factoral consequentialists. I have, of course, argued that factoral consequentialism is the inevitable outcome if one embraces a maximizing version of act consequentialism. But it is important to bear in mind that foundational consequentialists need not be *act* consequentialists at all, not even if they are maximizers. That is, foundational consequentialists—even maximizing foundational consequentialists—need not pick *acts* as the primary evaluative focal point; they could pick something else instead. And as we saw in the case of foundational egoism, the choice of focal point can make a significant difference in terms of what emerges at the factoral level.

Consider, for example, the possibility of maximizing *rule* consequentialism. According to this foundational view, the evaluative standpoint provided by maximizing consequentialism is used in the first instance, not to evaluate acts, but rather to evaluate rules. Roughly speaking, we ask what set of rules would lead to the best possible results. Acts are then evaluated only indirectly, in terms of whether or not they conform to the optimal rules. Obviously enough, all of this is quite similar to the approach of rule *egoism*—insofar as it is rules rather than acts that are directly evaluated by the relevant foundational machinery. But where rule egoists evaluate the rules in terms of their impact on the agent's own individual well-being, rule *consequentialists* evaluate the rules instead in terms of their impact on the overall good.

Since rule consequentialists evaluate acts in terms of rules, and rules in terms of the overall good, they remain true to the foundational consequentialist thought that it is consideration of the overall good that provides the *ultimate* basis for the justification of the genuine normative factors (whatever they turn out to be).

Less obvious—but equally important—they also remain true to the maximizing approach to the good, in that a given act is permissible only if it conforms to the *optimal* set of rules, the rules that would lead to the *best* possible outcome. Admittedly, individual *acts* are not evaluated directly in terms of whether or not they produce the greatest possible contribution to the overall good; on the contrary, they are evaluated in terms of their conformity to the rules. But this shouldn't be taken to show that the rule consequentialist approach isn't genuinely maximizing. It only shows that it is maximizing with regard to the *rules* rather than with regard to the acts. And this is exactly as we should expect, given the choice of rules rather than acts as the primary evaluative focal point.

What all of this shows, of course, is that the choice of maximizing consequentialism at the foundational level does not in and of itself commit you one way or another as far as the choice of focal point is concerned. You certainly *can* be a maximizing act consequentialist; but it is equally true that you can be a maximizing rule consequentialist. And if it is indeed rule consequentialism that is embraced, then we should expect this to have a significant impact at the factoral level. So let us ask: what sort of factoral theory would rule consequentialism support?

(We should, however, note that a rule consequentialist doesn't *have* to be a maximizing rule consequentialist. Assuming that nonmaximizing attitudes to the good are indeed coherent, then one could, for example, be a satisficing rule consequentialist instead, or even a respect rule consequentialist. Presumably, these would support rather different factoral theories from maximizing rule consequentialism. For simplicity, however, I am going to put these possibilities aside.)

Given our earlier detailed discussion of the differences between rule and act egoism (in 6.2), we can be relatively brief, for the same basic structural points apply here as well. The place to begin is by reminding ourselves that even *act* consequentialists can take a lively interest in moral rules. Admittedly, what standard (maximizing) act consequentialism most directly supports is factoral consequentialism. But even factoral consequentialists can go on to accept secondary rules (as we saw in 2.6), evaluating them in terms of their usefulness in guiding the agent to perform the act that best promotes the good.

Of course, any rules derived in this way will be mere rules of thumb—permissibly violated whenever doing so would lead to better results overall. It is precisely at this point that the difference between rule and act consequentialism becomes significant. For rule consequentialism asserts that an act is permissible if and only if it *conforms* to the optimal set of rules. Accordingly, it is never permissible to *violate* those rules, not even if doing so, in some particular case, might produce better results overall. In short, what makes rule consequentialism unique is not its interest in rules per se, but rather the *status* it assigns to those rules.

This is not yet to say what the *content* of those inviolable rules will be. That is, it still needs to be established *which* rules would lead to the best results overall. But given our earlier discussions of closely related issues (especially in 2.6 and 6.2), it seems plausible to suppose that the optimal set of rules will be similar to the familiar rules of commonsense morality. Perhaps this won't be true in every detail (certain rules may need to be modified or even rejected), and in any event, the matter turns on complex empirical questions that we cannot try to adjudicate here. But the fact remains that most rule consequentialists have found it plausible to suggest that, at least in general terms, the optimal set of rules will be similar to the rules of commonsense morality.

Note, however, that many of the familiar rules of commonsense morality appear to take the form of *constraints:* they forbid various acts (harm doing, lying, promise breaking, and so forth)—even if greater good would come in some particular case from performing acts of the prohibited type. If rules of this sort are indeed among the members of the optimal set of rules, then—given the rule consequentialist's insistence that a given act is permissible only if it *conforms* to the optimal rules—it will follow that the relevant types of acts are forbidden, even when performing them would lead to better results overall. Which is to say, rule consequentialism supports *constraints* at the factoral level. (And this means, of course, that we have yet another case in which foundational teleology supports factoral deontology.)

Furthermore, it seems plausible to suggest that rule consequentialism will generate *options* as well. The thought here is that it can be counterproductive if the moral rules are too demanding. If morality demands that people do all the good that they possibly can, then everyone will constantly fall short, and in the long run this may lead to a general disdain or disregard for the moral rules. Ironically enough, people might actually do *more* good if the moral rules demand somewhat less of them. As usual, the empirical issues here are complex, but it does at least seem possible that a relatively modest principle of beneficence might actually produce more good than a more demanding requirement.

If all of this is right, then rule consequentialism will generate both options and constraints, in intuitively familiar forms. In short, rule consequentialism will support commonsense deontology. Not surprisingly, then, many people have found rule consequentialism to be a particularly attractive theory. Apparently, it allows you to combine independently attractive thoughts—maximizing foundational consequentialism, on the one hand, and factoral deontology, on the other—that might otherwise seem incompatible.

At least, this is what the advocates of rule consequentialism have typically urged. Against this, however, critics have often argued that in point of fact there is *no* possible outcome for rule consequentialism other than *factoral* consequentialism (or a set of rules equivalent to it). After all, the basic idea of rule consequentialism is that the right thing to do is to conform to the optimal set of rules. Now the key word here is "optimal." It is only the *optimal* rules that are to be obeyed—those that would lead to the very best possible results. But what rule could possibly lead to better results than the factoral consequentialist principle itself—the rule which commands us to do the act with the best results! Obviously enough, if people were to obey this rule, if they did perform the acts with the very best results overall, then the results would have to be better than they would be were people to obey some alternative rule which gave different instructions.

So the optimal set of rules will actually contain exactly one rule—the principle of factoral consequentialism (or else, a set of rules equivalent to it). And since *rule* consequentialism says that an act is permissible if and only if it conforms to the optimal rules, it follows that for rule consequentialism an act is permissible if and only if it conforms to the factoral consequentialist principle that requires you to perform the act which best promotes the overall good. Which is to say, despite all the arguments to the contrary, rule consequentialism must generate factoral consequentialism!

(This argument is sometimes summarized as saying that rule consequentialism "collapses" into act consequentialism. Strictly, however, rule consequentialism and act consequentialism will still differ as foundational theories, in that the two select different primary focal points. Rather, the two "collapse" at the factoral level—with both supporting *factoral* consequentialism.)

The same argument can be stated in a slightly different way. Suppose that some set of rules, R, were proposed as the optimal set. And imagine that in some cases, conformity to R would rule out performing an act that would lead to better results overall. Consider now an alternative set of rules, R', which is just like R in terms of what it commands, except that in those cases where R forbids the actions with the best results, R' modifies R so as to require the relevant acts. (Similarly, if R ever merely permits the act with the best results, but does not require it, R' requires the act in question.) Obviously, R and R' would give the same commands in all cases except where R' modifies R, and by hypothesis, in those cases where they differ, obeying R' would lead to better results overall. Thus, obeying R' rather than R leads to better results, and so R cannot truly be the set of optimal rules after all: it is R' rather than R that is optimal. Thus the only way that a set of rules can be truly optimal is if it never forbids acts that lead to the best results, and indeed never fails to require such acts. But this means that the optimal set of rules must give commands identical to factoral consequentialism. And since rule consequentialism requires you to conform to the optimal set of rules, it will require you to conform to factoral consequentialism.

Is this argument sound? Is factoral consequentialism indeed the inevitable result of rule consequentialism? To settle this question, I think, we will first need to distinguish between different versions of rule consequentialism. For a great deal will turn on how, precisely, the optimal rules are to be selected.

To see this, consider the fact that rules, in and of themselves, have *no* consequences whatsoever. Rules only have results that can be measured and compared when they are taught, believed, accepted, endorsed, and acted upon—or, at the very least, when they are rejected, debated, scorned, misapplied, and flouted. Either way, we might say that rules only have results when they are *embedded*. Strictly, then, it doesn't even make sense to talk about which set of *unembedded* rules has the best results, or would have the best results. We can only ask which set of rules would have the best results were they embedded. But that means that there is a further question that we need to ask first, namely, *how* are the rules to be embedded? That is, what is the embedding *like*? For the fact of the matter is, we can imagine different ways that rules could be embedded, and there is no reason to assume that the rules that would have the best results with one kind of embedding are the same as the rules that would have the best results with a quite different kind of embedding.

So what *kind* of embedding is envisioned by rule consequentialism? When we "test" the rules, to compare their results, what kind of conditions are we testing them under? Not surprisingly, different rule consequentialists offer different proposals here. Some begin with the simple thought that, since rule consequentialism holds that people are morally required to obey the optimal rules, the appropriate test is to consider the results that would follow if the given set of rules were actually *obeyed*. Accordingly, the embedding conditions can be thought of along lines that are quite *idealized*. We can ask, for example, what rules would have the best results if *everyone* accepted them, understood them, were motivated to act on them, and *conformed* to them flawlessly. Obviously, no one is suggesting that such embedding conditions represent the situation in the real world. The thought is simply that insofar as we are interested in determining what the best rules are, we should ask what rules would have the best results were those rules perfectly obeyed. Accordingly, we can call this approach *ideal* rule consequentialism.

In contrast, the relevant embedding conditions can be thought of along lines that are far more *realistic*. Those who prefer this alternative approach argue that, in the real world, *no* set of rules would be accepted by *everyone*, and even those who accept the rules will not always be motivated to obey them; and even if they are motivated to obey them, they may misunderstand the implications of the rules in any given case, or they may simply fail to execute their intentions flawlessly (they might, for example, trip at the crucial moment). Accordingly, one might ask, instead, what rules would have the best results if *most* (but not all) people accepted them, and if those who did accept them were *typically* (but not always) motivated to obey them, and so forth. On some approaches along these lines, the relevant, hypothetical levels of conformity, understanding, motivation, and the like might be fixed. But on other versions the relevant lines will be allowed to "float": the more demanding the rules, the less often people will be motivated to act on them; the more complex the rules, the more often people will misunderstand their implications, and so on. So the test might be something like this: what rules would have the best results given realistic assumptions about the extent to which the rules would be taught, accepted, and conformed to? We can call an approach of this second kind *realistic* rule consequentialism.

Obviously enough, there is actually a range of more or less realistic embeddings to chose from. And all of them still represent at least a limited degree of idealization. For the question asked by the rule consequentialist is always, in effect, which set of rules *would* have better results were something about the world *changed*: for example, were the given rules taught, and as a result of this, were some people to come to believe the rules, and at least sometimes come to act on the rules, and so forth. But for our purposes, at any rate, it will suffice to distinguish between (perfectly) ideal rule consequentialism—which tests competing rules under conditions of perfect conformity—and (relatively) realistic rule consequentialism—which tests the rules under conditions of less than perfect conformity.

We are now in a position to return to the argument that rule consequentialism inevitably supports factoral consequentialism. That argument began by noting, correctly, that if the purportedly optimal rules were not equivalent to factoral consequentialism, there would have to be cases in which they would forbid (or fail to require) the act with the best results. Accordingly, if we modified those rules exactly to the extent of *requiring* the acts in question in such cases, then it would have to the case that were such modified rules perfectly obeyed, the results would be better than they would be were the original rules obeyed. Up to this point, the argument seems impeccable; in any event, let's suppose that it's right. But what, exactly, is supposed to follow from this?

If we are *ideal* rule consequentialists, it does seem to follow that the original rules are not genuinely optimal after all. For ideal rule consequentialists ask which rules would have the best results under the assumption of *perfect* conformity to the rules. And the argument certainly does seem to show that the modified rules would have better results than the original rules—*provided that* we compare the results under the assumption that the rules are being perfectly obeyed. Thus, if perfect conformity is indeed the appropriate embedding condition for testing the various competing rules, then it certainly looks as though no set of rules that diverges from factoral consequentialism could truly be optimal. (After all, given that factoral consequentialism always requires you to perform the act with the best results, perfect conformity to factoral consequentialism would necessarily produce the best results of those available.) Accordingly, if the version of rule consequentialism that is endorsed is ideal rule consequentialism, then it does seem as though the inevitable outcome is factoral consequentialism (or a set of rules equivalent to it).

Now in point of fact, I think that there is still a flaw in this argument, although it is subtle, and difficult to see. (I'll try to describe it later in this section.) But whatever the merits of the argument, it is important to see that, at best, it is only plausible provided that we are indeed talking about ideal rule consequentialism. If, instead, it is *realistic* rule consequentialism that is under consideration, then the corresponding argument shouldn't seem tempting at all.

After all, even if it were true that, under the ideal embedding assumption of *perfect* conformity, factoral consequentialism would have better results than some alternative set of rules, nothing at all would follow about which would have better results under more *realistic* embedding conditions. Indeed, often enough, rules that do quite well under the assumption of perfect conformity will do comparatively poorly under more realistic testing conditions. This is because ideal embedding allows us to simply *assume* perfect conformity (as part of the relevant test). And if we do this, then it doesn't matter how complex our moral rules are, whether they are easily misunderstood, how difficult it is to determine which concrete act fulfills the rules, or how hard it may be to motivate someone to perform the required act. All of these issues are simply abstracted away; they are irrelevant to determining the results of the rules. But under realistic testing conditions, these problems return with a vengeance, and they may have a significant impact on the results. Rules that would have good results were they obeyed *perfectly* might in fact be too complicated to remember, or they might be too easily misunderstood, or misapplied, or disregarded. In contrast, simpler rules, or less demanding rules, rules less easily misapplied or disregarded, might—under realistic embedding conditions—do better overall.

Thus it could well be that the familiar rules of commonsense deontology—incorporating both constraints and options—are indeed the rules that would have the best results overall, if the appropriate testing conditions are realistic ones. Admittedly, factoral consequentialism would have better results under the assumption of perfect conformity. But for the realistic rule consequentialist, this simply isn't the *relevant* embedding condition for comparing the results. Rather, we must bear in mind the fact that under *realistic* conditions factoral consequentialism will often be misapplied or simply disregarded. (On the one hand, given the difficulty of identifying the act with the best results, acts that actually lead to significantly bad results may often be chosen. And on the other hand, given that the demands of factoral consequentialism are so great, many people may grow disdainful of morality, or unconcerned about it altogether.) It is of course a complex empirical question *which* set of rules would actually have the best results under realistic embedding conditions, but it does at least seem a live possibility that the optimal rules will be similar to the familiar rules of commonsense morality. In sum, if it is realistic rule consequentialism that is at issue, then there is no reason at all to think that factoral consequentialism must be the inevitable result, and there is at least some reason to think that the result might well be similar to commonsense deontology.

(Although we did not discuss it at the time, it should be obvious that a similar set of issues arises for rule *egoism*. That is, it could be argued—along lines similar to those given here—that rule egoism inevitably supports *factoral* egoism. In evaluating the merits of this argument, it would presumably be important to distinguish between ideal and realistic rule egoism. Indeed, generalizing even further, it seems likely that whatever our foundational theory, if we accept rules as the primary evaluative focal point, it will be important to distinguish between ideal and realistic versions of the approach. And whatever our foundational theory, it will be important to ask whether the *ideal* rule version must give the same results, at the factoral level, as the *act* version.)

Suppose we grant, then, that rule consequentialism (at least, in its realistic versions) need not support factoral consequentialism. If this is right, then of course the choice between rule and act consequentialism will be a significant one. On what grounds should the choice be made? Obviously enough, one potential basis for choice is the very fact that they have different factoral implications. Those who find deontology attractive at the factoral level may well view this as reason to prefer (realistic) rule consequentialism. (Of course, those who don't share these intuitions, or don't give them much weight, won't find this a compelling argument.)

What *other* reasons are there for choosing between rule and act consequentialism? Given our earlier discussion of rule egoism, it's not surprising to learn that act consequentialists often accuse rule consequentialists of *rule worship*. After all (the objection goes), given the commitment to the foundational consequentialist thought that goodness of results provides the ultimate basis for our normative theory, how can it ever be appropriate to require an agent to conform to a mere rule—even though breaking that rule would admittedly lead to better results overall? And by this time, presumably, the rule consequentialist's reply to this charge won't be surprising either: mere commitment to foundational consequentialism does not, in and of itself, mandate a particular choice concerning the primary evaluative focal point. In effect, the charge of rule worship implicitly presumes that it is acts rather than rules that are to be directly evaluated by appeal to the overall good; thus, it simply begs the question against the rule consequentialist.

It must be admitted, however, that the charge of rule worship often has considerable intuitive force. Consider, for example, the fact that once the optimal rules are selected, rule consequentialism demands that we continue to obey those rules—even when others are *not* doing so. Yet obeying the rules in the face of general noncompliance on the part of others might well lead to disaster. For example, it might be that a rule requiring pacifism would have the best results if *everyone* were to obey it, or perhaps even if *enough* people obeyed it. But for all that, it might still be the case that refusing to use force, to defend oneself or to defend others, might have disastrous results in a world in which virtually *no one else* conforms to pacifism. And requiring conformity to the rules, even when doing so would lead to disaster because others are disregarding the rules, certainly does seem to constitute rule worship.

It is, I think, fairly easy to feel the force of this worry about rule consequentialism and situations of noncompliance. Nonetheless, stating the objection carefully—and trying to nail it down—is actually a surprisingly complicated matter. The best place to start, perhaps, is by emphasizing the fact that rule consequentialism always presupposes *some* general level of conformity when testing rival rules.

Imagine, then, that some rule is a member of the optimal set of rules. What this means, of course, is that on the whole, conformity to the rule leads to good results. But all that this guarantees is that the rule has good results when *enough* people obey it. For example, if we are ideal rule consequentialists, all that is guaranteed is that the rule would have good results if *everyone* were to obey it. Of course, if we are realistic rule consequentialists, we won't assume perfect conformity when testing rules. But here too, *some* particular level of conformity will be assumed. Thus, even if we are realistic rule consequentialists, it might be that all that is guaranteed is that the rule would have good results provided that *most* people obey it—or perhaps provided merely that *many* people obey it. Obviously, the precise level of conformity assumed will depend on the particular version of rule consequentialism we adopt.

But regardless of the *precise* degree of conformity assumed in assessing a rule's results, the fact remains that a rule's being optimal merely guarantees that the results will be good provided that *enough* people obey it. And what this means, of course, is that in a situation in which *too few* people are conforming to the rule, then if some particular agent were nonetheless to obey the rule—whether by himself, or as part of an overly small group—this could lead to quite bad results, indeed disaster. That is to say, even an optimal rule, a rule that might well have wonderful results given sufficient conformity, might well have disastrous results if obeyed in a situation where the level of noncompliance is too high.

But what, then, should we say in the face of such a situation? Imagine that you know full well that—given the abnormally high level of noncompliance—*your* obeying the rule would lead to disaster. According to the rule consequentialist, however, this fact isn't the least bit relevant: the optimal rules simply must be obeyed—come what may. Thus you are still required to obey the rule, even though you know that this will lead to horrible results. Indeed, you are still required to obey the rule, despite the fact that you know that you are in a situation (one of noncompliance) for which the rule has not been designed—a situation for which the rule is woefully inadequate. But this surely does appear to be rule *worship*.

Some rule consequentialists, presumably, will simply stick to their guns, steadfastly requiring obedience to the ill-fated rule. They may well admit that this feature of their theory will strike many as counterintuitive. But they will insist that given the various other advantages of rule consequentialism, it remains on balance an extremely plausible theory. (Recall again the observation from 1.3, that *no* theory is likely to be altogether without its counterintuitive aspects. The question, rather, is which theory provides the best fit with our various intuitions overall.)

Many other rule consequentialists, however, prefer to argue that if a given rule would lead to disaster if acted upon in the face of widespread noncompliance, then the rule cannot truly be one of the optimal rules in the first place. Stating the same point more positively, they argue that any genuinely optimal rule will have to be sensitive to the potential significance of noncompliance, and so will have a clause specifying the special behavior that is appropriate in situations where noncompliance is sufficiently widespread. To revert to our initial example, although an optimal rule might forbid violence for *most* situations, there might still be a clause allowing an exception in cases when enough others are unjustifiably disobeying the various moral rules. In particular, there might be a clause allowing the use of force in cases of self-defense. (Or—more narrowly—it might be that self-defense is only allowed in the face of *widespread* violence, that is, only when large numbers of people are disobeying the rules.)

Accordingly, the rule consequentialist can insist that it is indeed always obligatory to conform to the optimal rules—no matter how many others are or are not conforming. But conforming to the optimal rule in a situation of general *noncompliance* may well require a different kind of behavior than would be required by the rule in situations with *higher* levels of compliance. (Of course, since what is required is conformity to the optimal *set* of rules, there may be no need for an explicit noncompliance clause for each individual rule; it may suffice, for example, if there is a single general rule that specifically governs situations of noncompliance.)

If something like this approach is available to the rule consequentialist, then it may well answer the objection. But although the desire to include special clauses (or special rules) to deal with cases involving noncompliance is understandable, it is not at all obvious whether rule consequentialists are in a position to properly *evaluate* alternative clauses, so as to see which ones should be included in the (genuinely) optimal rules. Roughly speaking, the problem is this: any given version of rule consequentialism examines a proposed rule only under its favored testing conditions. Accordingly, it can hardly be in a position to see what the results of the rule would be if those conditions didn't obtain. And this means that rule consequentialism will be unable to provide adequate evaluation of rules or clauses specifically intended to govern such situations.

This objection is a subtle one, so let's spell it out more fully. As we have seen, any given version of rule consequentialism specifies a set of embedding conditions, and it tests rules under the assumption that its favored embedding conditions obtain. (It asks: what would the results of this rule be if such and such were the case?) Now obviously enough, when it comes to testing the noncompliance clauses, what we are primarily interested in are the results of such clauses in situations of noncompliance. But these are precisely situations in which the favored embedding conditions *don't* obtain. "Noncompliance," after all, was defined as being *less* than the level of compliance assumed by the relevant embedding conditions, whatever they are. (And as we noted, even realistic rule consequentialists assume *some* level of compliance when testing rival rules.)

Accordingly, what we *need* to do is to ask what the results of the noncompliance clauses would be if the embedding conditions didn't hold. But, of course, rule consequentialism doesn't do this. Instead, as always, it ends up asking what the results of the rules would be if the favored embedding conditions *did* obtain. In effect, it ineptly tries to test the *noncompliance* clauses by seeing what the results of these clauses would be if people were *compliant!*

Admittedly, these results—if any—are relevant too. (For example, even in situations of perfect compliance, people may be comforted by the thought that there are rules governing situations of noncompliance.) Obviously, however, such secondary effects of noncompliance clauses are likely to be of minor importance in comparison to the effects that such clauses have in situations of actual noncompliance. But *these* effects, it seems, simply can't be captured by the rule consequentialist; he is limited to testing rules under the assumption that the favored embedding conditions *do* obtain. And this means that the rule consequentialist isn't really in an adequate position to *evaluate* rival noncompliance clauses. Even if the rules selected by the rule consequentialist as optimal *do* have noncompliance clauses, there is no reason to believe that these clauses will deal with situations of noncompliance in anything like a satisfactory manner. The relevant clauses simply won't have been tested under the appropriate conditions.

To illustrate this difficulty, let's assume, once again, that the optimal rule would forbid violence—provided that enough other people are obeying this rule too. (It is easy enough to see how an ideal rule consequentialist might be attracted to such a rule; but even a realistic rule consequentialist might favor pacifism provided that *enough* other people were avoiding the use of force.) We are also imagining that some sort of clause is to be included to govern the situation of noncompliance, where too many people are disobeying this rule. But what reason do we have to think that the noncompliance clause will be a plausible one? How do we know that the noncompliance clause won't require, say, singing show tunes, rather than defending yourself?

Suppose, first, that we are ideal rule consequentialists, testing the rule that requires pacifism, except in cases of unjustified violence, where *singing* is required. What would be the results of this presumably unacceptable rule? Well, if we are ideal rule consequentialists, then the relevant question is what the results would be if *everyone* were to obey this rule. But, of course, if everyone were to obey such a rule, there would be no violence, and so the absurd noncompliance clause would never even come into play. It appears that ideal rule consequentialism is simply incapable of testing the noncompliance clause under the relevant circumstances—situations of non-compliance. And this means it is not in a position to guarantee *suitable* noncompliance clauses.

Although it is less obvious, the very same problem arises for the realistic rule consequentialist as well. For even the realistic rule consequentialist tests rules under the assumption that *some* appropriate level of conformity obtains. Even if we continue to assume—for the sake of the example—that pacifism is indeed optimal provided that this stipulated level of conformity does exist, we will still want to rule out a clause that requires singing when the use of force is *too* widespread. But when the realistic rule consequen-tialist tries to test this rule, the question that gets asked is what the results of the rule would be if *enough* people obeyed it (that is, if the stipulated level of conformity existed). Obviously, however, if enough people are obeying it, the noncompliance clause never even comes into play, and so the potentially disastrous effects of singing in the face of widespread violence are never detected. Thus, here too we will fail to test noncompliance clauses under the relevant circumstances—that is, when *too few* people are obeying the rules. And so, once again, rule consequentialism will not be in a posi-tion to guarantee suitable noncompliance clauses.

Of course, some realistic rule consequentialists will insist, plausibly, that since the level of compliance assumed by their favored embedding condi-tions is significantly less than perfect conformity, their testing conditions will already include the existence of a fair amount of unjustified violence, and so the optimal rule may already allow for the use of force in self-defense. But although this might disarm the particular example we have been using to illustrate the point, the theoretical objection remains: there will be *some* level of compliance assumed by the rule consequentialist when testing rules, and this means that rule consequentialism is unable to test the effects of noncompliance clauses in situations where compliance falls *below* that level.

Whatever the merits of this objection, it should be noted that it only works if we assume—as we have been assuming—that any given version of rule consequentialism will appeal to a single, fixed set of favored embed-ding conditions. (The favored embedding conditions may vary from theory to theory, but they are fixed within a given theory.) Accordingly, it may be possible to escape this line of argument, if there is some way to devise a version of rule consequentialism that doesn't do this. For example, perhaps the rule consequentialist should look for rules that would have good results under *more* than one set of embedding conditions. (It obviously won't do, however, to look for the rules that have the best results under *all* embedding conditions: there is no reason to think that any rules at all can pass this test.) Alternatively, perhaps there is a way of specifying appropriately "flexible" embedding conditions—where, for example, the level of compliance assumed varies with the content of the rule or clause being tested. If there can be versions of rule consequentialism along these lines, then they might well escape the objection we have been considering. Although I won't try to develop either of these proposals here, the potential advantages of these more complex versions of rule consequentialism should certainly be kept in mind.

(Having worked through the details of this last objection, we are now in a position to return to a piece of unfinished business and see why even *ideal* rule consequentialism need not lead to factoral consequentialism. The original argument, it will be recalled, claimed that if a given set of rules ever differs from factoral consequentialism, then it would necessarily have worse results—provided that we are assuming perfect conformity. Since this *is* the relevant embedding condition for ideal rule consequentialism, the conclusion seemed to follow that the optimal rules could never differ from factoral consequentialism. But in fact, all that actually follows is that the optimal rules must give the same instructions as factoral consequentialism in cases of perfect compliance. If the rules differ from factoral consequentialism *only* with regard to cases of *less* than perfect compliance, then this fact may never even be picked up by ideal rule consequentialism, which, after all, only tests the results of rules under the assumption that everyone is conforming perfectly. Accordingly, the rules selected as optimal by ideal rule consequentialism need not be identical to factoral consequentialism across the board.)

Before leaving the discussion of rule consequentialism, there is one final complication that should be noted. As we have seen, all versions of rule consequentialism require you to obey the optimal rules. But we have not yet explicitly asked whether the optimal rules must be exactly the *same* for everyone. That is, is each of us required to obey the very same set of moral rules—a moral code fixed across all societies and all times—or can the rules that we are required to obey vary from society to society?

The question being raised here—of universally binding moral rules versus *relativism*—should not be confused with the distinction between general and special obligations (see 4.3). Even if someone believes that the very same basic moral rules are binding upon everyone, they can certainly still accept the existence of special obligations. It might be, for example, that if I have harmed you, I have a special obligation to compensate you, an obligation that others lack. But one who believes in universal moral rules will think that *all* harm doers have such obligations or, more generally, that it is true of everyone that *if* you have harmed anyone, then you have a special obligation to compensate; it doesn't depend on what society you happen to live in. Similarly, everyone must keep their promises (if any), meet their parental obligations (if any), and so on. So belief in special obligations is quite compatible with belief in universal moral rules. The question we are raising now, however, is whether it is indeed *true* that the same basic moral rules apply to everyone.

Up to this point, we have been implicitly assuming that the optimal set of moral rules is indeed a fixed one—constant for all individuals. And this assumption has been reflected in the specific embedding conditions that we have previously considered. For example, we have imagined ideal rule consequentialists asking what rules would have the best results if *everyone* were to obey them. It may not be obvious *what* rules would do best on this test, but whatever they are, it will be that very same set of rules that each and every person is required to obey. The same thing is true for the various versions of realistic rule consequentialism that we have discussed. Of course, with realistic embedding conditions we don't simply assume perfect conformity—we take into account that there will be imperfect compliance, failures of understanding and motivation, and so forth. Still, we have imagined realistic rule consequentialists asking what single set of rules would have the best results under such realistic embedding conditions; and although here too it may not be obvious *what* rules would do best on this test, *everyone* is be required to obey those very same rules (whatever they turn out to be).

Nonetheless, it would be quite easy to design alternative embedding conditions—and thus different ways of identifying optimal rules—that allowed for the possibility that the optimal rules might vary from society to society. We could, for example, ask what rules would have the best results if everyone in the individual agent's *society* were to conform to the rules. (This would still be a kind of ideal embedding—since it still assumes perfect conformity *within* the society.) Or we could ask (more realistically) what rules would have the best results if *most* people in the agent's society were taught the rules, understood them, were motivated, and so on. By relativizing the rules to those that would have the best results if they were obeyed (whether perfectly, or imperfectly) by the members of the agent's *society*, the door becomes open to the possibility that the optimal rules may *vary* for different societies. And if this were indeed the case, then such a *relativized* rule consequentialism would yield different requirements at the factoral level for the members of the different societies. (Of course, whether this possibility is actually realized or not will depend on whether or not the relevant circumstances do differ sufficiently from society to society.)

It is important to keep in mind that despite this relativization of the optimal rules, it is still a version of rule *consequentialism* that is being described here: we are still looking for the best results overall, counting everyone equally, not just the members of the agent's society. That is, even though the rules that you are required to obey may differ, depending upon what society you are a member of, the rules themselves are still assessed in terms of the *overall* good, not just the good of your particular society. (Of course, we can imagine a still different foundational theory—halfway between foundational egoism and foundational consequentialism—which *would* be concerned solely with the good of the agent's society. But this is not the view under consideration here.)

Once this possibility of relativizing the optimal rules to the agent's society is noted, an even more radical possibility becomes apparent as well. Perhaps we should allow for the possibility of optimal rules that would vary from *individual* to individual, even within the same society. We could, for example, ask what rules would have the best results if the given *agent* were to obey them perfectly. Alternatively, we could ask what rules would have the best results if the agent generally *tried* to act on them. Either way, we would be individually "customizing" the rules, looking for those that best reflect the individual agent's particular circumstances and abilities. No doubt, for most of us, the individually optimal rules would be fairly similar; nonetheless, some significant differences at the factoral level might still emerge.

Once again, it is important to bear in mind that the view under discussion remains rule consequentialist. That is, despite being individualized, the rules would still be assessed in terms of their impact on the *overall* good— not just the agent's own welfare. Thus, even a view of this last kind should not to be confused with rule *egoism,* which does assess rival rules solely in terms of their impact on the individual agent's well-being.

(On the other hand, the current discussion does point, yet again, to another set of issues relevant to rule egoism. In our earlier discussion of rule egoism, we implicitly assumed that the appropriate question is: what rules would have the best results for the agent, given that the *agent* acts on the rules? But one might look, instead, for the rules that would have the best results for the agent given that *everyone*—or perhaps, everyone in the agent's society—acts on the rules. It is interesting to note that rule egoism is generally put forward in a form that allows for individually customized rules, while rule consequentialism is typically put forward in a form that requires the same set of rules for everyone. But as far as I can see, nothing in foundational egoism per se, and nothing in foundational consequentialism per se, mandates these standard choices.)

Since there is nothing especially problematic, from a logical point of view, about relativizing the rules (whether to the individual or to society), the choice between such a relativized approach and one that holds out for a fixed set of rules must be made on other grounds. Presumably, some metaethical conceptions will support a picture of morality as a single set of universal rules, binding on all individuals. Others may support relativism of one or another form. As usual, however, exploring such metaethical considerations would take us far beyond the scope of this book, and so we must leave the issue here.

There are, then, a variety of issues that must be faced in any attempt to work out a fully articulated version of rule consequentialism. Nor should we lose sight of the fact that rule consequentialism and act consequentialism are not at all the only ways of developing a foundational consequentialist approach. In principle, it seems, foundational consequentialism could be combined with the choice of any number of other primary evaluative focal points instead. Thus we could have virtue consequentialism, or motive consequentialism, or institution consequentialism, and so on for each of the other evaluative focal points. In each case, the evaluative standpoint provided by foundational consequentialism is used to directly evaluate items of the preferred type; and the various other focal points are then evaluated indirectly, in terms of the primary set of evaluations.

Unfortunately, we lack the space to investigate these various other forms of foundational consequentialism. (We would quickly face a variety of complications similar to those that arose for act and rule consequentialism.) But this should not be taken to suggest that act consequentialism and rule consequentialism are the only interesting or plausible versions of foundational consequentialism. While I do think it fair to say that these two represent the most common attempts to work out a foundational consequentialist approach, the comparative neglect of other versions of foundational consequentialism may reflect little more than a common failure to recognize the full range of possibilities.

There are, indeed, even more possibilities than we have already noted. For up to this point I have spoken as though a given foundational theory must chose a *single* focal point to be the *primary* focal point, directly evaluating only items of that single favored type, while all other focal points are evaluated indirectly, in terms of the favored set of evaluations. In fact, however, it seems possible for a foundational theory to evaluate the items of *more* than one type directly. For example, a theory might evaluate both rules *and* virtues directly, evaluating the other focal points in terms of these *two*. Obviously, this expands the range of possibilities even further.

Indeed, it seems possible for a theory to evaluate *all* focal points directly, rather than evaluating any of them only indirectly. Thus, instead of evaluating acts indirectly, in terms of conformity to the best rules, or evaluating rules indirectly, in terms of promotion of the best acts (not to mention even more elaborate possibilities, such as evaluating acts in terms of conformity to the rules promulgated by the best institutions), we might simply evaluate acts, rules, motives, institutions, virtues, and so on, all of them directly in terms of the evaluative standpoint provided by the foundational theory.

When combined, for example, with foundational consequentialism, this would result in what we might call *direct* consequentialism (since *all* focal points are evaluated directly). Obviously enough, the direct consequentialist would generate the same evaluations of acts as the act consequentialist, the same evaluations of rules as the rule consequentialist, the same evaluations of virtues as the virtue consequentialist, and so on down the line for each of the other evaluative focal points. At the same time, however, the direct consequentialist would differ in crucial ways from each of these other positions: for example, unlike the rule consequentialist, the direct consequentialist would never claim that the right act must conform to the optimal rules even when breaking the rules would lead to better results overall; on the contrary, since acts are to be evaluated directly, the direct consequentialist will insist that in such a case the right act to perform is the one that best promotes the overall good. (Thus, although the direct consequentialist and the rule consequentialist would *favor* the same rules, their views concerning the *significance* of those rules would differ.) Similarly, unlike the *virtue* consequentialist, the direct consequentialist would never claim that it is never permissible to violate the virtues; on the contrary, doing so would be permissible whenever it would lead to the best results.

It may not be apparent, however, how direct consequentialism differs from *act* consequentialism, given that both directly evaluate acts in terms of the goodness of their results. This means, of course, that when it is a matter of evaluating *actions*, the judgments of the two theories must be identical. Nonetheless, in principle at least, the assessments of the other focal points may still differ. For direct consequentialists evaluate *all* focal points directly, asking, simply, which rules would have the best results, which virtues would have the results, which institutions would have the best results, and so on. In contrast, *act* consequentialists—as we have characterized their position—evaluate these other focal points only *indirectly*, in terms of the best acts.

No doubt, even here, the substantive evaluations produced by the two views will often be fairly similar. A great deal will depend, for example, on how, exactly, the act consequentialist's evaluations of rules are derived from the evaluations of acts. But from a logical point of view, if nothing else, the difference remains important.

I should note, however, that since the distinction between act consequentialism and direct consequentialism is often overlooked, my use of these labels to mark out two distinct positions is somewhat idiosyncratic. Accordingly, many who call themselves act consequentialists may actually be direct consequentialists—given the way I have defined these positions. And many others may not have recognized the need to choose between the two.

# 7

---

# DEONTOLOGICAL
# FOUNDATIONS

## 7.1  Contractarianism

Teleological foundational theories all begin with the claim that the ultimate basis of normative ethics lies in terms of the significance of some central good or goods. Despite the fact that different teleological theories go on to appeal to different goods, this exclusive concern with the (relevant) good suffices to give teleological theories something of a common structure.

In contrast, deontological foundational theories as a group have rather little in common (see 6.1). They do, of course, all share the thought that teleological approaches are inadequate: the relevance of the basic normative factors, they hold, cannot ultimately be explained solely in terms of such an exclusive appeal to the good; other fundamental concepts must be brought in as well (or instead). As we shall see, however, there is such divergence among deontological foundational theories concerning what exactly the relevant further concepts are, and what the ultimate explanation should look like, that the resulting theories form a rather strikingly heterogeneous group.

Of course, as I've previously noted, the suggestion is sometimes made that what unites deontological foundational theories is the fact that they all yield deontology at the *factoral* level as well. But as we have already seen, even teleological foundational theories can—if properly spelled out—support factoral deontology. And in any event, as we shall soon see, it is far from obvious that the foundational theories typically thought of as deontological do indeed always support deontology at the factoral level.

In short, other than the common rejection of teleology at the foundational level, there is, I think, nothing significant that unites the various forms of foundational deontology. Inevitably, then, the various deontologi-

240

cal theories must simply be inspected one at a time, and evaluated on the basis of their individual merits. That's what we will try to do in this final chapter: examine some of the most important deontological foundational theories, and consider their strengths and weaknesses. But it is important to bear in mind, as we begin to do this, that our survey will not be exhaustive. Accordingly, given the striking differences from one deontological theory to the next, any attempts to generalize from this sample must be made with considerable caution.

(In contrast, as I have suggested, the various teleological foundational theories have a great deal in common. Thus, even though foundational egoism and foundational consequentialism do not *exhaust* the class of teleological theories—there are, after all, other goods beside the individual or the overall good on the basis of which a teleological theory might be constructed—these two are quite representative of teleological approaches as a whole.)

Now one important deontological approach begins with the thought that morality guides our interactions in a world in which we can affect others, and they can affect us. What we need, then, are reasonable principles to govern such interaction. But what, exactly, marks a principle as being a reasonable one for this purpose? This approach suggests, plausibly, that a given principle is a reasonable one if and only if it would be reasonable to *agree* to that principle (that is, to choose that principle to be one of the principles that govern interaction). But since everyone will be bound by the rules—not just me, or you—the appropriate test is whether or not *everyone* can agree to them. Accordingly, the question to ask is this: what rules would a *group* of reasonable people choose to govern their interaction?

This approach is known as *contractarianism*. The name comes, of course, from thinking of the members of the group as seeking to establish the terms of a *social contract,* one agreed upon by all parties, and binding upon all parties. Following common practice, we can call the parties to the contract, those attempting to come to an agreement, the *bargainers.* (Although common, in one way this term is unfortunate, for it may suggest that there is an inevitable need for compromise and bargaining here, in the absence of which there can be no agreement. In fact, however, the extent of the initial disagreement, if any, will depend on the details of the theory.) According to contractarianism, then, the valid moral rules are those that *would* be agreed to by the bargainers; and the terms of the contract are binding *by virtue of* the very fact that they would be agreed upon.

It is this last point that makes contractarianism a foundational theory. After all, one could presumably accept the claim that if everyone would agree to some principle, this is *evidence*—perhaps even decisive evidence—that the principle is binding, while still insisting that the agreement is not itself the *basis* of the principle's being binding. But if we were to do this, we would no longer be offering an *explanation* of the relevance of the normative factors, which is precisely what a foundational theory attempts to do. Accordingly, we should understand contractarians as holding that the ultimate *basis* of the normative factors (whatever they turn out to be) is the agreement of the bargainers.

Clearly, all of this still leaves a large number of details to be worked out. Most importantly, of course, we will eventually want to know what sort of factoral theory is supported by contractarianism. But the first thing we must settle is this: what exactly are the bargainers trying to reach an agreement *about*?

I have, of course, been writing as though the contractarian's question is this: what *rules* would be agreed upon by the bargainers? In writing this way I have been following the common practice, which is to think of contractarianism along the lines of *rule contractarianism*. Understood in this way, rules provide the primary evaluative focal point of the contract. Other focal points are then evaluated only indirectly, in terms of the agreed-upon rules. For example, rule contractarians typically hold that a given *act* is permissible if and only if it conforms to the agreed-upon rules.

In principle, however, there seems to be no reason why a contractarian could not select some *other* focal point as primary. As far as I can see, there is nothing in the basic contractarian idea—the idea of agreement as the ultimate basis of normative ethics—that dictates the choice of rules as primary. Thus, it seems, we could have *act contractarianism,* which would hold that a given act is permissible if and only if the bargainers would agree to its performance; other focal points would then be evaluated indirectly, perhaps in terms of how well they promote the agreed-upon acts. Or we could have *virtue contractarianism,* which would hold that the desirable character traits are those that would be approved of by the bargainers; a given act might then be held permissible so long as it doesn't violate the virtues (see 6.3). Or we could have *motive contractarianism,* or *institution contractarianism,* and so on, for each of the other evaluative focal points.

For each such theory, the standpoint provided by contractarianism—namely, that of the agreement of the bargainers—would be used to directly evaluate items of the favored type, while all other focal points are evaluated indirectly. Presumably, however (recalling the point made at the end of 6.5), there might also be more complicated contractarian theories as well, with two or more focal points evaluated directly. And there is even the possibility of *direct contractarianism,* where *all* focal points would be evaluated directly in terms of what the bargainers would think of them.

As we saw in the discussion of foundational teleology, the choice of focal point can have significant implications in terms of what a given foundational theory supports at the factoral level. In the light of this, it seems likely that this choice will have significant implications for deontological foundational theories as well. In particular, then, there is no reason to as-

sume that contractarianism would have the same results at the factoral
level, regardless of what choices are made concerning focal points. Thus it
should not be assumed without argument that rule contractarianism is the
only version of contractarianism worth investigating. Nonetheless, the fact
remains that contractarianism is almost always presented in the form of
rule contractarianism; and so, in what follows, we are going to restrict our
attention to this version as well.

With the choice of focal point in place, it might seem as though the natural next question to ask is just which rules would be agreed upon by the
bargainers. But, in fact, we are not in a position to answer this question, at
least not until we know something more about what the bargainers are *like*.
After all, we can imagine the bargainers being characterized in a number of
different ways, and presumably different *kinds* of bargainers might settle
upon rather different terms. So we need to know how, exactly, the bargainers are to be conceived.

Now this may seem like a peculiar question to ask. Since talk of what the
*bargainers* would agree to is just a somewhat fanciful way of talking about
what *we* would agree to (if we were bargaining over the terms of the contract), doesn't it follow that the bargainers should simply be thought of as
being like *us*?

But this simple answer may indeed be too simple. We began the discussion of contractarianism, after all, with the thought that it mattered what
kinds of rules *reasonable* people would agree to. (Even if unreasonable or
irrational people *would* agree to some set of rules, that would hardly be
reason to think the rules valid!) And so, presumably, at the very least the
bargainers must all be assumed to be reasonable. But to make this stipulation is already to embark on something of an idealization. The contractarian, it seems, is not necessarily asking what sorts of rules we would agree to
*as we are;* for it might well be the case, in fact, that some of us are *not* reasonable. The question, rather, is what we would agree to *if we were* all reasonable.

Once it is seen that the contractarian conceives of the bargainers in at
least partially idealized terms, it becomes an open question just how far this
process should go. For example, should we imagine the bargainers as being
*perfectly* rational in their deliberations—unlimited in their capacity to follow complex logical arguments, and capable of grasping even the most subtle of scientific theories? Or should we imagine instead that the bargainers
are more "normal" in their intelligence, largely rational, but limited in
what they can grasp, and capable of making mistakes in their reasoning?
Obviously enough, perfectly rational bargainers might well settle upon a
different set of rules from that preferred by imperfectly rational bargainers.

Similarly, there are questions concerning what, exactly, the bargainers are
assumed to *know.* Should we imagine the bargainers as being in possession
of complete and perfect scientific knowledge, with perfect information

about all relevant details of society and the world? Do they have, in particular, a clear and accurate grasp of the causal implications of adopting one
set of rules rather than another? Or—more realistically—should we imagine the bargainers as possessing only incomplete and imperfect empirical
knowledge? (Should we even go so far as to allow for the possibility that
the deliberations of the bargainers might sometimes be guided by *mistaken*—but perhaps widely held—beliefs concerning the potential effects of
rival sets of rules?)

Clearly, the bargainers can be conceived along fairly *idealized* lines (perfect information and perfect rationality), or along more *realistic* lines (limited information and imperfect rationality). And thus we face a choice between *ideal contractarianism,* and *realistic contractarianism.* Ideal
contractarians hold that the valid moral rules are those that would be
agreed upon by *ideal* bargainers. No one is suggesting, of course, that people in the real world are perfectly rational, or in possession of perfect information. But the thought is simply that, insofar as we are interested in determining what the genuinely binding moral rules are, we should ask ourselves
what rules we would agree to if we *were* perfectly rational and perfectly informed. In contrast, realistic contractarians insist that valid moral rules are
those that could be agreed upon by people much more like *us*—that is, people with at best limited information and rationality.

(The contractarian's need to choose between ideal and realistic characterization crops up in a second place as well. We are to imagine the bargainers
(suitably characterized) as picking rules to govern our interactions. But in
what terms do "they" think of *us*? For example, what assumptions do they
make about the extent to which we will *obey* the rules they pick? Do they
look for the rules that would be best if we were to *conform* to them—that
is, conform to them perfectly? Or, alternatively, do they select rules on the
assumption that our compliance will be flawed and imperfect? Clearly, the
distinction between ideal and realistic embedding conditions (introduced in
6.5) will be relevant for the contractarian as well.)

It is, of course, obvious that this contrast between ideal and realistic contractarianism is something of a simplification. At the very least, there is a
range of possibilities here, rather than a simple dichotomy. It is also worth
noting that some contractarians will want to characterize the bargainers at
least partially in terms of what they do *not* know. For example, it might be
suggested that each bargainer should be thought of as being completely ignorant concerning the details of his or her own actual identity. (Stipulating
that the bargainers know nothing about their own individual talents, or
their own particular place in society, guarantees that individual bargainers
cannot simply hold out for rules that would favor themselves. Note, incidentally, that since such utter self-ignorance is completely unrealistic, this is still
to think of the bargainers in highly *idealized* terms, albeit negative ones.)
And, of course, any number of combinations of realism and idealization—

both positive and negative—are possible as well. Thus, to mention only one possible combination, the bargainers might be thought of as being perfectly rational, but possessed of only ordinary empirical knowledge, except for the assumption of complete ignorance concerning their own identities.

Beyond the need to characterize the rationality and knowledge of the bargainers, there is also a need to say something about their *motivation*. The bargainers are trying to reach an accord concerning the rules. But what, exactly, motivates their deliberations? Is each person simply looking for the rules that hold out the greatest promise of promoting their own individual well-being? If so, then we are imagining the bargainers as *psychological egoists*—motivated solely by consideration of what is in their own self-interest. Of course, the contractarian need not think that this is a particularly accurate description of normal human psychology; rather, it may simply be another kind of negative idealization. Alternatively, perhaps the bargainers should be thought of as being interested in promoting a variety of personal goals and projects, concerned not only with their own welfare, but also with the well-being of family and friends, as well as with various other, more impersonal goals. Or perhaps the bargainers should be thought of as being altogether impartial, motivated to find rules that will equally promote the well-being of all.

Indeed, should we go so far as to think of the bargainers as being motivated in part by their own individual *moral beliefs?* Perhaps each bargainer is attempting to hold out for the rules that come closest to reflecting her own views concerning what morality requires. Alternatively, perhaps we should think of the bargainers as having no moral beliefs whatsoever, so that bargaining can proceed completely on nonmoral grounds, and moral considerations will have a place solely as the *outcome* of the bargain. (If we *did* allow the bargainers to be motivated by their moral beliefs, wouldn't this contradict the contractarian claim that the ultimate basis for the validity of the rules lies in the very fact that they would be agreed upon? After all, doesn't contractarianism imply that prior to or independently of agreement, no moral beliefs are *correct?* But the contractarian can properly point out that people certainly *have* varying moral beliefs—regardless of whether or not these would be agreed upon—and so we can certainly think of the bargainers as *using* their own moral beliefs to guide their deliberations.)

A related issue is this: should all of the bargainers be thought of in the very same terms? That is, is there a single favored characterization of the bargainers, with all of the bargainers to be conceived of as being exactly similar to one another? In real life, of course, people are different: they know different things, they are motivated by different things, and they are rational to differing degrees. Obviously, therefore, any approach that does think of the bargainers as being qualitatively identical must assume a fair amount of idealization.

But even with idealization, there is no logical requirement that all the bargainers be of the very same (idealized) type. We could, for example, imagine the bargainers as being of several *different* (idealized) kinds. Perhaps some of the bargainers are conceived of as being perfectly rational, while others are only imperfectly rational; some are egoistically motivated, while others have direct concern for strangers; some are fully informed, while others are occasionally misinformed. It seems quite plausible to think that such *many-type* contractarianism would lead to rather different results than would the simpler, *single-type* versions.

Even with single-type contractarianism, however, the bargainers need not be indistinguishable from one another. After all, to take a simple example, even if we assume that all bargainers are perfectly rational, egoistically motivated, and in possession of perfect information, if each bargainer knows *who* she is, each will have somewhat different preferences (since each will be concerned only with her *own* specific well-being). Generally, to get complete qualitative similarity among the bargainers, we will need a *very* high level of idealization, including some crucial elements of mandatory ignorance.

Of course, if the bargainers *were* characterized in such a way as to make each one perfectly similar to the other (or at least, perfectly similar with regard to anything that might influence their deliberations), then each bargainer would deliberate in exactly the same way, and so would favor exactly the same rules. In such a case, obviously enough, reaching *agreement* among the bargainers would be a trivial matter: by hypothesis, once a given bargainer decided what rules she herself favored, all of the other bargainers would necessarily favor the very same rules. Nonetheless, the fact that the bargainers would reach agreement remains important. According to the contractarian, after all, what *grounds* the validity of the rules is the very fact that they would be agreed upon by appropriately specified bargainers. Characterizing the bargainers in such a way as to make them qualitatively identical may suffice to make agreement easy to reach, but as far as the justification of the rules is concerned, it is the agreement itself that is crucial.

For other versions of contractarianism—where the bargainers cannot be assumed to be qualitatively identical—the rules initially favored by one bargainer may differ from those favored by others. As a result, reaching agreement here will not be a trivial matter, and there may be a need for compromise and genuine *bargaining* if any kind of agreement is to be reached at all. It is here, of course, that the bargainers earn their name.

Indeed, given *sufficient* variability among the bargainers, it seems possible that unanimity—which we have been assuming up to this point—may be impossible to achieve, even if we assume that the bargainers are reasonably willing to compromise. Accordingly, some contractarians may insist that valid rules need not be accepted by *all* suitably characterized bargainers; perhaps it would suffice if *enough* of the bargainers could agree to the

rules. Thus, different kinds of majorities, or supermajorities, might be required, instead of unanimity.

In principle, of course, even with many-type theories with a great deal of
initial disagreement among the bargainers, nothing rules out the possibility
that we as theorists should be able to determine (through reflection) precisely what rules the group of bargainers would agree upon. In practice,
however, as greater variability is allowed among the bargainers, it becomes
considerably more difficult to "calculate" what the terms of the agreement
would be (or whether there would even be an agreement). Not surprisingly,
then, most contractarian theories impose a fairly high degree of similarity
in the characterization of the bargainers; and many-type theories, although
not unheard of, are rather rare.

One final issue that we have yet to consider (in the context of contractarianism) is whether there is a single set of moral rules, binding upon all, or
whether instead the rules are somehow *relativized* (see 6.5). Up to this
point, I have been implicitly assuming that there is indeed a single set of
rules; accordingly, I have been writing as though the question is what, if
anything, we could all agree to. We are to imagine *all* of us as bargainers
(suitably characterized), trying to find rules that will be *binding* upon all of
us. Obviously enough, if contractarianism is thought of in these terms, it
generates a single set of rules, with the very same rules valid for all.

But contractarianism can easily be presented in such a way as to allow
for the possibility that different rules might be binding upon members of
different societies. Thus, instead of imagining a *single* contract agreed upon
by *everyone,* we might have a *separate* contract for each society. We could,
for example, ask what rules the members of a given *society* would agree
upon, plausibly holding that the terms of such a contract would be binding
solely upon those who had agreed to it, that is, the members of the given
society. This would allow for the possibility that different societies would
reach different agreements, and so the rules binding upon the members of
one society might differ from the rules binding upon the members of another society. (Whether this possibility would actually be realized or not,
however, would depend on a variety of issues, including whether the societies are sufficiently different, and whether the bargainers are conceived of
in such a way that they have knowledge of the relevant differences—if
any—in their societies.)

Other, more exotic possibilities are available as well. For example, we
might introduce socially relativized rules while still including *everyone*
among the bargainers. That is, we might ask whether we could *all* agree to
one set of rules for the members of one society, while preferring a different
set of rules for the members of another society. This might yield rather different results from the first approach to social relativism. Or we could even
have a version of contractarianism that allows for *individually* relativized
rules. We might, for example, imagine all of us among the bargainers, but

allow the bargainers to agree upon *different* rules for different individuals—"customizing" the rules, in effect, to meet the special circumstances and talents of the given individual.

As far as I can see, nothing in the contractarian idea per se settles the issue as to whether or not we should allow relativization of the moral rules (whether at the social or at the individual level). Apparently, then, this is a choice that must be made on independent grounds.

It should by now be obvious that the number of possible versions of contractarianism is so large that we cannot possibly begin to consider all of them here. Even if we continue to restrict our attention to rule contractarianism, and even if we assume—if only for simplicity—that relativizing the rules is to be rejected, we cannot try to adjudicate among all the various ways of characterizing the bargainers, nor can we try to investigate what each approach would yield at the factoral level. But it may be helpful to consider—even if only briefly—one or two examples, to see how some particular combinations might be motivated, and what they might plausibly be thought to yield.

Some contractarians begin by emphasizing the empirical fact that others can hurt me, and that I need their cooperation if I am to succeed. In the absence of moral cooperation, they note, we all lose. (If each of us is free to harm others—to lie, cheat, and steal—then we end up in a "war of all against all.") It is in my own self-interest, then, to try to come to some agreement with others, jointly settling upon an appropriate set of rules to guide and constrain our interactions. Of course, since I too will have to obey these rules, this certainly will impose a cost on me; I will no longer be free to act however I choose. Nonetheless, the advantages I gain from the fact that others too are limiting their behavior in conformity with these rules may far outweigh the costs. Overall, then, agreeing to obey the rules may be a rational thing for me to do—even from the point of view of my own narrow, self-interest—provided that others are agreeing to obey the rules as well. And since the situation of others is quite similar to my own in this matter, it seems that imposing a well-chosen set of moral rules can be *mutually beneficial*—and so there is reason to hope that an agreement can indeed be reached.

This line of thought motivates the contractarian approach through an appeal to largely egoistic considerations. (The fact that the rules are indeed *mutually* beneficial is of no direct concern to me; it simply gives me reason to think that an agreement is possible.) And it suggests that the appropriate way to think of the bargainers may be like this: egoistically motivated (since I want to find the rules that are to my own greatest advantage), but perfectly rational and fully informed (since I want to find the rules that are *truly* to my own greatest advantage).

A quite different approach to motivating contractarianism begins by emphasizing the fact that when I act I can affect the lives of others in ways they may not approve of. Thus I may infringe their autonomy, their ability to control their own lives. Of course, as a matter of brute empirical fact, I might well have the power to do this, regardless of what others think. But there is a sense in which if I do take advantage of this brute differential in power—without first seeing whether these differences can be justified— then I may be acting *unfairly*. Accordingly, fairness and a concern for the autonomy of others may dictate that I should give all those that I can affect a voice in determining how I shall act. But, of course, the situation is symmetrical: others can affect me as well. Thus *each* of us should have a voice in determining how all others who can affect us should act. This in turn supports the thought that each of us should limit our behavior, by seeing to it that we conform to rules that could be agreed upon by all of us.

If contractarianism is motivated in this second way, how should the bargainers be conceived? One possibility is this. Given that a concern for fairness and autonomy drives the move to a contractarian approach, perhaps the bargainers themselves should be thought of as having a concern for fairness and autonomy. It need not be their sole motivation, of course; the bargainers might well be primarily interested in finding ways to promote, say, their own individual projects and goals. But at the same time, each bargainer might think it important to find rules that it would be *reasonable* for all to accept, since such acceptance is essential if the autonomy of others is to be truly respected.

Alternatively, it might be suggested that there is actually no need at all to have the bargainers themselves concerned with either autonomy or fairness. It might be claimed, after all, that the contractarian framework itself guarantees that everyone's autonomy is respected, by giving everyone a vote. This would leave it open, if we wanted, to conceive of the bargainers as being egoistically motivated. The fairness of the agreement might then be assured by stipulating that the bargainers are to be ignorant of their actual identities (who they are in real life), making it impossible for any coalition of bargainers to hold out for rules that would unfairly favor their own particular group.

What might one or another of these versions of contractarianism yield at the factoral level? Typically, the suggestion is that something like commonsense morality is generated. The reasons for this should, by now, be familiar. We have seen repeatedly how the rules of commonsense morality tend to have good results overall. In any given situation, of course, any particular individual might find himself sacrificing rather than gaining, by virtue of his conformity to these rules. But the rules are impartial, and in the long run they work to everyone's advantage: they protect us from the threat of unprovoked harm, and they provide us with essential tools for attaining the fruits of interpersonal cooperation. Regardless of whether the motivation of the bargainers is completely egoistic, or at least in part driven by regard for the autonomy of others, it does not seem implausible to suggest that what the bargainers will agree upon will be—at least in broad strokes—similar to the familiar rules of commonsense morality.

Of course, there may well be differences of detail in the particular rules that would be agreed upon in the different versions of contractarianism that we have just considered. This would hardly be surprising, given the differences in the ways that the bargainers are characterized.

For example, on the first approach—where the bargainers are egoistically motivated but in possession of full information—requirements to aid others might be fairly limited. No doubt, any of us might unexpectedly find ourselves in suddenly threatening situations from which we would need to be rescued. So, at the very least, a minimal duty to rescue is likely to be agreed upon even here. But it is not at all clear that any more demanding principle of beneficence would be agreed to. After all, those who are well positioned in society will realize that they are unlikely to be the beneficiaries of such a principle, while they would be regularly called upon to aid others. And so, as bargainers, they are unlikely to agree to any principle that makes significant demands in this regard.

In contrast, on our second approach, far more demanding principles of beneficence might emerge. On the one hand, if the bargainers are conceived of as being directly concerned for the autonomy of others, then they may not be willing to agree upon principles that would leave some lacking the resources necessary to lead an adequate life. And on the other hand, even if the bargainers are thought of as being egoistically motivated, provided that it is also stipulated that they are ignorant of their actual identities, then even the wealthy (who will not realize that they are wealthy) may be unwilling to take the risk that they will end up needing assistance that is not to be provided. Either way, then, the bargainers might agree upon a principle of beneficence that is, in fact, fairly demanding. Thus, even if both versions of contractarianism would end up supporting something *similar* to commonsense morality at the factoral level, the results of the two approaches may still differ—perhaps even differ appreciably—in the details.

Unfortunately, we can't take the space to explore the factoral implications of contractarianism all that much further. But it may be helpful to briefly consider a few more examples.

One area that it is particularly interesting to consider from the point of view of contractarianism is that of duties to oneself. As we saw (in 4.5), it is not at all clear whether there are any genuine moral duties that one owes directly to oneself. Many people find the suggestion that there are such duties rather implausible, although it is not obvious on what ground such duties are to be ruled out. Interestingly, an appeal to contractarianism might provide the answer. It might be suggested, for example, that egoistically motivated bargainers would never agree to impose any *self-regarding* duties. After all, while it makes perfect sense for me to care about whether someone is free to harm *others* (since I might *be* one of the others), if someone merely wants to harm *himself*—what is that to me? Why should I object? So I will have no reason to support a rule that forbids harming oneself. Similarly, why should I care whether others keep their promises to themselves, and so on? Perhaps, then, egoistically motivated bargainers will restrict themselves to imposing other-regarding duties; there may simply be no duties to *oneself* at all.

Does this mean that those who do believe in the existence of duties to oneself must reject contractarianism? Not necessarily. For perhaps egoistically motivated bargainers would indeed want to impose some duties to oneself after all. Obviously enough, there is no danger that I might harm myself against my own will. But even deliberately self-imposed harm can still leave me worse off overall. Perhaps, then, bargainers truly concerned to maximize their own individual welfare *would* find it reasonable to require that no one deliberately harm himself.

Furthermore, as we know, not all versions of contractarianism characterize the bargainers as egoists. If, for example, the bargainers are thought of as having a direct concern for autonomy, this might make a difference here as well. Perhaps each bargainer will insist on a requirement that everyone respect not only the autonomy of others, but also their own autonomy. This would be, in part, a self-regarding duty—a duty to oneself—and there might well be other such duties as well.

Another topic worth considering from the perspective of contractarianism is that of self-defense. Most people believe it permissible to harm or even kill aggressors if this is the only way to avoid being harmed themselves. One attractive feature of contractarianism is that it appears to offer a simple and compelling justification for this view. We have seen how it could be rational for the bargainers to agree to restrictions on their own behavior, in exchange for the benefits that accrue when others obey the very same rules. But why would the bargainers ever agree to rules protecting even those who do not themselves obey the rules? On the contrary, what rational bargainers would agree to are presumably rules protecting only those who obey; the rules themselves might specify that if someone breaks the rules, they forgo the protections normally provided by the rules. In short, attacking an unprovoked aggressor will be completely justified; self-defense will be permitted by the very rules the aggressor is trying to violate.

On the other hand, as we saw (in 3.3), the common view about self-defense is rather surprisingly complex. Most people think that even against a deliberate aggressor, one is required to use the minimal amount of force necessary to fend off the attack. Can this feature too be justified by contractarianism? Why should the bargainers agree to extend any protection at all to those who are violating the rules? And what about the fact that many people think it permissible to harm innocent threats, and innocent shields of threats? Would appropriately characterized bargainers agree to rules permitting harm in each of these cases as well? Contractarianism does seem to offer a promising approach to the topic of self-defense; but it's clear that providing a full account of self-defense along contractarian lines will require some further work.

Now all of the examples that we have just been considering fit comfortably with the general suggestion that contractarianism generates something like commonsense morality at the factoral level. Of course, as each of these examples shows, there are many questions that cannot be quickly resolved, and the precise implications of contractarianism at the factoral level will depend on the specific details of the particular version of contractarianism being considered. Still, it has seemed plausible to many that a suitable version of contractarianism could be found that would indeed support commonsense morality.

Nonetheless, it would be too hasty to assume that contractarianism *must* support something like commonsense deontology at the factoral level. For it seems likely that at least *some* versions of contractarianism would actually support consequentialism at the factoral level. Indeed, this might even be the case for one of the versions of contractarianism that we have already considered. For example, suppose that the bargainers are egoistically motivated and perfectly rational, but ignorant of their own identities. Each bargainer is only interested in promoting her own well-being. But since she doesn't know who she *is*, the best she can do is to try to promote *everyone's* well-being. Similarly, since she doesn't know which party (if either) she might be in cases of conflict—where one of two people can be helped, but not both—she stands the greatest chance of promoting her own well-being overall if she favors helping the one who has the most at stake. In short, it might be reasonable for such a bargainer to agree to a *consequentialist* principle—requiring everyone to promote the overall good, counting the well-being of all equally. Thus, far from generating commonsense deontology, this version of contractarianism might yield a consequentialist system that includes neither options nor constraints.

Obviously, many details of this argument are controversial. For example, it assumes that bargainers who don't know their actual identities will assume—when deliberating—that they have an equal chance of being any given person in society. And it assumes that bargainers are willing to take sizable risks in order to gain a chance at significant benefits. It may also assume that the bargainers deliberate on the assumption of ideal embedding conditions (again, see 6.5). But for present purposes there is no need for us to try to defend these assumptions; we can simply build them in as part of the favored characterization of the bargainers. The point is simply that there do appear to be versions of contractarianism that would support consequentialism at the factoral level.

If this is right, then despite the fact that contractarianism is a deontological *foundational* view, not all versions of contractarianism support *factoral* deontology. This mirrors the observation of the last chapter, that certain teleological foundational views will actually *support* deontology at the factoral level. Apparently, then, the choice between teleology and deontology at one level does not dictate the corresponding choice at the other level.

But in any event, it is clear that different versions of contractarianism can have rather different implications at the factoral level. By altering the ways the bargainers are characterized, we can achieve quite varying factoral results.

It is important to keep this point in mind, for people often have a rather narrow view about what a contractarian approach can yield. For example, it is often suggested that contractarianism cannot accommodate the common belief that we have obligations to future generations, that is, to people not yet born. The thought here is that since the unborn will not be among the bargainers, the bargainers will have no reason to agree to any rules protecting the interests of those future generations.

In fact, however, there are several ways that obligations to future generations might be accommodated within a contractarian framework. The bargainers might, for example, be characterized as directly concerned about the well-being of any descendants they might have. Or we might stipulate that the bargainers—although strictly egoistically motivated—are ignorant of the fact that they are contemporaries (thus they will have reason to be concerned about the impact that the actions of one generation might have upon the interests of later generations). Or we might simply prefer a version of contractarianism in which the group of bargainers includes members of *all* generations—not just the current one. For our purposes, luckily, there is no need to choose among these rival approaches, nor to trace out their precise implications. I list them simply to illustrate the more general claim, that it is important not to underestimate the resources available to the contractarian.

Of course, regardless of the precise factoral implications of this or that particular version of contractarianism, many people find the very idea behind the contractarian approach implausible. Perhaps the most commonly voiced objection to contractarianism per se is that it is premised upon a historical fiction. After all, at no point in history has there ever actually been anything remotely like a joint bargaining session in which everyone tries to reach an agreement concerning what the rules of morality should be.

In and of itself, however, this historical observation need not be damning. The contractarian can simply insist that the contract is to be thought of as a *hypothetical* one. That is to say, we don't ask what people *have* agreed to, but only what they *would* agree to (under the right conditions).

But now it might be objected that such merely hypothetical agreement can have no moral force. No doubt, if an agreement *were* made, this would give each of us reason to obey the terms of that agreement; but no such agreement has actually transpired. And the mere fact that we *would* agree to something under certain conditions gives us no reason at all to think we actually *are* bound by the terms of this imaginary agreement.

This objection seems to presuppose that the real force of contractarian-ism derives from the importance of keeping one's *promises*. The thought, apparently, is that agreements are binding by virtue of being a kind of promise. But promises are only binding when they are actually *made;* the mere fact that you *would* make a promise under certain conditions does not suffice to obligate you. Accordingly, the mere fact that the bargainers would agree to some particular set of rules is morally irrelevant. Given that the agreement is a merely hypothetical one, it cannot be the source of the moral relevance of the rules in question (assuming that they are, indeed, rel-evant at all).

Some contractarians are sympathetic to this line of thought, and so they try to show that in the relevant ways an agreement actually *has* been made. Of course, it would be quite implausible to suggest that there has ever been anything like a worldwide convention, with everyone explicitly bargaining over the terms of a moral contract. But it is not obviously implausible to suggest that people generally do actually engage in moral practices, and this behavior may constitute a sort of implicit promise to continue to do so.

One problem with this reply, however, is that at best it seems to bind only those who are already acting morally. For if it is moral behavior that constitutes the implicit promise to continue to act morally, then those who violate the rules of morality have made no implicit promise, and so—by this account—would have no obligation to obey those rules. Clearly, this would be an unattractive implication for any account of the foundations of normative ethics.

In light of this difficulty, contractarians eager to ground moral obligation in actual practice might prefer to appeal instead to the principle of *fair play*. According to this principle, it will be recalled, if an agent has freely and knowingly received the benefits of an on-going mutually beneficial practice to which others have contributed, then the agent is obligated to do his fair share as well—to do his part to keep the practice going. The suggestion, then (similar to one already noted in 4.4), would be that we should think of all of morality as a mutually beneficial practice in which most of us are con-tinuously participating. Since even those who refuse to act morally receive the benefits that arise from the fact that the *rest* of us keep the practice go-ing, by fulfilling our duties, *everyone* is obligated to obey the various moral principles.

If contractarianism is construed along these lines, is *agreement* still the ul-timate grounding for normative ethics? Perhaps, so long as we understand that on this view it isn't a matter of *explicit* agreement, but rather a matter of implicit agreement constituted by our actual practices. Of course, on such a view there is a sense in which the relevant agreement need not be unani-mous—since the practice can and does exist even in the face of less than unanimous support. But to the extent that it is plausible to suggest that if someone freely and knowingly receives the benefits of a practice, then they have implicitly agreed to contribute to that practice, there is perhaps a sense in which everyone may have agreed to abide by morality after all.

However, the very fact that the benefits of morality must be *freely* and *knowingly* received, before the principle of fair play can generate any obligations, may point to a difficulty for this approach. To say the least, it is not obvious that these conditions are met in the case of everyone who benefits from morality. And so it is not obvious that an appeal to the principle of fair play will really succeed in grounding an obligation upon *everyone* to obey the rules. Nonetheless, it might be that such an approach will succeed in obligating *enough* people so as to minimize the force of this objection.

Of course, there may be other problems as well. For example, any attempt to ground morality in terms of what we have *actually* agreed to will be somewhat limited in its ability to criticize our actual moral practices. Moral rules that are not already part of actual moral practices cannot be legitimately appealed to (they will have no weight, since they haven't already been agreed upon). On the other hand, despite this limitation, this does not mean that every aspect of our actual behavior must be judged to be morally acceptable. For we may well be able to identify the principles underlying our actual practices, and then recognize that we often fail to live up to the very principles which we have implicitly embraced.

Perhaps, then, it would be possible to produce a reasonably plausible version of contractarianism which is based upon actual—even if only implicit—agreement. But this is not to say that contractarians *must* in this way abandon appeal to merely hypothetical agreement. For the contractarian need not admit that merely hypothetical agreement can have no justificatory force. It is certainly true that the mere fact that one would agree to do something does not by itself constitute having (actually) promised to do it. But critics of hypothetical contractarianism may be too quick to conclude that it is therefore strictly irrelevant to note what one *would* agree to. On the contrary, the fact that everyone would agree to something under appropriately specified conditions may indeed warrant the conclusion that we are obligated to keep to the terms of that hypothetical agreement—and obligated by virtue of that very fact.

How could this be? The precise answer will depend on the details of the favored version of contractarianism. But for the sake of illustration, let's briefly reconsider an approach whose motivation we have already sketched. Suppose, then, that contractarianism is motivated by appeal to considerations of autonomy and fairness. According to a view of this sort, the very fact that suitably specified bargainers would agree to a set of rules means that those rules would properly respect the autonomy of all, and would constitute the terms of a fair bargain. From this point of view, it doesn't matter at all whether or not such an agreement has ever actually taken place. The point is that the terms of such an agreement would be fair—fair *by virtue of* the very fact that everyone would agree to them under appropriate conditions. Thus, from the standpoint of this version of contractarianism, merely hypothetical agreement suffices: provided that the rules *would* be agreed to (by suitably characterized bargainers), we are bound to obey them.

Obviously, this is not to say that all versions of contractarianism would remain attractive even when it is understood that the relevant agreement can only be a hypothetical one. (And for those versions of contractarianism that appeal to fairly idealized characterizations of the bargainers, there is no alternative but to think of the agreement as merely being a hypothetical one.) But it may suffice to show that at least some versions of contractarianism may remain plausible, despite the fact that the agreements on which they turn have never actually taken place.

## 7.2  Universalizability

For contractarians, the key idea in the foundations of ethics is that of agreement. But this is not the only alternative available to foundational deontologists. A quite different approach begins with the claim that the truly binding moral rules will be equally binding upon everyone—they will be *universal*. This is, of course, a thought shared by many different approaches in ethics. But for the advocates of this new approach, the concept of universality provides the *key* to determining the valid moral rules. The suggestion is not merely that universality is a necessary feature of valid moral rules. Rather—and more ambitiously—the claim is that valid moral rules are the only ones that are *capable* of being universal moral rules, the only rules that we can continue to endorse while taking seriously the thought that they are supposed to be universally binding.

Thus—according to this new approach—the universality of genuine moral rules provides us with a test as to whether or not a given proposed rule is genuinely binding: we look to see whether the rule truly could be universalized, whether it is *universalizable*. The claim, then, is that if we consider a rule that is not, in fact, a valid moral rule, we can discover this fact by seeing that it is not universalizable; the lack of validity is demonstrated by the very fact that it cannot be properly universalized. In contrast, if a rule *can* be appropriately universalized, it follows that it is indeed universally valid, since *only* valid rules can be universalized.

At a minimum, then, universalizability is thought to provide a test—indeed a decisive test—of validity. But we are interested in foundational theories of normative ethics, theories which attempt to *explain* the relevance of the normative factors. So we should also understand the advocates of this new view to be making a further claim, that universalizability is the ultimate *basis* of normative ethics.

Let's call this foundational view *universalizability*. (No doubt, a more natural name for this view would be *universalizabilism;* its advocates would then be *universalizabilists*. But for obvious reasons these terms are rarely used, and I shall avoid them.)

Now one part of this view—the "negative" half—may be relatively easy to accept: if universality is indeed an essential feature of valid moral rules, then rules that cannot be universalized will lack validity *by virtue of* that very fact. Of course, in thinking about this claim, it is important not to confuse the question at issue—the universalizability of valid moral rules—with the distinction between general and special obligations (see 4.3). Even special obligations, after all, may be governed by basic principles that are universally binding. Promising, for example, can generate special obligations; nonetheless, one can consistently insist that *everyone* is bound by the rule that says you must keep your promises (if you've made any). Thus, the claim being made by the current foundational view is not that all obligations are general, but that all basic moral rules are universally binding. And if this is right, obviously enough, then it does seem to follow that rules that *cannot* be universalized will lack validity by virtue of that very fact.

But it is also important to see that a more ambitious, "positive" claim is being made by this approach as well: according to this view, for valid moral rules, the validity of those rules is grounded in the very fact that they *can* be universalized. In effect, a given rule's suitability to *be* a universally binding moral rule is what makes it be the case that the rule is indeed universally binding.

It will have been noted that in introducing this view I have been assuming that universalizability is used, in the first instance, to evaluate *rules*. That is, we first look to see whether a given rule can be universalized or not. Presumably, once the valid moral rules are identified in this way, we can then go on to evaluate other focal points, such as acts, indirectly—in terms of these rules. We might, for example, say that an act is permissible if and only if it conforms to the valid rules. But only the rules themselves are evaluated *directly* in terms of universalizability. In short, I have been presenting universalizability in the form of *rule universalizability*. This is indeed the standard version of universalizability among moral philosophers, and for most of what follows I will restrict our attention to it. Eventually, of course, we will want to ask whether and to what extent a universalizability approach can be combined with the choice of other focal points as primary. But for the time being, at any rate, let us assume that what is at issue is indeed the universalizability of rules.

(It is certainly a striking fact that foundational deontologists have generally chosen rules as the primary evaluative focal point of their theories, while modern foundational teleologists have most commonly focused on acts. Nonetheless, as we have seen, teleological theories *can* select rules—or other focal points—to be primary. And at least one deontological view—contractarianism—can be presented in an act version. So it is not at all obvious whether there is anything more than historical accident behind this generalization.)

A second thing to note about the way in which I have introduced universalizability is that I have been deliberately rather vague about what exactly it is to test whether a given rule is universalizable. The basic idea, I hope, is clear enough: we check whether a given rule could be truly valid by trying to take seriously the claim that the proposed rule is *universally binding*. That is, we somehow suppose (for the sake of argument) that the rule really is universal, and then we look to see whether something "goes wrong" when we try to make this assumption. But what, exactly, do we do when we imagine (if only for the sake of argument) that the rule is universal? And what, exactly, is it that is supposed to go "wrong" when we conduct this thought experiment on rules that are not genuinely valid?

To answer these two questions is to fill in the most important details of the universalizability approach. For the first question—what it is that we do when we try to imagine the rule to be universal—there is, I think, a standard answer: we try to imagine everyone *acting* on the rules. We are, after all, testing to see whether the given rule can truly be universally binding—a rule that everyone is morally required to act upon. So the *first* thing that we do is to try to imagine that everyone does indeed act upon the rule in question, just as they are required to do.

Although this is the standard answer, it is not the only possibility. For example, instead of trying to imagine a world in which everyone *acts* on the rule in question, we might try to imagine a world in which everyone *accepts* the rule. Of course, if everyone does accept the rule, then most people would probably act on it, at least much of the time. But in this second approach, unlike the first, we would leave open the possibility that in some cases one or more people might actually fail to act on the rule, perhaps because they lack adequate motivation, or because they misunderstand what the rule requires. (In effect, this second approach allows for realistic embedding (see 6.5), while the standard approach assumes ideal embedding.)

Both approaches seem worthy of investigation; and presumably they will at least sometimes support different results. However, for simplicity, let's assume that the standard answer is indeed the more plausible one, and restrict our attention to universalizability tests that ask us to imagine everyone *acting* on the rule in question. This still leaves the second question unanswered: what exactly is it that is supposed to go *wrong* when we try to imagine everyone acting on rules that are not, in fact, valid?

To this second question there is no standard answer. Rather, different advocates of universalizability answer it in different ways, yielding different versions of the universalizability test. Each specific version of the universalizability test will direct our attention to a different proposal concerning what exactly it is that might go "wrong" when we try to imagine everyone acting on a rule. But this means that there is a third question that will need answering as well. If the relevant sort of thing does go wrong, then we are supposed to conclude that the rule in question is not genuinely universally binding after all. But how, exactly, does this follow? Why does the fact that the given thing goes wrong (when we imagine everyone acting on the rule) make it legitimate to infer that the rule is not universally *valid*? More simply still: why is the test—as specifically spelled out—a *good* test as to whether or not a given rule is genuinely universally binding?

Presumably, the answer to this third question will depend on the answers to the first two, in particular to the second. Different versions of universalizability direct our attention to different things that might go wrong when we try to imagine everyone acting on a rule. What we will need, then, is a specific account of how the fact that things go wrong in that *particular* way demonstrates that the rule in question is not genuinely valid after all.

One final introductory remark. It is generally assumed that it is appropriate to test individual rules in isolation, one at a time. Presumably, however, what we are ultimately interested in finding is the complete *set* of valid rules. And it seems conceivable that a rule might pass when tested in isolation, but not when tested along with other plausible rules. If so, then instead of testing the universalizability of rules one at a time, perhaps we ought to test competing *sets* of rules, universalizing all the members of a given set at the same time. Nonetheless, in what follows, I'll leave this potential complication aside.

Now in many ways the most straightforward suggestion concerning what might go wrong, when we try to imagine a world in which everyone acts on a given rule, is this: it might simply be *impossible* for everyone to act on the rule in question. That is, when we *try* to imagine a world in which everyone conforms to the rule, we find this cannot actually be done: we discover that it isn't actually possible for *everyone* to conform. (It might of course still be possible for some, or even most, people to act on the rule, or even for all people to act on it, at different times; what is impossible—we are supposing—is that everyone act on it, all the time.) The particular universalizability test that would correspond to this proposal is this: if it is literally impossible for everyone to act on a given rule, then that rule is not, in fact, valid.

To say the least, it is not obvious that many rules would fail this test. How often is it literally impossible for everyone to act on a given rule? Accordingly, it doesn't seem especially plausible to suggest that this particular universalizability test will suffice to rule out all morally illegitimate rules. But that doesn't mean that there is any problem with the test so far as it goes. That is, so long as we are willing to allow for the possibility that there may be more than one morally relevant thing that can go wrong when we try to universalize a rule, there is no need to insist that any single proposal does all the work by itself. Thus advocates of the current proposal might want to concede that we will need to supplement it—find further ways that something can go wrong when we try to universalize a rule. All that they must insist upon is that impossibility is *one* relevant thing that can go wrong.

This proposal does seem intuitively plausible. But why, exactly, should we believe it? That is, why *must* it be the case that if a rule is genuinely universally valid, then it must be possible for everyone to act on that rule? The most natural defense of this claim, I suppose, is this. There is a plausible and widely held view that "ought implies can". According to this view, a given agent can be morally *required* to perform a given act only if the agent *can* perform the act; if it is actually impossible for that particular agent to perform the act in question, then she cannot truly be required to do it (all things considered). Suppose we grant this. What follows? Well, what seems to follow is that if a rule is truly *universally* valid, then it must be possible for *everyone* to act on it. For if the rule is truly universally binding, then everyone is required to act upon it, and so—since ought implies can— everyone must be *able* to act upon it, even in a situation in which everyone else is acting upon the rule too. Therefore, if it isn't really possible for everyone to act upon the rule, it can't truly be the case that everyone ought to act upon it: the rule cannot truly be a universally binding one.

Incidentally, this explanation appears to show that the impossibility in question need not be a *logical* impossibility. Mere empirical impossibility would suffice to demonstrate that a rule was not truly universalizable. For when we say that ought implies can, we mean more than that it must be logically possible for the person to perform the act; it must also be empirically possible. Thus even if there is no logical or conceptual incoherence involved in imagining everyone acting on the rule, provided that there could be circumstances in which it would be *physically* impossible for everyone to act on the rule, the rule cannot truly be universally binding. For if it were universally binding—valid for everyone, in all situations—then it would have to be valid even under the particular empirical circumstances in question, circumstances in which—by hypothesis—it would not be possible for everyone to act upon the rule. Apparently, then, even mere empirical impossibility (indeed, even the possibility of such an impossibility) will suffice to show that a given rule is not universally valid.

This entire line of argument, however, seems open to the following objection. At best, ought implies can applies only to moral *requirements:* if someone is required to perform a given act, then it must be possible for that person to perform the act; and so, if a rule requiring *everyone* to perform some act is valid, it must be possible for everyone to perform the act. But what about rules that merely assert that it is *permissible* (but not obligatory) to perform a certain act? Why must it be possible for everyone to perform the act in question even for a rule of *this* sort? After all, it doesn't seem especially plausible to insist that "*may* implies can": an act can certainly be morally permissible even though the agent who is permitted to perform the act cannot in fact do it. So even if it is impossible for everyone to perform a given act, this won't show that a rule permitting (but not requiring) the act in question is illegitimate.

But this objection may presuppose too narrow a notion of what it is for everyone to act on a given rule. Obviously enough, for rules that *require* a particular act, a world in which everyone conforms to the rule will indeed be a world in which everyone performs acts of the particular type in question. Similarly, for rules that *forbid* a particular act, if everyone conforms to the rule, then everyone will avoid performing acts of that type. But for rules that merely *permit*—but do not require—a given type of act, a world in which everyone conforms to the rule need not be a world in which everyone actually performs acts of the type in question. On the contrary, everyone conforms to a merely permissive rule regardless of *what* they do!

Since you "act on" a permissive rule regardless of whether or not you perform the type of act it permits, any world at all will count as a world in which everyone conforms to the rule. So even if it is impossible for everyone to *perform* the given type of act, this gives us no reason at all to think that it is impossible for everyone to *act on* the rule—that is, to conform to it. Thus, the objection fails. Despite the claims of the objection, the universalizability test doesn't improperly fail merely permissive rules on the admittedly irrelevant ground that it may be impossible for everyone to perform the act permitted by the rule. On the contrary, this version of the universalizability test inevitably *passes* all such rules.

Indeed, so long as any world at all is possible—and obviously enough, at least one world, the real world, is possible—then for every merely permissive rule whatsoever, it will be possible for everyone to act on the rule, *regardless of its content*. No matter what the rule permits, so long as it is merely permissive, it will be possible for everyone to act on it. And what this means, of course, is that absolutely every merely permissive rule passes this version of the universalizability test.

Now were this version thought to be complete—were someone to hold that so long as it is possible for everyone to act on a rule, that rule is valid—this would clearly be a devastating implication. No plausible moral theory could hold, for example, that the rule that says absolutely everything is permissible is a sound moral rule. But as we have already seen, those who think that impossibility is *one* of the things that can go wrong when we try to universalize a rule need not think that it is the only thing that can go wrong. So even if it is true that an appeal to impossibility will not be sufficient—all by itself—to rule out all illegitimate rules, there is still no reason to doubt that this version of universalizability is correct so far as it goes. At a minimum, then, if it would be impossible for everyone to act on a given rule, then indeed the rule cannot be valid. Still, if we are to have a complete account of the foundations of normative ethics—a test adequate to rule out all illegitimate rules—we will need to find further things that can go wrong (when we try to universalize) beyond sheer impossibility. But what else might we appeal to?

One common suggestion is this. Even if it would be *possible* for everyone to act on a given rule, the results of everyone doing so might still be quite undesirable. In particular, the results might be bad for me—adversely affecting my overall well-being. So this points to a second possible proposal concerning what might go "wrong" when I imagine everyone acting on a given rule: the results of everyone doing so might be bad for me. Corresponding to this is a second possible version of the universalizability test: if everyone's acting on a given rule would be bad for the individual agent, then the rule in question is not, in fact, a valid one.

The thought at work here may be something like this. Often, an individual agent is content to act on a rule (or set of rules) provided that she is the *only* person (or one of only a few) who is doing so. That is, she may attain some benefit from acting in the way she proposes—but her attaining that benefit may depend crucially on her being something of an exception: were everyone to act on the very same rules that she wants to act upon, the benefit might well be lost, and she might even end up worse overall. In a case like this, clearly, what the agent *wants* is to play by one set of rules while others have to play by a quite different set of rules. But if the rules are only attractive provided that not everyone is acting upon them, then they cannot be morally legitimate. For moral rules are universal—equally valid for everyone. Thus if the agent is *unwilling* to endorse the rules even for a situation in which everyone is going to be acting upon them, it follows that the rules are not, in fact, morally legitimate ones.

This second approach to universalizability might be buttressed by appeal to many of the same sorts of considerations that motivated foundational egoism. That is, it might be agreed that ultimately morality must be concerned with what is good for the individual agent. But where foundational egoism tried to base normative ethics on this thought alone, our current approach also emphasizes the fact that genuine moral rules are universal—valid for everyone if valid for anyone. Accordingly, it might be suggested, if all we do is ask whether it would be good for the agent if *she* were to act on the rule being tested, then we're not asking precisely the right question. Rather, we should ask whether it would be good for the agent if *everyone* were to act on the rule in question. And this is exactly the question raised by the current version of universalizability.

(There is, of course, a version of rule egoism that raises the very same question (as noted in 6.5). This shouldn't surprise us. Distinct foundational theories begin with rather different basic ideas, but in the course of elaborating them we may find ourselves also drawing upon ideas that are more central to some other approach. As a result, the final products may sometimes be indistinguishable, except for points of emphasis. Inevitably, this will sometimes make the "proper" classification of a fully developed theory somewhat arbitrary.)

Of course, an agent might find the prospect of everyone's acting on a rule undesirable for a variety of reasons, and not merely because it would be bad for the agent's overall level of well-being. Assuming that we reject psychological egoism—the view that people are only concerned with their own well-being—then agents might have any number of reasons for finding some outcome unattractive. Thus you might be unwilling to endorse everyone's acting on some rule, even if the results of this would not be particularly bad *for you*. And so this points us in the direction of a third possible version of the universalizability test, in which rules are to be rejected *whenever* the agent cannot, on reflection, endorse them as valid for everyone, in all situations. Adverse impact on her own well-being may be one common ground for the agent's refusing to endorse a given rule as universal; but it need not be the only such ground.

Like the second approach, this new version of universalizability draws upon the idea that moral rules must be ones that can be *endorsed* by the agent. For in many cases, of course, no one is in a position to force the agent to conform to morality; this is something the agent will have to freely choose to do. Thus, it might be suggested, the genuine rules must be ones that the agent can—on due reflection—accept. But when we combine this with the thought that to accept a rule as a *moral* rule is to view it as something universally binding, we are led to the view that valid moral rules must be ones that the agent can endorse even for the situation in which everyone is acting upon them. And this is precisely the question raised by our third version of universalizability.

One potential difficulty with both the second and the third version of the universalizability test is that it seems possible that the results might differ from individual to individual. For example, if everyone were to act on a given rule, this might be bad for me, but good for you. Similarly, it might be that on reflection I find the prospect of everyone's acting on the given rule unattractive, while you are quite prepared to endorse the rule in all circumstances whatsoever. But if this is right, then whether a given rule passes these two versions of universalizability will depend on the specific person using the test. (In contrast, the first version didn't have this feature: whether or not it would be *impossible* for everyone to act on the rule is not something that can vary from person to person.)

Perhaps the most obvious suggestion to make here is that whether a given rule is valid for a given agent does indeed depend on the results of *his* (properly) applying the test. This would be to allow for the possibility of relativism at the individual level: the rules binding upon one person might not be binding upon another. (Of course, whether this possibility is actually realized or not will depend on whether people are truly *sufficiently* different that the universalizability tests really do yield different results. At first glance, no doubt, it may seem obvious that they are; but appearances might be deceptive.)

However, this suggestion would be a rather uncomfortable one for an advocate of universalizability to accept. After all, the key idea used to motivate universalizability was the claim that valid moral rules are *universal—*

equally binding upon everyone. How can one start with the claim that universality is fundamental to all of normative ethics and then end up endorsing a theory that allows for the possibility of individually relativized rules? The combination of ideas seems incoherent.

Of course, even if this is right, that doesn't necessarily prove that either of these tests is mistaken. Strictly speaking, there is no *logical* contradiction in combining relativism and universalizability tests. That is, even if relativism is true, it might still be the case that which rules I am bound by is a matter of seeing, say, whether it would be bad for me if *everyone* were to act on these rules. The problem only arises when we try to explain why this test is a *good* test. Obviously enough, if we are going to combine universalizability tests with relativism, we will need an account that can motivate such tests *without* appealing to the claim that the valid moral rules are universal (for if they are, relativism is false). To be honest, I don't know what this alternative account would look like. But that hardly shows that no such account could be offered.

Still, the fact remains that the most plausible motivation for a universalizability approach appeals to the claim that moral rules are indeed universal. And so any suggestion that leads to relativism is one that is likely to be resisted. Now the problem with the second and third proposals arose from the fact that the particular things that could go wrong (when universalizing) were things that could go wrong for one person without going wrong for everyone. Presumably, then, we could avoid relativism by restricting ourselves to things that will only go wrong for someone if they go wrong for absolutely everyone. This may mean rejecting the second and third proposals—or, perhaps, modifying them.

Think again about the second proposal. The appeal to what would be bad *for me* was problematic, since what is bad for me might not be bad for you. Perhaps, then, we should appeal instead to what is bad *overall*. (Of course, what is bad overall may not be bad *for* everyone; that is, it may not be to everyone's personal disadvantage. But the fact that it is bad *overall* will not vary from person to person. So this should avoid relativism.) Thus, instead of running a universalizability test in terms of the agent's own individual good, we might instead run the test in terms of the *overall good*. This suggests the following version of the test: if everyone's acting on a rule would produce bad results overall, then the rule is not, in fact, valid. (Once again, it will be noted that this test is the same as that used by a particular teleological theory, in this case, ideal rule consequentialism. And so we see, again, how rather different starting points can lead to much the same end product.)

Presumably, this fourth version of the universalizability test would be motivated by appeal to the twin thoughts that morality is impartial, and so must be concerned with the good of all, and that moral rules are universal. Together these may support the view that the genuinely valid moral rules must have good results overall, even when everyone is acting on them.

Return now to the third version of the universalizability test, which held that a rule is not valid if the agent cannot, on reflection, endorse it as valid for everyone. Here, too, the problem was that it seemed possible that the prospect of everyone's acting on a given rule might be attractive to one agent but unattractive to another; one person's reason for rejecting a rule (when universalized) might have no weight for someone else. Perhaps, however, we could restrict the grounds for endorsing or rejecting the rule to those that would necessarily appeal to *all* agents (at least, insofar as they are rational). For example, all rational agents presumably prefer efficient means to achieving their goals. But in some cases it might be that if everyone were to act on a given rule, this would make it more difficult for everyone to achieve their goals—including goals that might be assigned by the very rule in question. If so, then everyone would have reason to refuse to endorse the rule (as valid for everyone). And this suggests a fifth version of the universalizability test: if all rational agents have reason to reject the rule as binding upon everyone, then it is not, in fact, valid. (This is, of course, similar to yet another of our foundational theories, this time to a certain highly idealized version of contractarianism.)

This final version of the universalizability test might well incorporate one or more of the earlier versions. It might plausibly be suggested, for example, that all rational agents will have reason to reject a rule if it is literally impossible for everyone to act on it. And it might even be claimed that all rational agents have reason to reject any rule that would have bad results overall if everyone were to act on it. Nonetheless, the current test might still be provided with its own justification, one stressing the thought that valid moral rules must be ones that it is *rational* to accept. And since they are binding upon everyone, they must be rules that *everyone* can rationally accept—even for the situation in which everyone is acting on them. Thus, if all rational agents would have reason to reject a rule as binding upon everyone, then the rule is not, in fact, a valid one.

There are, of course, still other versions of the universalizability test. But these are among the most important. In some cases, presumably, all of these approaches might agree in rejecting a proposed rule. For example, suppose that in order to get out of a tight situation, I make a promise that I have no intention of keeping. It is reasonable to think that any rule that required me to make such an insincere promise would fail several, and perhaps all, of the universalizability tests that we have discussed.

After all—it might be argued—if everyone made promises that they had no intention of keeping, the mere fact that someone had made a promise would give you no reason to believe them, and so the practice of making promises would be severely damaged, and perhaps even disappear. This would clearly be a bad result overall, and so the proposed rule would be rejected by our fourth test. But it would also be a bad result for me (I've often benefited from the practice of promising), and so the proposed rule would be rejected by our second test as well. The rule may also fail the third test, since it's unlikely that, on reflection, I'd be willing to endorse the rule as valid for everyone. And the same thing may be true for the fifth test: arguably, all rational agents would have reason to reject the rule. Indeed, even the first test might fail the proposed rule, for it might be argued that it is literally impossible to make a promise in a world in which no one would believe you, and the practice of promising has disappeared.

In at least some cases, then, there might be a fair amount of agreement among the various versions of the universalizability test. But this hardly shows that different versions of the test will give the same answers in *every* case. And, in fact, given the rather different concerns of each of the tests— the different things that can go wrong—it seems likely that in at least many cases different tests will pass and fail different rules.

Consider, for example, a rule that says that I need not make any sacrifices to aid others. There certainly doesn't seem to be anything impossible about everyone's acting on such a rule, so it seems to pass the first test. Of course, if no one made sacrifices to aid others, the results would be very bad overall, and so the fourth version of the test would presumably reject such a rule. On the other hand, if I am sufficiently wealthy and independent, the results of everyone's acting on such a rule might not be bad *for me* (it frees me from the need to make costly sacrifices), and so the second test might well pass the rule. Despite this, however, I might be unwilling to endorse a rule that might leave others without necessary aid, and so the third test might well fail the rule. That still leaves the fifth test, which asks whether all rational agents have a reason to reject the rule in question. Admittedly, it's not obvious what the correct answer here is; but even without settling this last question, I think we've seen enough to agree that not all versions of universalizability yield the same answers in all cases.

In the light of this, it is likely to be rather important which particular universalizability tests are to be accepted. But this is a matter which I am going to have to leave unresolved. I have tried to say enough to give some sense of the distinct motivations that might be thought to support the individual tests. But I will not try to settle the controversial question of what combination of tests (or which single test) is the most plausible one overall.

This makes it difficult to say anything satisfactory in a general way about the factoral implications of universalizability. Not surprisingly, many advocates of universalizability claim that their own favored version of the theory yields something like commonsense morality at the factoral level (though they often differ about the details). Others believe that universalizability supports factoral consequentialism. I won't try to settle this debate either. I only want to emphasize the point that it seems likely that different versions of universalizability will yield different results at the factoral level, and there is no good reason to assume that *all* of these versions generate factoral deontology. Thus we have, I believe, yet another case where a deontological foundational view—here, universalizability—need not support deontology at the factoral level.

It should probably be noted, however, that some critics of universalizability have argued that universalizability won't actually have *any* factoral implications at all. They claim that any rule whatsoever can be universalized—since, obviously enough, no matter what the rule says, one can always insist that everyone should obey it. Thus (they conclude) the requirement that valid rules be universalizable fails to eliminate any rules at all; and so it cannot support any one particular factoral theory rather than another.

But this objection rests on a misunderstanding of what the universalizability tests come to. No advocate of universalizability believes that a rule is shown to be universalizable by the mere fact that someone does or could insist that everyone should obey it. On the contrary, as we have seen, investigating the universalizability of a given rule involves trying to imagine a world in which everyone acts on that rule, and seeing whether certain relevant things go wrong when we do this. The mere fact that someone could *say* that everyone should act on a rule gives us no reason at all to believe that the given rule would actually pass the specific universalizability tests that we have described. (We can't even be confident that it would pass the third version of the test: perhaps, after adequate reflection, the agent would actually be unwilling to endorse the rule as binding upon everyone.) Accordingly, the claim that universalizability is necessarily "empty"—unable to rule anything out—seems to me mistaken.

On the other hand, it still might be the case that there are certain *kinds* of rules that universalizability tests are ill suited to evaluate. For example, recall (from 6.5) the need for rules (or clauses of rules) telling us how to act in situations of general *noncompliance*—situations where too many people are failing to conform to morality. One potential problem with rule consequentialism, I argued, was that it had difficulty testing such rules in the right way. Unfortunately, it seems possible that the very same problem may arise—and for the very same reason—for universalizability. For when we ask ourselves whether something would go wrong if everyone were to act on a given rule, we are obviously imagining a world with perfect conformity to the rule. But when it comes to evaluating noncompliance clauses, what we primarily need to be considering are the implications of such clauses in situations of *less* than perfect conformity. And this, it seems, universalizability cannot do; it is limited to asking whether anything goes wrong with the rule when *everyone* is acting on it.

There may, however, be ways to meet this difficulty. Consider again the thought that valid moral rules are universal. One implication of this—the one we have been emphasizing—is that valid moral rules are binding upon everyone. This points in the direction of universalizability tests in which we ask whether anything (of the relevant sort) goes wrong when everyone acts on the rules. But another implication of the universality of valid moral rules seems to be that such rules should be valid in every *situation*. This may point in the direction of further universalizability tests, where we ask whether anything (of the relevant sort) goes wrong when we think of the rules as being *valid* in every situation—including situations of less than perfect conformity. It seems at least possible, therefore, that even rules specifically intended to govern noncompliance can be properly evaluated, provided that we attend to the full implications of universality. However, I won't try to pursue the details of how these further tests might be spelled out.

Before leaving the topic of universalizability, let's return to a question I earlier put aside—the extent to which this approach can be combined with a different choice of primary evaluative focal point. On the face of it, as far as I can see, there is no reason why the evaluative standpoint provided by universalizability must be used in the first instance to evaluate *rules*. Other kinds of focal points could easily be tested as well, or instead, by seeing whether anything would go wrong if an item of that kind were universalized. For example, it certainly seems as though we could have *motive universalizability,* in which we might test a given motive by asking whether anything would go wrong if *everyone* had that motive. Or we could have *virtue universalizability,* asking whether anything would go wrong if everyone had that character trait. Similarly, or so it seems, we could have *intention universalizability,* or *norm universalizability,* and so on, for any number of other focal points.

In abstract terms, the general idea behind universalizability seems to be this: we test specific items—particular motives, social norms, rules—by asking whether anything (of the relevant sort) would go wrong if that particular kind of item were universal. In principle, it seems, so long as it makes sense to think of a particular type of item as being universal—as certainly seems to be the case for motives, norms, intentions, and so on—there is no reason why we could not have a version of universalizability directly evaluating items of that particular type. If this is right, then a commitment to universalizability does not, in and of itself, mandate a particular choice of focal point. As usual, the choice of focal point must be made on independent grounds. Rule universalizability may be by far the most common version of universalizability, but it seems that other versions are possible, and worthy of consideration.

What about the possibility of *act universalizability?* Interestingly, there is a popular moral test that might be best understood along these lines. One way that people often attempt to challenge the action of another is by asking the question, "What if everyone did that?" The idea here seems to be that we are to try to imagine everyone doing that *kind* of act. And the unstated assumption seems to be that if we do try to imagine everyone's acting in this way, something will go wrong. Realizing this, we are supposed to draw the desired conclusion, namely, that the action cannot be legitimate after all. Now if this is indeed the way that the challenge behind the question is supposed to function, then it seems that we are evaluating actions *directly*—and we are evaluating them in terms of their universalizability. In short, we seem to have a version of act universalizability.

Of course, even if this is right, several things remain obscure about this popular test. The most obvious is that it is not at all clear what it is that is supposed to go *wrong* when we try to imagine everyone's acting like that. Is it supposed to be impossible for everyone to act in that way? Or is it, rather, that if everyone were to act that way the results would be bad for the agent, or bad overall? Is it simply that after adequate reflection we are supposed to be unable to endorse everyone's acting in the given way? Or is it, perhaps, that we are supposed to see that anyone rational would have reason to oppose everyone's acting that way? As far as I can see, despite the popularity of the test, there is no *common* understanding concerning what, exactly, it is that goes wrong when we try to imagine everyone's acting in a way that is not, in fact, permissible.

A second problem is this. Faced with a particular action, we are supposed to imagine a world in which everyone acts like that. But what, exactly, is it for everyone to act like *that*? Presumably, we are imagining everyone performing that *kind* of act—an act of that *type*. But any given action will be of *many*—indeed infinitely many—different types. How do we determine what the *relevant* act type is? Suppose, for example, that I strangle my mother with my bare hands on a Wednesday evening to inherit her money. For the purposes of universalization, what *kind* of act have I performed? Have I killed my mother? Killed a parent? Killed a woman? Killed someone? Killed someone's mother? Have I strangled someone? Strangled someone with my bare hands? Killed a relative on a weekday? Used my hands to make money? Exerted myself on a Wednesday evening? I have, of course, done all of these things (and many more). But which type of act is the *relevant* type? What is it for everyone to perform an act of *that* type? This is sometimes known as the problem of the *relevant act description*.

There is, I think, no standard solution to this problem. So far as I can see, nothing in the common practice tells us the proper way to determine the relevant act description. But this is not to say, of course, that no solution to the problem is possible. For example, one suggestion would be that the relevant description of the act is the one that captures what the agent *intends* to be doing. (Presumably, many features of my act are quite irrelevant to my intentions.) According to this suggestion, then, I am supposed to imagine everyone performing acts with the particular features that I intend my particular act to have. (Clearly, such an approach would be rather similar to—although perhaps not quite identical with—intention universalizability.) However, one difficulty with this approach is that there could easily be features of an agent's act that intuitively seem to be morally relevant but which are not among the features of the act that the agent intends. If so, then testing the permissibility of the act solely on the basis of the *intended* features may fail to take into account some of the morally relevant features of the act.

A more radical suggestion might be that *every* accurate act description is, in principle, relevant: my act must be universalizable no matter *how* it is described. According to this view, if there is even a single (accurate) description of the act such that something (of the relevant sort) would go wrong were everyone to perform an act of *that* type, then the act is impermissible. Obviously enough, an approach of this sort completely avoids the problem of finding the *single* relevant act description to universalize. Unfortunately, it faces its own difficulties: it may run the risk of inappropriately condemning certain morally permissible acts. (For example, if I kill an aggressor in self-defense, then one accurate description of what I have done is that I have killed someone. But what if everyone were to go around killing people?)

In the light of all of this, it should be clear that the popular question "What if everyone did that?" cannot stand on its own. Various details still need to be filled in, in plausible ways; but to do this is to go well beyond anything implied by the question itself. At best, it seems, asking "What if everyone did that?" does nothing more than point us in the general direction of an act universalizability theory.

The same thing may well be true for another popular (indeed, extraordinarily popular) principle, *the golden rule:* "do unto others as you would have them do unto you". Although here too the proper interpretation of this principle is less than transparent, it does not seem implausible, on the face of it, to view the golden rule as a kind of universalizability test. What's more, universalizability seems to be directed, in the first instance, to the evaluation of *acts*. We are, it seems, told to do those *acts* that are of such a kind that we would want to have others perform them as well. In short, the golden rule appears to be yet another version of act universalizability.

(I should perhaps note that people sometimes distinguish between the "positive" version of the golden rule—the one I have just quoted—and a "negative" version which instructs you *not* to do unto others what you would not have them do unto you. And sometimes it is claimed that unlike the positive version, the negative version can generate only negative duties. I find this claim implausible—it requires putting rather a lot of weight upon the word "do"—but won't try to argue against it here. For simplicity, however, let's stick to the positive version.)

In the light of our previous discussion, three points about the golden rule seem especially worth making. First, the problem of finding the relevant act description seems to arise here as well. You are to ask whether you would want others to "do unto you" the same sort of thing that you are "doing unto" them. But what, exactly, is it that you are *doing* to the others? Which features of your act are relevant? What *kind* of act are you to imagine others doing to you? There may well be a plausible solution to the problem of relevant act descriptions, but as far as I can see, the golden rule itself does not offer any particular help here at all.

Second, what exactly is it that is supposed to go *wrong* when you imagine others doing to you the same sort of thing as you are doing to them? The golden rule asks you whether you "would have them" acting in this way toward you. The matter is hardly clear, but the idea may be that you are supposed to ask whether their acting in this way would be bad for you. Or perhaps—less narrowly—you are supposed to ask whether you are willing to endorse their acting in this way. Although it would be unfair to claim that the golden rule gives no guidance here at all, it does seem fair to suggest that the precise nature of the test could stand to be somewhat clearer.

But a third point should be raised as well, which is that it is not altogether clear that the golden rule should indeed be understood as a genuine *universalizability* test. After all, the golden rule only asks you to imagine a world in which the *particular* people you are acting toward in a certain way act in that same way *toward you*. In effect, the golden rule asks you to think about a world with *role reversal*: the actions stay the same, but the relevant parties switch places. This is considerably narrower than stipulating full-scale universalization of the act in question. Instead of imagining a world in which *everyone* acts in the given way (to *lots* of people), we only have to imagine a world in which the particular people you are interacting with act in the given way (and only to you). Perhaps, then, the golden rule should not be construed as a universalizability test at all.

On the other hand, imagining role reversal is certainly *compatible* with trying to imagine full universalization. And it is difficult to see what might motivate the relevance of role reversal as a moral test other than an implicit appeal to the idea of universality. Perhaps, then, the golden rule merely means to be drawing your attention to the particular implication of universalization that is most likely to meet with your disapproval. If so, then it may be plausible to view the golden rule as a version of universalizability after all (although, perhaps, only an implicit version).

## 7.3 The Ideal Observer

It is a striking fact about ethics that although everyone has deeply held views about it, none of us think that *all* of our moral beliefs are exactly correct—that every single moral judgment we ever make is flawless. Why is this? The answer, obviously, is that we all recognize that we can make mistakes; we are imperfect as moral judges. For example—although we may not realize it at the time—often enough we fail to possess empirical information that might be relevant to making a particular moral judgment, or to evaluating some general moral principle. Or we might get caught up in the emotional turmoil of some situation, and this might cloud our thinking. We might be unwittingly biased with regard to some individual, or prejudiced on some issue. Or we might make a slip in some complex chain of reasoning, or fail to consider the logical implications of a position we are entertaining. Clearly, there are a number of ways in which our own moral judgment can—and often does—go wrong.

But we can imagine the possibility of an ideal moral judge—someone who observes a situation, evaluates it, and renders moral judgments, but who is free of the various shortcomings, both cognitive and noncognitive, that limit our own ability to make moral judgments. We might, for example, imagine someone who is perfectly rational and who knows all the relevant facts, someone who is impartial and benevolently disposed. For the moment, the precise list of qualifications isn't as important as the very idea of such an ideal moral judge. Armed with this idea, we might plausibly suggest that the valid moral judgments are those that would be rendered, not by flawed and imperfect moral judges like ourselves, but rather by such an ideal observer. By itself, of course, this claim is merely an epistemological one; it says nothing about what it is that grounds or explains the validity of the valid moral judgments. But a further claim might be added as well. It could be suggested that the valid moral judgments are valid *by virtue of* the very fact that they would be endorsed by a suitably specified ideal observer. This is the basic claim of the *ideal observer theory* of the foundations of normative ethics.

Obviously enough, the evaluative standpoint provided by the ideal observer theory can be combined with different choices of evaluative focal point. We could, for example, have an *act ideal observer theory,* where we ask whether or not a given act would meet with the approval of the ideal observer. Or we could have a *virtue ideal observer theory,* a *rule ideal observer theory,* a *norm ideal observer theory,* an *institution ideal observer theory,* and so on. For theories of this simple sort, only items of the favored type are evaluated directly by the ideal observer. Other types of focal point can be evaluated as well, of course, but this is done only indirectly, in terms of the evaluations of the primary evaluative focal point. Presumably, however, there can also be more complicated versions of the theory, with more than one focal point evaluated directly by the ideal observer. And it certainly seems as though we could easily have a *direct ideal observer theory* as well, with all focal points whatsoever being evaluated directly by the ideal observer.

As usual, it seems likely that the precise choice of focal points will make a difference to what emerges from the ideal observer theory at the factoral level. But—again, as usual—for simplicity, we are going to restrict ourselves to the *rule* version of the theory. Accordingly, we can say that an act is permissible if and only if it conforms to the set of rules that would be favored by a suitably specified ideal observer.

Not surprisingly, the most pressing question for the ideal observer theory is exactly which qualities go into characterizing a suitably ideal observer.

Presumably, for each quality that we want to require of an ideal observer, we must be prepared to argue that to lack that quality is to have a flaw from the moral point of view—or, at least, a flaw for the purposes of making moral judgments. Unfortunately, there is no consensus concerning what, precisely, the relevant requirements come to.

I do think that most advocates of the ideal observer approach would agree that the ideal observer should be perfectly rational and in complete possession of all relevant factual information. It is less clear, however, whether there are any further strictly cognitive features that are necessary as well. For example, should we require that all information be equally present before the mind's eye? Should we require that all facts be imagined vividly?

Matters are even more controversial when we attempt to characterize the ideal observer's motives. A common suggestion is that the ideal observer should be impartial—favoring no particular individual or group of individuals. Somewhat more broadly, perhaps we should require that the ideal observer have no *ties* to particular people—or times or places. But this merely guarantees that the ideal observer won't "play favorites"; nothing yet assures us that the ideal observer will even *care* about what happens to anyone. Perhaps, then, we should also insist that the ideal observer must be benevolent, with a loving concern for all. Or perhaps we should even require that the ideal observer feel a sympathetic identification with absolutely everyone.

Assuming that we can arrive at—and defend—a satisfactory specification of what the ideal observer must be like, we can then say that the valid moral rules are those that would be *endorsed* by a suitably ideal observer. But what, precisely, is the reaction of the ideal observer that we have in mind when we say this? This, too, is a matter of some controversy. On some views, the judgments of the ideal observer are quite literally that—judgments. That is, when we say that the ideal observer "favors" a rule, or "endorses" it, we mean that she *believes* it—she believes that the rule is a valid one. On other views, however, the relevant reaction of the ideal observer is less strictly cognitive: "endorsing" is more like *approving* of a rule, being in favor of the rule, having a "pro attitude" toward the rule. Still other views try to identify a reaction that is more specifically moral in its character. It might be, for example, that when the ideal observer thinks about rules that are in fact valid, they strike her in a specifically moral way—perhaps as rules that ought to be acted upon.

(Each of these approaches faces its own problems, but I want to mention only one. Suppose that when the ideal observer endorses a rule she *believes* it valid. Now according to the ideal observer approach, the validity of a given rule is a matter of being endorsed by the ideal observer. Does this mean, then, that when the ideal observer endorses a rule as valid, what she believes about it is that she endorses it? Does she believe that it is valid by *virtue* of the fact that she believes it valid?)

So far, I have repeatedly spoken about *the* ideal observer. Presumably, however, there could be more than one individual who met the various requirements, whatever they are. That is, in principle at least, there might be a *group* of ideal observers. But this points to a potential difficulty for the ideal observer approach. For if we say that the valid rules are those that would be endorsed by *the* ideal observer, there is an implicit assumption that it doesn't matter which ideal observer we appeal to. We are assuming, in effect, that all ideal observers would agree, that they would endorse the very same rules. If this is so, of course, then we can make do in our theorizing with just a single one of them. We can continue to talk about what "the" ideal observer would endorse—for this will just be a convenient way of referring to what any given one of them would endorse.

But is it indeed legitimate for us to assume that all ideal observers will agree in this way? Is there anything in the characterization of what makes someone an ideal observer that guarantees that anyone at all who met those qualifications would agree with anyone else who met the same qualifications? Obviously, absent a complete specification of the relevant qualifications, we can't rule this possibility out. But I think it must also be admitted that it is at least far from obvious whether any of the qualifications we have already considered—whether alone, or in combination—will have this effect.

Suppose, then, that not all ideal observers would endorse the very same rules. What then? If ideal observers would disagree among themselves—presumably not over everything, but at least occasionally—then we cannot continue to talk, indifferently, about which rules "the" ideal observer will endorse. It will make a difference which particular ideal observer we appeal to. But by hypothesis, despite their disagreement, all of them are *ideal* observers; so there can be no reason to single out *one* of them for special attention. How, then, shall we select the valid moral rules?

The easiest part of the solution, I think, is to look for those areas—whatever they are—where all ideal observers would *agree*. We can certainly still hold, at a minimum, that if all ideal observers whatsoever would endorse a given rule, then that rule is valid. Similarly, if all ideal observers reject a rule, it is invalid. But what about those rules where there is no agreement—where some endorse the rule while others do not? Are such rules valid, or invalid?

At this point, various proposals might be made. Let me mention three. First, it could be held that rules *forbidding* various acts must have the agreement of all ideal observers if they are to be valid. On this first approach, then, if no rule forbidding a given act would be endorsed by all ideal observers, that act would not be forbidden, and so would be permitted. And this would mean, in effect, that merely permissive rules wouldn't actually require agreement at all. Since disagreement over whether to forbid would automatically result in permission, even a single ideal observer would be able to guarantee that the given type of act was permissible.

Alternatively, of course, one could hold that rules *permitting* various acts must have the agreement of all ideal observers if they are to be valid. On this approach, in contrast, since disagreement over whether or not to permit would automatically result in prohibition, any given ideal observer would be able to guarantee that a given type of act was *forbidden*. And so, on this second approach, rules forbidding acts could be valid, even in the absence of agreement. Note, however, that this might easily—perhaps too easily—lead to moral dilemmas, where every alternative open to the agent is forbidden (see 5.4). So perhaps the first approach is preferable.

A quite different approach would be to require the ideal observers to iron out their initial differences. Perhaps we should imagine the ideal observers being asked to *come* to some agreement, compromising where necessary. Even if there are initial areas of disagreement, then, sufficient bargaining might allow the ideal observers to reach a consensus concerning what the rules should be. (Obviously enough, if this third approach were the one we adopted, the ideal observer theory would at this point be quite similar to a kind of contractarianism—one with highly idealized bargainers. On the other hand, in normal versions of contractarianism, the bargainers are themselves identical to the individuals who will be bound by the terms of the agreement; that's not the case with ideal observers. Would this difference affect the terms of the agreement reached?)

Clearly, whichever solution we adopt, the ideal observer theory becomes more complicated if we have to allow for the possibility of disagreement among the ideal observers. And as I have already indicated, it is not obvious that we are entitled to rule this possibility out. Nonetheless, let us suppose—if only for simplicity—that all ideal observers *would* agree about which rules to endorse. This will allow us to revert to our initial practice of referring simply to the reactions of *the* ideal observer.

Very well, then, what sorts of rules would the ideal observer endorse? What should we expect to emerge, at the factoral level, from the ideal observer approach? Presumably, the answer will depend on how, precisely, the ideal observer is characterized. It may also depend on what, exactly, we mean by "endorsing." And we have, of course, left these matters unresolved.

Nonetheless, it is noteworthy that many advocates of the ideal observer theory have believed that such an approach supports consequentialism at the factoral level. In particular, it is often thought that the ideal observer theory supports *utilitarianism* (factoral consequentialism combined with a welfarist theory of the good). It is easy enough to see why such a conclusion seems plausible. The ideal observer is typically thought of as being benevolently disposed and impartial—equally concerned for the well-being of all. Thus, faced with situations in which not everyone's well-being can be promoted, the ideal observer will prefer the outcome in which overall well-being is promoted as much as possible. And this suggests that the ideal observer may endorse a rule requiring agents to promote the overall good, where this is measured in terms of the total amount of well-being (counting everyone's well-being equally). In short, the ideal observer will endorse a utilitarian principle.

It seems, then, that the path from the ideal observer theory to a utilitarian version of consequentialism is short and direct. Partly because of this fact, I believe, many moral philosophers would hesitate to classify the ideal observer theory in the way that I have, that is, as a *deontological* foundational theory. This would be a reflection of the common assumption that foundational theories that are truly deontological must support deontology at the factoral level as well. We have, however, already seen that this common assumption, although natural, is mistaken. (Contractarianism, for example, is a standard example of a deontological foundational view; yet certain versions seem to support factoral consequentialism.) Thus, even if the ideal observer theory does support factoral consequentialism, by itself this gives us no good reason to deny that the ideal observer theory is a deontological foundational view.

What is relevant, rather, is the fact that—unlike teleological foundational theories—the ideal observer theory does not make the notion of the good the single, dominant concept in explaining the basis of normative ethics. On the contrary, obviously, the ideal observer theory starts with the idea of a suitably specified ideal observer. Concern for the good may well come in (via the ideal observer's impartial concern for the well-being of all); but it can hardly be claimed that the notion of the good is the single, fundamental concept appealed to by an ideal observer theory. Accordingly, it does seem to me appropriate to view the ideal observer theory as a genuinely deontological approach to the foundations of normative ethics. And this will be true regardless of what this approach happens to support at the factoral level.

But this is not to say that we should so readily agree that the ideal observer theory does indeed support factoral consequentialism. In fact, the argument for that conclusion can be challenged in at least two places. First, even if it is true that the ideal observer will be concerned solely with the overall good (measured in terms of the total level of well-being, counting everyone equally), it does not yet follow that the ideal observer will simply endorse a rule requiring agents to promote the overall good. At best, all that follows is that the ideal observer will evaluate rival rules in terms of which rule would have the best results. And as our discussion of rule consequentialism revealed (in 6.5), it is far from obvious whether a consequentialist principle is indeed the rule whose results would be best. It certainly seems possible—at least, in the absence of further argument—that consequentialist concerns on the part of the ideal observer would actually lead her to favor rules more like those of commonsense morality, in which case the ideal observer approach would support deontology at the factoral level, rather than consequentialism.

(Note, however, that had we been considering *act* ideal observer theories, rather than *rule* versions, this objection might have been less successful. For if the ideal observer is evaluating individual *acts* solely on the basis of their results—their effect on overall well-being—then presumably she will always endorse the act with the best results. Once again, then, we see how the choice of primary evaluative focal point can have an impact on the factoral implications.)

Beyond this, the argument also assumes that the ideal observer will be concerned *solely* with the overall good (measured in terms of total well-being). Presumably, the ideal observer's impartiality and benevolence will indeed mean that potential impact on everyone's well-being will be at least *one* of the features in terms of which the ideal observer evaluates rival rules. But this does not yet give us reason to conclude that this will be the *only* feature that interests her. It might be that various other features influence her as well. At the very least, absent a *complete* specification of the ideal observer's characteristics, we can't yet be sure that other concerns may not motivate her beyond benevolence. And at any rate, it may beg the question to assume that no specific concerns could emerge from the assumption of perfect rationality. That is, perhaps a perfectly rational being would necessarily be concerned with *various* features of a rule (for example, its universalizability)—and not just its results. If something like this is right, then we have even less reason to assume that the ideal observer will endorse or reject rules on the basis of a simple consequentialist point of view. In sum, the rules that would be endorsed by an ideal observer might well be deontological in nature.

Again, this is not to say that the rules *would* be deontological, but only that they might be. For all that I have argued, it might still turn out that a suitably characterized ideal observer would indeed endorse utilitarianism, or some other consequentialist principle. But settling the matter, I think, would require a complete specification of the qualities necessary to be an ideal observer, along with a detailed argument concerning the ideal observer's deliberations.

Of course, this last way of putting the point assumes that the ideal observer does indeed go through something that can reasonably be called *deliberation*. That is, I assume that the ideal observer's endorsements of particular rules are the result of reflection and thought; they are not mere "knee jerk" or "mindless" reactions. Rather, the ideal observer *assesses* the rules, attending to their various attractive and unattractive features, comparing them to alternatives. In effect, the ideal observer considers arguments for and against various rules, and endorses the particular rules that she does on the basis of the weightier arguments.

But if this is right, it might be objected, isn't the appeal to the ideal observer herself unnecessary? That is, why can't we simply drop all mention of the ideal observer, and instead appeal directly to the various arguments that influence her? Of course, we can assume that the ideal observer—being perfectly rational, and fully informed, and so forth—is moved only by sound arguments and weighty considerations. But whatever those arguments are (the objection continues), surely it is the arguments themselves that justify the choice of the particular rule in question. Put another way: the rule itself is valid *because* of those facts and considerations (whatever they are) that move the ideal observer. But it is not the fact that they move the ideal observer that makes these considerations sufficient to justify the rule; they do that directly. And this means that the ideal observer has no actual role to play in grounding the validity of the rules. In short, valid rules are not valid by virtue of the fact that the ideal observer endorses them; rather, the ideal observer endorses the rules because—as an ideal observer—she recognizes their validity. As a theory of the foundations of normative ethics, then, the ideal observer theory is misguided. At best, it takes an account of a plausible heuristic device, useful for discovering valid moral rules, and mistakes it for an account of the basis or explanation of the validity of those rules.

Although troubling, this objection may not be decisive. For even if we can explain why ideal observers make the particular endorsements that they do, by appeal to the particular arguments that they find persuasive, it could still be the case that reference to the endorsement of the ideal observer should not be eliminated. That is, the content of morality could still be fixed by the very fact that an ideal observer would endorse it. Such a claim might be supported by appeal to particular metaethical views concerning the nature of moral facts. For example, moral facts might partially consist in, or depend upon, facts about the reactions of suitable moral observers. (Consider, as an analogy, the familiar view that facts about color depend in part upon facts about how a suitably specified "standard observer" would respond when viewing things under "normal conditions." Here, too, it seems, the reference to the relevant reaction on the part of the observer is something that cannot be eliminated.) Clearly, such metaethical conceptions are controversial, but their possibility shows that ideal observer theories need not be misguided. The references to the ideal observer may be more than a heuristic; it could well be the case that valid rules are indeed valid by virtue of the very fact that the ideal observer would endorse them.

It is probably worth pointing out, however, that even if this is so, and references to the ideal observer cannot be eliminated, advocates of the ideal observer theory need not believe that any genuinely ideal observers actually exist. The claim, rather, is simply this: valid moral rules are valid by virtue of the fact that they *would* be endorsed by an appropriately qualified ideal observer. Even if there are, in fact, no truly ideal observers, this doesn't threaten the theory.

On the other hand, it should go without saying that the ideal observer theory is quite compatible with a belief that there actually *are* individuals who meet all the relevant qualifications. And, in point of fact, many people have thought that this is so. More precisely, many people have believed in the existence of *one* being who would presumably qualify as an ideal observer: God. (Of course, there would be no logical inconsistency in claiming that God fails to meet some requirement relevant to characterizing ideal observers. But I presume that most theists believe that God meets the legitimate requirements, whatever they are.)

Obviously enough, not everyone who believes in the existence of God accepts the ideal observer theory. Indeed, many who believe in the existence of God don't even think that God is the ultimate source of morality. (God might well be the supreme moral teacher, without being the *author* of morality.) But for those who do believe that God is the ultimate source of morality, the ideal observer theory is one important way of making sense of this claim. For if the valid moral rules are those that would be endorsed by an ideal observer, and if there is indeed a God, then the valid moral rules are those that are endorsed by God. They are valid by virtue of the very fact that God endorses them. Thus, when presented in theological terms, the ideal observer theory becomes the *divine command theory*: valid moral rules are valid by virtue of the fact that God commands them.

I do not mean to claim that the divine command theory *must* be understood in terms of the ideal observer theory. Sometimes, for example, it is suggested that God's commands are morally binding by virtue of the fact the God is the creator of everything. And sometimes it is suggested, more narrowly, that God's commands are morally binding by virtue of the specific fact that God created *us*. Unfortunately, we cannot take the space that would be necessary to try to adjudicate between these and other possible suggestions. I simply want to underline the fact that thinking of the divine command theory in terms of the ideal observer theory is one potentially attractive possibility. If God's commands are indeed morally binding, this may be by virtue of the fact that God is, say, all knowing, perfectly rational, impartial, and loving; in short, God's commands might be binding by virtue of the fact that God is an ideal observer.

Finally, I should note that although I have restricted my discussion to ideal *observers*—ideal judges who stand outside the situation, evaluating it, with no particular ties to particular individuals—other, near relatives to this approach are possible as well. We could, for example, imagine each agent having an *ideal adviser*—someone who takes the particular agent's interests and goals to heart, but who is perfectly rational, fully informed, and free of prejudice and bias (unlike normal agents). Or we could imagine the agents themselves being perfected in appropriate ways—and then deliberating with perfect rationality, on the basis of perfect information, and so on. That is, we might have an *ideal agent* (or ideal deliberator) theory. Presumably, theories of either of these kinds might yields results somewhat different from those supported by the ideal observer theory; establishing a connection to a particular individual might well influence what, exactly, gets endorsed. Accordingly, it would be well worth exploring how these alternative approaches would differ from the ideal observer theory itself. Unfortunately, these too are questions that we must leave unanswered.

## 7.4  Reflection

A fourth deontological approach to the foundations of normative ethics begins with the simple thought that the contents of a morality that is appropriate for creatures like us will depend on what creatures like us are *like*. Were we sufficiently different, in significant ways, morality itself would have to be different as well: morality must adequately reflect the nature of the beings that fall under its domain. Thus, if we want to know what the contents of morality come to, we can make progress on this question by thinking about which of our features would appropriately play a role in determining the content of morality. A morality appropriate for creatures of *that* kind will need to reflect these facts about what we are like. More particularly, then, by getting clear about our morally central features, and thinking about what kind of morality would appropriately reflect those features—what kind of morality would best take them into account and respond to them most adequately—we can determine what the content of morality must be. Morality will have the particular content that it does by virtue of the very fact that by doing so it most adequately reflects the nature of the creatures that fall under its domain.

Any given theory of this type will first need to identify particular features—whether our rationality, our ability to feel pain, our autonomy, our social nature, or what have you—and claim that these particular features are the ones that must be adequately reflected by morality. And it must then go on to argue that particular aspects or details of morality can be justified and explained by thinking of them as appropriate responses to the significance of the favored features. Not surprisingly, then, the major concerns of any such theory will be to articulate the favored list of morally relevant features to be reflected, and to demonstrate how various conceivable contents of morality would, in fact, reflect these features. In principle, it seems, different theories of this kind might well have rather little in common, beyond the very fact that they all agree that morality is to be explained in terms of adequately reflecting relevant features of the creatures under its domain.

For this reason, perhaps, theories of this general sort are not typically thought of as *forming* a general approach to ethics. The philosophical literature does not normally group these various specific theories together as distinct versions of a single underlying approach. They are not normally examined and discussed as a group, nor is there a standard name for approaches of this general kind. Nonetheless, it does seem to me helpful to think of the various specific theories of this type as indeed being different ways of developing the same basic idea—namely, that the ultimate basis of normative ethics is a matter of adequately reflecting the nature of the creatures governed and protected by morality. We can call theories of this sort *reflection* theories.

As usual, I should note, commitment to the reflection approach seems to be compatible with any choice of evaluative focal point. We could, for example, have a *virtue reflection theory,* asking which particular character traits would best reflect our natures. Or there could be an *act reflection theory,* asking whether particular acts appropriately reflect the relevant facts concerning what we are like. Similarly, it seems, there could be an *institution reflection theory,* a *norm reflection theory,* a *direct reflection theory,* and so on. Presumably, the choice of evaluative focal point could have a significant impact on what emerges at the factoral level. But having noted this point, I am, once again, going to put it aside. In what follows, I will simply talk about what *content* morality must have if it is to adequately reflect our natures. Most of the examples, however, will concern evaluating various possible rules and requirements in this light.

One general concern about reflection theories is that they may seem to be incompatible with a belief in the universality of morality. After all, if morality must reflect what we are like, then—given that we are, in fact, rather different from one another—doesn't it follow that the contents of morality must vary from person to person? In particular, if what we are like determines what morality requires of us, then won't we have to reject the view that the same moral requirements are binding upon everyone? Of course, not everyone does accept the belief in the universality of morality. But for those that do, doesn't this rule out a reflection approach?

In thinking about this objection, the first thing to bear in mind is that variation is presumably acceptable at a *derivative* level. For example, you may have an obligation to meet Elana at the park, having promised her that you would do this, while I have no such obligation, having made no such promise. Here, although our specific obligations vary from person to person, this presumably doesn't threaten the belief in the universality of morality, for the same *basic* moral requirement—that one keep one's promises—applies to both of us. If reflection theories are to truly threaten universality, they will have to do this at the level of basic moral principles.

The second thing to bear in mind is that any given reflection theory specifies only particular features as being morally significant: an adequate morality must appropriately reflect *those* features. Variation per se will have no moral significance whatsoever. Thus it doesn't really matter that we are "rather different" from each other. So long as we are all similar in terms of the *relevant* features, morality might appropriately reflect those features, while still being the same—in terms of the basic principles—for all of us.

A further point to bear in mind is this. When someone claims that the same basic moral requirements are binding upon everyone, they are already implicitly restricting the set of beings to which moral requirements apply. After all, no one thinks that moral requirements are binding upon everything that exists in the universe. The thought, rather, is that the same moral requirements are binding upon all *moral agents*. But what *kind* of thing can be a moral agent? Not everything, obviously: not specks of dust, nor chairs, nor even lions. Only certain kinds of things have the features necessary to be something subject to moral requirements in the first place. At the very least, then, we will want to know what features something must have to be a moral agent. And presumably, it is the very fact that particular moral agents have these relevant features (whatever they are) that explains the fact that they are indeed moral agents.

Clearly, nothing in any of this yet threatens a belief in the universality of morality. But a reflection theorist might do nothing more than add to this the further thought that if we think about the *kind* of thing that can be a moral agent, then we might be able to learn something about the *content* of morality. This might not be true, obviously, but in and of itself it poses no threat to a belief in the universality of morality.

Of course, pursuing this line of thought requires taking a stand concerning just which features are necessary for something to be a moral agent—subject to moral requirements. This is, not surprisingly, a controversial matter, and I won't try to settle it here. One common proposal is this: to be a moral agent one must be a *rational* agent—that is, a being who can deliberate about its actions, and about standards for evaluating those actions, and who makes choices with an eye toward meeting the standards that seem, on reflection, plausible. Note that if being a rational agent in this sense *is* necessary for being a moral agent, this will support the intuition that neither specks of dust, nor chairs, nor even lions can be moral agents. It will also support the plausible suggestion that very young children cannot be moral agents either—that they have no moral requirements binding upon them.

A reflection theorist who accepts the claim that moral agents must be rational agents might try to derive some—or all—of the content of morality from this fact. For example, such a theorist might argue that since moral agents must be rational agents, shaping their behavior with an eye to the standards that seem to them plausible, moral requirements must be ones that it would be reasonable for moral agents to *accept* as legitimate standards for governing their behavior. This might then lead to a form of contractarianism. Or the reflection theorist might argue that since moral agents are rational agents, they must act on reasons—and since reasons for action are themselves universal, moral requirements must be ones that could be universal. And this might then support a version of universalizability. I won't try to assess the plausibility of either of these arguments. For now, the point is simply that either of these approaches is fully compatible with a belief in the universality of morality; and this reinforces my claim that there need not be any conflict between accepting the universality of morality and accepting a reflection approach.

It should be noted, of course, that many people do not think that being a rational agent is *sufficient* for being a moral agent. (It might be necessary without being sufficient.) Perhaps some rational agents are free from moral obligations. Perhaps further features are necessary, beyond rational agency, before something is subject to moral requirement. For example, it might be that in order to be subject to moral requirements one must feel emotions of various sorts (perhaps sympathy, or empathy), or one must have needs that one cannot fulfill, or be vulnerable to attack by others; or perhaps one must be a social animal and identify, in part, with others. Depending on which, if any, of these proposals we accept, we might be led to rather different conceptions of what kinds of requirements can be reasonably thought to be binding upon moral agents. But again, the immediate point is simply this: one can accept the claim that morality is universal—binding upon *all moral agents*—while still endorsing the thought that the content of morality reflects the relevant facts about what moral agents are *like*.

So a reflection theorist need not reject the claim that the same basic moral requirements are binding upon all moral agents. But that is not to say that a reflection theorist must *accept* this claim either. For it certainly seems possible for a reflection theorist to hold that there are different *kinds* of moral agents, and that depending upon what kind of agent you are, you face different moral requirements. The idea here, of course, would be that differences between the various types of moral agent are morally significant, and morality must appropriately reflect these differences by imposing different requirements upon the differing types of agent. Of course, there might still be considerable overlap in the requirements faced by the various types of agent—reflecting the fact that all moral agents necessarily share certain common features. But there could be variation as well, and whatever variation did exist would be a reflection of the relevant *differences* among the different kinds of agent.

(One might try to reconcile even a view of this sort with the universality of morality by claiming that the *basic* moral requirements actually *all* take the form of conditionals: if you are an agent of a certain kind, then you must do such and such; but if you are an agent of a second kind, then you must do this and that; and so on. The claim, then, would be that the very same *conditional* requirements are binding upon all moral agents. But if this is right, then it seems that *any* form of relativism can be reconciled with a belief in the universality of morality, and so it will no longer be clear what such a belief really comes to.)

Even if he does allow for the possibility that different kinds of moral agents would face different moral requirements, the reflection theorist might still insist that all *human* moral agents are of the very same kind. That is, the reflection theorist might simply be arguing for the *logical* possibility of different kinds of moral agents. But as a matter of empirical fact, it might well be that only one type of moral agent actually exists. Or, perhaps, if there were going to be another type of moral agent, we would have to find creatures quite unlike us: angels, for example, or Martians, or some such. At any rate, as far as human beings are concerned, it could still be the case that all human moral agents face the very same moral requirements.

But then again, the reflection theorist need not be satisfied with noting mere logical possibilities. He might insist, more ambitiously, that even among humans there are different types of moral agents—facing different moral requirements. If we are indeed sufficiently different from one another, in morally relevant ways, then this will have to be reflected by an adequate morality.

To illustrate some of these possibilities—and to have a more developed example of the reflection approach before us—consider the following argument. Each of us views the world from our own individual perspective, our own personal point of view. From this standpoint, we care more about certain individuals than others, and we are more concerned with certain goals and projects than others. My own personal point of view differs from yours—not only because we know different things, and see, hear, and touch the world from different particular locations, but also because we have different loves, ambitions, and concerns. What's more, the value I assign to things—the importance they take on from my personal point of view—typically differs from the value they might be assigned from a more objective, impartial point of view. For example, I care more about the members of my family, even though, objectively speaking, the well-being of my children is of no more moral importance than the well-being of strangers.

Given the disproportionate weight that I assign to things from my personal point of view, I will typically find it difficult to be motivated to act in an impartial manner. I will have a natural inclination to favor my loved ones, and to pursue those projects and goals that are of personal significance to me—even when a more objective standpoint might oppose my making these choices. In effect, the personal point of view results in a kind of "bias" in favor of my various interests, concerns, family, and friends.

Some reflection theorists think that these facts about the nature of the personal point of view are morally significant, and must be appropriately reflected in an adequate morality. Suppose we grant this. How might morality best reflect these facts? One plausible suggestion is that morality can best reflect the nature of the personal point of view by granting a certain amount of freedom from the demands of a completely impartial standpoint. We must be given a certain amount of "space" in which we are free to pursue our individual interests and concerns, even when doing so may not produce the greatest amount of good overall. There must be limits on the sacrifices that morality can demand of us. In a word, morality must grant us *options*—permission to act in less than optimal ways.

Suppose, for the moment, that this argument is sound. This means that there are limits to the requirements that morality imposes upon us. Certain acts that might otherwise be required are not in fact required of us, for such overly demanding requirements would fail to adequately reflect the nature of the personal point of view. It is because of the fact that we *have* a personal point of view that the moral requirements binding upon us are *limited* in the way that they are.

Note, however, that this does not yet take any kind of stand concerning the universality of morality. The various possibilities that we have discussed still remain open. It might be argued, for example, that *all* moral agents necessarily have a personal point of view, with a corresponding bias in favor of their own interests and concerns. If so, then morality will have to grant options to all moral agents. Morality will appropriately reflect certain facts about what moral agents are like, by limiting the demands it makes of agents. But morality will still be universal—with the same basic moral requirements binding upon all moral agents.

Alternatively, perhaps the personal point of view is not necessarily biased in the way that I have described. It might, of course, still be true that all *humans* necessarily give disproportionate weight to their own projects and concerns; this might, for example, be a fact about human nature. Nonetheless, we might be able to imagine the possibility of a rational agent whose personal point of view *coincides* with the impartial standpoint of morality. Such a creature might not be human, but presumably it could still be a moral agent. Yet given that it lacked the bias, morality would not need to grant options to it, and so the moral requirements binding upon such a creature might be far more demanding than those imposed upon humans. If something like this is right, then different kinds of moral agents will be faced with different moral requirements (differing, at least, in terms of how demanding they are).

Or it might be that, even among humans, having a bias in favor of one's own interests and concerns is not inevitable. Perhaps such a bias, although common, is not truly a part of human nature. For example, perhaps certain moral or religious saints have been free of this bias. If so, then even among human beings there may be more than one *kind* of moral agent. For those few among us who are free of the bias, there will be a more demanding set of moral requirements. For the rest of us, however, morality will appropriately reflect the existence of the bias by granting us options.

Of course, no matter how widespread the bias is—whether it is merely common among humans, or shared by all moral agents whatsoever—it is certainly not uncontroversial that the appropriate way to reflect the bias, when it does exist, is by granting options. Options, after all, merely *permit* the agent to pursue her own interests rather than the overall good; but they don't actually *require* the agent to refrain from sacrificing her interests. Yet we could certainly imagine a moral theory that would, in fact, require the agent to promote her interests whenever this was permissible. Arguably, this might *better* reflect the nature of the personal point of view than would a system with options.

Nor should we be so quick to assume that, at the very least, when the bias does exist, the appropriate way to reflect this fact is by *permitting* (if not requiring) agents to promote their interests. Perhaps the existence of the bias is adequately reflected by a morality that simply recognizes that people will often fail to do as they are required to do; the mere fact that the bias makes it *difficult* to fulfill some otherwise plausible requirement may not yet show why the requirement should not, in fact, be imposed. (This last position may be especially plausible if it is indeed possible for us to overcome the bias, as certain individuals may have done.)

Obviously, then, for the reflection theorist to argue for the existence of options, on the grounds that this best reflects the nature of the personal point of view, will not be a trivial matter. Even if we grant that facts about the nature of the personal point of view must be appropriately reflected by an adequate morality, it is not at all obvious what the facts are, and how they should be reflected. Filling in the details of a reflection argument requires canvassing alternative ways the relevant facts might be reflected, and arguing for the superiority of one approach over another. Unfortunately, pursuing these details lies well beyond the scope of our present discussion.

Note that all the examples of reflection arguments that we have considered so far concern ways in which the content of morality is determined, at least in part, by the need to reflect certain facts about our natures as moral *agents*. For example, it was suggested that morality must reflect the fact that moral agents are rational agents, or it must reflect the fact that as agents our deliberations are influenced by the personal point of view. But it is important to bear in mind that we fall under the domain of morality in at least *two* capacities. On the one hand, of course, we are capable of acting—we are agents—and so morality offers us directives, and in various ways the content of morality may have to reflect what we are *like* as agents. On the other hand, we are also creatures who can be acted upon—we are *patients*—and so morality also offers us protection: we may only be treated in ways that morality permits; other forms of behavior constitute mistreatment.

Recalling a term from an earlier discussion (in 5.3), we can say that as patients we make *claims* upon the behavior of others (which correspond to requirements on the parts of those others to treat us appropriately). Plausibly enough, then, what we are like as *patients* may need to be reflected by morality as well, in the kinds of claims that we can legitimately make. For example, if morality does not allow us to make certain specific claims upon the behavior of others, this might fail to reflect significant facts about our natures. And, of course, some conceivable claims might be implausible, having no appropriate basis for creatures like us.

Of course, talk of claims and talk of requirements are simply two different ways of looking at the very same moral facts—the former from the perspective of the claim holder, the patient, and the latter from the perspective of the agent. But for all that, thinking about the two roles—agent and patient—may still be analytically useful. For it could be that certain aspects of morality are best explained in the light of thinking about us as agents, and what does and does not reflect our abilities and limitations as agents. Other aspects, meanwhile, might better be explained in the light of thinking about us as patients, and what does and does not reflect our vulnerabilities and needs as patients.

Admittedly, any aspect of morality explained by the need to reflect our natures as agents will at the same time have to be compatible with reflecting our natures as patients. Similarly, any aspect of morality explained in terms of reflecting our natures as patients will, at the very least, have to be compatible with reflecting our natures as agents. There cannot be claims where the corresponding requirements would fail to reflect the nature of the agents; and there cannot be requirements where the corresponding claims would fail to reflect the nature of the patients. But despite this fact, it still might be that explaining some particular aspect of morality is primarily a matter of attending to our natures as patients, or attending to our natures as agents, but not both.

The point is fairly easy to see if we briefly consider the moral status of (nonhuman) animals. Most people are inclined to think that animals can make claims upon our behavior. This obviously doesn't mean that they can *assert* those claims; it simply means that certain ways of treating animals are morally illegitimate. For example, it would be morally unacceptable to hurt a cat simply for the pleasure of hearing it scream. And it is wrong, presumably, because of what cats are *like*—in particular, perhaps, because of the fact that they can feel pain. Generalizing from this example, it might be suggested that all animals have a claim against us not to be subjected to gratuitous pain. Morality reflects this morally relevant fact about animals as patients by granting them the particular claim that it does.

Obviously, not everyone accepts the claim that animals count from the moral point of view. Some hold that it is permissible to treat animals any way at all that serves our purposes, however trivial. (Of course, for any particular animal, there may be restrictions arising from the claims of other *people*—for example, the animal's owner; but the animal itself is not the source of any claims.) I believe this view is mistaken, although, unfortunately, the arguments are too complex to review here. But for our immediate purposes, the relevant point is simply this: those who deny that animals count from the moral point of view do not similarly deny that *people* count! Presumably, then, they must think that there are morally relevant differences between people and animals—and they must hold that these differences are appropriately reflected by morality when it grants people rights but denies them to animals. At least, this is the sort of account that a reflection theorist would want to see in defense of this view.

Even among those people who think that animals do count—that they are the source of legitimate claims—most believe that animals do not count in the same *ways* that people count. That is, the most common view is that people can make certain kinds of claims that animals cannot. For example, even if it is impermissible to cause an animal gratuitous pain, it might not be impermissible to *kill* an animal, provided this is done painlessly. In contrast, of course—special circumstances aside—even if it is done painlessly, it is forbidden to kill a *person*. According to this view, then, people have a right not to be killed; but this is a right that animals lack.

Alternatively, it might be that animals too possess a right not to be killed, but it lacks the special force that this right has in the case of people. It might be, for example, that although it would normally be wrong to kill an animal, it is permissible to kill an animal for the sake of promoting some greater good. In contrast, as we have seen, most of us believe that it is forbidden to kill a person (special circumstances aside), even if doing so would promote the greater good overall. On this view, then, people would have *deontological* rights, while animals would not. (Very roughly, then, while deontology would govern the treatment of people, something more like consequentialism would govern the treatment of animals.)

There are, of course, other possible positions concerning how the rights of animals and the rights of people might differ. But whatever the precise nature of the proposed differences, the reflection theorist simply insists, plausibly, that if these differences are genuine, they must be explained in terms of underlying differences in the natures of animals and people. What sorts of differences might be relevant in this way? Perhaps it is the fact that although animals can certainly feel pain, they may not be sufficiently self-conscious to possess a belief in their own existence, and a desire for their lives to continue. Or it might be the fact that although animals can make choices, they lack the capacity to form an autonomous conception of how they want their lives to go.

Again, the point here is not to evaluate these various views. I offer them simply to illustrate the suggestion of the reflection theorist that some aspects of morality are best explained in terms of reflecting relevant facts about the nature of moral *patients*. In particular, according to the reflection theorist, if the claims that *we* can make are different from the claims that *animals* can make, these differences are a reflection of the fact that animals and people are different *kinds* of moral patients.

In some cases, then, the reflection theorist might want to argue that some particular aspect of morality is best explained in terms of reflecting the nature of the relevant moral patients. In other cases, meanwhile, explaining some other aspect of morality might be primarily a matter of reflecting the nature of moral agents. It should certainly be noted, however, that it could also easily be the case that for some elements, to explain why morality has the precise content that it does, we will need to appeal to what we are like both as agents and as patients. For example, given what we are like as patients, this might tend to support some particular kind of claim; but given what we are like as agents, this might tend to support various limitations on claims of that kind. In a situation like this, what ultimately emerges will presumably be a sort of *compromise*—a product of the need to adequately reflect our natures both as patients *and* as agents. However, even in a case like this, it may still prove useful to distinguish between our natures as agents and our natures as patients—to separate out the contribution that each makes—if we are to fully understand why morality has the particular content that it does.

An example may make this clearer. Suppose we ask: why is there any kind of requirement to aid others at all? A reflection theorist might begin to answer this question by noting the fact that we have needs, often central to our well-being, that we may be incapable of meeting on our own. Often, then, we need help. Furthermore, the needs of other people are *real;* they don't merely exist "for" the person who needs the help. After all, each of us is one person, among others, equally real. Perhaps, then, morality appropriately reflects these facts—that others may have needs, and these needs are quite as real as my own—by granting each of us a claim on the aid of others. Of course, were we (as agents) incapable of recognizing and being moved by the needs of others—were we unable to recognize the very fact that others are equally real—then a requirement to aid others could not be grounded. It would fail to reflect our nature as agents. But, in fact, we are capable of recognizing the reality of the needs of others, and we can be moved by this recognition. So a requirement to aid others is compatible with reflecting our nature as agents as well.

On the other hand, given the nature of the personal point of view (at least as it typically exists among humans) we are not normally prepared to give the needs of everyone equal weight: we have a natural bias in favor of our own interests and the needs of our loved ones. Perhaps, then (to return to an earlier suggestion), this fact about us should be reflected as well, by limiting the requirement to aid others, and granting us options to pursue our own interests. Again, were we incapable of being moved by our recognition of the needs of others, it might even be appropriate for these options to be unlimited. But the fact of the matter is that the personal point of view is not the only point of view we are capable of adopting. We can also adopt a more objective standpoint from which we can recognize the reality of the needs of others, and be moved by this fact. Morality reflects this, too, by imposing *limits* to our options. And the result of all of this—of reflecting the various relevant facts about our natures both as patients and as agents—is a principle of beneficence that is limited but not empty. We are required to aid others, but only within limits.

Once more, my aim here is not to evaluate the various details of this argument. I am simply trying to illustrate the way in which a reflection theorist might try to account for certain aspects of morality by repeated appeal to particular facts about what we are like—both as patients and as agents.

Note, however, that the reflection theorist need not believe that we can literally *derive* morality from these various facts about what we are like. The claim is that morality has the particular content that it does because this appropriately reflects relevant facts about us. But there doesn't have to be any suggestion that it is somehow *inconsistent* to recognize the facts in question while denying that morality has the particular content under consideration.

I emphasize this point, because often it is assumed that reflection theorists must believe that moral conclusions are somehow *entailed* by the relevant facts about what we are like. And then it is claimed that any argument of this sort inevitably makes a fundamental mistake. For according to a widely held metaethical view, no merely factual premises about what we are like—or for that matter, about anything else—could possibly entail moral conclusions: "you can't derive an ought from an is." The objection, then, is that this is precisely what reflection theories attempt to do: starting simply with empirical facts, they illegitimately attempt to derive moral conclusions.

Of course, not everyone accepts the claim that factual premises cannot entail moral conclusions. Obviously, reflection theorists who reject this claim won't be bothered by this objection at all. But it is important to see that one can accept the common metaethical claim without abandoning a commitment to a reflection approach. For there is no reason for the reflection theorist to deny that he appeals to substantive moral premises. Reflection theories, after all, start with the claim that an adequate moral theory will appropriately reflect the relevant facts about what we are like. This is, presumably, a substantive moral claim. And so are the additional specific claims that get made in the course of offering a given reflection argument— claims to the effect that some particular fact should be reflected by morality, or claims that some conceivable content of morality would best reflect the facts in question. There is no reason for the reflection theorist to deny that all of these are substantive moral claims. He simply insists that these are indeed the sorts of claims that are relevant to determining and explaining the specific content of morality.

But what, then, should guide our judgment here? What is it, exactly, for a particular aspect of morality to "appropriately reflect" some particular feature of moral agents or moral patients? The answer to this question certainly isn't obvious, and for this reason it does seem fair to suggest that reflection theories remain somewhat more difficult to pin down than the various other foundational theories that we have considered. And many particular claims—to the effect that a given conceivable content of morality would best reflect some particular feature—are often quite difficult to evaluate. But for all that, we often do seem capable of arguing for and against such claims; we certainly seem to have some feel for the notion of "appropriately reflecting." Obviously, this is not to deny that particular reflection claims are often quite controversial. But at the same time, it would be unfair to suggest that reflection claims are inevitably unmotivated and ad hoc. Consider, for example, the suggestion that options reflect the nature of the personal point of view, and in particular the bias in favor of our own interests and concerns. This claim is contestable, to be sure, but it hardly seems to be made up out of thin air, in the way that it would if we claimed, say, that the requirement to keep one's *promises* reflects the fact that we are all *mortal!*

It is difficult to say much more, in a general way, about reflection theories. The list of features that might be appealed to by a reflection theorist is rather open ended. And, in point of fact, the specific claims that have been offered by reflection theorists have varied tremendously. Indeed, as I have already noted, in part because of this sheer range and variety, reflection theories are not typically thought of as forming a single, general approach to the foundations of normative ethics.

Given the variety of possible reflection arguments, it is, I think, impossible to make any helpful generalizations about what such arguments would support at the factoral level. Obviously enough, it will all depend on the details. But it may be helpful to consider one final—extended—example of the reflection approach at work. What is particularly interesting about this last example is that rather than being concerned with only one or two aspects of morality, it points in the direction of a justification for a good many of the major elements of something like commonsense morality, and all in terms of reflecting a single—crucially significant—fact.

According to many reflection theorists, the central fact about us that needs to be reflected by an adequate morality is the fact that we are *autonomous.* We have the capacity to envision how we want our lives to go; and with an eye toward this vision we make plans, and then decide how to act so as best to put these plans into effect. Now it certainly does seem to be a highly significant fact about us that we are autonomous—that we are capable of having this kind of control over our own lives—and it doesn't seem implausible for the reflection theorist to argue that an adequate morality will have to appropriately reflect this fact. But what would morality have to be like if it were going to do this?

One natural suggestion is that there should be a prohibition against interfering with the autonomy of another. If I act in such a way as to reduce, or to undermine, the control that someone else has over their own life, then I harm them in a profound way. My act fails to reflect the fact that my victim has his own conception of how he wants his life to go and that—but for my action—he would have been better able to live as he has chosen. Of course, if I am forbidden to interfere with the autonomy of others, then this will inevitably diminish somewhat my own ability to achieve the life that I have chosen for myself. But here it might be suggested that the cost to the agent of having to refrain from interfering with another's autonomy will typically be considerably less than the cost to the victim of having his autonomy attacked. On balance, then, a prohibition against interfering with autonomy might be the "compromise" that best reflects the fact that everyone's autonomy is equally real—the patient's as well as the agent's.

Now if there is such a moral prohibition, then other prohibitions might be derivable from it. That is, it might be that interference with another's autonomy is the form of harm that is most fundamental from the moral point of view. Other familiar forms of harm—inflicting pain, causing bodily damage, murder, theft, and so on—might matter (when they do) just by virtue of the fact that normally such acts interfere with, or destroy, autonomy. And various other prohibitions might be justified in this way as well. For example, when we discussed the constraint against lying (in 4.1), we noted the possibility that lying to someone may interfere with their autonomy, by reducing their control over their life. Similarly, if I can't be counted on to keep my promises to you, this can render your plans ineffective, diminishing your ability to plan your future. Thus, requirements to keep one's promises and to refrain from lying might be based on autonomy as well.

Note, however, that if a person *consents* to a given form of treatment, then typically, at least, being treated in that way will not constitute a violation of autonomy. For example, if I harm you with your permission, or if I fail to act on a promise from which you have released me, this doesn't actually interfere with your autonomy: you are still in control of your life, deciding how it is to go. Therefore, if the content of morality is to be explained in terms of reflecting the importance of autonomy, we have a possible explanation of why consent has the moral significance we normally take it to have.

On the other hand, the mere fact that someone consents to something may not automatically guarantee that such consent was given autonomously. It might be, for example, that autonomy is only exercised if the person giving consent has at least a minimal competence at evaluating the alternatives; or it might be that an autonomous choice must be at least minimally rational. Evaluating these claims would require a more careful investigation of the nature of autonomy than we can undertake here. But if anything like this is right, then not all consent will be morally relevant.

And this issue, as we have seen (in 4.5), may be important for settling the possibility of duties to oneself. Normally, perhaps, it is morally permissible for me to act toward myself in any way that I choose—including harming myself. For in the normal case, this will simply be living my life the way I want to, and will pose no threat to my own autonomy. But in certain cases, my consent may not suffice to make my act permissible. This might be especially so for actions that would destroy my autonomy, leaving me unable to control my life in the future. For example, it might be forbidden to sell myself into slavery, or to take drugs that would leave me insane. In short, if morality is to adequately reflect our autonomy, this might actually require certain duties to oneself—and not merely duties to others.

Returning to our duties to others, will all such duties be negative—based on a prohibition against interfering with another's autonomy—or will there be positive duties as well? In particular, will there ever be a requirement to aid others? Some reflection theorists have argued that no such duty would emerge from the need to reflect our autonomy. Provided that morality forbids *interfering* with autonomy, it adequately reflects the fact that we are autonomous. But other reflection theorists argue that the mere absence of interference does not guarantee that someone has any *effective* control over their life. For they may still lack the basic resources necessary to have even a minimal chance of achieving the kind of life they would like to live. Perhaps, then, morality should also include a requirement to *aid* others—a requirement to help provide them with the resources necessary to have a life under their own control.

Even if this is right, however, such a requirement might still be limited. For if people are to *live* autonomously—to live as they choose to live—then they cannot be subject to perpetual demands on the part of morality. They must be given some "space" to do with as they wish. Sometimes, of course, someone may autonomously *choose* to promote the greater good; but they cannot be perpetually required to do this. In short, if morality is to fully reflect our autonomy, it must grant us options as well.

Obviously, every step of the argument I have just been reviewing can be challenged. For example, even if it is true that options are one way of reflecting our autonomy, it is not at all clear that they are the best way to do this; perhaps instead there should be requirement to promote the greatest overall balance of effective autonomy. And in any event, crucial details remain to be filled in. Even if there is a prohibition against interfering with another's autonomy, will this take the form of a *constraint,* or will it be a mere rule of thumb? Can the autonomy of one be violated to protect the autonomy of others? As usual, I won't try to evaluate the merits of the argument I have sketched, nor will I go any further in laying out the various ways that the details of the argument might be filled in. But I hope to have said enough to give a sense of how someone might try to argue for a variety of factoral conclusions, on the grounds that this is what morality must be like, if it is to adequately reflect what *we* are like.

Finally, it should perhaps be noted that there is a sense in which virtually *all* foundational theories can be understood as developing some particular version of the reflection approach. After all, talk of morality's "reflecting" what we are like is just a metaphor. If you strip it away, we may be left with little more than the claim that creatures under the domain of morality have the particular moral status that they do—both as patients and as agents— by virtue of certain relevant features that they possess. Arguably, every foundational theory shares this thought.

Nonetheless, even if this is true, foundational views can clearly differ considerably in terms of the emphasis they place upon this idea. No doubt, every theory holds that there is *something* about us that is relevant to determining *something* about the content of morality. But not every theory gives this idea pride of place. Reflection theories take this idea and place it at the foundation of all of normative ethics: morality has the content that it does because of what we are *like*.

## 7.5  Foundational Pluralism

With the discussion of reflection theories in place, I am going to bring our survey of deontological foundational views to a close. Obviously, this is not because we have now considered every possible deontological approach to the foundations of normative ethics. On the contrary, since deontological theories need share nothing more than the belief that an adequate account of the basis of normative ethics will appeal to further concepts beyond, or instead of, that of the good, there are, I think, an unlimited number of forms that deontological foundational theories could take. But the theories that we have considered are, I believe, the most significant ones; at the very least, they represent what I take to be the most important deontological theories that have been suggested in the philosophical literature. And so, taken together with the discussion of teleological theories from the previous chapter, our review of basic foundational theories is now complete.

Although I have tried to give a sense of the diversity of possible foundational views, there is at least one important respect in which the discussion has been misleadingly narrow. For in discussing foundational theories, I have assumed, in effect, that some single basic foundational approach (whatever it is) accounts for *all* of the content of normative ethics at the factoral level. That is, even though I allowed for pluralism at the *factoral* level—with more than one basic normative factor possessing intrinsic moral significance—as far as the discussion of *foundations* was concerned, I assumed that if an adequate account could be found at all, it would be a monistic one. Of course, I have made no attempt to settle the question as to *which* particular foundational theory provides the most plausible account of the foundations of normative ethics; but I did assume that we would only appeal to a *single* theory. Accordingly, each foundational theory was presented as making the claim that it—and it alone—was the ultimate source of all of normative ethics. This simplified the discussion; and in any event it certainly reflects the most common point of view.

But the possibility of *pluralism* at the foundational level should not be overlooked. For it might be that no single foundational approach truly accounts for everything at the factoral level; perhaps, instead, we must appeal to some combination of views. It might be, for example, that a complete account will need to appeal to several foundational theories, each one of which is able to explain the basis of *some* of the normative factors, but no one of which explains all of them. If something like this is right, then instead of being tightly unified, the foundations of normative ethics will be more like a patchwork quilt—joining together several distinct approaches.

Of course, even if foundational pluralism is right, there will still be a sense in which there is a single, correct account of the foundations of normative ethics—namely, the account that appropriately combines the right component accounts. But intuitively, at any rate, this merely "conjunctive" account will lack the kind of conceptual unity that has been present in the more monistic foundational theories we have been examining. For even though it is not at all uncommon, as we have seen, to appeal to several different concepts in the course of developing a given foundational theory, each of the foundational theories we have examined grows out of a single, root idea, which can be expressed in some basic claim. Nothing like this would be true for foundational pluralism. Rather, if foundational pluralism is correct, the best overall account would simply *add together* what intuitively strike us as being distinct foundational views.

Obviously enough, if something like foundational pluralism is right, then no single component approach can correctly claim to be "the" ultimate basis of normative ethics, insofar as this claim is naturally understood to mean that it is the exclusive and sole basis. Rather, some *set* of foundational theories will jointly lay claim to providing the ultimate basis of morality. Still, it could well be the case that each component approach provides the ultimate explanation for some of the normative factors, even though no single approach does this for all of them.

I certainly don't mean to suggest, however, that pluralism at the foundational level faces no particular difficulties. One important worry begins by recalling that a completely articulated factoral theory will need to do more than provide a list of the basic normative factors; it will also need to provide an account of how these various factors *interact*. In effect, there must be interaction principles (see 5.4) specifying the various ways in which one factor, or combination of factors, can outweigh (or be overridden by, or modify the impact of) another factor, or combination of factors. But what is it, exactly, that explains the basis of the sound interaction principles? That is, why do the various basic normative factors interact in the precise ways that they do, rather than in some alternative fashion? This is, of course, one of the questions that we would like an adequate account of the foundations of normative ethics to answer.

Now it seems clear that the various monistic accounts that we have discussed are, in principle, capable of answering this question. In most cases, presumably, the requisite interaction principles will already be included—whether explicitly or implicitly—among the various factoral implications of the given foundational theory. For example, having justified a set of moral rules, a foundational theory will have (perhaps only implicitly) justified the corresponding interaction principles. And of course, if necessary, a monistic foundational theory could always evaluate the relevant interaction principles directly, from the particular evaluative standpoint provided by the foundational theory in question. Thus, for example, we could look to see which interaction principles would be agreed upon by appropriately specified bargainers, or which could be universalized without anything (of the relevant sort) going wrong, or which would lead to the best results overall, and so on. Obviously, the details here will vary, depending on the particular foundational theory we appeal to, but in principle there is no reason why monistic foundational theories cannot readily provide an account of the sound interaction principles.

In contrast, it is less clear whether a foundational pluralist can similarly provide a plausible account of all the necessary interaction principles. Of course, it won't be especially problematic for the pluralist to justify interaction principles for cases where all of the relevant factors derive from the very same component account; in such cases, that same component account can provide the requisite interaction principles as well. But what about cases involving the interaction of factors that are ultimately grounded in two (or more) distinct component accounts? When these factors jointly determine the status of a given act, what is it that explains why they interact in the precise ways that they do? By hypothesis, in such cases, no single component account grounds all of the relevant factors; but how then is the pluralist going to explain the various interactions of factors "across" accounts?

One possibility, presumably, is that some third component account grounds the relevant "transcategorical" interaction principles. For example, it might be that even though one set of factors derives from a reflection approach, while another set of factors derives from contractarianism, the *interactions* of these two sets of factors are governed by principles justified by appeal to, say, the ideal observer. There is, of course, a danger that on closer inspection it will turn out that this third account actually provides the basis for *all* of normative ethics—and so the overall theory will not actually be pluralist after all—but it is certainly not obvious that some sort of solution along these lines is impossible.

Alternatively, perhaps the foundational pluralist should simply insist that there is no further explanation of the relevant transcategorical interaction principles. Perhaps factors deriving from the different component accounts simply have the particular weights relative to one another that they do, and interact in the particular ways that they do, and that is all that there is to say on this subject; there is no further, or deeper, explanation.

Such a position is, of course, somewhat similar to the view of the *nonfoundationalist* (see 6.1), who holds that once the basic normative factors have been described, and the basic interaction principles stated, there is no further explanation to be found at the foundational level at all. Like the nonfoundationalist, the foundational pluralist who adopts this second approach claims that transcategorical interaction principles have no foundational explanation. But despite this point of agreement, the difference between the foundational pluralist and the nonfoundationalist is still significant. For unlike the nonfoundationalist, foundational pluralists insist that for at least some of the content of normative ethics—although, perhaps, not all—we can indeed offer an explanation at the foundational level.

It may be helpful to think of the various alternative positions concerning the possibility of foundational explanation as forming a spectrum. Someone who is a *monist* at the foundational level believes that everything about the factoral level can be explained in terms of a single, unified foundational account. In contrast, foundational *pluralists* reject the possibility of such a unified account. Nonetheless, foundational pluralists still accept the possibility of explaining at least some of the content of the factoral level through appeal to one or more component foundational accounts. Indeed, some of these pluralists will claim that everything at the factoral level can be provided with a foundational explanation in this way. Other pluralists, however, will insist that at least some of the content of the factoral level has no deeper foundational basis. Perhaps this is true only for certain transcategorical interaction principles. If so, then much of the content of the factoral level will have an explanation at the foundational level, although not quite all of it.

Clearly, however, a pluralist might hold instead that a great deal of the content of the factoral level lacks a foundational explanation. For example, perhaps although many of the basic normative factors can be explained in terms of one or another component account, some cannot; some simply lack any deeper explanation at all. And many of the relevant interaction principles may lack a foundational explanation as well.

At the limit, one might hold the view that *no* basic normative factors and *no* interaction principles can be provided with any sort of explanation at the foundational level. And this, of course, is precisely the view of the nonfoundationalist.

Seen from this perspective, then, the nonfoundationalist holds a view at the extreme end of a range of possible positions. And although this fact by itself hardly shows that nonfoundationalism is incorrect, I suspect that on reflection most people will find that they are more attracted to one or another version of foundational pluralism. After all, even if not all of the content of normative ethics can be explained at the foundational level, it doesn't seem implausible to believe that at least some of it might well be amenable to foundational explanation. And perhaps even all of it can be, provided that we bear in mind that at the foundational level we need not be monists, but can appeal instead to several distinct foundational accounts as components of our overall foundational theory.

Of course, none of this is meant to imply that foundational pluralism is more plausible than foundational monism. I intend only to suggest that some who may initially find themselves attracted to nonfoundationalism—

thinking, mistakenly, that the only other option is foundational monism—might find that they prefer foundational pluralism to either of these. Many others, however, will find both pluralism and nonfoundationalism implausible; and so, despite the apparent heterogeneity of content at the factoral level, they may insist that there must be a single, unified account of the foundations of normative ethics.

I began this discussion of foundational pluralism by noting that it represented a possibility that we had previously neglected. I should perhaps mention another possibility of this sort as well—a possibility that I have up to this point deliberately left aside, for the sake of simplicity of presentation. In discussing foundational theories I have presented them as though each insists that it provides the *ultimate* grounding of normative ethics. That is, each theory purported to be the bottom level—that which explains and justifies everything else. But we might want to leave open the possibility that the best overall account of normative ethics is one in which the foundational theory that generates the factoral level can *itself* be explained and justified in terms of an even deeper or more fundamental foundational theory.

For example, although one might appeal to rule consequentialism, say, as the correct account of the sound moral rules—the valid moral rules being valid by virtue of the fact that they are the ones that would have the best results—it might be that the correctness of rule consequentialism can itself be explained by appeal to, say, contractarianism. That is, it might be that suitably specified bargainers would agree, not upon any particular rules, but rather upon the use of rule consequentialism as the correct way to evaluate particular rules. They might simply agree, that is to say, that the binding moral rules are those (whatever they turn out to be) that would have the best results. If an account like this were correct, then it is indeed rule consequentialism which would generate and explain the factoral level, but it is contractarianism which would ground and explain the validity of rule consequentialism.

Obviously, there are many other possibilities along these lines. Egoism, for example, might support and ground contractarianism, which in turn might generate the factoral level. Or the ideal observer might support universalizability. And, of course, once the possibility of a view like this is recognized, there is no obvious reason to insist that we must stop with a single deeper layer. There might even be several rounds like this, with one foundational theory generating a second, which generates a third, which might even generate a fourth, before—finally—the factoral level is generated. For example, egoism might support contractarianism, the bargainers might agree upon an ideal observer approach, the ideal observer might endorse rule consequentialism, and only then might consequentialism generate the various valid moral rules of the factoral level.

(I should note that the possibility of a view like this reveals the existence of yet another potential evaluative focal point: foundational theories themselves. In effect, the evaluative standpoint provided by a given foundational theory is being used to evaluate, not rules, or acts, but rather alternative foundational theories.)

There is, I suppose, a clear sense in which on any multilayered approach like this, the only component account that can truly lay claim to providing the *ultimate* basis of normative ethics is the bottom account. From this perspective, perhaps, we shouldn't even call the intermediate accounts "foundational." But be that as it may, the intermediate component accounts will still be a part of the correct overall theory of the foundations of normative ethics; they will indeed be essential elements in the correct explanation of the factoral level. For, by hypothesis, we are imagining an explanation that proceeds in layers, or levels—and it remains the case that a full account of normative ethics will need to note each of these layers, not just the bottom one: we are, after all, imagining that the bottom level doesn't generate the factoral level directly; it does so, rather, by way of first generating the intermediate levels. (More precisely, of course, each level generates the next in the series.) In any event, whatever we call the component accounts in such a multilayered theory, what is important to stress is the very possibility of theories with such a structure.

In one way, of course, multilayered theories of this sort simply represent another version of foundational pluralism. For all these theories make use of more than one component account in constructing the overall theory. But unlike the current theories, the pluralistic foundational theories I initially described kept all of the component accounts on the same level. In contrast, the multilayered theories I have just been describing have only one component account at any given level; but they appeal to more than one foundational level.

We could, presumably, combine both types of pluralism—creating a theory with several layers, with at least some of the layers containing more than one component account. (Pluralism at one level might then be grounded in monism at a deeper level; although, of course, this need not be the case.) However, having noted some of the more exotic structural possibilities that foundational pluralism opens up, we will, unfortunately, have to leave the matter here.

## 7.6  Possibilities

Suppose—if only for the sake of simplicity—that we agree to restrict our attention to monistic foundational accounts. What sorts of choices do we face? There is, of course, always the possibility that a new approach to the foundations of normative ethics—one that we have not considered—will be suggested and prove promising. But even if we limit ourselves to the basic foundational theories with which we began, it is worth emphasizing the fact that we face quite a large number of alternatives, indeed, far more than is often realized. For as I have tried to show, there are many different ways that any given theory can be developed. Foundational theories may begin with a simple, central idea, or basic claim; but as the details of the theory are worked out, numerous choices must be made, and inevitably this leads to a tremendous explosion in the number of possible alternative views. I think it fair to say that only rarely have more than a few of the many different versions of any given basic theory been explored.

I have been especially keen to stress the different ways in which foundational theories can be combined with various choices concerning evaluative focal points. The range of possibilities here is, I think, considerably greater than has normally been recognized; and many combinations that have to date received little or no attention may well be worth investigating.

Of course, my discussion of evaluative focal points has itself been far from systematic. (Indeed, so far as I know, nothing like a systematic study of evaluative focal points has ever been undertaken.) For example, although I have mentioned a fair number of potential focal points—acts, rules, motives, and character traits, among others—I have certainly made no attempt to offer a complete list of morally significant focal points. Similarly, although I have noted some of the different structures that are possible here—a given theory might, for example, evaluate all focal points directly, or several, or only one—I have done little by way of exploring these various possibilities, beyond the last. Nor have I done anything more than offer a few examples of the different ways that one type of focal point might be evaluated in terms of another. In short, the discussion of evaluative focal points has been both sketchy and incomplete.

Still, I hope I have said enough to give at least some sense of the range of possibilities here. There is, I believe, a common failure to appreciate the sheer range of choices available with regard to focal points. There is also a common failure to recognize the very fact that each foundational theory faces this same range of choices. As a result, many potentially interesting combinations are simply never considered. Yet it seems likely that at least some of these typically overlooked possibilities would merit more careful investigation.

All told, we have looked at six basic approaches to the foundations of normative ethics: egoism, consequentialism, contractarianism, universalizability, the ideal observer, and reflection. Which of these, if any, should we accept? (We might, of course, accept a single basic approach on its own, or we might accept several, as parts of a more complex, pluralistic theory; but again, I am leaving this complication aside.)

It will come as no surprise to learn that I am not going to try to settle this question here. Indeed, my own view is that I have not yet said enough about any of these theories to allow us to make a final, overall evaluation. It's not that such overall evaluations are impossible; it is simply that still more needs to be said, beyond what I have been able to say here.

My goal, rather, has been the somewhat more modest one of trying to give some sense of each theory's strengths and weaknesses. I have tried to say enough to make each of these theories appear plausible—or, at least, to give some sense of why so many people have found each approach attractive. Of course, even here, my level of success has probably been somewhat mixed. No doubt, many people will find one or more of these theories quite implausible as accounts of the basis of ethics—utterly unattractive, and perhaps even bizarre. Yet each of them, I think, begins with a root idea or basic claim that is not without its intuitive appeal, even if, on reflection, we decide that some alternative approach is superior.

Philosophical theories are often something like works in progress. This is, I think, especially true for the foundational theories as they have been presented here. I have repeatedly noted areas in which various crucial details remain to be worked out, and questions remain to be answered. What shape the answers should take is something that is often far from settled. It is, in large part, because the theories as we have been considering them are so incomplete, that final judgments concerning their merits are probably premature.

On the other hand, even works in progress can be held up for evaluation, however tentative. For each basic theory, I have tried to give a sense of some of the intuitive objections and difficulties it faces. Doubtless, many people will find that they have already seen enough to leave them unsympathetic to one or another approach. Some objections may well seem damning; it may be clear that there is little prospect of finding an answer capable of adequately repairing the damage.

Making much the same point in a more positive vein, many will find that one or another foundational approach seems to them sufficiently plausible and promising, perhaps even compelling, that they are inclined to think that something along these lines must be right—even if much work remains to be done to develop the theory fully.

It is, of course, important to bear in mind that in evaluating foundational theories we must consider not only the intrinsic plausibility of these theories (as well as their intuitive drawbacks) but also how well they fit with our various other views. I have, for example, several times noted ways in which a given foundational theory may draw support from a particular *metaethical* claim, or from some more general metaethical picture concerning the purpose of morality. And these remarks have only scratched the surface. Ultimately, I suspect, the plausibility or implausibility of any given foundational theory will turn in large part on our metaethical views concerning the nature of morality and its place in the world. Indeed, as I have already noted (in 1.1), I doubt that there is any sharp line to be drawn between metaethics and normative ethics. But in any event, we will certainly want our metaethical theories and our normative ethical theories to cohere.

Within normative ethics itself, it will also be important to have harmony between our foundational theories and our *factoral* theories. And for this reason, of course, a foundational theory will also be plausible to the extent that it generates views concerning the factoral level that we can, on reflection, find acceptable. An adequate foundational theory must yield a plausible list of basic normative factors and plausible interaction principles. And for those cases where questions concerning the factoral level have remained controversial and unsettled, we can hope that an adequate foundational theory will resolve the controversies in illuminating and plausible ways.

I have, therefore, tried to say at least something about the factoral implications of each of our basic foundational theories. But as I have also tried to show, much depends on the details of how the theories are filled in, and so I have typically done nothing more than sketch one or two possible lines of argument. It is, I think, worth emphasizing the point that in no case have I offered anything like a complete argument concerning the factoral implications of any of our foundational theories.

Indeed, it is probably worth pointing out that *most* philosophical discussions concerning the factoral implications of various foundational views are similarly sketchy and incomplete. After all, even for a fully specified foundational view, it will typically be far from trivial to argue for specific factoral conclusions. The relevant arguments are often subtle and complex, and they may draw upon controversial philosophical or empirical assumptions. And these difficulties are multiplied considerably when we then bear in mind that most people accept several basic normative factors, involving a variety of distinct interaction principles. It would be difficult to investigate more than a few such specific factoral implications with care.

Given this fact, it is rather striking how often it is claimed—and claimed with some confidence—that this or that favored foundational theory supports something like commonsense morality at the factoral level. Such confidence is surprising, for the claim is rarely supported with anything more than a few sketchy arguments—illustrating in rather rough outline how at best one or two familiar principles might be derived.

But then again, perhaps this fact shouldn't surprise us after all. Most people begin their moral theorizing thinking that something at least roughly similar to commonsense morality is correct. (Were this not true, of course, the view wouldn't deserve the name "commonsense morality.") People may disagree with one another concerning some of the details—and people can obviously be uncertain, in their own minds, about individual issues—but generally, most start out with the belief that, in at least broad outline, something like commonsense morality is on the right track. But when they turn to the search for a foundational view, obviously enough, among other things they are looking for a view that will have what they take to be plausible results at the factoral level. And this means, of course, that they start out trying to find foundational views that will generate something at least roughly similar to commonsense morality. Given all of this, it probably should not surprise us that most people believe that their favored foundational views do, in fact, support something like commonsense morality. But for this very reason, we should never lose sight of the fact that foundational views can take on something of a life of their own, and once they are developed they may actually lead in rather unexpected directions.

Accordingly, we should not be too quick to assume that a foundational view that seems plausible in its own right will necessarily lead in the direction of commonsense morality. I have more than once tried to show how at least one version of a given foundational view—even deontological foundational views—might be thought to support consequentialism at the factoral level. And of course, it might well be that even more exotic and less familiar views are what actually emerge from the most plausible foundational theory. Once we spell out the theory, and look with some care to see what factoral view it actually supports, we might find ourselves rather surprised. And yet, if the foundational view is itself sufficiently attractive, we might be prepared to follow this view and accept its factoral implications, even if these are somewhat counterintuitive. This is especially so, if the foundational view can challenge our initial factoral beliefs in plausible and compelling ways.

It is also worth recalling, in this regard, that our overall assessment of a foundational view—or indeed any normative theory—is always at least in part a comparative affair. It might well be that no moral theory escapes all philosophical objections, that no moral theory is without its counterintuitive implications. It is rather unlikely, I think, that we will be able to find a moral theory that gives us everything we initially want, without exacting any significant costs in terms of modifying or even abandoning some of our initial views. Rather, what we should hope for is to find a moral theory that provides what is, on balance, an attractive and plausible position.

Thus people may start out looking for a defense of their ordinary, commonsense moral views—but they may end up having justified views rather different from the ones with which they began. Of course, they may not even always realize this: it takes a certain amount of open-mindedness, and a willingness to follow a plausible line of argument to its logical conclusion. But in principle, at any rate, moral reflection and the attempt to arrive at an adequate moral theory might lead you to a position rather removed from where you started. This possibility is one we face as soon as we begin to do moral philosophy.

Moral philosophy begins with the question: how should I live? Moral wisdom begins with the realization that I may not already know the answer.

# SUGGESTED READINGS

This final chapter contains suggestions for further reading. (Since the book contains no footnotes, when the main text has specifically borrowed from some particular work, that will be noted here as well.) I have tried to make some suggestions for each of the topics discussed in the book, but I have not attempted anything like complete bibliographies; the references that follow are highly selective. It should also be borne in mind that for the most part the works mentioned here were written *by* professional philosophers *for* professional philosophers, so many of them will make for rather difficult reading.

Individual works are referred to by author and title; more complete bibliographical information can be found in the References section.

## Chapter 1: Preliminaries

### 1.1    *What Normative Ethics Is*

A standard (although somewhat dated) treatment of the problems of metaethics can be found in Brandt, *Ethical Theory.* On the particular issue of whether or not there are moral facts, a useful selection of recent articles can be found in Sayre-McCord, *Essays on Moral Realism.* Good examples of applied ethics can be found in Singer, *Practical Ethics* (a single, sustained work), and in the following anthologies: Regan, *Matters of Life and Death*; Sterba, *Morality in Practice*; and Rachels, *Moral Problems.*

For the thesis that metaethics and normative ethics are independent of one another and that philosophers should be concerned solely with the former, see Ayer, *Language, Truth and Logic,* chapter 6.

Given the focus of the book, many topics in moral philosophy will not be considered here. Rachels, *The Elements of Moral Philosophy,* is a very clear and readable introduction to the field that also treats several issues I will not be discussing at all; Feldman, *Introductory Ethics,* covers much of the same material at a slightly more advanced level. For something far more inclusive, *A Companion to Ethics* (edited by Singer) is a collection of almost fifty essays covering the scope of moral philosophy. Finally, the *Encyclopedia of Ethics* (edited by Becker and Becker) has entries for hundreds of issues in moral philosophy.

One of the most important topics I won't discuss involves questions surrounding free will and responsibility, and praise and blame. Some good works here are Wolf,

*Freedom Within Reason;* Fischer's anthology, *Moral Responsibility;* Watson's anthology, *Free Will;* and particularly for discussion of praise and blame, Donagan, *The Theory of Morality,* chapter 4. For discussion of the moral status of animals, see the references for 2.3.

## 1.2     What Normative Ethics Is Not

As I've noted, the book you are reading doesn't discuss the history of ethics at all. For a short recent treatment of this topic, see Nelson, *Morality: What's in It for Me?* Sidgwick's *Outlines of the History of Ethics* is a classic.

In distinguishing normative ethics from other concerns, I relied heavily upon our having a working understanding of the concepts of "ought" and "should" (and related notions, such as "permitted," "required," and "forbidden"). But what do these notions really mean? These are good metaethical questions. See Sidgwick, *The Methods of Ethics,* Book I, chapter 3, and Gibbard, *Wise Choices, Apt Feelings.* I also relied on our having a notion of the moral point of view (and how it differs from other standpoints). See Baier, *The Moral Point of View,* and also Gibbard again.

For the rationality of morality, see Sidgwick's *Methods,* the "Concluding Chapter." Kant is the most important advocate of the view that moral demands are demands of rationality as well. His *Groundwork of the Metaphysics of Morals* is one of the most significant works in moral philosophy—but it is also one of the most difficult. Two more recent advocates of this view are Nagel, *The Possibility of Altruism,* and Gauthier, *Morals by Agreement.*

## 1.3     Defending Normative Theories

The problem of observation and ethics is discussed by Harman in *The Nature of Morality,* chapter 1, as well as by several of the writers in Sayre-McCord, *Essays on Moral Realism.*

The general approach to justification in ethics that I endorse is similar to the notion of "reflective equilibrium" described by Rawls in *A Theory of Justice.* See also Gibbard, *Wise Choices, Apt Feelings,* and DePaul, *Balance and Refinement.* An example of someone who wants to give intuitions about cases very considerable weight is Thomson, *The Realm of Rights,* Introduction. For someone who wants to give them very little weight, see Hare, *Moral Thinking.* A lengthy discussion of justification in ethics (including the problem of observation) can be found in Brink, *Moral Realism and the Foundations of Ethics,* especially chapter 5.

## 1.4     Factors and Foundations

Discussions of particular factors and foundational theories are plentiful, and references will be given below as they come up in the text. However, systematic surveys of both the basic normative factors and the rival foundational theories are rather rare. The book that comes closest to my own approach—in terms of the basic organization and framework—is Donagan, *The Theory of Morality* (although this endorses many conclusions I would reject). A classic examination of the normative factors endorsed by commonsense morality can be found in Sidgwick, *The Methods of Ethics,* Book III. Two other important discussions are Hume, *Enquiry Concerning the Principles of Morals,* and Kant, *The Metaphysics of Morals,* part II, the Doctrine of Virtue.

Once one entertains a picture of normative ethics with several morally relevant factors, the structural possibilities get quite complex (for example, factors can override, outweigh, or undermine one another, or interact in a variety of other ways). An illuminating—but extremely abstract and difficult—discussion of these matters can be found in Nozick, "Moral Complications and Moral Structures" (which also appears in abbreviated form as chapter 5, section 3, of Nozick's *Philosophical Explanations)*.

Chapter 3 of Scheffler, *Human Morality,* considers some of the ways in which moral theory might or might not enter into practical deliberation.

# Chapter 2: The Good

## 2.1    Promoting the Good

A very clear discussion of some of the different ways that the notion of the "outcome" of an act can be understood (that is, more narrowly or more widely) can be found in Vallentyne, "Teleology, Consequentialism, and the Past." Although using different vocabulary, and a somewhat different approach, Feldman's *Doing the Best We Can* argues, in effect, for the widest reading of "outcome" (that is, complete world histories).

The concept of intrinsic value and the distinction between intrinsic value and instrumental value are surprisingly difficult matters to get completely clear about. A classic essay is Moore, "The Conception of Intrinsic Value." An important (but difficult) discussion is Korsgaard, "Two Distinctions in Goodness." Lemos, *Intrinsic Value,* is a recent treatment of the topic.

## 2.2    Well-Being

A brief, but influential, recent discussion and classification of rival theories of well-being can be found in Appendix I to Parfit's *Reasons and Persons.* The most sustained contemporary discussion of well-being is Griffin, *Well-Being,* especially parts I and II. (Griffin ultimately adopts a kind of preference theory of well-being.)

Versions of hedonism go back to antiquity. In the modern era, the classic statement of quantitative hedonism can be found in Bentham, *An Introduction to the Principles of Morals and Legislation.* Bentham held that "pleasure for pleasure, pushpin is as good as poetry" (pushpin was a sort of simple-minded children's game). His view was criticized by Mill, who argued for qualitative hedonism in *Utilitarianism,* chapter 2. (The example of the contented pig comes from Mill, as does the suggestion that the best test for distinguishing higher from lower pleasures is to ask the experts.) Another classic—and unusually clear—statement of quantitative hedonism can be found in Sidgwick, *The Methods of Ethics,* Book II. A recent advocate of quantitative hedonism is Brandt, *A Theory of the Good and the Right,* chapter 13.

The story of the deceived businessman is an expansion of an example given by Nagel in "Death." The experience machine was introduced by Nozick in *Anarchy, State and Utopia,* pp. 42–45. Interesting reflections on experience machines can be found in Glover, *What Sort of People Should There Be?,* chapters 7 and 8, and in Unger, *Identity, Consciousness and Value,* chapter 9.

Preference theories of well-being are largely taken for granted in contemporary economic theory, especially welfare economics. An ideal preference theory is defended in Griffin, *Well-Being,* and is discussed sympathetically (although ultimately rejected) by Brandt, *A Theory of the Good and the Right.*

Objective theories of well-being have had few contemporary defenders, although they seem to be making something of a comeback. The classic objective theory is Aristotle's, in the *Nicomachean Ethics.* Kraut's "Two Conceptions of Happiness" provides a helpful comparison of Aristotle's views with modern ones. Hurka's *Perfectionism* is a recent, philosophically sophisticated, defense of that view. (It should be noted, however, that Hurka sees perfectionism as an alternative to a theory of welfare, rather than as the best account of welfare.) Scanlon's "Preference and Urgency" argues (roughly) that benefit to others should be measured in terms of an objective scale, rather than in terms of individual preference.

## 2.3    The Total View

If we accept the total view, I noted, we can often make comparisons more easily if, instead of comparing entire totals, we consider only the incremental benefits (or benefits and losses). These two approaches will give the same answers—*provided* that all the same people exist in the two outcomes being compared. If the population varies, however, the two views can come apart, and we may have to choose between them. (They'll only come apart, however, if one holds the further view that being caused to exist cannot count as a benefit—not even if your life is worth living.) Unfortunately, the issues involved are too complex to consider here. But see Parfit, *Reasons and Persons,* part IV, and appendix G. Indeed, population ethics raises a host of fascinating and extraordinarily difficult problems. (The choice between the total view and the average view—discussed briefly in the text—is only one of these.) Parfit's discussion of these problems is groundbreaking and unsurpassed. (The phrase "different number cases" comes from Parfit.)

Skepticism about interpersonal comparisons of utility is one of the working assumptions of much contemporary welfare economics (which is not to say that such skepticism is well defended in that literature). Sensible remarks in defense of the possibility of interpersonal comparisons can be found in Griffin, *Well-Being,* part II, and in Hare, *Moral Thinking,* chapter 7. A recent, but difficult, collection of papers on this issue is *Interpersonal Comparisons of Well-Being,* edited by Elster and Roemer.

In arguing for the total view, I have been assuming that "the numbers count" (for example, the outcome is better if you save two people's lives rather than just one, and this is a morally relevant factor in determining what you should do). This assumption has been provocatively challenged by Taurek, in "Should the Numbers Count?" Several replies to Taurek can be found in *Ethics: Problems & Principles,* edited by Fischer and Ravizza.

The equal moral status of animals has been forcefully defended by Singer. Singer's *Animal Liberation* offers a popular treatment of the topic; his *Practical Ethics* provides a philosophically more sophisticated discussion, chapters 3 and 5. *Animal Rights and Human Obligations,* edited by Regan and Singer, is a helpful collection.

## 2.4    Equality

There is a vast literature on equality. A useful collection is *Equality: Selected Readings,* edited by Pojman and Westmoreland. Two especially interesting essays are Nagel, "Equality," and Williams, "The Idea of Equality." A very modest egalitarian position—where equality is only a tie breaker—is adopted by Sidgwick, *The Methods of Ethics,* pp. 416–17. Most other egalitarians take a stronger position.

A superb discussion of the nature of equality, and different methods of measuring inequality, can be found in Temkin, *Inequality.* A briefer statement of Temkin's approach can be found in "Inequality." Parfit, *Equality or Priority?,* also illuminatingly compares and evaluates various egalitarian positions, ultimately opting for a moderate version of weighted beneficence (the label for this position is Parfit's).

A maximin distributive principle is defended by Rawls in *A Theory of Justice.* It should be noted, however, that Rawls's particular principle concerns the distribution of certain basic resources, rather than well-being. Likewise, some egalitarians have argued that what matters morally is not equality of well-being but equality of resources. See Dworkin, "What Is Equality?" especially part I. (It should also be noted that Rawls's principle is only intended to govern choices between basic social institutions; it is not offered as a general moral principle. Similarly, some "resource egalitarians" only intend to be making claims about the appropriate distributive concerns of social and political institutions.)

McKerlie, "Equality and Time," presents an interesting defense of the claim that there is value in having equality at any given moment (as opposed to a view that holds that equality matters only when comparing whole lives). Further discussion of the proper "unit" of egalitarian concern can be found in Temkin, *Inequality,* chapter 8.

The term "welfarism" comes from Sen, "Utilitarianism and Welfarism" (although my use of the term does not coincide exactly with Sen's).

## 2.5    Culpability, Fairness, and Desert

A good introduction to the topic of desert is Feinberg, "Justice and Personal Desert." The most wide-ranging study of the subject is Sher's *Desert.* Donagan, *The Theory of Morality,* chapter 4, examines the nature of culpability and blameworthiness. Feinberg's "Sua Culpa" similarly explores the nature of fault, responsibility, and culpability. (These two essays by Feinberg are included in his *Doing and Deserving,* along with several other papers of his that treat related topics.)

Kant's moral philosophy represents a classic statement of the retributivist position. Unfortunately, the discussion of this issue is scattered throughout his works; but see the first paragraph of the First Section of the *Groundwork of the Metaphysics of Morals,* as well as part 2, section 49e of The Doctrine of Right in *The Metaphysics of Morals.* (The reader should be warned, however, that these works are extremely difficult.) A contemporary defense of retributivism is Murphy, *Retribution, Justice and Therapy.* Most discussions of retributivism take place in the context of potential justifications for punishment. See Honderich, *Punishment: The Supposed Justifications.*

## 2.6    Consequentialism

The term "consequentialism" was introduced by Anscombe, in "Modern Moral Philosophy." Anscombe, however, used the term much more broadly than is common nowadays. Scheffler's use of "consequentialism" in *The Rejection of Consequentialism* is more typical of recent writing. Although stating the basic idea behind consequentialism is fairly easy (see, for example, Scheffler, pp. 1–2), finding a satisfactory precise formulation is not. A good discussion of some of the complications—with a proposed solution—is Feldman's *Doing the Best We Can*. See also, Regan, *Utilitarianism and Co-operation*.

The classics of the utilitarian tradition are Bentham, *An Introduction to the Principles of Morals and Legislation;* Mill, *Utilitarianism;* and Sidgwick, *The Methods of Ethics,* especially Book IV. Mill's work is the most accessible (it was written as a popular exposition of utilitarianism); Sidgwick's is the most philosophically sophisticated. Two important recent defenses of utilitarianism are Smart, "An Outline of a System of Utilitarian Ethics," and Hare, *Moral Thinking*. A short statement of Hare's approach can be found in "Ethical Theory and Utilitarianism."

There is a huge literature on utilitarianism. Two recent collections are *Utilitarianism and Beyond,* edited by Sen and Williams, and *The Limits of Utilitarianism,* edited by Miller and Williams. A particularly influential essay is Williams, "A Critique of Utilitarianism." (This essay has been published along with Smart's in *Utilitarianism: For and Against*.)

It is only fairly recently that moral philosophers have started exploring the strengths and weaknesses of consequentialism per se (as opposed to those of the particular consequentialist theory, utilitarianism). Three significant works in this vein are Scheffler, *The Rejection of Consequentialism;* Parfit, *Reasons and Persons,* especially part I; and Slote, *Common-Sense Morality and Consequentialism*. A number of important articles have been collected in *Consequentialism and Its Critics,* edited by Scheffler, and in *Consequentialism,* edited by Pettit. A good, clear critique of consequentialism can be found in Donagan, *The Theory of Morality,* chapter 6.

Ethical egoism is by far the best-known individualistic teleological theory. *Morality and Rational Self-Interest,* edited by Gauthier, contains several interesting articles on various conceptions of egoism. As noted in the text, the distinction between individualistic theories and universalistic theories is somewhat difficult to make precise, since an individualistic theory might not be concerned with what is good for the agent, but rather with what is good from a point of view whose content is defined relative to the agent (for example, what is good for the agent's mother). Careful articulation of the distinction will thus appeal to the difference between agent-neutral and agent-relative evaluations. These more technical terms are explained in Nagel, *The View from Nowhere,* pp. 152–154 ff., and in Parfit, *Reasons and Persons,* p. 27 and passim.

The classic account of the consequentialist's use of rules is given in Mill, *Utilitarianism*. A quite subtle discussion can be found in Sidgwick's *Methods,* Book IV. A brief modern statement is Smart, "Extreme and Restricted Utilitarianism." A fuller recent account is Hare, *Moral Thinking*.

## Chapter 3: Doing Harm

### 3.1    Deontology

The organ transplant case and the case of the angry mob have both been widely discussed. The transplant case was originally introduced by Foot in "The Problem of Abortion and the Doctrine of the Double Effect." It is discussed by Thomson in "Killing, Letting Die, and the Trolley Problem" and in *The Realm of Rights*. The case of the angry mob was introduced by McCloskey, "A Note on Utilitarian Punishment." It is discussed by Smart in "An Outline of a System of Utilitarian Ethics," and by Donagan, *The Theory of Morality,* pp. 203–204. But there are in fact dozens, if not hundreds, of examples meant to make a similar point. Most discussions (particularly critical discussions) of consequentialism or utilitarianism consider one or more examples of this sort.

For a standard attempt to defuse such an example, see Smart, "Outline." For criticism of such attempts, see Donagan, *The Theory of Morality,* chapter 6, section 5. Hare has written the most about the various options open to the consequentialist. "What Is Wrong with Slavery?" argues that once we tell a plausible story in which slavery will actually have the best results, it no longer seems intuitively unacceptable. *Moral Thinking* offers a "recipe" for producing anticonsequentialist examples and for defusing them. Typically, Hare criticizes the appeal to intuitions in such arguments.

The various consequentialist replies I have surveyed in the text do not quite exhaust the possibilities. Consequentialists can also stress the risk of bias and calculation error if one is prepared to break the rules—and they point to this as part of a consequentialist justification for agents having a general unwillingness to break the rules. There is also the danger that breaking the rules will lead others to break them in circumstances where doing so would *not* be justified—and this too supports hesitation about breaking the rules. For more on this, and similar points, see Hare, *Moral Thinking;* Smart, "Extreme and Restricted Utilitarianism"; and Sartorious, *Individual Conduct and Social Norms.* Many of these ideas were introduced by Sidgwick in *The Methods of Ethics,* Book IV.

The characterization of deontology in terms of the priority of the right over the good goes back to Kant, in the *Critique of Practical Reason.* In contemporary writing the phrase has been popularized by Rawls; see *A Theory of Justice,* pp. 446–452.

There are almost as many deontological theories as there are critics of consequentialism. Kant is the classic exponent of a deontological system; unfortunately, his work is extremely difficult to read and understand. But see the *Groundwork* and the *Metaphysics of Morals.* Many contemporary moral philosophers accept some form of deontology, but few have attempted to articulate and defend entire deontological theories. Two accessible exceptions are Donagan, *The Theory of Morality,* and Fried, *Right and Wrong,* especially part I. Nagel, *The View from Nowhere,* chapters 8–10, defends the basic elements of a deontological outlook. Thomson's *The Realm of Rights* is an extended exploration and defense of that part of deontological morality that concerns rights.

I have suggested using the term *constraints* for prohibitions that rule out performing various kinds of acts even when such acts are necessary to promote the overall good. It should be noted, however, that prohibitions of this sort get called by a number of different names in the contemporary philosophical literature: for example, Nozick, *Anarchy, State and Utopia,* uses the term "side-constraints"; Scheffler, *The Rejection of Consequentialism,* talks about "agent-centered restrictions"; and Nagel, *The View from Nowhere,* writes about "deontic restrictions." (These are, I should also note, perhaps the three most important contemporary discussions of constraints per se.)

## 3.2   Thresholds

A large number of deontologists are sympathetic to the thought that constraints have thresholds. But almost no one has discussed the nature of these thresholds in any kind of detail. The most important exception is Thomson, *The Realm of Rights* (from whom the distinction between infringing and violating a constraint comes as well). Interesting discussions of some of the relevant issues can be found in Brennan, "How Is the Strength of a Right Determined?" and "Thresholds for Rights."

Kant is the classic defender of an absolutist approach to constraints. See, for example, the *Groundwork* and "On a Supposed Right to Lie from Benevolent Motives." Prominent recent advocates of (deontological) absolutism include Anscombe, "Modern Moral Philosophy," and Donagan, *The Theory of Morality.* Finnis, *Moral Absolutes,* is a defense of deontological absolutes from the standpoint of the Christian moral tradition. A forceful consequentialist attack on absolutism is Bennett's "Whatever the Consequences." A useful collection of articles on this topic is *Absolutism and Its Consequentialist Critics,* edited by Haber. Many deontologists continue to embrace the language of absolutism despite the fact that they actually seem to endorse moderate deontological positions (see, for example, Fried, *Right and Wrong*) or are at least open to its possibility (for example, Nozick, *Anarchy, State and Utopia*—see the footnote on p. 30).

An interesting discussion of alternative deontological approaches to risk can be found in Thomson, "Imposing Risks." Also helpful is *Values at Risk,* edited by MacLean. Much of the debate about imposing risk involves issues concerning consent. See section 3.3.

## 3.3   The Scope of the Constraint

Many important issues surrounding the nature of harm and harm doing are discussed helpfully in Feinberg, *Harm to Others.* (It should be noted that this work— the first volume of Feinberg's four-volume work, *The Limits of the Criminal Law*— is primarily concerned with certain issues in the philosophy of law; but in the course of defending its main thesis, Feinberg illuminatingly examines a number of topics relevant to normative ethics proper.) An interesting discussion of Feinberg's views can be found in Thomson, "Feinberg on Harm, Offense, and the Criminal Law." Thomson also discusses these topics in *The Realm of Rights.* A narrow interpretation of "doing harm" is defended in Donagan, *The Theory of Morality,* chapter 2, section 2.

The relevance of consent to moral constraints is discussed by Brock in "Moral Prohibitions and Consent." Feinberg examines the issues in detail in *Harm to Self,* and somewhat more—under the topic of exploitation—in *Harmless Wrongdoing* (volumes 3 and 4, respectively, of *The Limits of the Criminal Law*). Thomson argues against the relevance of hypothetical consent in *The Realm of Rights,* chapter 7, section 5. The example of George trapped by the tree comes from Thomson as well. In "Paternalism and Rights," Brennan examines the possibility that thresholds might be lower in cases where the constraint is violated for the sake of the person being harmed.

Possible justifications for self-defense are examined by Thomson in "Self-Defense and Rights," "Self-Defense," and *The Realm of Rights,* chapter 4. Uniacke's *Permissible Killing* is an extended treatment of the topic. McMahan's "Self-Defense and the Problem of the Innocent Attacker" is especially helpful. Innocent threats are discussed in the McMahan essay as well as in Fletcher, "Proportionality and the Psychotic Aggressor," and Kamm, "The Insanity Defense, Innocent Threats and Limited Alternatives." The permissibility of harming both innocent threats and innocent shields of threats is noted by Nozick, *Anarchy, State and Utopia,* pp. 34–35. (The tank example comes from Nozick, as do the expressions "innocent threat" and "innocent shield of a threat.") Quinn connects the justification of self-defense and punishment in "The Right to Threaten and the Right to Punish." Honderich, *Punishment: The Supposed Justifications,* is a critical survey of standard accounts of the permissibility of punishment. A fascinating discussion of the permissibility of punishment can be found in Nozick, *Anarchy, State and Utopia,* chapter 4. For the distinction between excuses and justifications, see Austin, "A Plea for Excuses."

## 3.4    Doing and Allowing

The literature on the do/allow distinction is tremendous. Two very helpful collections are Steinbock, *Killing and Letting Die,* and Fischer and Ravizza, *Ethics: Problems & Principles.* Many of the papers cited below are reprinted in one or both of these.

Many deontologists sympathetic to the distinction between doing and allowing simply draw upon our intuitions, rather than attempting to offer an analysis. But there are several striking exceptions. Quinn, "Actions, Intentions, and Consequences: The Doctrine of Doing and Allowing," attempts to articulate and defend a general account of the do/allow distinction. McMahan, "Killing, Letting Die, and Withdrawing Aid," is especially focused on trying to offer an account adequate to handling cases like that of turning off the artificial respirator. Kamm, "Killing and Letting Die: Methodological and Substantive Issues," does not set out to offer a general analysis of the distinction, but she considers a large number of points relevant to creating and defending such an account. (Kamm's paper is also the most difficult of the three.) See also Kamm's *Morality, Mortality,* volume 2, part 1.

Criticisms of the do/allow distinction can be found in Bennett's "Whatever the Consequences" and "Morality and Consequences." Bennett argues that an adequate analysis makes it easy to see that the distinction lacks moral relevance. He also attacks the relevance of the distinction through the use of examples similar to that of the drowning cousin. The drowning cousin example itself comes from Rachels, "Active and Passive Euthanasia."

Trammell, "Saving Life and Taking Life," has attempted to defend the do/allow distinction from arguments like that based on the example of the drowning cousin (among other things, he makes the suggestion that the cases may still differ, even if we're unable to detect this). Kamm, "Non-consequentialism, the Person as an End-in-Itself, and the Significance of Status," pp. 366–367, suggests that it may indeed be possible to detect moral differences in such cases if we focus instead on how it would be permissible to treat the agent. In "Killing and Letting Die," Kamm also suggests that the do/allow distinction can still have intrinsic significance, even if its effect varies from context to context. See also *Morality, Mortality,* volume 2, part 1. I have argued for a similar point in "The Additive Fallacy." I have, however, criticized both the do/allow distinction and the constraint against doing harm in *The Limits of Morality,* chapter 3.

## 3.5    Intending Harm

The trolley car problem was introduced by Foot in "The Problem of Abortion and the Doctrine of the Double Effect" (the case of the poison gas in the hospital comes from this article as well). But it came to prominence through Thomson's "Killing,

Letting Die, and the Trolley Problem." Thomson returned to the topic in "The Trolley Problem" and in *The Realm of Rights,* chapter 7. Quinn examines a large number of such cases in "Actions, Intentions, and Consequences: The Doctrine of Doing and Allowing" and in "Actions, Intentions, and Consequences: The Doctrine of Double Effect," as does Kamm in "Harming Some to Save Others" and *Morality, Mortality,* volume 2, part 2.

The doctrine of double effect—equivalent to a constraint against intending harm—is defended by Anscombe, "Modern Moral Philosophy"; Nagel, *The View from Nowhere,* chapter 9; Fried, *Right and Wrong,* chapter 2; and Quinn, "Actions, Intentions, and Consequences: The Doctrine of Double Effect." It is criticized by Donagan, *The Theory of Morality,* chapter 5, section 3; Bennett, "Morality and Consequences"; and Davis, "The Doctrine of Double Effect: Problems of Interpretation." I have myself attacked the constraint against intending harm in *The Limits of Morality,* chapter 4.

## Chapter 4: Other Constraints

### 4.1   Lying

A general discussion of the morality of lying can be found in Bok, *Lying.* Fried offers a number of different justifications for a constraint against lying in *Right and Wrong,* chapter 3. An interesting discussion of lying and the violation of autonomy is Hill's "Autonomy and Benevolent Lies." (For the idea of autonomy in general, see Dworkin, *The Theory and Practice of Autonomy,* and Hill, *Autonomy and Self-Respect,* as well as the essays in *The Inner Citadel,* edited by Christman.) The most famous defender of absolutism with regard to lying is Kant, who holds that one cannot tell a lie even in the would-be murderer example; see "On a Supposed Right to Lie from Benevolent Motives."

### 4.2   Promises

Interesting discussions of promising can be found in Thomson, *The Realm of Rights,* chapter 12; Prichard, "The Obligation to Keep a Promise"; and—more briefly—Donagan, *The Theory of Morality,* pp. 90–94. The significance of promising for solving problems of reliance and reassurance is emphasized by Scanlon, "Promises and Practices," as it was by Hume in *A Treatise of Human Nature,* Book III, part 2, section 5. Warnock, *The Object of Morality,* defends a veracity account of promising.

It has sometimes been argued that—appearances to the contrary notwithstanding—utilitarians would not be able to establish a practice of promise keeping or truth telling. See Hodgson, *Consequences of Utilitarianism.* Utilitarian replies can be found in Regan, *Utilitarianism and Co-operation,* chapter 4, and Lewis, "Utilitarianism and Truthfulness."

The uptake requirement is discussed at length in Thomson, *The Realm of Rights,* (from which the name for this condition is taken). The connection between promising and contracts is explored in Fried, *Contract as Promise.* The example of the cabin damaged during the storm comes from Feinberg, "Voluntary Euthanasia and the Inalienable Right to Life."

## 4.3    Special Obligations

The obligation to compensate for harm done underlies much of what is known as tort law. A brief introduction to some of the philosophical issues in this area can be found in Murphy and Coleman, *The Philosophy of Law,* pp. 167–189, with more extended discussion in Coleman's *Risks and Wrongs.* Thomson's "Remarks on Causation and Liability" is a fascinating investigation of why causing harm is a necessary condition for liability. I examine some of the complications underlying the special obligation to compensate in "Causation and Responsibility."

Several of the essays in Thomson's *Rights, Restitution and Risk* explore the claim that constraints can leave behind traces and residues, even when overridden; Thomson notes that this may explain the requirement to compensate in "Rights and Compensation." The proposal to derive the requirement to compensate from a requirement to minimize the harm you do was made (in discussion) by Heidi Malm.

The claim that there are no pure positive duties is often an important element in libertarian writings. Nozick's *Anarchy, State and Utopia* is the most influential recent philosophical defense of libertarianism.

The duty to rescue is discussed in Fried, *An Anatomy of Values.* Singer's "Famine, Affluence and Morality" defends a general requirement to promote the good; it also criticizes many of the distinctions upon which a more narrow duty to rescue might be based. The same thing is done at greater length in Unger's lively *Living High and Letting Die.*

Gratitude is discussed by Kant in The Doctrine of Virtue in *The Metaphysics of Morals.*

## 4.4    Conventions

The classic discussion of role based obligations is found in Bradley, "My Station and Its Duties." An interesting contemporary exploration is Hardimon, "Role Obligations."

The principle of fair play—sometimes called the principle of fairness—was introduced by Hart, "Are There Any Natural Rights?" and given wide currency by Rawls, *A Theory of Justice,* sections 18 and 52. It is subjected to sharp attack by Nozick in *Anarchy, State and Utopia,* pp. 90–95. Attempts to resist this attack—in part through a more careful statement of the principle—can be found in Simmons, *Moral Principles and Political Obligations,* and Klosko, *The Principle of Fairness and Political Obligation.*

The classic conventionalist account of property-related obligations is Hume, in *A Treatise of Human Nature,* Book III, part 2, sections 1 and 2. Thomson, *The Realm of Rights,* chapter 13, is a contemporary conventionalist. Locke offers the classic defense of property-related obligations as natural in the second of *Two Treatises of Government.* Nozick's *Anarchy, State and Utopia* is an influential contemporary statement of this position; see, especially, chapter 7. Becker's *Property Rights* is a clear, critical survey of the various possible justifications for property regimes. Hare's "What Is Wrong with Slavery?" approaches the question posed in its title from a utilitarian standpoint.

## 4.5    Duties to Oneself

A brief survey of traditional duties to oneself can be found in Donagan, *The Theory of Morality*, pp. 76–81. Kant's defense of duties to oneself can be found in The Doctrine of Virtue, in *The Metaphysics of Morals*. The suggestion that cases where my current self affects my later self should be seen as similar to ones where one person affects another comes from Parfit, *Reasons and Persons;* see part III, especially chapters 14 and 15. Beauchamp's "Suicide" is a survey of the issues on this topic.

For the duty of self-respect, see Hill, "Servility and Self-Respect" and "Self-Respect Reconsidered."

## Chapter 5: Further Factors

## 5.1    Demanding Too Much

For a brief history of views concerning the category of the supererogatory, see Heyd, *Supererogation*. The recent debate on the extent to which consequentialism and other moral theories are too demanding began with Urmson's "Saints and Heroes." Influential statements of this objection to consequentialism can be found in Williams, "A Critique of Utilitarianism" and "Persons, Character and Morality." In "Famine, Affluence and Morality" and in *Practical Ethics,* chapter 8, Singer agrees that consequentialist considerations can have quite demanding implications; but he argues forcefully for accepting them. Historically, the opposing view—that consequentialism is not normally especially demanding—was held by Mill in *Utilitarianism*. Unger's *Living High and Letting Die* argues that (initial appearances to the contrary notwithstanding) even our ordinary moral values already commit us to a very demanding requirement to aid others.

Those readers troubled by the fact that millions of people will die this year, who could have been saved for a few dollars each, might want to consider making a contribution to Oxfam. In the United States, the address is: Oxfam America, P.O. Box 4215, Boston MA 02211–4215.

## 5.2    Options

Scheffler's *The Rejection of Consequentialism* provides the most sustained attempt to defend options. See also his *Human Morality*. Other interesting discussions of options can be found in Slote, *Common-Sense Morality and Consequentialism* (the distinction between agent-favoring and agent-sacrificing options is drawn here), and in Nagel, *The View from Nowhere,* chapter 10. I argue at length against the possibility of successfully defending options in *The Limits of Morality*. The fact that moderate deontologists face a violation of transitivity (if they explain options in terms of cost to the agent, but reject options to do harm) is pointed out by Kamm in "Supererogation and Obligation"; see also *Morality, Mortality,* volume 2, chapter 12.

It should be noted that options get called by a number of different names in the philosophical literature. For example, Scheffler refers to them as "agent-centered prerogatives"; and Nagel calls them "agent-relative permissions."

## 5.3    Rights

The literature on rights is enormous. Two helpful anthologies are Lyons, *Rights,* and Waldron, *Theories of Rights.* The classic analysis of different types of rights is Hohfeld, *Fundamental Legal Conceptions* (although Hohfeld was concerned with legal rather than moral rights, most of his distinctions carry over straightforwardly). A wonderful contemporary discussion is Thomson, *The Realm of Rights.* A brief treatment of some of the main issues can also be found in Feinberg, *Social Philosophy,* chapters 4–6.

Consequentialists have often been hostile to rights. Bentham called them "nonsense on stilts"! Mill, however, thought them unproblematic; he defends an enforceability conception of rights in *Utilitarianism,* chapter 5. A recent defender of a consequentialist account of rights is Sumner, *The Moral Foundation of Rights.*

## 5.4    Interaction

Nozick's "Moral Complications and Moral Structures" (reprinted, in abridged form, in *Philosophical Explanations,* chapter 5, section 3) is an illuminating but difficult discussion of the various ways in which factors can interact.

For a detailed attempt to establish the impossibility of moral dilemmas for the innocent arising within commonsense morality, see Donagan, *The Theory of Morality,* chapter 5. An argument for the existence of dilemmas can be found in Sinnott-Armstrong, *Moral Dilemmas.* A valuable collection of articles on the topic is Gowans, *Moral Dilemmas.* The distinction between prima facie duties and duties all things considered was drawn by Ross, in *The Right and the Good,* chapter 2.

Particularism is defended by Dancy in *Moral Reasons,* especially chapters 4–6.

# Chapter 6: Teleological Foundations

## 6.1    Foundational Theories

Many theorists don't draw a sharp distinction, in the way that I have suggested, between factoral theories and foundational theories. One contemporary work that does is Donagan, *The Theory of Morality.* Examples of nonfoundationalism can be found in Prichard, "Does Moral Philosophy Rest on a Mistake?" and Ross, *The Right and the Good.*

## 6.2    Egoism

Hobbes's *Leviathan* is the classic modern statement of foundational egoism. A contemporary defense of rule egoism can be found in Kavka, *Hobbesian Moral and Political Theory,* chapter 9 (Kavka interprets Hobbes as a rule egoist). The charge of "rule worship" was made by Smart, in "Extreme and Restricted Utilitarianism." (Smart was actually criticizing rule consequentialism—see 6.5—rather than rule egoism; but the criticism seems at least as apt against the latter as the former.)

## 6.3    Virtues

The classic statement of virtue egoism is Aristotle's *Nicomachean Ethics.* In fact, however, much of ancient moral philosophy can be interpreted as some form of virtue egoism, and one striking contrast between much modern moral philosophy and what came before is the shift from virtues to rules or acts as the primary evaluative focal point. In "Modern Moral Philosophy," Anscombe argues forcefully that this shift away from virtue represents a shortcoming of the modern approach. Other contemporary advocates of a return in ethics to a focus upon virtue are Foot, *Virtues and Vices* (especially the title essay); Geach, *The Virtues;* and Wallace, *Virtues and Vices.* (It should certainly be noted, however, that not all advocates of virtue are virtue egoists.) For the difficulty of demarcating a class of particularly moral virtues (as opposed to the broader class of desirable character traits), see appendix IV of Hume's *Enquiry Concerning the Principles of Morals.*

## 6.4    Act Consequentialism

The classic modern statement of act consequentialism (more particularly, act utilitarianism) is Mill's *Utilitarianism.* In effect, Mill argues for factoral utilitarianism on the basis of foundational utilitarianism, though Mill—like many other theorists—doesn't much distinguish between the two levels. (Indeed, it must be admitted that in construing act consequentialism as a foundational theory, and thereby distinguishing it from factoral consequentialism, I am going against the trend of much contemporary and classical writing, including that by many consequentialists.)

The possibility that foundational consequentialism might support constraints if only it had the right kind of theory of the good is raised—and rejected—by Nozick in *Anarchy, State and Utopia,* chapter 3. McMahon defends a kind of sophisticated consequentialism in "The Paradox of Deontology."

The idea of a satisficing (as opposed to maximizing) consequentialism is introduced by Slote in "Satisficing Consequentialism"; and the distinction between satisficing, maximizing, and other attitudes to the good is investigated more generally in Slote's *Beyond Optimizing.* Interestingly, the latter also argues that the common-sense notion of rationality includes *constraints* on the pursuit of one's individual good. Pettit's "Consequentialism" distinguishes between "promotion" approaches to the good (like maximizing) and "honoring" approaches (similar to what I have called "respect"). But full-blown, explicit *defenses* of a "respect" version of act consequentialism are hard to come by. Nonetheless, something at least similar to this position is suggested (albeit in completely different terms) by some remarks made by Finnis in *Moral Absolutes.*

## 6.5    Rules

Although Mill is generally interpreted as an act utilitarian, Urmson argues, in "The Interpretation of the Moral Philosophy of J.S. Mill," that he is actually a rule utilitarian. Smart disputes this interpretation in "Extreme and Restricted Utilitarianism." (As I've already noted, the charge of rule worship also goes back to Smart.) The foremost contemporary advocate of rule utilitarianism is Brandt, *A Theory of the Good and the Right.* A shorter statement of Brandt's views can be found in "Some Merits of One Form of Rule-Utilitarianism." Important contributions to the debate over whether or not rule consequentialism collapses into act consequentialism can be found in Lyons, *Forms and Limits of Utilitarianism;* Gibbard, "Rule Utilitarianism: Merely an Illusory Alternative?"; and Regan, *Utilitarianism and Co-*

*operation.* Regan is also relevant for the possibility of solving the noncompliance problem for rule consequentialism by appeal to flexible embedding conditions.

Motive consequentialism is discussed by Adams in "Motive Utilitarianism."

## Chapter 7: Deontological Foundations

### 7.1    Contractarianism

The major classic contractarians in ethics are Hobbes, *Leviathan;* Rousseau, *On The Social Contract;* and Kant, The Doctrine of Right, in *The Metaphysics of Morals.* (It should be noted, however, that all three of these authors primarily use the contractarian approach to address issues in political philosophy.) Hobbes motivates the contractarian approach along boldly egoistic lines (the phrase, "the war of all against all," is his); for Rousseau and Kant, the motivation is more in terms of a regard for autonomy. A very helpful commentary on Hobbes's moral theory is Kavka, *Hobbesian Moral and Political Theory.* The most important contemporary contractarian in the Hobbesian tradition is Gauthier, *Morals by Agreement.* Rawls, *A Theory of Justice,* is by far the most influential contemporary contractarian work; it develops the Rousseauian and Kantian tradition. Rawls's work too is concerned largely with political issues; but Richards, *A Theory of Reasons for Action,* extends the Rawlsian framework to explicitly address issues of individual morality. Scanlon offers another (broadly Kantian) defense of contractarianism in "Contractualism and Utilitarianism." As we might expect, these authors differ from one another in how they characterize the bargainers. For example, Rawls characterizes bargainers as being ignorant of their identities; Gauthier and Scanlon reject this. Rawls and Gauthier characterize bargainers along (roughly) egoistic lines; Scanlon rejects this, too. The fact that certain versions of contractarianism may yield factoral consequentialism is noted by Rawls (see pp. 150–183).

### 7.2    Universalizability

The most important philosophical advocate of universalizability is Kant, in the *Groundwork.* Unfortunately, Kant's position is quite complex, and the proper interpretation of many parts of his view is a matter of considerable controversy, so I have not tried to discuss a view precisely like his in the text. (However, it seems likely that Kant would be sympathetic to the first and fifth of our universalizability tests.) Kant is also extremely difficult to read on one's own. A very helpful commentary on his moral view as a whole is Paton, *The Categorical Imperative.* The best work focusing on the universalizability strand in his thought is Onora Nell (now O'Neill), *Acting on Principle.* Also helpful is Korsgaard, "Kant's Formula of Universal Law." Kant believed universalizability would support factoral deontology. The examples of the insincere promise and the requirement to aid others are two of those discussed by Kant in the *Groundwork.*

Hare, *Moral Thinking,* argues for something similar to the second and third versions of the universalizability test. Hare believes that universalizability supports factoral consequentialism, in particular, utilitarianism. Singer's *Generalization in Ethics* is a defense of something similar to the fourth version of the universalizability test. *Morality and Universality,* edited by Potter and Timmons, is a recent collection of essays on universalizability. A brief discussion of the golden rule can be found in Singer's "Golden Rule."

## 7.3     The Ideal Observer

The classic statement of an ideal observer theory is Smith, *The Theory of Moral Sentiments*. Firth's "Ethical Absolutism and the Ideal Observer" is the most influential contemporary defense. Useful discussion of the ideal observer theory can be found in Brandt, *Ethical Theory*, chapter 7, and Carson, *The Status of Morality*, chapter 2.

Various versions of the divine command theory are discussed in the essays in *Divine Commands and Morality*, edited by Helm. Adams, "A Modified Divine Command Theory of Ethical Wrongness," is especially useful in the current context. The worry that valid rules are not valid by virtue of the ideal observer's endorsement, but rather that the ideal observer endorses valid rules because she recognizes their validity, is a version of the objection that Plato raises to divine command theories in the *Euthyphro*.

## 7.4     Reflection

Some interesting general remarks about reflection approaches to morality, as well as the distinction between reflecting the nature of agents and reflecting the nature of patients, can be found in Nozick, *Philosophical Explanations*, chapter 5, sections 1 and 2. In *Anarchy, State and Utopia*, pp. 35–42, Nozick entertains the suggestion that consequentialism is appropriate for animals, deontology for people. (Further readings on the moral status of animals can be found in the references for section 2.3 above.)

The claim that options reflect the nature of the personal point of view is defended by Scheffler in *The Rejection of Consequentialism*. The proposal that the requirement to aid others is a reflection of the equal reality of the needs of others—as well as our ability to recognize and be moved by this fact—is made by Nagel in *The Possibility of Altruism*. See also Nagel's *The View from Nowhere*, chapter 9, and *Equality and Partiality*.

Kant's moral philosophy is a classic source of the view that the content of morality is determined by the need to reflect our autonomy. See, for example, *The Groundwork of the Metaphysics of Morals*, section II. Once again, however, the reader should be warned that Kant is extremely difficult to understand. (I should also note that he does not express himself in the language I have used in this section. He speaks instead of the importance of always "respecting" the "rational nature" of oneself and of others. And although Kant does indeed talk about a principle of autonomy, he means something somewhat different by this.) The observant reader will have been struck by the fact that Kant is a classic source of ideas not just for reflection theories but also for contractarianism and universalizability; in many ways he is the father of modern deontological ethics.

## 7.5     Foundational Pluralism

The existence of an irreducible pluralism at the foundations of normative ethics is defended by Nagel in "The Fragmentation of Value."

It is rather uncommon for a foundational theory to be explicitly presented as a multilayered account; still, it can often be illuminating to think of theories in these terms. For examples, see the works by Harsanyi, Hare, Gauthier, and Kant.

# REFERENCES

Philosophical classics that are readily available in various editions are listed below, but no specific edition is cited.

Adams, Robert. "A Modified Divine Command Theory of Ethical Wrongness." In *The Virtue of Faith,* pp. 97–122. Oxford, 1987.

_____. "Motive Utilitarianism." *Journal of Philosophy* 73 (1976): 467–481. Reprinted in Pettit, *Consequentialism,* pp. 71–86.

Anscombe, G.E.M. "Modern Moral Philosophy." *Philosophy* 33 (1958): 26–42.

Aristotle. *The Nicomachean Ethics.*

Austin, J. L. "A Plea for Excuses." In *Philosophical Papers,* pp. 175–204. Oxford, 1961.

Ayer, A. J. *Language, Truth and Logic.* 2d edition, 1946. Reprint, Dover, 1952.

Baier, Kurt. *The Moral Point of View.* Cornell, 1958.

Beauchamp, Tom. "Suicide." In Tom Regan, ed., *Matters of Life and Death,* 3d ed., pp. 69–120. McGraw-Hill, 1993.

Becker, Lawrence. *Property Rights.* Routledge & Kegan Paul, 1977.

Becker, Lawrence, and Charlotte Becker, eds. *Encyclopedia of Ethics.* 2 vols. Garland, 1992.

Bennett, Jonathan. "Morality and Consequences." In Sterling McMurrin, ed., *The Tanner Lectures on Human Values,* Vol. 2. Cambridge, 1981.

_____. "Whatever the Consequences." *Analysis* 26 (1965–1966): 83–102. Reprinted in Fischer and Ravizza, *Ethics: Problems & Principles,* pp. 93–106.

Bentham, Jeremy. *An Introduction to the Principles of Morals and Legislation.* 1781.

Bok, Sissela. *Lying: Moral Choice in Public and Private Life.* Pantheon, 1978.

Bradley, F. H. "My Station and Its Duties." In *Ethical Studies,* 2d ed., pp. 160–213. Oxford, 1927.

Brandt, Richard. *Ethical Theory.* Prentice-Hall, 1959.

_____. "Some Merits of One Form of Rule-Utilitarianism." In *Morality, Utilitarianism, and Rights,* pp. 111–136. Cambridge, 1992.

_____. *A Theory of the Good and the Right.* Oxford, 1979.

Brennan, Samantha. "How Is the Strength of a Right Determined?" *American Philosophical Quarterly* 32 (1995): 383–392.

_____. "Paternalism and Rights." *Canadian Journal of Philosophy* 24 (1994): 419–440.

_____. "Thresholds for Rights." *Southern Journal of Philosophy* 33 (1995): 143–168.

Brink, David. *Moral Realism and the Foundations of Ethics.* Cambridge, 1989.

Brock, Dan. "Moral Prohibitions and Consent." In Myles Brand and Michael Bradie, eds., *Action and Responsibility,* pp. 110–121. Bowling Green, 1980.

Carson, Thomas. *The Status of Morality.* Reidel, 1984.

Christman, John, ed. *The Inner Citadel: Essays on Individual Autonomy.* Oxford, 1989.

Coleman, Jules. *Risks and Wrongs.* Cambridge, 1992.

Dancy, Jonathan. *Moral Reasons.* Blackwell, 1993.

Davis, Nancy. "The Doctrine of Double Effect: Problems of Interpretation." *Pacific Philosophical Quarterly* 65 (1984): 107–123. Reprinted in Fischer and Ravizza, *Ethics: Problems & Principles,* pp. 199–212.

DePaul, Michael. *Balance and Refinement: Beyond Coherence Methods of Moral Inquiry.* Routledge, 1993.

Donagan, Alan. *The Theory of Morality.* Chicago, 1977.

Dworkin, Gerald. *The Theory and Practice of Autonomy.* Cambridge, 1988.

Dworkin, Ronald. "What Is Equality?" *Philosophy & Public Affairs* 10 (1981): 185–246, 283–345.

Elster, Jon, and John Roemer, eds. *Interpersonal Comparisons of Well-Being.* Cambridge, 1991.

Feinberg, Joel. *Doing and Deserving.* Princeton, 1970.

_____. "Justice and Personal Desert." In *Doing and Deserving,* pp. 55–94.

_____. *The Limits of the Criminal Law.* Vol. 1, *Harm to Others;* Vol. 2, *Offense to Others;* Vol. 3, *Harm to Self;* Vol. 4, *Harmless Wrongdoing.* Oxford, 1984–1988.

_____. *Social Philosophy.* Prentice-Hall, 1973.

_____. "Sua Culpa." In *Doing and Deserving,* pp. 187–221.

_____. "Voluntary Euthanasia and the Inalienable Right to Life." *Philosophy & Public Affairs* 7 (1978): 93–123.

Feldman, Fred. *Doing the Best We Can.* Reidel, 1986.

_____. *Introductory Ethics.* Prentice-Hall, 1978.

Finnis, John. *Moral Absolutes: Tradition, Revision, and Truth.* Catholic University of America, 1991.

Firth, Roderick. "Ethical Absolutism and the Ideal Observer." *Philosophy and Phenomenological Research* 12 (1952): 317–345.

Fischer, John Martin, ed. *Moral Responsibility.* Cornell, 1986.

Fischer, John Martin, and Mark Ravizza, eds. *Ethics: Problems & Principles.* Harcourt Brace Jovanovich, 1992.

Fletcher, George. "Proportionality and the Psychotic Aggressor." *Israel Law Review* 8 (1973): 367–390.

Foot, Philippa. "The Problem of Abortion and the Doctrine of the Double Effect." In *Virtues and Vices,* pp. 19–32. Reprinted in Fischer and Ravizza, *Ethics: Problems & Principles,* pp. 59–67.

_____. *Virtues and Vices.* University of California, 1978.

Foot, Philippa, ed. *Theories of Ethics.* Oxford, 1967.

Fried, Charles. *An Anatomy of Values.* Harvard, 1970.

_____. *Contract as Promise.* Harvard, 1981.

_____. *Right and Wrong.* Harvard, 1978.

Gauthier, David. *Morals by Agreement.* Oxford, 1986.

Gauthier, David, ed. *Morality and Rational Self-Interest.* Prentice-Hall, 1970.

Geach, Peter. *The Virtues.* Cambridge, 1977.

Gibbard, Allan. "Rule-Utilitarianism: Merely an Illusory Alternative?" *Australasian Journal of Philosophy* 43 (1965): 211–220. Reprinted in Pettit, *Consequentialism*, pp. 189–198.

_____. *Wise Choices, Apt Feelings.* Harvard, 1990.

Glover, Jonathan. *What Sort of People Should There Be?* Penguin, 1984.

Gowans, Christopher, ed. *Moral Dilemmas.* Oxford, 1987.

Griffin, James. *Well-Being.* Oxford, 1986.

Haber, Joram, ed. *Absolutism and Its Consequentialist Critics.* Rowman & Littlefield, 1994.

Hardimon, Michael. "Role Obligations." *Journal of Philosophy* 91 (1994): 333–363.

Hare, R. M. "Ethical Theory and Utilitarianism." In H. D. Lewis, ed., *Contemporary British Philosophy.* Allen and Unwin, 1976. Reprinted in Sen and Williams, *Utilitarianism and Beyond*, pp. 23–38.

_____. *Moral Thinking.* Oxford, 1981.

_____. "What Is Wrong with Slavery?" *Philosophy & Public Affairs* 8 (1979): 103–121.

Harman, Gilbert. *The Nature of Morality.* Oxford, 1977.

Harsanyi, John. "Morality and the Theory of Rational Behavior." In Amartya Sen and Bernard Williams, eds., *Utilitarianism and Beyond*, pp. 39–62. Cambridge, 1982.

Hart, H.L.A. "Are There Any Natural Rights?" *Philosophical Review* 64 (1955): 175–191.

Helm, P., ed. *Divine Commands and Morality.* Oxford, 1981.

Heyd, David. *Supererogation.* Cambridge, 1982.

Hill, Thomas. "Autonomy and Benevolent Lies." In *Autonomy and Self-Respect*, pp. 25–42.

_____. *Autonomy and Self-Respect.* Cambridge, 1991.

_____. "Self-Respect Reconsidered." In *Autonomy and Self-Respect*, pp. 19–24.

_____. "Servility and Self-Respect." In *Autonomy and Self-Respect*, pp. 4–18.

Hobbes, Thomas. *Leviathan.* 1651.

Hodgson, D. H. *Consequences of Utilitarianism.* Oxford, 1967.

Hohfeld, Wesley. *Fundamental Legal Conceptions as Applied in Judicial Reasoning.* Yale, 1919.

Honderich, Ted. *Punishment: The Supposed Justifications.* Penguin, 1969.

Hume, David. *Enquiry Concerning the Principles of Morals.* 1752.

_____. *A Treatise of Human Nature.* 1739.

Hurka, Thomas. *Perfectionism.* Oxford, 1993.

Kagan, Shelly. "The Additive Fallacy." *Ethics* 99 (1988): 5–31. Reprinted in Fischer and Ravizza, *Ethics: Problems & Principles*, pp. 252–271.

_____. "Causation and Responsibility." *American Philosophical Quarterly* 25 (1988): 293–302.

_____. *The Limits of Morality.* Oxford, 1989.

Kamm, Frances. "Harming Some to Save Others." *Philosophical Studies* 57 (1989): 227–260.

_____. "The Insanity Defense, Innocent Threats and Limited Alternatives." *Criminal Justice Ethics* 6 (1987): 61–76.

_____. "Killing and Letting Die: Methodological and Substantive Issues." *Pacific Philosophical Quarterly* 64 (1983): 297–312.

_____. *Morality, Mortality.* 2 vols. Oxford, 1993 and 1996.

_____. "Non-consequentialism, the Person as an End-in-Itself, and the Significance of Status." *Philosophy & Public Affairs* 21 (1992): 354–389.

_____. "Supererogation and Obligation." *Journal of Philosophy* 82 (1985): 118–138.

Kant, Immanuel. *Critique of Practical Reason.* 1788.

_____. *Groundwork of the Metaphysics of Morals.* 1785.

_____. *The Metaphysics of Morals.* 1797.

_____. "On a Supposed Right to Lie from Benevolent Motives." 1797.

Kavka, Gregory. *Hobbesian Moral and Political Theory.* Princeton, 1986.

Klosko, George. *The Principle of Fairness and Political Obligation.* Rowman & Littlefield, 1992.

Korsgaard, Christine. "Kant's Formula of Universal Law." *Pacific Philosophical Quarterly* 66 (1985): 24–47.

_____. "Two Distinctions in Goodness." *Philosophical Review* 92 (1983): 169–195.

Kraut, Richard. "Two Conceptions of Happiness." *Philosophical Review* 88 (1979): 167–197.

Lemos, Noah. *Intrinsic Value: Concept and Warrant.* Cambridge, 1994.

Lewis, David. "Utilitarianism and Truthfulness." In *Philosophical Papers,* Vol. 2, pp. 340–342. Oxford, 1986. Reprinted in Pettit, *Consequentialism,* pp. 219–222.

Locke, John. *Two Treatises of Government.* 1690.

Lyons, David. *Forms and Limits of Utilitarianism.* Oxford, 1965.

Lyons, David, ed. *Rights.* Wadsworth, 1979.

McCloskey, H. J. "A Note on Utilitarian Punishment." *Mind* 72 (1963): 599.

McKerlie, Dennis. "Equality and Time." *Ethics* 99 (1989): 475–491.

MacLean, Douglas, ed. *Values at Risk.* Rowman & Allanheld, 1985.

McMahan, Jeff. "Killing, Letting Die, and Withdrawing Aid." *Ethics* 103 (1993): 250–279.

_____. "Self-Defense and the Problem of the Innocent Attacker." *Ethics* 104 (1994): 252–290.

McMahon, Christopher. "The Paradox of Deontology." *Philosophy & Public Affairs* 20 (1991): 350–377.

Mill, John Stuart. *Utilitarianism.* 1861.

Miller, Harlan, and William Williams, eds. *The Limits of Utilitarianism.* Minnesota, 1982.

Moore, G. E. "The Conception of Intrinsic Value." In *Philosophical Studies,* pp. 253–276. Routledge & Kegan Paul, 1922.

Murphy, Jeffrie. *Retribution, Justice and Therapy.* Reidel, 1979.

Murphy, Jeffrie, and Jules Coleman. *The Philosophy of Law.* Rowman & Allanheld, 1984.

Nagel, Thomas. "Death." In *Mortal Questions,* pp. 1–11.

\_\_\_\_\_. "Equality." In *Mortal Questions,* pp. 106–127.

\_\_\_\_\_. *Equality and Partiality.* Oxford, 1991.

\_\_\_\_\_. "The Fragmentation of Value." In *Mortal Questions,* pp. 128–42.

\_\_\_\_\_. *Mortal Questions.* Cambridge, 1979.

\_\_\_\_\_. *The Possibility of Altruism.* Oxford, 1970.

\_\_\_\_\_. *The View from Nowhere.* Oxford, 1986.

Nell, Onora (O'Neill). *Acting on Principle.* Columbia, 1975.

Nelson, William. *Morality: What's in It for Me?* Westview, 1991.

Nozick, Robert. *Anarchy, State and Utopia.* Basic Books, 1974.

\_\_\_\_\_. "Moral Complications and Moral Structures." *Natural Law Forum* 13 (1968): 1–50.

\_\_\_\_\_. *Philosophical Explanations.* Harvard, 1981.

Parfit, Derek. *Equality or Priority?* University of Kansas, 1995.

\_\_\_\_\_. *Reasons and Persons.* Oxford, 1984.

Paton, H. J. *The Categorical Imperative.* Hutchinson, 1958.

Pettit, Philip. "Consequentialism." In Peter Singer, ed., *A Companion to Ethics,* pp. 230–240. Blackwell, 1991.

Pettit, Philip, ed. *Consequentialism.* Dartmouth, 1993.

Plato. *Euthyphro.*

Pojman, Louis, and Robert Westmoreland, eds. *Equality: Selected Readings.* Oxford, 1997.

Potter, N., and M. Timmons, eds. *Morality and Universality: Essays in Ethical Universalizability.* Reidel, 1985.

Prichard, H. A. "Does Moral Philosophy Rest on a Mistake?" In *Moral Obligation,* pp. 1–17.

\_\_\_\_\_. *Moral Obligation.* Oxford, 1928.

\_\_\_\_\_. "The Obligation to Keep a Promise." In *Moral Obligation,* pp. 169–179.

Quinn, Warren. "Actions, Intentions, and Consequences: The Doctrine of Doing and Allowing." In *Morality and Action,* pp. 149–174. Reprinted in Fischer and Ravizza, *Ethics: Problems & Principles,* pp. 145–161.

\_\_\_\_\_. "Actions, Intentions, and Consequences: The Doctrine of Double Effect." In *Morality and Action,* pp. 175–193. Reprinted in Fischer and Ravizza, *Ethics: Problems & Principles,* pp. 179–190.

\_\_\_\_\_. *Morality and Action.* Cambridge, 1993.

\_\_\_\_\_. "The Right to Threaten and the Right to Punish." In *Morality and Action,* pp. 52–100.

Rachels, James. "Active and Passive Euthanasia." *New England Journal of Medicine* 292 (1975): 78–80. Reprinted in Fischer and Ravizza, *Ethics: Problems & Principles,* pp. 111–115.

\_\_\_\_\_. *The Elements of Moral Philosophy.* 2d ed. McGraw-Hill, 1993.

Rachels, James, ed. *Moral Problems.* Harper & Row, 1979.

Rawls, John. *A Theory of Justice.* Harvard, 1971.

Regan, Donald. *Utilitarianism and Co-operation.* Oxford, 1980.

Regan, Tom, ed. *Matters of Life and Death.* 3d ed. McGraw-Hill, 1993.

Regan, Tom, and Peter Singer, eds. *Animal Rights and Human Obligations.* 2d ed. Prentice-Hall, 1989.

Richards, David. *A Theory of Reasons for Action.* Oxford, 1971.

Ross, David. *The Right and the Good.* Oxford, 1930.

Rousseau, Jean-Jacques. *On the Social Contract.* 1762.

Sartorious, Rolf. *Individual Conduct and Social Norms.* Dickenson, 1975.

Sayre-McCord, Geoffrey, ed. *Essays on Moral Realism.* Cornell, 1988.

Scanlon, Thomas. "Contractualism and Utilitarianism." In Amartya Sen and Bernard Williams, eds., *Utilitarianism and Beyond,* pp. 103–128. Cambridge, 1982.

_____. "Preference and Urgency." *Journal of Philosophy* 72 (1975): 655–669.

_____. "Promises and Practices." *Philosophy & Public Affairs* 19 (1990): 199–226.

Scheffler, Samuel. *Human Morality.* Oxford, 1992.

_____. *The Rejection of Consequentialism.* Oxford, 1982.

Scheffler, Samuel, ed. *Consequentialism and Its Critics.* Oxford, 1988.

Sen, Amartya. "Utilitarianism and Welfarism." *Journal of Philosophy* 76 (1979): 463–489. Reprinted in Pettit, *Consequentialism,* pp. 15–42.

Sen, Amartya, and Bernard Williams, eds. *Utilitarianism and Beyond.* Cambridge, 1982.

Sher, George. *Desert.* Princeton, 1987.

Sidgwick, Henry. *The Methods of Ethics.* 7th ed. Macmillan, 1907.

_____. *Outlines of the History of Ethics.* 6th ed. Macmillan, 1931.

Simmons, A. John. *Moral Principles and Political Obligation.* Princeton, 1979.

Singer, Marcus. *Generalization in Ethics.* Knopf, 1961.

_____. "Golden Rule." In Lawrence Becker and Charlotte Becker, eds., *Encyclopedia of Ethics,* pp. 405–408. Garland, 1992.

Singer, Peter. *Animal Liberation.* Avon, 1975.

_____. "Famine, Affluence and Morality." *Philosophy & Public Affairs* 1 (1972): 229–243.

_____. *Practical Ethics.* Cambridge, 1979.

Singer, Peter, ed. *A Companion to Ethics.* Blackwell, 1991.

Sinnott-Armstrong, Walter. *Moral Dilemmas.* Blackwell, 1988.

Slote, Michael. *Beyond Optimizing.* Harvard, 1989.

_____. *Common-Sense Morality and Consequentialism.* Routledge & Kegan Paul, 1985.

_____. "Satisficing Consequentialism." *Proceedings of the Aristotelian Society* 58 (1984): 139–163. Reprinted in Pettit, *Consequentialism,* pp. 351–376.

Smart, J.J.C. "Extreme and Restricted Utilitarianism." Reprinted in Foot, *Theories of Ethics,* pp. 171–183; and in Pettit, *Consequentialism,* pp. 175–188.

_____. "An Outline of a System of Utilitarian Ethics." In J.J.C. Smart and Bernard Williams, *Utilitarianism: For and Against.* Cambridge, 1973.

Smith, Adam. *The Theory of Moral Sentiments.* 1759.

Steinbock, Bonnie, ed. *Killing and Letting Die.* Prentice-Hall, 1980.

Sterba, James, ed. *Morality in Practice.* 5th ed. Wadsworth, 1997.

Sumner, L. W. *The Moral Foundation of Rights.* Oxford, 1987.

Taurek, John. "Should the Numbers Count?" *Philosophy & Public Affairs* 6 (1977): 293–316. Reprinted in Fischer and Ravizza, *Ethics: Problems & Principles,* pp. 214–227.

Temkin, Larry. "Inequality." *Philosophy & Public Affairs* 15 (1986): 99–121.

_____. *Inequality.* Oxford, 1993.

Thomson, Judith Jarvis. "Feinberg on Harm, Offense, and the Criminal Law." *Philosophy & Public Affairs* 15 (1986): 381–395.

_____. "Imposing Risks." In *Rights, Restitution and Risk*, pp. 173–191.

_____. "Killing, Letting Die, and the Trolley Problem." In *Rights, Restitution and Risk*, pp. 78–93. Reprinted in Fischer and Ravizza, *Ethics: Problems & Principles*, pp. 67–77.

_____. *The Realm of Rights*. Harvard, 1990.

_____. "Remarks on Causation and Liability." In *Rights, Restitution and Risk*, pp. 192–224.

_____. "Rights and Compensation." In *Rights, Restitution and Risk*, pp. 66–77.

_____. *Rights, Restitution and Risk*. Harvard, 1986.

_____. "Self-Defense." *Philosophy & Public Affairs* 20 (1991): 283–310.

_____. "Self-Defense and Rights." In *Rights, Restitution and Risk*, pp. 33–48

_____. "The Trolley Problem." In *Rights, Restitution and Risk*, pp. 94–116. Reprinted in Fischer and Ravizza, *Ethics: Problems & Principles*, pp. 279–292.

Trammell, Richard. "Saving Life and Taking Life." *Journal of Philosophy* 72 (1975): 131–137. Reprinted in Fischer and Ravizza, *Ethics: Problems & Principles*, pp. 116–121.

Unger, Peter. *Identity, Consciousness and Value*. Oxford, 1990.

_____. *Living High and Letting Die*. Oxford, 1996.

Uniacke, Suzanne. *Permissible Killing: The Self-Defence Justification of Homicide*. Cambridge, 1994.

Urmson, J. O. "The Interpretation of the Moral Philosophy of J. S. Mill." In Foot, *Theories of Ethics*, pp. 128–136.

_____. "Saints and Heroes." In A. I. Melden, ed., *Essays in Moral Philosophy*, pp. 198–216. University of Washington, 1958.

Vallentyne, Peter. "Teleology, Consequentialism, and the Past." *Journal of Value Inquiry* 22 (1988): 89–101.

Waldron, Jeremy, ed. *Theories of Rights*. Oxford, 1984.

Wallace, James. *Virtues and Vices*. Cornell, 1978.

Warnock, G. J. *The Object of Morality*. Methuen, 1971.

Watson, Gary, ed. *Free Will*. Oxford, 1982.

Williams, Bernard. "A Critique of Utilitarianism." In J.J.C. Smart and Bernard Williams, *Utilitarianism: For and Against*. Cambridge, 1973.

_____. "The Idea of Equality." In Peter Laslett and W. G. Runciman, eds., *Philosophy, Politics, & Society*, 2d ser., pp. 110–131. Blackwell, 1962.

_____. "Persons, Character and Morality." In *Moral Luck*, pp. 1–19. Cambridge, 1981.

Wolf, Susan. *Freedom Within Reason*. Oxford, 1990.

# About the Book and Author

Providing a thorough introduction to current philosophical views on morality, *Normative Ethics* examines an act's rightness or wrongness in light of such factors as consequences, harm, and consent. Shelly Kagan offers a division between moral factors and theoretical foundations that reflects the actual working practices of contemporary moral philosophers.

The first half of the book presents a systematic survey of the basic normative factors, focusing on controversial questions concerning the precise content of each factor, its scope and significance, and its relationship to other factors. The second half of the book then examines the competing theories about the foundations of normative ethics, theories that attempt to explain why the basic normative factors have the moral significance that they do.

Intended for upper-level or graduate students of philosophy, this book should also appeal to the general reader looking for a clearly written overview of the basic principles of moral philosophy.

Shelly Kagan is professor of philosophy and Henry R. Luce Professor of Social Thought and Ethics at Yale University. He is the author of *The Limits of Morality*.

# Index

absolutism, 73, 75, 79–81, 84, 93–94, 114–116, 122, 130, 148, 169, 173. *See also* thresholds
acts as evaluative focal point, 198–199, 204, 214, 238, 242, 257, 268–271, 272, 277, 281, 300
  in consequentialism. *See* consequentialism, act
  in egoism. *See* egoism, act vs. rule
aid to others, 132–135, 150–151, 154–163, 207, 250, 266, 275–277, 289, 293. *See also* options
allowing harm, 94–100, 102–105, 168. *See also* doing harm
animals (nonhuman), 7, 47–48, 170–172, 287–288
applied ethics, 3, 19
Ari, 121, 124, 126
autonomy, 106, 111–113, 249–251, 291–293
average view, 46–47, 61

beneficence, 133, 250, 277. *See also* aid to others; weighted beneficence

Captain Hook and the Lost Boys, 86
character traits. *See* virtues
Chuck, chopping up. *See* organ transplant case
claims. *See* rights
commonsense morality
  and consequentialism, 67–69, 118, 157–158
  and constraints, 72–75, 78
  and contractarianism, 249–253
  defined, 25

as deontological, 73–75, 78, 118
and egoism, 63–64, 196–202
and foundational theories, 302–303
and ideal observer theories, 276
and options, 160, 163–166
and reflection theories, 291–293
and universalizability, 266
compensation, 122–123, 128–132, 150, 177
conflicting duties, 180–183, 201, 211. *See also* moral dilemmas
consent, 88–90, 116, 121, 147–148, 161–162, 173, 292
consequences. *See* goodness of outcomes
consequentialism
  act, 214–223, 239
  and the calculation objection, 66–68
  and choice of focal point, 214, 223–224, 238–239
  and constraints, 72–78, 216–218, 220, 221–222, 225
  and contractarianism, 252
  as demanding too much, 154–161
  direct, 238–239
  and doing vs. allowing, 94–100
  vs. egoism, 63–64
  at the factoral level, 60–63, 213–215, 218–219
  at the foundational level, 213–224
  and ideal observer theories, 275–277
  and maximizing, 218–224
  objective vs. subjective, 65–66
  and options, 160–161, 219–221, 225
  as permitting too much, 75–77, 153, 157–160
  and respect, 221–222